The Myth of American Inequality

The Myth of American Inequality

How Government Biases Policy Debate

PHIL GRAMM, ROBERT EKELUND,
AND JOHN EARLY

ROWMAN & LITTLEFIELD
Lanham • Boulder • New York • London

Published by Rowman & Littlefield
An imprint of The Rowman & Littlefield Publishing Group, Inc.
4501 Forbes Boulevard, Suite 200, Lanham, Maryland 20706
www.rowman.com

86-90 Paul Street, London EC2A 4NE

Distributed by NATIONAL BOOK NETWORK

Hardcover edition 2022

British Library Cataloguing in Publication Information Available

Library of Congress Cataloging-in-Publication Data

Names: Gramm, Phil, author. | Ekelund, Robert B. (Robert Burton), 1940– author. | Early, John (Mathematical economist), author.
Title: The myth of American inequality : how government biases policy debate / Phil Gramm, Robert Ekelund, and John Early.
Description: Lanham : Rowman & Littlefield, [2022] | Includes bibliographical references and index. | Summary: "Everything you know about income inequality, poverty and other measures of economic well-being in America is wrong. In measuring income inequality, poverty and other indexes of well-being our government does not count two-thirds of all transfer payments that are received or any of the taxes paid. When we get our facts straight poverty has virtually been eliminated, income inequality is lower than it was in 1947 and America is still the great land of opportunity"— Provided by publisher.
Subjects: LCSH: Income distribution—United States. | United States—Economic conditions. | Poverty—United States.
Classification: LCC HC110.I5 G688 2022 (print) | LCC HC110.I5 (ebook) | DDC 339.20973—dc23/eng/20220325
LC record available at https://lccn.loc.gov/2022014078
LC ebook record available at https://lccn.loc.gov/2022014079

ISBN: 978-1-5381-6738-0 (cloth : alk. paper)
ISBN: 978-1-5381-9013-5 (pbk. : alk. paper)
ISBN: 978-1-5381-9014-2 (ebook)

∞™ The paper used in this publication meets the minimum requirements of American National Standard for Information Sciences—Permanence of Paper for Printed Library Materials, ANSI/NISO Z39.48-1992.

Contents

Preface to the Paperback Edition

Phil Gramm

For the last two hundred years, and to an ever-increasing degree since the dawn of the information age, both the lessons we draw from history and our perception of the world we live in are based to a significant degree on statistical measures. Using published government data, we show in this book that the Census Bureau does not count two-thirds of all transfer payments to households as income to the beneficiaries. The omitted payments from over one hundred government programs range from refundable tax credits where the beneficiary receives a check from the Treasury, to food-stamp debit cards loaded with credits to spend on food, to Medicaid where the government simply pays the families' medical bills. More than $1.9 billion worth of transfer payments going mostly to low-income Americans are not counted as part of their income. The Census also does not subtract taxes paid when calculating income inequality, even though taxes reduce spendable income by $4.4 trillion annually, and 82 percent of those taxes are paid by the top 40 percent of income earners. The result of these decisions is to distort fundamentally the measures of both income inequality and poverty.

The hardback edition of this book was rated as one of the five "best of the year in political argument, history and analysis" in 2022 by the *Wall Street Journal*. We have made presentations on the book at Harvard, the University of Chicago, Stanford, and numerous other universities, think tanks, and civic organizations throughout the country. As we had hoped, the book has spawned a debate in the country and Congress on the inadequacy of the basic economic measures of America's wellbeing.

With the official measure of poverty now discredited both by the findings of this book and the absurdity of the official poverty rate rising when welfare benefits rocketed during the pandemic, the Census Bureau is promoting an alternative measure to the official poverty measure. We have added a section in chapter 6 of this paperback edition to show that while the official measure has not shown progress in reducing poverty in over fifty years because the Census does not count the payments from most anti-poverty programs as income to the recipients, the new Census measure would tie the poverty thresholds to median household spending so that significant reductions in poverty could not come from economic growth but only from redistributing income. We have also added a section to chapter 8 with new data on the ability of adult children to rise out of the income quintiles of their childhood, which shows that the American dream is alive and well and comes true far more often than conventional data show.

We have proposed in numerous meetings with lawmakers that the Census Bureau be forced to count all transfer payments as income to the recipients. We have also urged Congress to require the Census to reduce income by taxes paid when measuring income inequality and to use better price indexes when calculating poverty thresholds and measures of wellbeing expressed in real dollar values. There is growing support in Congress for these changes.

The purpose of this book is to start a debate, not to end a debate, and we continue to challenge the Census Bureau and other statistical agencies of the federal government to respond to the findings of this book. Today Americans continue to have debates about poverty and income inequality that are based on statistics that have virtually no relationship to reality. Any political consensus in America will depend first on getting our facts straight. When Senator Bernie Sanders says that the growth of income inequality in America is "obscene . . . immoral, un-American and un-sustainable" and official government data show clearly that when you count transfer payments as income to the recipients and taxes as income lost to the taxpayer, income inequality in America is actually slightly lower today than it was in 1947, it is hard to have a meaningful debate. The truth can make us free only when we know the truth.

We believe that if you read this book, you will have a clearer picture of the real America that you live in. As we present the facts on whether the rich pay their fair share of taxes or whether the American dream is alive and well, you will find that getting the facts straight shows you how our great country and its unparalleled economic system have produced a cornucopia of plenty that has in fact been widely shared.

Preface

Phil Gramm

The lessons of history and our perception of the present have profound effects on the future. In the last two hundred years, and to an ever-increasing degree since the dawn of the information age, both history and our perception of the world we are living in are based to a significant degree on statistical measures. We may have the ability through our direct observations to perceive our own well-being, but we rely on standard statistical measures like inflation-adjusted gross domestic product, economic growth, productivity, and the poverty rate to form a perception of our national well-being and mean household income, average hourly earnings, and income distribution to gauge our own relative well-being.

It is hard to overstate the importance of getting our facts straight concerning basic statistical measures of well-being. Public policy, the role of government, and ultimately our freedom and happiness depend on knowing the facts. The truth can make us free only if we know the truth. Since this book is about getting our facts straight, and since getting the facts straight will affect our prosperity, freedom, and happiness, the subject matter of this book is vitally important.

This book is a joint effort by three authors with different political views who have had three very different careers. I first met Bob Ekelund in the summer of 1967 when we both arrived as newly minted assistant professors in a publish-or-perish economics department at Texas A&M University, which had recently achieved national ranking and aspired to become one of the best economics departments in the country. We did not perish. I left economics to do good, first as a member of Congress and then as a member of the Senate. On turning sixty, with the budget balanced, America prosperous, and the Cold War won, I decided that I would never have a better opportunity to quit politics while I was ahead. I went into finance to do well, first in investment banking and now in private equity.

Bob stayed in academics and has had an extraordinary career writing some two hundred peer-reviewed articles and thirty books on subjects ranging from economic history to the economics of advertising, from the history of economic thought to mercantilism, and from the economic origins of Roman Christianity to the economics of art. He is professor and eminent scholar emeritus at Auburn University.

In a conversation two years ago, Bob and I started talking about how American statistics measuring economic well-being seemed to be at variance with the world we lived in. Based on that initial conversation, we started to look more closely at the various statistical measures of well-being produced by the Census Bureau and by the Bureau of Labor Statistics.

During that study we discovered the work of John Early, a distinguished applied statistician and economist with a lifetime of experience in the very subject we were trying to understand. John has twice served as assistant commissioner of the Bureau of Labor Statistics, directed operations of a global consultancy, was chief strategy officer at a Fortune 100 company, and is currently president of Vital Few, LLC. Bob and I quickly concluded that we would never live long enough to understand the American system of collecting and reporting statistics at anything like the level of understanding present in John's work. Fortunately, we were able to convince John to join our effort.

This is not a book written by three different people and pieced together. We researched, analyzed, and wrote it jointly. It is a joint effort to understand what is wrong with America's measures of economic well-being, why they are wrong, and how we can fix them. While we each have our own opinions and political views, we share a desire to get the facts straight. We believe that we have come close to doing that in this book.

This book has benefited greatly from the research and technical assistance provided by Mariel Peterson, Mike Solon, and Mark Thornton. If we have succeeded in getting the facts straight and following the right trail in doing so, it is largely because of the quality of research and assistance that they have provided.

We have tried not to be pedantic, but we also wanted to provide enough detail to make clear that we are not being fast and loose with the facts. Getting the facts straight reveals the extraordinary accomplishments of the American economy under good policy and bad, in producing a cornucopia of plenty, which has in fact been widely shared.

CHAPTER 1

Introduction

OFFICIAL STATISTICAL MEASURES UNDERSTATE AMERICA'S WELL-BEING

The wisdom of Mark Twain was never more evident than when he reportedly said, "It ain't what you don't know that gets you into trouble. It's what you know that ain't so."[1] That simple truth applies to individuals and nations alike. History is replete with examples of where nations had conceptions of their well-being that were significantly different from the reality of the world in which they lived.

Believing Your Eyes, Not Government Statistics

The *Economist* magazine in 2020 summed up the contemporary public assessment of income inequality as follows: "It is a truth universally acknowledged that inequality in the rich world is high and rising."[2] This view permeates the American political and economic debate and is generally accepted across American society. While few are as blunt as Senator Bernie Sanders, he expresses what appears to be the uniform opinion of all major elements of the Democratic Party and some in the Republican Party when he says, "The obscene and increasing level of wealth and income inequality in this country is immoral, un-American and unsustainable."[3]

According to the Census Bureau, the average income of the top 20 percent of households in America in 2017 was 16.7 times higher than the average income of the bottom 20 percent of households, and income inequality has grown more or less consistently since World War II. The Census Bureau also finds that the percentage of Americans living in poverty has been largely unchanged since the War on Poverty was implemented in the mid-1960s.[4] The Bureau of Labor

Statistics (BLS) data on inflation-adjusted average hourly earnings for production and nonsupervisory workers led the Pew Institute to note in August 2018, "In real terms average hourly earnings peaked more than 45 years ago."[5]

If this doesn't sound like the America you live in, that is because it's not. There are at least three dead giveaways to the fact that the official measurements of the economic well-being of Americans are wrong. The most obvious clue is that from the ramp-up of funding for the War on Poverty in 1967 to 2017, annual government transfer payments to the average household in the bottom 20 percent of the income distribution rose more than fourfold in inflation-adjusted dollars from $9,677 to $45,389.[6] And yet the official poverty measures tell us that the percentage of people living in poverty hardly changed during that fifty-year period.

Another clear indication that the numbers are wrong was an admission by Census itself. The annual Census report on income and poverty showed that median household income was down 2.9 percent in 2020 and 3.3 million additional Americans had fallen into poverty.[7] These numbers failed the laugh test in a year when federal spending, mostly on transfer payments, rose almost 50 percent and personal savings exploded. The Census explained that its income measure didn't count stimulus checks, since many were paid as refundable tax credits, and didn't count any other noncash benefits like food stamps. Census reported that if it had counted some of these missing payments, median household income would have risen by 4.0 percent instead of falling 2.9 percent, and the poverty rate would have fallen 2.6 percent instead of rising 1.0 percent.[8]

The final clue that the official numbers do not reflect reality is that while highly publicized numbers from the Bureau of the Census on household income inequality show that in 2017 the bottom 20 percent of households had an average income of $13,258,[9] other, less publicized data from the Bureau of Labor Statistics show that these same households spent $26,091 on consumption—two times more than their income.[10] Households in the second 20 percent income group spent 11.0 percent more than their Census income. Census also reports that the top 20 percent of households had average annual income of $221,846, but BLS reports they consumed only $116,998.

Clearly there is something wrong here. The bottom 20 percent can consume more than twice its Census income only because the Census does not count two-thirds of transfer payments as income for those who receive them. The Census report that the top 20 percent of households averaged 16.7 times as much income as the bottom 20 percent can be reconciled with the BLS report that they only consumed 4.5 times as much only by adding the value of transfer payments received to the income of the bottom 20 percent and subtracting the taxes paid by the top 20 percent.

This book will document that these illogical and contradictory findings are the product of historical decisions made by the Census Bureau over the last seventy-five years that have undercounted income. In measuring income, the Census Bureau chooses not to count over two-thirds of all transfer payments made by federal, state, and local governments as income to the recipients of those transfer payments. In 2017, federal, state, and local governments redistributed $2.8 trillion, 22 percent of the nation's earned household income, with 68 percent of those transfer payments going to households earning in the bottom 40 percent.

Remarkably, the Census Bureau chooses to count only $0.9 trillion of that $2.8 trillion in government transfer payments as income for the recipients of those transfers, counting only eight of the more than one hundred federal transfer payment programs and only a select number of state and local transfer payment programs. Excluded from the measurement of household income are some $1.9 trillion of government transfers—programs like refundable tax credits, where beneficiaries get checks from the Treasury; food stamps, where beneficiaries buy food with government-issued debit cards; and numerous other programs such as Medicare and Medicaid, where government directly pays the bills of the beneficiaries.

Americans pay $4.4 trillion a year in federal, state, and local taxes, 82 percent of which are paid by the top 40 percent of household earners. Even though most households never see this money, because it is withheld from their paychecks, the Census Bureau does not reduce household income by the amount of taxes paid when it measures income inequality.

The net result is that in total the Census Bureau chooses not to count the impact of more than 40 percent of all income, which is gained in transfer payments or lost in taxes. The Census data-collection process is the finest in the world, but the assumptions it makes concerning what to count as income distort every statistical measure that incorporates its measure of income. The Census Bureau is accurately measuring what it has chosen to measure, but it is *not* measuring the *right* things. In this book, we add the missing pieces to the Census data to get a more complete picture. Paradoxically, the missing pieces come from official government sources that are collected but not used in the official measure of income.

In this book we will show that when all transfer payments, not counting government's administrative costs in making the transfers, are counted as income of the recipients of those payments and when all taxes paid are counted as income lost to the taxpayers, the measurement of income inequality in America is profoundly altered. Accounting for all transfer payments and taxes yields a measure of income inequality that is only one-fourth as large as the official

Census measure. Whatever your value judgments are about the desirable amount of income redistribution in a free society, it is much harder to argue that the distribution of income is unfair when the ratio of the income for the top 20 percent of households to the bottom 20 percent is 4.0 to 1 rather than the 16.7 to 1 ratio found in the official Census numbers.

As we will show in this book, when you include all transfer payments and taxes and look at changes in income inequality over time, you find that income inequality is not rising. It has in fact fallen by 3.0 percent since 1947 as compared to the 22.9 percent increase shown in the Census measure.

The official measure of the poverty rate, which uses the Census Bureau definition of income, does not count two-thirds of all transfer payments as income to the recipients. As a result, for more than fifty years, the measured income of low-income Americans has been substantially understated. As we will show, when you count all transfer payments as income to the households that receive the payments, the number of Americans living in poverty in 2017 plummets from 12.3 percent, the official Census number, to only 2.5 percent. There are certainly people who are physically or mentally unable to care for themselves and have fallen through the cracks in the system that delivers transfer payments, but, for all practical purposes, poverty due to a lack of public or private support has been virtually eliminated in America.

America's fundamental measures of well-being—hourly earnings, median household income, the poverty rate, gross domestic product, and productivity—are adjusted for inflation using official price indexes to enable meaningful comparisons over time. Measuring changes in prices would be relatively simple if people always bought the same goods and services and those goods and services did not vary in quality over time. The problem is that consumer preferences are constantly changing, new products are introduced, changes in relative prices induce consumers to change the market basket of goods and services they buy, and goods and services change in quality, sometimes in ways that dramatically alter their value.

Today, incredibly, our government uses *five* different price indexes to adjust for changes in consumer prices when it measures economic well-being, when it adjusts government transfer-payment benefit levels for inflation, and when it adjusts the tax brackets in the tax code for inflation. The inflation rate in the post–World War II era as measured using three of these price indexes is significantly greater than the rate using the other two indexes. The price indexes used to adjust tax brackets for inflation and in measuring real gross domestic product and productivity are, respectively, the Chained Consumer Price Index, produced by the Bureau of Labor Statistics, and the Personal Consumption Expenditure Price Index, produced by the Commerce Department, Bureau of Economic Analysis. These two indexes are very similar and yield approximately the same measure of inflation. They are also universally judged to be more accurate than the three indexes used in adjusting indexed government transfer payments for inflation and adjusting individual measures of well-being, such as hourly earnings, household income, and the poverty rate for inflation.

Their greater accuracy comes from measuring what consumers are actually buying at the same time the prices of those items are collected, thereby capturing the gains in well-being that individuals achieve in response to changes in relative prices. During most of the postwar period, the market baskets used to measure consumer price changes in the other three official price indexes have been as much as a decade out of date. As a result, when Americans responded to a fall in the relative price of air travel in the mid- to late 1960s and started to fly more instead of using surface transportation, these other three consumer price indexes missed most of the benefits gained by consumers because the weightings in the market basket for air travel and surface transportation did not reflect what was actually being bought. The same type of distortion occurred as consumers shifted more recently to cell phones when they became cheaper relative to landlines.

If the most accurate inflation measures had been employed to adjust for inflation in indexed transfer benefits and in individual measures of well-being, government spending would have decreased, real hourly earnings and real median household income would have been found to be much higher, and the poverty rate would have been significantly lower.

As will be shown in this book, reducing these overstatements of inflation and the associated understatements of well-being would be quite significant. But numerous academic studies and the Bureau of Labor Statistics itself have also documented yet another set of equally important overstatements of inflation that have yet to be fully corrected for in any of the official price indexes. These additional overstatements arise from the introduction of new and improved products and services, where the value of the new items is not fully accounted for in our official measures of inflation. Delays in introducing new products into the price index miss the dramatic price declines and quality improvements from the early models and the benefits from replacing older products that are inferior and even more expensive.

For example, the cell phone was first introduced as a specific item in the Consumer Price Index in 1998. But because the device was only included in the Consumer Price Index fourteen years after its first public sale, the index never captured the initial 75 percent drop in cell phone prices or the value of their lighter batteries and longer-lasting charge. No government metric comes close to capturing the full value of modern communications technology. Official price indexes have also missed most of the increased efficiency and efficacy of minimally invasive medical treatments and pharmaceuticals and the greater comfort, safety, and size of our homes.

In this book, we will show how claims that real hourly earnings and real median household income have stagnated in postwar America and that the poverty rate has remained unchanged for fifty years are solely the result of a failure by the statistical agencies of the American government to count most transfer payments as income and to use the most accurate available price indexes to adjust for inflation. Every significant measure of economic well-being expressed in terms of dollars is higher than the official measure shown in government statistics.

The Romantic / Victorian-Era View of British Industrialization

While it may seem hard to believe that we could have such a misconception of our general level of well-being and the progress we have achieved in postwar America, it is hardly unique in history for nations to fail to recognize economic progress that is occurring in their midst. There is probably no greater example of the public's misperception of the world they were living in than that of Victorian England, from about 1830 to 1900. Popular perception and even the history subsequently written about the period are highly colored by novels and poems focused on the plight of factory workers and the squalid living conditions in urban nineteenth-century England. Yet this outpouring of indignation and outrage occurred in what, at that point in history, was the beginning of a golden age of human material achievement, especially for workers.

Victorian literature paints a "worst of times" portrait of England in the midst of the Industrial Revolution, with emotional novels and poems that cry out against the poverty, exploitation, and human want of the period. A novel and a poem, both published in December 1843, are among the best-known examples.

Charles Dickens's *A Christmas Carol*, one of the most popular books ever written, tells the story of Ebenezer Scrooge, a coldhearted, wealth-hoarding financier who is visited by four apparitions on Christmas Eve night. The ghost of his partner, Jacob Marley, who is forced to wander the world because he had shown so little compassion for his fellow human beings during his life, comes to tell Scrooge of the horrors that await him in death. Scrooge is then visited by the ghosts of Christmas past, present, and future. Scrooge awakens to a world of poverty, with the unemployed eating potatoes that have fallen off a wagon and people living in squalor, and to the danger of not recognizing the twin threats, personified by two small children, of Want and Ignorance. Their neglect would doom civilization. Thomas Hood's poem "The Song of the Shirt," published in the 1843 Christmas issue of *Punch* magazine, portrays the conditions faced by women sewing in British sweatshops. This despairing poem is a plea to the privileged to understand the dire conditions that workers endure in industrial workshops. The seamstress is compared to a slave as she sews from morning to night. The poet draws an analogy between the wearing out of men's shirts and other clothing and the wearing out of her body: "Oh, Men, with Sisters dear! / Oh, men, with Mothers and Wives! / It is not linen you're wearing out, / But human creatures' lives!" Hood's poem contains one of the most moving lines ever written: "Oh God that bread should be so dear and flesh and blood so cheap."

According to Dickens and Hood, the urban workplace was nothing more than a prison with rewards of a crust of bread, threadbare clothes, and a rented hovel for shelter. So persuasive is Victorian-era literature with its picture of poverty and misery that a twenty-first-century French academic, Thomas Piketty, cites *Germinal*, *Oliver Twist*, and *Les Misérables*, fiction from the era, as empirical "evidence" since the misery portrayed is so vivid that it "did not spring from the imagination of their authors."[11]

Poets and writers extolled the virtues of rural life and emphasized the dignity of rural workers. By contrast, the theme that city life was evil found voice in William Blake's poem "London": "I wander thro' each charter'd street, / Near where the charter'd Thames does flow. / And mark in every face I meet / Marks of weakness, marks of woe."[12] Rural life and nature were viewed by Blake and William Wordsworth as life affirming, filled with fresh air, sunshine, morality, and beauty, in contrast to the dehumanizing evils of city living for poor workers.

Friedrich Engels, whose father owned large textile mills in Salford, England, and in Germany, in 1845 wrote a book titled *The Condition of the Working Class in England*. In it he expressed nostalgia for rural life and claimed people didn't have to work so hard in rural areas. His bleak picture of Victorian England carried over into the rallying cry of the "Communist Manifesto" that he wrote with Karl Marx in 1848: "Workers of the world unite. You have nothing to lose but your chains. You have the whole world to gain."

These Romantic critiques are simply astonishing given the actual economic record of the period. The economy was awakening from a millennial-long slumber. While Romantic literature paints a dark Victorian landscape, the era in fact marked mankind's turning of the tide from economic stagnation and pervasive poverty to a secular increase in prosperity that still dominates the world we live in.

We can appreciate the true achievements of the Industrial Revolution in England during the Victorian era only by understanding that from the fall of Rome in 476 until the Enlightenment of the seventeenth and eighteen centuries, economic growth, wages, and living conditions were largely stagnant. The Enlightenment liberated mind, soul, and property, empowering people to think their own thoughts, worship their own gods in their own way, and benefit from the fruits of their own labor and thrift. Labor and capital came to serve their owners, rather than the crown, guild, church, and village. Labor and capital were recognized as private property and not as communal assets subject to involuntary sharing. These fundamental changes unleashed the explosion of knowledge and production that drives human flourishing to this day.

The British Parliament stripped away the leaching influence of royal charters and initiated reforms that ultimately allowed businesses to incorporate simply by meeting preset capital requirements. Parliament further established that its laws, created through a process of open deliberation, would govern business, not the corrosive influences and rampant cronyism that were pervasive in the medieval marketplace.

Human effort surged, capital accumulated, and knowledge and productivity exploded. Agrarian and handicraft production gave way to mechanization. Rural populations and rural life gave way to urban society as people left rural areas for what they perceived to be a better life in the cities. The movement of people began before the end of the eighteenth century and accelerated markedly by the 1830s. By the mid-nineteenth century, urban dwellers accounted for half the total population of England.

Poverty in rural England had been largely hidden. The poor lived in villages off the road or in the forest, and even a rundown mud shack, when viewed at a distance across the creek, looked picturesque. When huge numbers of relatively poor people flooded into the cities in search of a better life, they were painfully visible. Many authors of both fiction and philosophy in the Victorian era had apparently seen little of rural poverty, and that view of real life in rural areas appears to have been from the veranda of a manor house. But farm and village workers saw the poverty and hopelessness of rural life up close and personal, and while poverty and hardship were visible everywhere in the cities, the potential rewards for moving there were great.

A recent study by Professor Gregory Clark provides a clear picture of the stagnation of wages from 1200 until 1800.[13] For some six hundred years real (inflation-adjusted) wages of skilled craftsmen and their unskilled apprentices were basically unchanged, rising and falling based on the economic conditions of the times. Wages rose after the Black Death due to a reduced supply of labor, only to recede over time. Real wages in 1800 were about what they had been in 1209. According to Clark, a revolution in economic production accelerated beginning around 1800, and the quality of human life in Great Britain experienced more rapid improvement than had ever occurred in recorded human history. Wages that had been stagnant for six hundred years started to rise rapidly (see Figure 1.1). Then, during the Victorian era from 1840 to 1900, the real wages of skilled builder craftsmen increased by 113 percent, and the real wages of unskilled builder helpers rose by 124 percent.[14]

Professor N. F. R. Crafts, of the London School of Economics, showed a similar result for real per capita income (in 1970 US dollars). In England, it rose

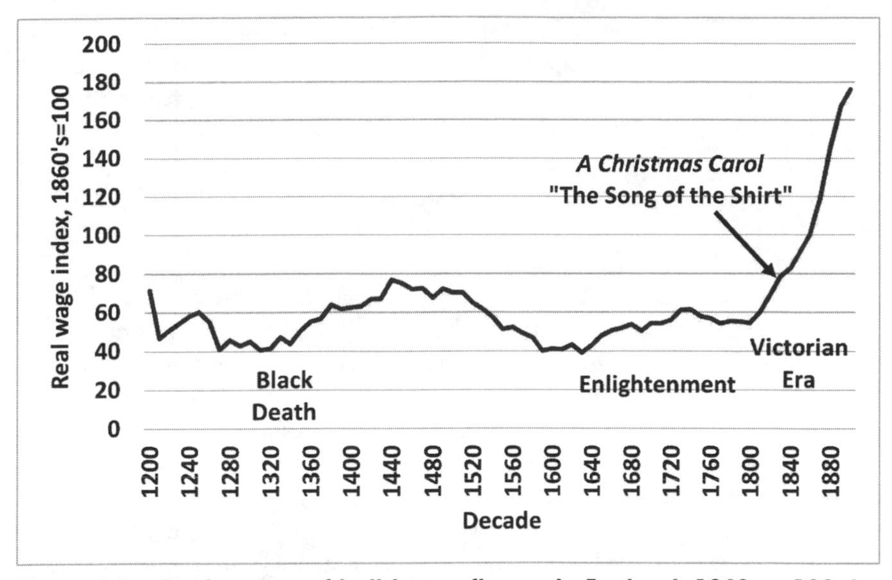

Figure 1.1. Real wages of builder craftsmen in England, 1860s = 100, by decade 1200-1900.

Source: Constructed from data from Table A-2 in Gregory Clark, "The Condition of the Working Class in England, 1209–2004," *Journal of Political Economy* 113, no.6 (2005): 1324–25. http://www.journals.uchicago.edu/t-and-c.

from less than $500 in 1830 to over $1,200 in 1900.[15] A new era of human achievement had begun.

Life expectancy for males rose by 20 percent, from 40.2 years to 48.5 years, from 1841 to 1901. For females, it rose by 24 percent, from 42.2 years to 52.4 years.[16] The literacy rate, which was 64 percent for men and 53 percent for women in 1830, improved to an almost-universal 98 percent for both by 1900.[17] An Index of the Quality of Life for Victorian Children and Youths, which combined metrics for the mortality rate in the first five years of life, a body-mass index to measure adequacy of nutrition, a wage index, school enrollment, female literacy, and household size, more than doubled from 40.9 in 1840 to 93.5 in 1900, where 1914 equaled 100.[18]

Children had worked as field hands and servants since the beginning of settled agriculture more than ten thousand years before. There is no evidence that child labor was more pervasive in urban areas during the early nineteenth century than it had been in rural areas. But there is overwhelming evidence that the movement from the farm to the factory led to a dramatic reduction in child labor. As economic historian Clark Nardinelli concluded, "Technological change reduced the demand for child labor and increasing income reduced the supply. The Factory Acts, then, did not cause the long-term decline in child labor."[19] The broad-based abundance created by the Industrial Revolution during the Victorian era produced widespread school attendance and almost-universal literacy. In closing the ugly ten-millennial chapter of child labor by the end of 1900, the Industrial Revolution ushered in a new chapter of childhood nurturing and learning.

Even within the existing city population, the arrival of factories and the opportunities they produced was a liberating influence. In 1851, one-third of young women living in London were employed as servants in rich and middle-class households.[20] Life "below stairs" was generally miserable, with hard work, long hours, low pay, and physical punishment. The basement environment even in the finest homes was often infested with vermin, damp, and unhealthy. The factories offered higher pay, shorter hours, better working conditions, and even more fresh air.[21] As a result, a Victorian complained in 1872, "It was now necessary . . . to allow their maids to go to bed at ten o'clock every night, and to give them an afternoon out every other Sunday, or no servant would stay."[22]

Of course, there was still poverty and suffering—just as there had always been. As the poor flooded into the cities, the population of London exploded from 1 million in 1800 to 6.7 million in 1900. The causes of many common diseases were not yet known, water and sewer systems were in their infancy, and housing was crowded. But by the time that Dickens and Hood wrote, enormous improvements had already been made, and the unprecedented trend of continuing improvement had been set in place, improvements that would not have been possible without the liberation of the Enlightenment and the increased abundance produced by the Industrial Revolution.

In short, in a period with economic data showing wages, per capita income, mortality, morbidity, and the general condition of human life improving at never-before-seen rates, we had an unprecedented, incredible outpouring of passion over the living and working conditions of the poor. It is important to recognize the sources of these attacks on industrialization and economic development. Their philosophical basis rested in writings that extolled a "return to nature" and a kind of perfectibility of human nature in a rural setting. Poor people in rural Britain sought greater prosperity and freedom, not an opportunity to commune with nature. Not only did they believe their prospects were better in the cities, but any objective reading of the economic data of the Victorian era proves conclusively that they were right.

Getting Our Facts Straight

Like in the Victorian era, today the public and its opinion leaders almost uniformly believe a description of American society that just "ain't so." They believe with almost religious fervor that income inequality is large and growing and that most Americans are not much better off than they were in the mid-1970s. Unlike in the Victorian era, when British statistics consistently showed the actual progress being made, current beliefs are fostered and abetted by generally used official statistics that do not count most transfer payments as income, do not adjust for the impact of taxes on income, and overstate the general inflation rate. This book is our effort to show that the picture of inequality and economic stagnation since the mid-1970s is inaccurate because, as a country, we do not have our facts straight. Getting the facts straight largely requires only that we use all the available statistics collected by our statistical agencies to count all income received and taxes paid and to adjust their value over time for inflation using the most accurate measures available. The facts are hiding in plain sight in official data sources and generally agreed-upon research. The analysis in this book simply applies them.

In the detailed analysis below, we try to set the record straight on the current state of income inequality and the nation's general well-being. We try to do more than just correct the numbers. We try to show why our more complete estimates comport better with the world we live in than the official statistics do. We try to understand and explain the historical forces that made the world we live in.

Using income measures that count all transfer payments and taxes and using the most accurate available measure of inflation, we look at the top of the income structure, the rich, and whether they bear their "fair share" of the tax burden. We also evaluate their contribution to economic progress and the general well-being. We look closely at economic mobility and the economic changes across racial and ethnic groups, age groups, and income classifications that have occurred in the last fifty years. Finally, we look at the policy implications of the findings of this book.

The resulting picture shows a very different and better America than the one that is currently portrayed in the official statistics of the nation and described by advocates across much of the political spectrum. In postwar America, we have experienced strong and widely shared prosperity. Some government policies contributed to those results, and other policies inhibited them. But for almost three-quarters of a century, America has largely managed, in the words of Adam Smith, to overcome "not only the disease but the absurd prescription of the doctor." We find this picture both enlightening and reassuring, and we hope that you will come to share that conclusion.

Since we are presenting information that is different from many of the official statistics of the US government, we examine the data in detail so that the reader can assess the underlying data and the methods used to calculate it, not just the results of our adjustments. We have tried to achieve a balance that is neither too pedantic nor too obscure. For those who want to dig deeper, we provide key data in an online technical appendix (https://vitalfewllc.com/research). Our goal in this book is to start a debate not to end one. The star of this book is the American economic system and its ability in good times and bad to deliver the goods. We hope at the conclusion of this book you will share our conviction that we are still indeed blessed to live in the greatest country in the history of the world and capable of making it even greater.

CHAPTER 2

Inequality in Producing and Consuming in America

Plato's admonition that "a man is only as good as his facts" applies today to the income measure used by the US Bureau of the Census to calculate income inequality and the poverty rate in America. The world's premier statistical agency, calculating the most important economic measure of the country's well-being, using the most sophisticated and accurate techniques available, produces a distorted picture of reality by choosing to measure the wrong things.

Almost three-quarters of a century ago, the Census established a procedure for measuring income by counting only "cash" payments—currency, check, or direct deposit to a recipient's bank account—as income. Because in 1947 over 90 percent of all employment compensation and government assistance was received in cash payments and it was difficult to measure the value of noncash payments, the decision was made to define income simply as the total of all cash payments received. At the time, cash payments received were reasonable approximations of total income. Since then, however, the value of employer-paid benefits has expanded, and the War on Poverty has created an explosion of new programs, such as Medicare, Medicaid, food stamps, housing subsidies, and numerous others that have not been classified as cash payments. None of these new sources of income have been counted as income by the Census. Unlike the uncertainties concerning the value of noncash payments in 1947, the Census and other government agencies now collect and report data on all employer-paid benefits and noncash transfer payments. But, even with detailed information reported separately by various government entities, the Census continues to follow a procedure established seventy-four years ago and does not count noncash payments as income.

In 2017, the average household with earned income in the bottom 20 percent of all households received more than $45,000 in government transfer payments; yet, remarkably, Census failed to count nearly $32,000 of those transfers as income to the recipients. This substantial omission has caused the Census calculations of income inequality and the poverty rate to be seriously overstated. In addition, the expanding number and size of these transfer payments has caused the overstatement of inequality and poverty to grow over time.

Food stamps began as a pilot program in 1961 and became a standardized nationwide income-subsidy program in 1964.[1] Initially beneficiaries were required to buy food stamps at a price lower than their store value. But the purchase requirement was eliminated in 1977, and beneficiaries now receive free debit cards that they can spend on the food of their choice. Because the debit cards can be used only for food, the Census has considered them "in-kind" payments, and their value is not counted as income for the recipients of the debit cards.

Medicare and Medicaid began in 1967. Government pays physicians and hospitals for services consumed by beneficiaries, but because the beneficiaries do not touch the money, Census counts these programs as in-kind and does not count the benefits as income for the beneficiaries.

The Housing and Urban Development Act of 1968 greatly expanded the number and size of housing subsidies for low-income households. Since the payments go to the landlords or to local governments that manage the public housing projects, Census does not count payments from any of those programs as income either.

The Earned Income Tax Credit began in 1975. It has since been expanded, and an additional Child Tax Credit has been added. These tax credits are refundable. The tax filer receives money from the US Treasury for the full value of the tax credit in excess of any income tax liability. Census does not count this money as income, classifying it as a "negative tax."

In 1947, government transfer payments were only about 2.5 percent of total personal income, and the Census counted more than 90 percent of those payments as income to the recipients. By 1979, transfer payments had risen to 11.8 percent of the nation's personal income, and less than half of those transfer payments were counted as income by the Census. By 2017, transfer payments were a whopping 18.2 percent of all personal income, but Census counted only one-third of those transfers as income to the households that received them.

There are now at least one hundred federal programs that each spend more than $100 million annually providing transfer payments to households, as well as an uncounted number of smaller programs. Of that total number, Census counts only eight in its measure of income and chooses not to count the others as income to the recipients. The majority of state and local transfer payments are similarly not counted by the Census. The result is that today two-thirds of all government transfer payments to individuals and households are not counted by Census in its income estimates.[2]

The Census measure has also failed to account for all federal, state, and local taxes, which total 34.1 percent of all household earned income. For some purposes, estimates of income before taxes are useful, but they are totally inappropriate for measuring income inequality. Income paid in taxes is income lost, and in most cases, income never received, because it is deducted before most income is paid. Households in the top fifth of income earners lose 35.2 percent of their pretax income to taxes of all kinds; those in the bottom fifth of earners lose only 7.5 percent.[3] Therefore, any claim about income inequality that does not adjust for these vast differences in taxes paid is extremely misleading. Once again, Census simply measures the wrong things. When the War on Poverty produced an explosion in new transfer payments that were not paid in cash, the old 1947 definition of income, which counted only cash payments, produced income estimates that were increasingly inaccurate representations of economic reality. Because the Census does not take account of taxes, all income differences are overstated by even more, and the magnitude of that overstatement has only grown as the tax burden has expanded and become more progressive. The problem is that Census uses "money income" to measure income inequality and poverty as if it were an accurate measure of the totality of income. The result of these and other, lesser shortcomings is a gross overstatement of both income inequality and poverty. This chapter corrects for these deficiencies using available data sources, 99 percent of which are official government data, and demonstrates that getting our facts straight makes a crucial difference.

Except where otherwise indicated, data in this book relate to households. Since 1967, the Census Bureau has collected and published data based on the household, which is defined as a group of individuals who share in a common housing unit. Prior to 1967, the Census reported income by families and unrelated individuals. When analyzing incomes, households are typically classified into five groups according to their earned income. These five groups are called quintiles, and each has 20 percent of all households. Going forward, this book will typically use the term "quintile" when referring to these income groups.[4]

When analyzing income differences, it is helpful to keep two characteristics of income distributions in mind. First, income quintiles simply divide the population into fifths, and each fifth must always contain exactly 20 percent of the nation's households. Thus, when one household moves upward in its quintile ranking, another household must, of necessity, fall into a lower quintile even though that household's income may have stayed the same or even risen. One can never increase or decrease the proportion of households in a quintile, and no matter how high the income of all American households may rise, there will always be 20 percent of American households in the bottom quintile and 20 percent in the top.

Second, income distributions, such as those in Table 2.1, which will be discussed shortly, exist only for a single calendar year. Individual households are constantly moving among the income quintiles based on where they are in their economic life cycles, the decisions they make, and many other factors. Americans have always been highly mobile in terms of their income. For example, a student in medical school may be in the bottom quintile of earned income but ten years later could easily be in the top quintile. In fact, one study found that between the ages of twenty-five and sixty, more than 75 percent of Americans had incomes that put them in the top quintile for at least one year.[5] This income mobility will be analyzed in more detail in Chapter 8.

Failure to appreciate these two characteristics can lead to statements such as "the poor became poorer" or "the rich became richer." These statements are inherently misleading because many of the poor and many of the rich were different people at the two points in time being compared. If the breadwinner in a low-income household earns a big promotion to be a manager and the household income rises to the middle quintile, its higher income does not show up as increased income for the bottom quintile. The increase in the income of the household does not make the poor appear richer because the household is now counted in the middle quintile. Similarly, if a CEO in a major company chooses to become a teacher and his or her household income drops from the top to the middle quintile, this change never shows up as the rich becoming poorer.[6]

Income Produced versus Ability to Consume

Income inequality in America is most pronounced at its source, the extraordinary inequality in the contributions Americans make to the nation's production of goods and services. In 2017, the most recent year for which we have complete data, the 20 percent of households with the lowest earned income on average earned $4,908. That is less than 5 percent of the $102,093 average earned by American households. Among the top 20 percent of households with the highest incomes, the average household earned $295,904, 60 times as much as the average household in the bottom 20 percent (see Table 2.1).

The earned-income data in Table 2.1 show the average values of contributions to the nation's production of goods and services by households in each quintile. More than 88 percent of all income earned by American households in 2017 was paid in wages, salaries, and employment benefits, so it is hardly surprising that employment income was the source of most of the overall inequality in income earned by American households. The average household in the top quintile had wage and salary income that was 96 times greater than the average wages and salaries for households in the bottom quintile.

Table 2.1. Average earned household income and its components by earned income quintile, 2017 (dollars)

		Average household income and components			
			Total compensation		
Quintile earned household income	*Maximum earned income in quintile*	*Total earned income*	*Wages and salaries, including self-employed*	*Employer-paid benefits*[a]	*Earned income from saving and investing*
Bottom	18,026	4,908	2,211	2,218	480
Second	46,655	30,931	19,605	9,941	1,384
Middle	87,171	66,148	46,171	17,672	2,306
Fourth	147,336	112,563	81,766	25,829	4,968
Top	n/a	295,904	212,494	33,781	49,629
Average		*102,093*	*72,451*	*17,888*	*11,754*
Ratio					
Top to bottom		60.3	96.1	15.2	103.4
Top to middle		4.5	4.6	1.9	21.5
Middle to bottom		13.5	20.9	8.0	4.8

Notes:

a. Benefits and payroll taxes paid by employer. Includes employer-paid defined-benefit retirement benefits and employer contributions to 401(k) or IRA accounts (but not earnings from those accounts, which are owned by the employee and are part of earned income from saving and investing), employer-paid health insurance premiums, and any other employer-paid benefits. Also includes cash income from sources that are not otherwise specified. Miscellaneous could be anything, but severance pay is likely the largest. Miscellaneous constitutes less than 0.5 percent of benefits.

n/a = not applicable.

Sources: Calculated from US Census Bureau, Current Population Survey, Annual Social and Economic Supplement, March 2018 (data for 2017), public-use file. "The Distribution of Household Income, 2015," Congressional Budget Office, March 2018, data files "54646-additional-data-for-researchers." Extreme-poverty adjustments based on Bruce D. Meyer et al., "The Use and Misuse of Income Data and Extreme Poverty in the United States," Working Paper no. 25907, National Bureau of Economic Research, May 2019.

There are two primary reasons why average wage and salary income in the bottom quintile was so low, at $2,211 per household. First, households had fewer workers than in other quintiles. Half of the adults were retired. And among the prime work-age persons in the quintile—those between the ages of eighteen and sixty-five who were not full-time students and not retired—only 36 percent worked. Second, those who did hold jobs worked only 17.3 hours per week, or less than half as many hours as the average worker in the other quintiles. In contrast, the average top-quintile household earned $212,494 in wages and salaries because almost all their prime work-age adults worked, as did many of their retired and students, and, on average, they worked 38.6 hours per week. The factors producing earned-income inequality and the forces that have caused that inequality to grow in postwar America will be analyzed in detail in Chapter 5.

As shown in Table 2.1, benefits paid for by employers, like health insurance and retirement, were much more evenly distributed than wages and salaries. Employer contributions to defined contribution retirement plans are counted as income at the time of the payment because the employee owns the value in the plan. For defined benefit plans, the employer benefits are counted at the time they are paid out, and they are a significant part of the employer benefits for retirees in the bottom quintile. Overall, the top quintile of households earned benefits only 15 times larger than the bottom quintile. Income earned from saving and investing includes payments from 401(k)s, IRAs, private annuities, dividends, capital gains, rent, and interest payments. They were 103 times greater for the top quintile than for the bottom quintile of households. Income from saving and investing constituted a larger share of the income in the highest-income households because higher wages and salaries make it easier for them to save a greater proportion of their income. Also, on average, workers in top-quintile households had longer work histories with more years to save and invest. This greater share of income from saving and investing, however, still accounted for only 17 percent of the difference in earned income between the top and bottom quintiles. In Chapter 7, we will see that income from saving and investing made up a significantly larger share of the earnings for a few extremely high-income households, but for more than 99.9 percent of all American households, wage and salary income provided the dominant share of their earnings. And differences in earnings from work accounted for the vast majority of the inequality in earned income.[7]

The estimates in Table 2.1 make four major improvements on the earned-income components of Census Bureau estimates of income. The most important is adding the value of all employer-paid benefits. Just as Census has excluded in-kind transfer payments to lower-income households, it has also excluded in-kind employer benefits—the most significant being employer contributions to medical insurance premiums.[8] Second, the income from investing adds capital gains from asset sales, which Census excludes. Third, wage and salary income counts additional kinds of incentive and performance compensation that Census does not capture completely. These three improvements come from estimates developed by the Congressional Budget Office (CBO), which drew on detailed Internal Revenue Service (IRS) data and other surveys.[9] All three of these CBO enhancements added disproportionately to the measure of income in the higher quintiles.

The fourth, and smallest, improvement to the Census numbers was to adjust reported income of the so-called extreme poor (with less than $2 per day per person in money income) at the bottom of the income distribution. A research team of academic economists and Census Bureau staff audited the Current Population Survey data using administrative records and other data sources to check the accuracy of the reported income of those who reported extraordinarily low incomes. They found that 90 percent of these individuals were misclassified as extremely poor. Half of them were not even poor, and some were in the middle income quintile.[10] In total, all four improvements added 14.9 percent to the Census income estimate for the bottom quintile and 36.0 percent to the estimate for the top quintile. The net effect of the improvements was to make the measured difference in earned income between the top and bottom 18.3 percent more unequal.

Government Transfer Payments

The resources available to American households are not determined only by the $13.0 trillion of income they earn producing value with their labor and with the investment of the fruits of their thrift. The total resources available for consumption are also determined by the $2.8 trillion of government transfer payments received, $0.2 trillion of private transfer payments, and the $4.4 trillion of taxes paid. After receiving transfer payments and paying taxes, American households in 2017 had $11.7 trillion of available income, one-fourth of which had been redistributed through taxes and transfer payments.

Table 2.2 shows federal, state, and local transfer payments, which totaled $2.8 trillion and accounted for almost 22 percent of all household income in 2017. Over 41 percent of those transfers payments went to bottom-quintile households, and 27 percent went to households in the second quintile. Transfer payments made from more than one hundred different federal programs constituted 93 percent of all government transfers.[11] (See Appendix A for a list of the major federal transfer payment programs.) The remaining 7 percent came from programs funded by states and municipalities.

Table 2.2. Government transfer payments per household, 2017 (current dollars)

		Federal program transfer payments per household[a]							
Earned income quintile	*Total government transfer payments per household*	*Total federal program transfer payments*	*Social Security Old-Age and Survivors Insurance*	*Medicare*	*Social Security Disability*	*Medicaid and CHIP*[b]	*Food stamps (SNAP*[c]*)*	*Other federal transfer payments*	*Total state and local program transfer payments per household*
Bottom	45,389	41,783	10,958	7,986	2,575	9,634	1,504	9,126	3,606
Second	29,793	27,757	6,885	4,720	1,349	7,056	726	7,021	2,037
Middle	17,850	16,760	4,723	3,724	827	3,893	187	3,406	1,090
Fourth	9,738	9,369	3,315	2,604	608	1,706	91	1,044	370
Top	7,282	7,073	2,875	2,360	569	796	—	473	209
Average	*22,010*	*20,548*	*5,730*	*4,279*	*1,207*	*4,617*	*502*	*4,214*	*1,462*
Ratio[d]									
Bottom to top	6.2	5.9	3.8	3.4	4.5	12.1	n/a	19.3	17.3
Middle to top	2.5	2.4	1.6	1.6	1.5	4.9	n/a	7.2	5.2
Bottom to middle	2.5	2.5	2.3	2.1	3.1	2.5	8.0	2.7	3.3

Notes:

a. For programs such as Medicaid that are administered by states but funded in total or in part by the federal government, the state contributions to the funding are counted under the total program and reflected in the federal program total so that the program totals are correct. Program beneficiaries get a single benefit, not separate checks from the two levels of government. State and local totals are for exclusively state and local programming.

b. CHIP: Children's Health Insurance Program.

c. SNAP: Supplemental Nutrition Assistance Program.

d. Inverted compared to most other tables.

n/a = not applicable.

Sources: Calculated from US Census Bureau, Current Population Survey, Annual Social and Economic Supplement, March 2018 (data for 2017), public-use file. "The Distribution of Household Income, 2015," Congressional Budget Office, March 2018, data files "54646-additional-data-for-researchers." "Table 3.12. Government Social Benefits," US Bureau of Economic Analysis, National Income and Product Accounts, July 31, 2018. Social Security Administration, *Annual Statistical Supplement to the Social Security Bulletin, 2017*, Board of Trustees, Federal Old-Age and Survivors Insurance and Federal Disability Insurance Trust Funds, Washington, DC, 2018. Social Security Administration, *The 2018 Annual Report of the Board of Trustees of the Federal Old-Age and Survivors Insurance and Federal Disability Insurance Trust Funds*, Washington, DC, June 5, 2018, Table II.B1, 7. The Boards of Trustees, Federal Hospital Insurance and Federal Supplementary Medical Insurance Trust Funds, *2018 Annual Report of the Boards of Trustees of the Federal Hospital Insurance and Federal Supplementary Medical Insurance Trust Funds*, Washington, DC, June 5, 2018, Table II.B1, 11. "CRS Report: Welfare Spending the Largest Item in the Federal Budget," US Senate Budget Committee, Washington, DC, 2013. "Spending for Federal Benefits and Services for People with Low Income, FY 2001–2011: An Update of Table B-1 from CRS Report R41625," Congressional Research Service, October 16, 2012. US Census Bureau, American Housing Survey, 2017 National—Housing Costs—All Occupied Units, Tenure Filter: Renter. https://www.census.gov/programs-surveys/ahs/data/interactive/ahstablecreator.html. "Federal Student Loans: Education Needs to Improve Its Income-Driven Repayment Plan Budget Estimates," GAO-17-22, US Government Accountability Office, November 2016. "Fair-Value Estimates of the Cost of Federal Credit Programs in 2019," Congressional Budget Office, June 2018, https://www.cbo.gov/system/files?file=2018-10/54095-2019fairvalueestimates.pdf. "Disbursements 2017," Universal Services Administrative Company, https://www.usac.org/li/about/process-overview/stats/historical-support-distribution.aspx. "Table 2.1—Receipts by Source: 1934–2022" and "Table 2.5—Composition of 'Other Receipts': 1940–2022," Office of Management and Budget, https://www.govinfo.gov/app/collection/budget/2018/BUDGET-2018-TAB. "Table 1. State and Local Government Finances by Level of Government and by State: 2016," US Census Bureau, 2016 Annual Surveys of State and Local Government Finances.

The five largest federal transfer payments are broken out separately. The portion of the senior population that met the minimum age of sixty-two, satisfied the required history of qualifying earnings, and elected to start its benefits received transfer payments from Social Security Old-Age and Survivors Insurance. Disabled individuals under the full retirement age of sixty-six received benefits from Social Security Disability Insurance (DI). Individuals over age sixty-five with the required taxed earnings history and all DI beneficiaries were eligible to receive Medicare transfer payments to pay all or part of their medical bills.

These Social Security and Medicare benefits were paid for by taxes collected from the current working population, with more taxes being collected from those in the higher quintiles based on their greater earnings. This transfer of earnings from workers in higher quintiles to retired individuals in lower quintiles is a major factor in reducing income inequality. In addition to these transfers from one generation to earlier generations, there are transfers within a generation of workers. The Social Security system grants disproportionately higher benefits to low-income workers for every dollar they paid in taxes. The net result is that Social Security retirement benefits, relative to Social Security taxes paid, are five times greater for low earners than for high earners.[12]

The impact of Medicare benefits on reducing income inequality is even more pronounced because every Medicare beneficiary receives the same hospitalization insurance coverage (Part A), irrespective of the amount of income they earned and Medicare taxes they paid while working. As a result, in 2017 on average, bottom-quintile earners received a Medicare hospitalization benefit twenty-three times larger relative to the taxes they paid than was received by top-quintile earners.

Medicare beneficiaries are assessed premiums to cover medical and drug benefits (Parts B and D), just as with any other insurance. However, these premiums are heavily subsidized with transfer payments from general revenues. Disability beneficiaries and about 20 percent of elderly beneficiaries with the lowest incomes pay no premium because they are fully covered by subsidies. Another two-thirds of elderly beneficiaries receive subsidies that pay for 75 percent of their premiums, and the top earners receive subsidies that fund 20 percent of their premiums.

Elderly beneficiaries with low incomes and all disabled beneficiaries pay no deductibles or coinsurance for their care. The government payments for these deductibles and coinsurance were all part of the transfer payments reported in Table 2.2 and part of the reason the transfers are so much larger for the bottom quintile. Disability transfer payments under Social Security were made to individuals in 9.8 percent of all nonsenior households. Bottom-quintile households were four times more likely to receive disability payments than households in the top quintile. Since 1972, eligibility standards for disability benefits have been systematically loosened, causing the number of disability beneficiaries to rise more than five times faster than the working population and increasing the redistribution of income from working individuals to those receiving disability benefits. This increase in disability transfers has occurred despite a sharp decline in work-related injuries, medical advances enabling more individuals to overcome their disabilities, and the Americans with Disabilities Act requirement for employers to make much greater accommodations for workers with disabilities.[13]

Medicaid pays medical bills for families and individuals with income up to 138 percent of the federal poverty guidelines. The Children's Health Insurance Program (CHIP) pays medical bills for children in families with too much money to qualify for Medicaid up to 150 percent of the poverty guidelines.[14] A few households in higher quintiles receive Medicaid and CHIP benefits owing to a variety of special situations, such as a family being enrolled in Medicaid or CHIP during a spell of unemployment followed by several months of employment in the same year. Also benefits can be paid to eligible individuals who are in a household but not in the immediate family of a high-income householder.[15]

The next largest transfer program, food stamps (officially known as the Supplemental Nutrition Assistance Program, or SNAP), is one of twelve different federal programs providing food assistance to lower-income households. In 2017, it was a source of income subsidies totaling $63.7 billion in benefits for 42.3 million people, roughly one in eight Americans.

In addition to these five income transfer programs, some ninety-five other federal programs each distribute more than $100 million annually. They range from relatively large, broad-based initiatives like Temporary Assistance for Needy Families, Supplemental Security Income, student Pell Grants, and cash payments from refundable tax credits to more narrowly targeted transfers like the Rural Rental Assistance Program, the Indian Health Service, and the Title I Migrant Education Program.[16]

In total, these ninety-five programs and other smaller programs distributed an average of $4,214 to every household in America, with an average of $9,126 going to the bottom quintile of households and $7,021 to the second quintile (see Table 2.2). Even the middle and upper quintiles received some smaller amounts of these benefits.

Medicaid and a few smaller transfer payment programs are financed jointly by federal and state funds. Table 2.2 combines both the federal and the state funds for these programs under the federal heading because beneficiaries get a single combined benefit that is not differentiated by funding source, and the total for the program is of more interest than the exact source of the funds. But each of the fifty states, the District of Columbia, and many local governments also distribute transfer payments funded exclusively from their own taxes. These programs typically include public-assistance cash payments, a variety of nutrition and energy subsidies, public housing, a few state-tax refundable tax credits, and special assistance for children and the elderly. More than two-thirds of state and local transfer payments go to the bottom two quintiles, with small amounts to the others.

In Table 2.2, government transfer payments are valued at the actual dollar cost of the transfer payment and come from official government sources. Transfers like Social Security and food stamps are valued at the level of the cash deposit the government makes to a bank account or debit card.[17] Transfers like Medicare and rent subsidies are valued at the payment government gives to the service provider to pay some or all of a bill that the recipient household owes.[18] A small number of programs, such as school-based food programs and community health clinics, are valued at the cost of the actual service provided.[19] In all cases the transfer payment is the value actually transferred to the household and excludes administrative and overhead costs.[20]

This at-cost approach is simple and straightforward. The transfer amounts are in some cases below the true market value. For example, Medicare and Medicaid programs use government regulatory force and monopsony power in the market to compel physicians, hospitals, and other healthcare providers to accept payments that are not only below market value but also, in many cases, even below cost, thereby creating financial losses for providers on the sale of healthcare to government beneficiaries. In those cases, providers shift costs to privately insured and self-pay patients, raising their prices on average to 79 percent above government prices.[21] The transfer payments in Table 2.2 do not include the value of any costs shifted to the public by providers but simply assume that the transfer payment received is worth what government pays the provider. Note that transfer payments do not include general government services, like public education, public health, and law enforcement, that are provided to all the public generally without qualifying conditions.

Table 2.2 shows the magnitude of government transfers by quintile. The average household in the bottom quintile received an astonishing $45,389 in government transfer payments annually, more than nine times greater than its earned income. The second quintile received a total of $29,793 in government transfer payments, about two-thirds as much as the bottom quintile, and the middle quintile received $17,850.

As described at the beginning of this chapter, the Census Bureau counted only $0.9 trillion of the $2.8 trillion in government transfers made in 2017. Census included only eight of the more than one hundred federal transfer payment programs and counted only state and local public assistance programs that were paid directly to the beneficiaries in "cash."[22]

The Census justification for these significant omissions is that it only counts "cash" payments. Census has applied that same definition of income since 1947. Before the vast expansion of transfer payments that began after

1964 with Medicare and the War on Poverty, transfer payments were small, consisting mostly of Social Security and unemployment benefits,[23] both of which were counted by the Census as cash payments. After 1964, most new benefits were paid in forms the Census considered to be noncash, and as a result the Census income measure became increasingly inaccurate.

But even transfer payments that most folks would consider cash are ignored by Census. For example, the Earned Income Tax Credit and Child Tax Credit are refundable. That is, if the household income tax liability is smaller than the credit, then the Treasury sends a check for the balance to the tax filer. While this would seem to be a cash subsidy even by the Census definition, Census has decided to classify it as a negative tax. Then, since money income is counted by the Census on a pretax basis, it does not count the refunded part of the credit as income to the recipient. That decision eliminated $80 billion in cash paid to low-income households. The exclusion of food stamps and other nutrition programs because they are "not cash" seems impossible to justify. Just because the payment is on a debit card that can be used only for food does not make the $64 billion of taxpayer money worth zero, as the Census method implies.

Excluding other programs like energy and rent subsidies where government pays the utility company and the landlord in the beneficiary's name also seems unjustifiable. Excluding Medicare and Medicaid, the second- and third-largest government transfers, is similarly untenable. The calculations in Table 2.2 value these medical services at what government pays the providers to settle the medical bills that would otherwise need to be paid by the beneficiary. The government forces providers to accept artificially low prices for medical services purchased through Medicare and Medicaid. Since these artificial prices are estimated to be more than 44 percent below the market price, it is highly likely that the value of these services is, if anything, understated by using actual government payments.[24]

The implications of omitting these transfer payments when calculating measures of income inequality are huge. In 2017, Census omitted counting transfers that constituted 59 percent of total pretax income for households in the bottom quintile. Far more than half their pretax income was simply ignored. Census also ignored 34 percent, more than one-third, of the income received by the second quintile. In higher quintiles, the omissions of transfer payments fell sharply to only 14 percent in the middle quintile, 4 percent in the fourth quintile, and a virtually invisible 1 percent in the top quintile.[25] In these higher quintiles, most of the transfer payments were Social Security and Medicare. Obviously, when a computation excludes 59 percent of the income from the bottom quintile and only 1 percent of the income from the top quintile, the result will be a dramatically skewed measure of income inequality.

The statistics in Table 2.2 incorporate $1.9 trillion of annual transfer payments missing from Census calculations. These missing transfers have been obtained from official government sources such as the Department of Commerce Bureau of Economic Analysis National Income and Product Accounts, the US Government Accountability Office, the Office of Management and Budget (OMB), the American Housing Survey, the Annual Surveys of State and Local Government Finances, and the Congressional Research Service.[26] In addition to including entire programs omitted by Census, these sources have been used to make smaller adjustments to the reported Census numbers so that the total amount for each transfer payment is equal to the total amount actually paid to households by government.[27]

Private Transfers

Some households received additional resources, such as help from charitable organizations, private educational assistance, child support from an absent parent, regular payments from family or friends, or alimony. Americans donated 1.44 percent of gross domestic product to charity, by far the highest rate for any nation.[28] A little more than one-quarter of these charitable donations was directed to private households. Charitable assistance, family, and other sources for private transfers were relatively small, only about 7 percent as much as government transfers. Nevertheless, the bottom quintile received a meaningful average transfer of $3,313 per household from these sources (see Table 2.4).[29]

Census reports a little more than half the total—primarily in child support, alimony, and a limited amount of family and private charity support received in regular periodic payments. The remainder was derived from the Giving Institute's *Giving USA: The Annual Report on Philanthropy*.[30]

The Impact of Federal, State, and Local Taxes on Income Redistribution

To measure the actual resources available to American households, we need to subtract the taxes they paid from the $13.0 trillion they earned and the $3.0 trillion they received in transfers. Table 2.3 shows the average tax payments to federal, state, and local governments by household in each income quintile.

The top quintile on average paid $80,828 of federal taxes, more than eighty-three times as much as the bottom quintile. The federal personal income tax was the largest tax payment, with top-quintile households paying an average of $54,006, while the bottom two quintiles paid no federal income tax at all, in part because the Earned Income Tax Credit and the Child Tax Credit offset any income taxes that they would have otherwise owed. These credits are "refundable," which means that if the credit is larger than the taxes that would have been paid without the credit, the IRS sends a check for the extra unused credit. These cash payments for unused credits are counted as "other federal transfer payments" in Table 2.2. The middle quintile paid about 4 percent of all federal income taxes, the fourth quintile paid 13 percent, and the top quintile paid fully 83 percent of the total income tax bill.

Payroll taxes for each quintile are proportional to their earned wages and salaries up to the maximum income level subject to the respective taxes. Payroll taxes were thus a constant proportion of wages and salaries for the first four quintiles. Significant wage and salary income in the top quintile is above the maximum level subject to Social Security tax, so Social Security taxes constituted a smaller percentage of wage and salary income in the top quintile. But there are no income limits above which the Medicare tax does not apply, and the Affordable Care Act of 2010 added an extra 0.9 percent Medicare tax on wage and salary income above $200,000 ($250,000 for joint filers).

Almost half of the remaining federal taxes were excise taxes, mostly derived from sales of motor fuel, alcohol, tobacco, airline tickets, and telephone service. Because these taxes were paid as part of many common consumer purchases, they are proportional to household consumption rather than income. As a result, the top quintile paid only about seven times more in excise taxes than the bottom quintile. Customs and duties on imports were about one-quarter as large as excise taxes and were distributed similarly across the income quintiles. The "other" category also included gift and estate taxes, which constituted 11 percent of the total "other" category and were almost exclusively paid by the top quintile.

State and local taxes were only about 47 percent as much as federal taxes, and the associated tax burden was distributed differently among the quintiles. The two lowest quintiles paid more state and local taxes than federal taxes, while the other quintiles paid more in federal taxes.

The top quintile paid 8.6 times as much in state and local taxes as the bottom quintile, compared with 83.4 times as much in federal taxes. The major source for this difference is the federal personal income tax. It is much more "progressive" than state and local income taxes—that is, higher-income households pay proportionately much more than lower-income households. In addition, personal income taxes constituted more than half of federal taxes paid by households but only a little more than a quarter of state and local taxes. State and local taxes rely primarily on less progressive sales taxes, property taxes, miscellaneous taxes such as motor vehicle registration, and excise taxes on a range of items from alcohol to gasoline to cell phones.

Sales taxes constituted 40 percent of all state and local taxes paid by households. They are less progressive than income taxes because they are applied only to consumption and do not apply to many personal services. These regressive

Table 2.3. Federal, state, and local taxes per household, 2017

	Federal taxes per household				*State and local taxes per household*				
Earned income quintile	*Total federal*	*Personal income taxes*	*Payroll taxes*[a]	*Other*[b]	*Total state and local*	*Sales taxes*	*Personal income taxes*	*Property taxes and other taxes*[b]	*Total federal, state, and local taxes per household*
Bottom	969	—	332	637	3,027	1,171	8	1,847	3,996
Second	3,809	—	2,947	862	5,032	2,468	354	2,210	8,841
Middle	10,499	2,486	6,939	1,073	8,815	4,691	1,261	2,864	19,314
Fourth	22,382	8,527	12,289	1,565	12,652	5,721	2,702	4,229	35,034
Top	80,828	54,006	22,100	4,722	26,169	8,453	11,266	6,450	106,997
Average	*23,698*	*13,004*	*8,922*	*1,772*	*11,139*	*4,501*	*3,118*	*3,520*	*34,837*
Ratio									
Top to bottom	83.4	n/a	66.5	7.4	8.6	7.2	1345.3	3.5	26.8
Top to middle	7.7	21.7	3.2	4.4	3.0	1.8	8.9	2.3	5.5
Middle to bottom	10.8	n/a	20.9	1.7	2.9	4.0	150.6	1.6	4.8

Notes:

a. Social Security and Medicare taxes.

b. Excludes corporate income taxes. The Congressional Budget Office includes corporate income taxes in federal taxes, but it also adds 75 percent of them as benefit income and 25 percent as investment income that is in effect diverted to government before wages, salaries, or dividends are paid. Since the same values show up as both income and taxes, they don't affect the final result. Since they have no practical effect, this analysis diverges from the CBO at this point and does not include them.

n/a = not applicable.

Sources: Federal (all but 5 percent): "The Distribution of Household Income, 2016," Congressional Budget Office, July 2019, https://www.cbo.gov/publication/55413 (select "additional data for researchers"). Remaining 5 percent of Federal: "Budget of the United States Government," Office of Management and Budget, https://www.govinfo.gov/app/collection/budget/2018/BUDGET-2018-TAB. State and local: "Table 1. State and Local Government Finances by Level of Government and by State: 2016," *2016 Annual Surveys of State and Local Government Finances*, US Census Bureau, https://www2.census.gov/programs-surveys/gov-finances/tables/2016/summary-tables/16slsstab1a.xlsx. "Table 1. State and Local Government Finances by Level of Government and by State: 2017," *2017 Census of Governments: Finance*, US Census Bureau, https://www2.census.gov/programs-surveys/gov-finances/tables/2017/summary-tables/17slsstab1a.xlsx Additional computations derived from these sources.

tendencies have been somewhat mitigated because most states have not levied sales taxes on necessities such as food for preparation at home, medical care, and some apparel and have begun extending sales taxes to more services. The top-quintile households still paid 38 percent of all sales taxes, compared with 5 percent for the bottom quintile.

State and local personal income taxes were very progressive, with the average household in the top income quintile paying 1,345 times as much as the average household in the bottom quintile, but they were still less progressive than the federal personal income tax, which, on average, collected no taxes from households in the two lowest quintiles. The top quintile paid a smaller share of state and local income taxes than its share of the federal tax, but it still paid 72 percent of the total.

The largest among "other" state and local taxes was the property tax. Homeownership is so pervasive in America that somewhat more than half of all households in both the bottom and second quintiles owned their homes and, consequently, were assessed property taxes.

In total, the top quintile paid some 61 percent of all federal, state, and local taxes as compared to 20 percent paid by the fourth quintile, 11 percent paid by the middle quintile, 5 percent paid by the second quintile, and 2 percent paid by the bottom quintile.[31]

The estimates for federal taxes in Table 2.3 come primarily from the CBO, supplemented with data from OMB for the approximately 5 percent of taxes not included by CBO. State and local taxes are calculated from the Census Bureau's *2017 Annual Surveys of State and Local Government Finances.*

Income after Transfers and Taxes

Table 2.4 brings together earned income, government and private transfers, and taxes to calculate the total income after taxes for the average household in each income quintile. The average bottom-quintile household earned only $4,908 but received $45,389 in government transfers and $3,313 from private transfers, bringing its total income to $53,610. It paid $3,996 in payroll, excise, sales, property, and other taxes, which reduced its after-tax income to $49,613.

Second-quintile households earned on average $30,931 annually, more than six times as much as those in the bottom quintile. About 80 percent of these higher earnings came from a larger proportion of prime work-aged persons being employed and working more hours. Second-quintile households received about one-third less in government and private transfers, resulting in $62,765 of income before taxes. Although their income before taxes was $9,155 higher than the average for the bottom-quintile household, they paid more than half of that difference in higher taxes because a greater portion of their income was

Table 2.4. Average annual household earned income, transfer payments, and taxes and the resulting income after taxes by household earned income quintile, 2017

Earned income quintile	*Earned income*	*Government transfers*	*Private transfers*	*Income before taxes*[a]	*Federal, state, and local taxes*	*Income after taxes*	*Taxes as percentage of income before taxes*	*Income after taxes as percentage of earned income*
Bottom	4,908	45,389	3,313	53,610	3,996	49,613	7.5	1,010.9
Second	30,931	29,793	2,041	62,765	8,841	53,924	14.1	174.3
Middle	66,148	17,850	947	84,945	19,314	65,631	22.7	99.2
Fourth	112,563	9,738	865	123,166	35,034	88,132	28.4	78.3
Top	295,904	7,282	845	304,030	106,997	197,034	35.2	66.6
Average	*102,093*	*22,010*	*1,602*	*125,705*	*34,837*	*90,868*	*27.7*	*89.0*
Ratio								
Top to bottom	60.3	0.2	0.3	5.7	26.8	4.0	4.7	0.1
Top to middle	4.5	0.4	0.9	3.6	5.5	3.0	1.5	0.7
Middle to bottom	13.5	0.4	0.3	1.6	4.8	1.32	3.1	0.1

Note:
a. Earned income plus government and private transfers.

Sources: Tables 2.1, 2.2, and 2.3.

earned and, hence, subject to payroll and income taxes. As a result, the average second-quintile household had only 9 percent more income after taxes than the bottom quintile had.

The average middle-income household earned $66,148. The taxes it paid and the transfers it received almost exactly offset each other. The fourth quintile earned $112,563. Government and private transfers, primarily from Social Security and Medicare, added $10,603. Taxes took away $35,034, or 28 percent of that total income, leaving the average fourth-quintile household with only $88,132.

The top-quintile households earned, on average, $295,904. These earnings came from almost-universal employment of its prime work-aged members, who mostly worked full-time, and from a significant number who worked beyond the normal retirement age or while they were full-time students. Transfers from Social Security, Medicare, and private scholarships added less than 3 percent to their before-tax income. They paid $106,997 in taxes, which accounted for 61 percent of the taxes paid by all households. That reduced their after-tax income to $197,034, only 67 percent of what they had earned.

In addition to the combined effect of transfer payments and taxes on the distribution of income shown in Table 2.4, the next to the last column shows taxes as a percentage of income. The average tax rate rises steadily from 7.5 percent in the bottom quintile to 35.2 percent in the top quintile. These numbers show that at least up to the top 20 percent of income earners, the claim that high-income households pay a lower share of their income in taxes is wrong. Chapter 7 will show that even for households with extremely high incomes, the average tax rate paid continued to increase as average income rose even up to the top 0.1 percent of households.

The results of Table 2.4 are startling. The most surprising result is just how distorted the general perception of income distribution is when one takes full account of all transfer payments and taxes. While the average top-quintile household earned 60.3 times more than the average bottom-quintile household, it was left with only 4.0 times as much income after accounting for all transfer payments received and all taxes paid.

It is also startling how different these numbers are when compared to "official" government reports on income inequality. The Census Bureau's so-called money income is the official measure used to gauge income inequality in America. Because the Census measure of income does not count two-thirds of government transfer payments as income to the recipients and does not count taxes paid as income lost to the taxpayer, the Census measure of income inequality is grossly overstated. The Census publications for 2017 show a ratio of the average income for the top quintile to the average for the bottom quintile as 16.7 to 1.[32] That is more than four times larger than the 4.0 ratio that exists when all earnings, transfers, and taxes are counted.[33]

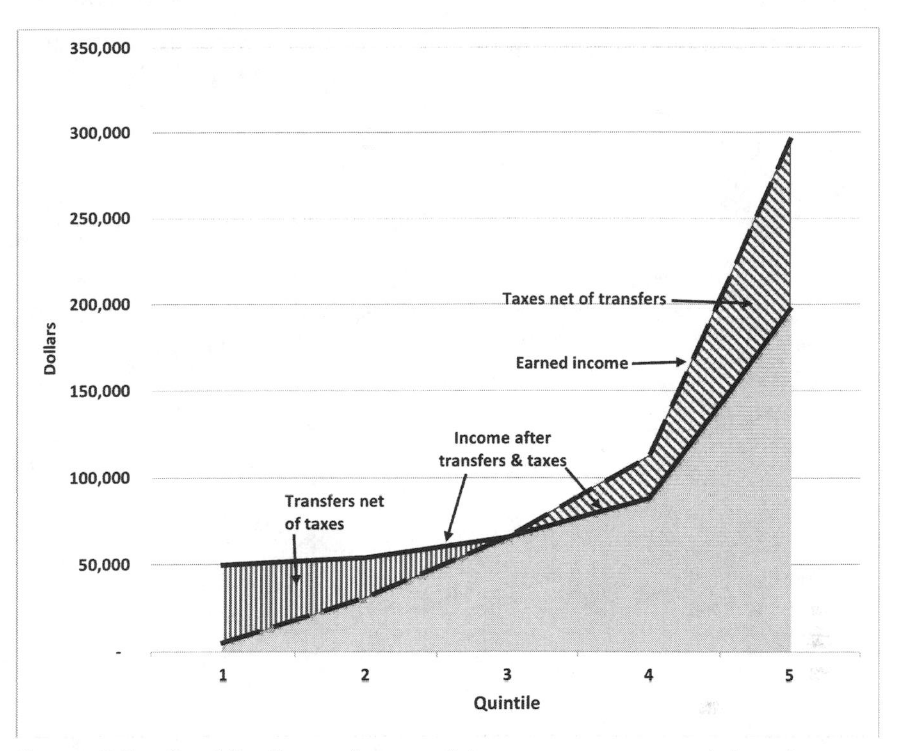

Figure 2.1. Contributions of earned income, government transfer payments, private transfer payments, and taxes to after-tax income, 2017.
Sources: Tables 2.1, 2.2, and 2.3.

Figure 2.1 displays the data from Table 2.4 visually. The dashed line shows earned income. The solid bold line shows income after all transfer payments and taxes. In the lower quintiles, the area filled with vertical stripes represents net transfers (total government and private transfers minus total taxes paid). In the upper quintiles, taxes exceed transfers, and the net-taxes area with diagonal stripes shows the reduction in income from taxes paid in excess of transfer payments received. The bold solid line is the resulting income after taxes and transfers.

An eye-catching result in Figure 2.1 is that the bottom quintile's average net income after transfers and taxes is $49,613, clearly within the range of what is generally considered the earned income of middle-income America, $46,656 to $87,171 (see Table 2.1). Government takes and redistributes enough resources to elevate the average bottom-quintile household into the American middle class.

Also note the stunning fact that the second quintile of households has an average net income after transfers and taxes that is only 8.6 percent above the average income of the bottom quintile. This means the second quintile is only slightly better off than the bottom quintile despite the fact that the second quintile earned more than six times as much, it had more than twice the proportion of its prime work-aged adults working, and they worked, on average, 1.8 times as many hours per week.

Effects of Household Size

The bottom quintile has on average only 1.69 people living in each household. The higher quintiles have 2.23, 2.51, 2.81, and 3.10, respectively. These differences are readily understandable because the lower income quintiles have disproportionate numbers of households headed by young people who have yet to marry or have children and by seniors whose children have left home and whose spouses may have died. The old stereotype of a poor household in America being composed largely of a single mother and a house full of children is fifty years out of date.

Figure 2.2 shows the effects of three different approaches to adjusting for household size applied to the more complete income measure counting all transfer payments received as income and all taxes paid as income lost. The first one, per household, makes no adjustment for household size.

The most direct method to adjust for household size is to divide total household income by the number of people in the household to get a per capita measure of the amount of income available. On that basis, the average bottom-quintile household receives $36,079 per capita. The higher quintile households have on average $32,447, $35,142, $40,549, and $78,837 per capita, respectively. On a per capita basis the top quintile has only 2.2 times as much income per person living in the household as the bottom quintile, a considerably smaller difference than the 4.0 times as much without any adjustment for household size. But the blockbuster finding is that on a per capita basis the average bottom-quintile household receives over 10 percent *more* than the average second-quintile household and even 3 percent *more* than the average middle-income household!

Per capita comparisons are used for many statistics, but we know that if two people combine their incomes and live together, they can achieve a higher standard of material well-being than if they lived separately. The Census Bureau and the Organisation for Economic Co-operation and Development (OECD) have each developed slightly different adjustments for household size that account for the economic value of shared resources. The measurements produced by using either of these two adjustments are very close to each other, so Figure 2.2 simply shows the result of using the average of the two methods.[34]

The average of the OECD and Census adjustment methods produces top-quintile average income that is 2.9 times greater than the average for the bottom quintile, compared with 2.2 times using the per capita method and 4.0 without

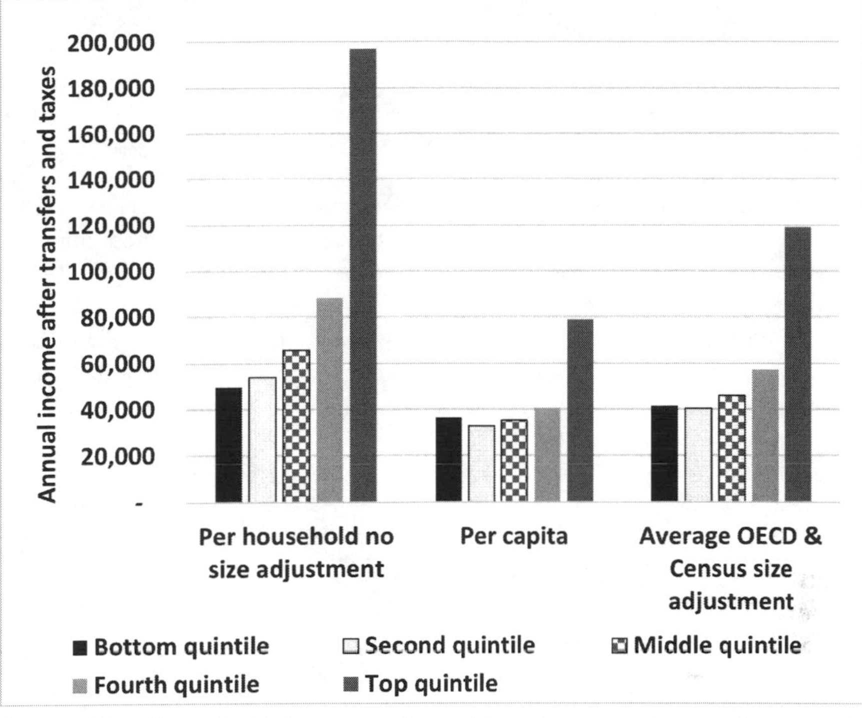

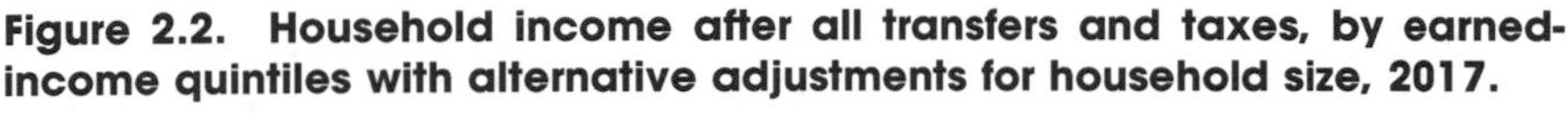

Figure 2.2. Household income after all transfers and taxes, by earned-income quintiles with alternative adjustments for household size, 2017.
Sources: Calculated from data sources for Tables 2.1, 2.2, and 2.3 using size adjustments described in the text.

any household size adjustment. Using OECD/Census adjustments, income after transfers and taxes for the second quintile is still less than for the bottom quintile—about 3 percent less rather than the 10 percent less with the per capita measure. However, with the OECD/Census adjustments, the middle-quintile income after transfers and taxes is somewhat greater than the income for the bottom quintile—but only by 11 percent.

The average second- and middle-quintile households worked more and earned more than those in the bottom quintile, and yet, extraordinarily, the bottom 60 percent of American households all received essentially the same income when we count all transfer payments received and taxes paid and adjust that income for household size. This virtual equality of incomes after transfer payments and taxes in the lowest 60 percent of households is the result of two factors. First, inflation-adjusted transfer payments have exploded by 269 percent per bottom-quintile household since funding for the War on Poverty ramped up in 1967. Second, the tax burden has been reduced for low-income households and raised for higher-income households. Adjustments for household size make this income equality even more pronounced.

This government-engineered equality of income for the bottom 60 percent of American households is a new dimension that must be addressed in future policy debates. Previously, almost all debate concerning income inequality has focused on the inequality between the top and bottom quintiles. The politics of envy based on income inequality has always been a hard sell in America. Few Americans resent Bill Gates, whose innovations made him mega-rich but also made the rest of us better off. Who resents Warren Buffet, who became one of the richest men in the world by raising the investment returns across multiple industries that in turn increased the growth of our retirement accounts? Texan George Mitchell, who invented fracking, combined several existing technologies to make oil and natural gas cheaper for the whole world while reducing carbon emissions as natural gas replaced coal in power generation. He received so small a share of the value he created that he deserves to be considered one of the great public benefactors of the twenty-first century.

Americans have tended to believe that people become rich because they work hard and are smart, but it is hard to see how a middle-income family with two adults both working would not resent the fact that other prime work-age people who are not working at all are just about as well off as they are. It might be fair that Bill Gates is rich, but it seems unjust that 60 percent of Americans have virtually the same standard of living despite dramatic differences in their work effort and levels of earned income.

Current State of Income Inequality in America

It is perfectly legitimate to debate how much income redistribution is appropriate in a free society. Those debates have a long and rich history, but it is much harder to argue that the top quintile of households gets too much and the bottom quintile gets too little when the top gets 4.0 times as much rather than the official Census measure of 16.7 times as much. When household income is adjusted for household size, it becomes even more difficult to claim that Americans suffer from "obscene" income inequality. In fact, a real question can be raised as to the fairness of current income redistribution policies that, after adjusting for household size, provide the average bottom-quintile household with about as many resources as the second and middle quintiles, even though prime work-age persons in the bottom quintile are less than half as likely to work and work only about half as many hours when they do work.

The incomplete numbers being used by the Census to measure income distribution distort the debate. As a country we need to get our facts straight. Debate on income distribution in America should center on facts that include not only the value of what is produced but also the total resources that are available to households after all transfer payments are made and all taxes are paid.

CHAPTER 3

Poverty in America

When the War on Poverty began more than fifty years ago, the proportion of Americans living in poverty according to the official measure set by government was falling rapidly. The number of Americans living in poverty had already fallen from 32.1 percent of the nation's population in 1947 to 14.7 percent in 1965. President Lyndon B. Johnson's policy had the stated goal of not only continuing the rapid reduction in poverty but also accelerating it dramatically. In his 1964 special address to Congress proposing the War on Poverty, he emphasized that it was more than a mere transfer of money to make poverty disappear: "The war on poverty is not a struggle simply to support people, to make them dependent on the generosity of others. It is a struggle to give people a chance. It is an effort to allow them to develop and use their capacities, as we have been allowed to develop and use ours, so that they can share, as others share, in the promise of this nation."[1]

On this second dimension of the policy, the nation has failed miserably. After spending on the War on Poverty ramped up, the official rate of poverty, in fact, stopped improving. For more than fifty years since then, it has simply oscillated within a relatively narrow range between 11.1 percent and 15.2 percent—rising a few points during recessions and dropping similar amounts during recoveries. See the line labeled "Official percent in poverty" in Figure 3.1 for the published Census measure of poverty, with its sharp declining trend prior to the War on Poverty, followed by the stagnant oscillations from then until the present.

To calculate the percentage of the population living in poverty, the Census Bureau applies a threshold below which a family is defined as poor—that is, lacking the resources needed to satisfy its minimum economic needs. That poverty threshold is compared to the actual "money income" of each family in the survey. If the family money income is less than the threshold that applies to families of its size and type, it is classified as poor, and all members of the family

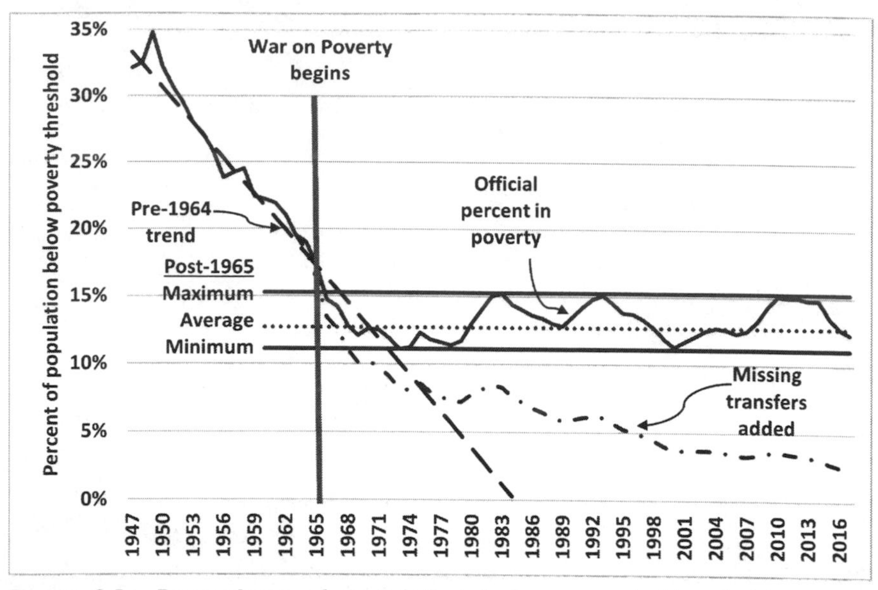

Figure 3.1. Percentage of population below poverty threshold, official Census measure and with missing transfer payments added, 1947–2017.

Sources: For 1959–2017: Table B-1 in Kayla Fontenot, Jessica Semega, and Melissa Kollar, "Income and Poverty in the United States, 2017," Current Population Reports, P60-263, US Census Bureau, September 12, 2018, https://www.census.gov/content/dam/Census/library/publications/2018/demo/p60-263.pdf. For earlier data: Gordon Fisher, "Estimates of the Poverty Population under the Current Official Definition for Years before 1959," US Department of Health and Human Services, Office of the Assistant Secretary of Planning and Evaluation, 1986. Chart updated with foregoing sources from John F. Early, "Assessing the Facts about Inequality, Poverty, and Redistribution," Policy Analysis no. 839 (Washington, DC: Cato Institute, April 24, 2018), 16. For sources of measure with missing transfer payments added, see Table 2.2.

are counted as poor people. For example, in 2017, a husband-wife family with two children under eighteen and Census money income below $24,858 would have been counted as four poor people. The number of poor people is divided by the total population to calculate the poverty rate. In 2017, 12.3 percent of the population met that definition for their respective family types. Official poverty rates have always been determined on a family basis, including families of one. Families of more than one are defined as being related by birth, marriage, or legal arrangements such as adoption. When Census switched to publishing most data on a household basis, poverty measures continued using families.

The US government established poverty thresholds for 1963 that defined minimum economic needs for each of forty-eight family types and sizes. The Social Security Administration began with the US Department of Agriculture (USDA) information on the cost of an economical, nutritionally adequate diet in 1963.[2] It then set the poverty threshold for each family type at three times the cost of the economical, nutritionally adequate diet for the relevant family type and size because a 1955 USDA food-consumption survey had shown that, on average, families spent one-third of their income after income and payroll taxes on food.[3] Since 1963, the thresholds have been updated every year, adjusting them by the percentage change in the Consumer Price Index for All Urban Consumers (CPI-U), which increased 701 percent between 1963 and 2017.

As shown in Chapter 2, the Census counted only about one-third of the total of all government transfer payments as income, but among those families that they classified as poor, Census counted only 12 percent of the total transfer payments they received. This lower percentage of counted transfers among the poor occurs because the vast majority of the uncounted transfer payments have income criteria that target them specifically toward the poor, such as food stamps, the refundable portion of the Earned Income Tax Credit, Medicaid, and most public housing subsidies.

Most of the uncounted programs did not exist in 1963, so their omission did not significantly distort the poverty measurement back then. But with the War on Poverty, the transfer payments that the Census did not count became the biggest sources of income for families that otherwise would have been poor. In 2017, the Census failed to count nearly $500 billion of government transfers received by families that Census counted as poor. Had those missing transfer payments been counted, the actual incomes for many of these families would have been well above the poverty thresholds.

Because most of the spending on massive transfer payments undertaken by the federal government to alleviate poverty was never counted in the official poverty measure, the poverty rate did not improve. Government transfer payments specifically targeted to alleviate poverty rose by 269 percent in real dollars per household in the bottom quintile. By 2017, transfer payments constituted 91 percent of before-tax income for the average household in the bottom quintile. When the Census Bureau applied the poverty thresholds to its income measure, the result was the official 2017 poverty rate of 12.3 percent. When the poverty rate is recalculated using official government data that incorporate a full accounting of all transfer payments as income,[4] the percentage of Americans living in poverty drops sharply to only 2.5 percent. The line labeled "Missing transfers added" in Figure 3.1 shows that when the transfer payments excluded by the Census are counted, the poverty rate has been in a fairly steady decline for the entire postwar period and has almost disappeared. The official definition of poverty is based on *annual* income. This choice of a reference time period is reasonable, but we should understand its implications. Census has estimated that less than one-quarter of the reported poor families have been poor for more than two years. However, more than twice as many families were poor for only two to eleven months as were poor for the entire year.[5] This relatively high mobility into and out of poverty is not surprising. Events like layoffs and illness may cause short periods of little or no income.

Some jobs, like farmwork, construction, and income-tax preparation, are seasonal, creating periods of low income for less than a year. (Chapter 8 will look at the nature of income mobility over different periods in more detail.)

For most situations, the fact that Census calculates the poverty rate based on families and not households has no substantial effect. In fact, 86 percent of households are composed of only a single family, with about two-thirds of them having two or more persons and one-third consisting of a single individual. But the calculation of poverty based on families rather than households produces an unusual and sometimes misleading result. When two unmarried, unrelated adults live together in a single household, each one of them (along with any of his or her children) is treated as a separate family. If one of the adults has income below the relevant poverty threshold, that person and any of his or her children will be counted as poor, even when the household income that supports them is far above the poverty level. As unbelievable as it may be, about 1 percent of the people counted as poor in the official poverty measure live in households in the top income quintile, which means a household with before-tax income greater than $157,328 can include people who are classified as poor. Another 1.7 percent of people officially counted as poor live in the fourth quintile of households, and 2.4 percent live in the middle quintile of households. These individuals would not be classified as poor if the poverty definition were based on households rather than families.[6]

Children and seniors within the ranks of poor families are frequently a focus of special concerns in the debates over poverty. Correcting the measure of income to include all transfer payments improves the pictures for these two groups significantly. The percentage of children living in poverty drops from 17.5 percent to only 3.1 percent. For people age sixty-five and over, the proportion in poverty falls from 9.2 percent to only 1.1 percent. Social Security, Medicare, Supplemental Security Income, food stamps, and other transfer payments have virtually eliminated poverty among seniors.

The official 2017 estimates show 13.6 percent of women living in poverty as compared with 11.0 of men. Calculations that count all transfer payments as income show the gap between the two is much smaller: 2.4 percent for women versus 2.0 percent for men. The differences based on race also narrow when all transfers received are counted as income. The Census data show 10.7 percent of Whites and 21.2 percent of Blacks are poor. Other races on average have 13.0 percent of their members classified as poor. Counting all transfer payments as income received, the relative poverty numbers fall to 2.3 percent for Whites, 3.5 percent for Blacks, and 2.5 percent for others. Counting all sources of income makes the differences in poverty rates among demographic groups much smaller than is portrayed in the official measures.

The current debate about poverty revolves around the belief that 12.3 percent of the population is poor. But once we recognize that the official numbers count a mere 12 percent of transfer payments received by poor families as income, the terms of the discussion change dramatically because only 2.5 percent of the population has a level of income that is consistent with the official *definition* of poverty. In this substantially smaller population of poor people, individuals who often lack the basic mental and physical capabilities to care for themselves and the children in their care become a far greater proportion of the total counted as poor. These special populations require specifically tailored programs to address their specific needs. Simply increasing the expenditure on food stamps or other subsidies generally does not address their problems.

Independent Validation of Poverty Estimates

These corrections to the official overstatements of poverty are validated by two other types of independent analysis. The first is a set of measurements based on what households consume. Consumption is a more direct measure of well-being, and it usually varies less than income over time. Because the majority of people who fall below the poverty thresholds do so for relatively short periods, their consumption does not show the same drop as their income because they draw on savings, borrow, or consume the stored value of assets like owned homes and automobiles until their economic situation improves. Consumption also captures a more complete view of available resources because it is not distorted by arbitrary definitions of what is counted as income.

Two academic economists, Bruce Meyer from the University of Chicago and James Sullivan from University of Notre Dame, have compared the consumption levels of poor American families over time. Meyer and Sullivan began their study with measures of family consumption levels in 1980. They then computed poverty thresholds for consumption that would yield the same poverty rate as the official income-based measure for 1980. In subsequent years, they adjusted these consumption thresholds for inflation and counted as poor those families that consumed amounts less than their consumption poverty thresholds for poor families in real-dollar terms.[7] They discovered that only 2.8 percent of people in 2017 consumed an amount of goods and services that would put them below the real-dollar consumption poverty level of 1980,[8] substantially fewer than the Census count of 12.3 percent of the population. These Meyer-Sullivan results use methods and data that are entirely different from those presented earlier in this chapter, and yet both methods yield the same conclusion—namely, that the current official measure of poverty is about four times larger than it should be.

A second line of inquiry about poverty measures looks at the actual standard of living of families officially classified as poor by Census and demonstrates that most of those defined by the Census as being poor actually have a standard of living more consistent with being middle income. Data from the Census American Housing Survey for 2011 showed that among the households that are officially defined as being poor, 42 percent owned their own home with, on average, three bedrooms, one and a half bathrooms, a garage, and a porch or patio. Half lived in single-family homes or townhouses, 40 percent in apartments, and 10 percent in mobile homes. Only 7 percent of the poor lived in housing classified as "crowded," and two-thirds had more than two rooms per person. The average poor American family lived in a home that was larger than the average for a middle-income French, German, or British family.[9]

Most of the poor lived in a house or apartment in good repair. A mere 1 percent of all housing for the poor was classified as "severely inadequate," only one-quarter as much as in 1975,[10] and most of that inadequacy was concentrated in public housing provided by local governments like New York City.[11] This significant reduction in inadequate housing is consistent with the smaller poverty estimates presented above.

Families defined as poor also had significantly greater amenities for daily living than those defined as poor fifty years ago. For example, 88 percent of poor households had air conditioning, compared with only 12 percent of the entire population that had air conditioning in 1964. Most families classified as poor had multiple color televisions, one-third with wide, flat screens. Two-thirds had cable or satellite television. One-quarter had a digital video recorder. More than half of those with children had a video game system such as Xbox or PlayStation.[12] Fifty-nine percent had internet access, and 72 percent had at least one computer.[13] Almost three-quarters had a car or truck, and 31 percent had two or more cars or trucks.[14]

Hunger and Food Assistance

In the early 1960s, evidence of significant hunger in America led to the Food Stamp Act of 1964 and the formation of the Senate Select Committee on Nutrition and Human Needs chaired by Senator George McGovern. By 1970, the select committee had led implementation of a number of expansions to the original food stamp program with a design that would assure that no poor family would need to spend more than 30 percent of its income on food—slightly better than the 33 percent used earlier for setting poverty thresholds. Total enrollment in the program had grown from 380,000 in 1964 to over 10 million in early 1971.[15] In fact, with these expansions, believing that the battle against hunger was succeeding, the select committee shifted its focus to improving the content of diets for all Americans.[16]

The success in defeating hunger among the poor was documented in 2009 by the Census Bureau. It reported that 96 percent of poor parents were confident that their children were never hungry at any time during the year, and 83 percent of poor families said that they always had enough food to eat.[17] Most poor children's consumption exceeded the recommended minimums for nutrients. In fact, poor and middle-income children consumed the same amounts of protein, vitamins, and minerals.[18] A USDA Agricultural Research Service report, titled "What We Eat in America," showed that for the years 2013–2014 there was no statistical difference in the calories consumed per person between families with incomes of less than $25,000 and families with incomes more than $75,000.[19]

The claims of significant hunger or malnutrition are misrepresentations of a USDA survey that reported 40 million people being "food insecure" in 2017.[20] The survey counted the number of people in households for which the respondent agreed with statements such as "We worried whether our food would run out before we got money to buy more at some time in the last 12 months." If, for a single day in an entire year, someone in the household had worried that they might not have enough money to buy food, then the respondent would count as having agreed that they were "food insecure." The government asked each respondent ten similar questions, eighteen questions if there were children in the household. If the response was positive on three or more, the entire family was classified as "food insecure."[21]

As surveyed by government, food insecurity is a state of mind, not an objective measure or medical condition of actual hunger and malnutrition. The direct, objective evidence cited above from both the Census and the USDA shows that the occurrence of actual hunger or malnutrition is far less frequent than the reported measure of food insecurity would suggest. In 2013, researchers at the Harvard School of Public Health conducted a random-assignment experiment to test the connection between actual food availability and the responses to questions on food insecurity. They found that when a household received a new and continuing subsidy of extra money to buy food, the attitude of people in the household about food security did not improve.[22]

This same phenomenon is reflected in the overall data on food stamps from 2009 to 2013. The United States was recovering from a recession. Unemployment declined by more than 20 percent. At the same time, the federal government loosened its eligibility standards for food stamps and aggressively recruited more beneficiaries, resulting in a 42 percent increase in the number of people receiving food stamps. It is astonishing that with increasing economic security and greatly expanded government subsidies for purchasing food, the measure of food insecurity hardly changed, declining by less than 3 percent. Clearly, the virtually unchanged feeling of food insecurity was an attitudinal measure unrelated to economic reality.

Among families defined as poor, hunger has been virtually eliminated, inadequate housing has all but disappeared, and the amenities of daily life have expanded. These data constitute definitive, independent verification of the vast historical reduction in poverty from 17.3 percent of our population as the War on Poverty began to only 2.5 percent in 2017.

Summing Up on Poverty

In the very few situations in which hunger and real poverty still exist today, there are generally underlying capability or behavioral issues that cannot be solved simply by expanding aggregate welfare spending. Chapter 6 will show that when the most accurate measures of price changes are used to make inflation adjustments to the poverty thresholds that define poverty, the poverty rate is even lower than the 2.5 percent shown in Figure 3.1.

Our success in virtually banishing poverty is an important victory and a tribute both to the power of our economic system to generate the world's largest national income and to the trillions of dollars in taxpayer support for low-income households. Yet the official statistics obscure these triumphs because federal statistical agencies continue to undercount transfer payments to low-income Americans and, in the process, overstate the poverty rate.

Except for a very few individual outliers who have special needs that income redistribution cannot meet, America's poverty program has virtually eliminated most poverty and raised most households to middle-income levels. But in another sense, the War on Poverty has been an abject failure because it has failed in President Lyndon Johnson's second main objective: "to give people a chance . . . to allow them to develop and use their capacities."[23] The explosion in transfer payments to low-income Americans since 1967 has induced twice as many prime work-age adults among the poor to stop working and accept government subsidies, exchanging development and use of their capabilities for idleness. Chapter 5 will explore that problem in considerable detail since it is the single largest cause of the rise in earned-income inequality.

CHAPTER 4

Trends in Income Inequality

The *Economist* magazine introduced a recent article on inequality with the following summary of conventional wisdom on the topic: "It is a truth universally acknowledged that inequality in the rich world is high and rising."[1] Chapter 2 evaluated the first half of that belief and showed that income inequality is considerably smaller than generally believed. This chapter tests the second half of the claim and looks at whether income inequality has in fact grown in postwar America.

Effect of Transfer Payments and Taxes over Time

Chapter 2 identified how Census has failed to count two-thirds of government transfer payments to households as income, neglected to deduct taxes as income lost to those who paid the taxes, and omitted some earned income such as capital gains and employer-paid benefits like medical insurance. Chapter 2 showed that in 2017, when all transfer payments, missing earned income, and taxes are accounted for, the average household in the top quintile had an income only 4.0 times greater than that of the average household in the bottom quintile. According to Census income estimates, that ratio was more than four times greater, 16.7 to 1.

The omission of a substantial majority of transfer payments and all taxes in calculating income inequality also has had a profound effect on the measured trend of income inequality over time. National Income and Product Accounts data from the Bureau of Economic Analysis show that from 1947 to 2017, total real transfer payments grew 211.9 percent faster than total real earned personal income. This huge divergence in the trend between transfers and earnings caused inequality of income after transfers to become significantly smaller over the last seventy years because a large share of transfer payments went to low-income households.

Taxes grew a less dramatic 7.1 percent faster than earned income over the last seventy years. But different types of taxes grew at substantially different rates. Income and payroll taxes rose 21.2 percent faster than income, while sales, excise, and property taxes rose 8.3 percent slower than income.[2] The US income tax system has become significantly more progressive over the last seventy years. Over the same seventy years, less progressive taxes, such as sales, excise, and property taxes, have collected a smaller share of the overall taxes. As a result, an increasing share of the tax burden has been shifted from low- and middle-income households to higher-income households, thereby reducing income inequality.

The decline of income inequality from larger transfer payments to the lower-income quintiles and higher taxes taken from the upper-income quintiles was partly offset by the effects of adding employer-paid benefits and other earnings omitted by Census such as capital gains, both of which grew somewhat faster than wages and salaries. But the net effect of trends in all four factors omitted by the Census has been to reduce income inequality over the last seventy years. For income after transfers and taxes reported in Chapter 2, the ratio of the top quintile to the bottom quintile was 4.0 to 1 in 2017. Seventy years earlier, in 1947, the ratio was 40 percent greater at 5.6 to 1. But because the Census income measure ignores most of the rise in transfer payments at the bottom and all the increasing tax burden at the top, its top-to-bottom ratio for the Census measure of income did the opposite and rose from 13.7 to 16.7.[3] Adding missed transfer payments, taxes, and other unreported income not counted by Census changes the seventy-year trend of inequality, as measured by the ratio of the top quintile to the bottom quintile, from the Census measure adding one-quarter more inequality to the more complete measure showing more than a one-quarter less inequality.

Figure 4.1 shows in more detail how this more complete accounting affected the trends in earnings, transfers, and taxes for each income quintile over the last seventy years. For simplicity, transfers are shown as net transfers (transfers minus taxes) when transfer payments received are greater than taxes paid. That is generally the case for most of the postwar period in the bottom two quintiles shown in Figure 4.1, except in the immediate postwar years. The difference is shown as net taxes when taxes paid exceed transfers received. That is the case for the top two quintiles shown in Figure 4.1. For the middle quintile, tax increases were slightly greater than transfer increases for most of the seventy years, but since 2009 transfer payments have grown more.

Before the War on Poverty, which posted its first big spending increase in 1967, transfer payments constituted about three-quarters of total income for the

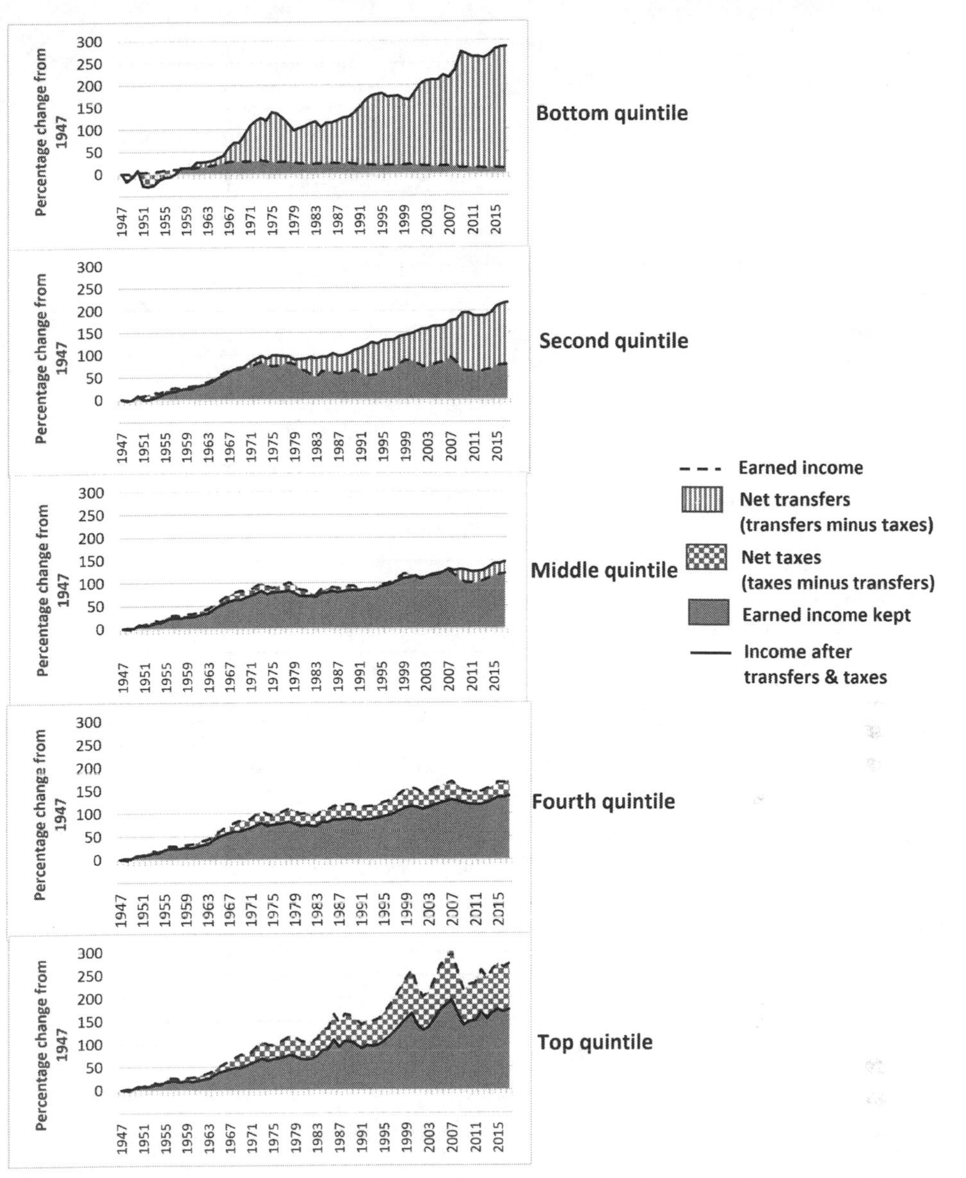

Figure 4.1. Cumulative percentage change from 1947 in real household income components, by quintile.

Note: Net transfers are transfer payments minus taxes when transfer payments are greater than taxes. Net taxes are taxes minus transfer payments when taxes are greater than transfer payments. Real dollars calculated using CPI-U.

Sources: Calculated from micro sources underlying Tables 2.1, 2.2, 2.3, and 2.4. Plus "The Distribution of Household Income, 2015," Congressional Budget Office, March 2018, data files "54646-additional-data-for-researchers." "Table 2.1—Receipts by Source: 1934–2022" and "Table 2.5—Composition of 'Other Receipts': 1940–2022," Office of Management and Budget, https://www.govinfo.gov/app/collection/budget/2018/BUDGET-2018-TAB. "Table 1. State and Local Government Finances by Level of Government and by State: 2016," US Census Bureau, 2016 Annual Surveys of State and Local Government Finances, https://www.census.gov/data/datasets/2016/econ/local/public-use-datasets.html. "Table 3.2. Federal Government Current Receipts and Expenditures," National Bureau for Economic Analysis, National Income and Product Accounts, https://apps.bea.gov/iTable/iTable.cfm?reqid=19&step=2#reqid=19&step=2&isuri=1&1921=survey. "Table 3.3. State and Local Government Current Receipts and Expenditures," National Bureau for Economic Analysis, National Income and Product Accounts, https://apps.bea.gov/iTable/iTable.cfm?reqid=19&step=2#reqid=19&step=2&isuri=1&1921=survey. Census series from "Table H-4. Gini Indexes for Households, by Race and Hispanic Origin of Householder: 1967 to 2017," US Census Bureau, https://www.census.gov/data/tables/time-series/demo/income-poverty/historical-income-households.html.

bottom quintile. Nearly half of bottom-quintile adults were of retirement age and receiving Social Security. About two-thirds of the prime work-age adults in the bottom quintile were working. The almost one-third who were not working were receiving some combination of unemployment insurance, workers' compensation, and relief payments, primarily from state and local government. Figure 4.1 shows that when the War on Poverty began, transfer payments to the bottom quintile grew very rapidly. But their average earned income actually declined very slightly, because while wages and benefits rose for those who worked, the proportion of bottom-quintile prime work-age persons who actually worked fell. By 2017, about the same proportion of the bottom quintile was of retirement age, but they were now receiving both Social Security and Medicare. The proportion of prime work-age adults who were not working had doubled, and they were receiving far larger transfer payments than the earlier generation. As a result, transfer payments in 2017 constituted 91 percent of the total income of the bottom quintile. At the same time, the bottom quintile benefited from a drop in its total tax burden from 19 percent of total income to less than 8 percent.

The second quintile also became more dependent on transfer payments. Transfers averaged about 21 percent of pretax income in the two decades following World War II, and taxes took about 24 percent of income. Because transfer receipts and tax payments largely offset each other in those early years, Figure 4.1 shows only minor changes in the amounts of net transfers or net taxes in the years before 1967, and most of the growth in after-tax income came from increases in earned income. After 1967, transfer payments began to grow faster than earned income. By 2017, transfer payments as a share of income for the second quintile had more than doubled and accounted for 51 percent of total before-tax income by 2017. The proportion of prime work-age individuals in the second quintile who worked declined from 90 percent to 85 percent from 1967 to 2017. Although the decline in employment was smaller than for the bottom quintile, earned income in the second quintile still dropped from about 79 percent of pretax income before 1967 to only 49 percent in 2017 because the growth in transfer payments was much larger than the increase in earned income. The second quintile's tax burden fell from an average of 24 percent before 1967 to only 14 percent of income in 2017.

In the middle quintile, growth in transfer payments and taxes almost offset each other for most of the seventy years, with taxes growing slightly faster until the 2008–2009 recession, after which the cumulate growth in transfer payments was faster. For the full seventy-year period, net transfer payments accounted for 6 percent of the growth in after-tax income for the middle quintile. Earned income grew strongly for both the fourth and the top quintiles, but taxes took 35.0 percent of that growth from the fourth quintile and 40.0 percent from the top quintile.[4]

The net effects of all these changes on the trend in income after transfers and taxes paint a very different picture from the one often claimed in political debates. Figure 4.1 shows that the bottom quintile, with its substantial expansion in transfer payments and reduced tax burden, experienced faster real-income growth than any other quintile, 285 percent over the seventy years. Its faster growth did not begin until the War on Poverty programs started, however. Before the War on Poverty, although earned income in the bottom quintile grew faster than in the other quintiles, its income after transfer payments and taxes grew about the same as the others because overall transfer payments were growing more slowly than earnings and because payroll taxes on the bottom quintile more than quadrupled.

The second quintile had the second strongest growth in real income after transfers and taxes. Its income rose 217 percent, with significant contributions from increased transfer payments and reduced taxes, both of which were more modest than those for the bottom quintile. Rising taxes reduced the top quintile's net income growth to only 174 percent after transfers and taxes, somewhat ahead of the 146 percent growth for the middle quintile and 137 percent growth for the fourth quintile.

Trends in the Gini Coefficient

Claims about increasing income inequality are often made using a statistic called the Gini coefficient, which is designed to equal 0.000 when every household has the same income and to approach 1.000 when a single household has all the income. It was designed as a measure of the amount of inequality, with larger numbers indicating greater inequality. A Gini coefficient between 0.000 and 1.000 approximates the proportion of income that would need to be redistributed to make all household incomes equal. For example, if the Gini coefficient were 0.300, then the amount of money that government would need to take from above-average households to give to the below-average households to make all incomes equal would be about 30 percent of all earned income.

The Gini coefficient for the Census income measure in 2017 was 0.482,[5] and the Gini coefficient for the more complete income after transfers and taxes from Chapter 2 was only 0.335. By not counting two-thirds of transfer payments, the effects of all taxes, and underreported income, the Census overstated actual income inequality by 44 percent, which is consistent with the difference between the ratio of the average income for the top quintile to that for the bottom quintile, as noted in Chapter 2. The 2017 Gini coefficient for earned income alone was 0.561. Earned income is more unequal than the Census income measure because earned income does not add any transfer payments at all to lower-income households, making the income of the two lower quintiles even lower. It also includes income from capital gains and employer-paid benefits that Census excludes, which makes the income for other quintiles, especially the top quintile, even higher. Reducing the bottom and increasing the top makes the measure of inequality for earned income greater.

Official government Gini coefficients for income inequality have been published by the Census Bureau since 1967. The dashed black line in the center of Figure 4.2 contains the published Census Gini coefficients, supplemented with coefficients from 1967 to 1947 that have been calculated from archived income

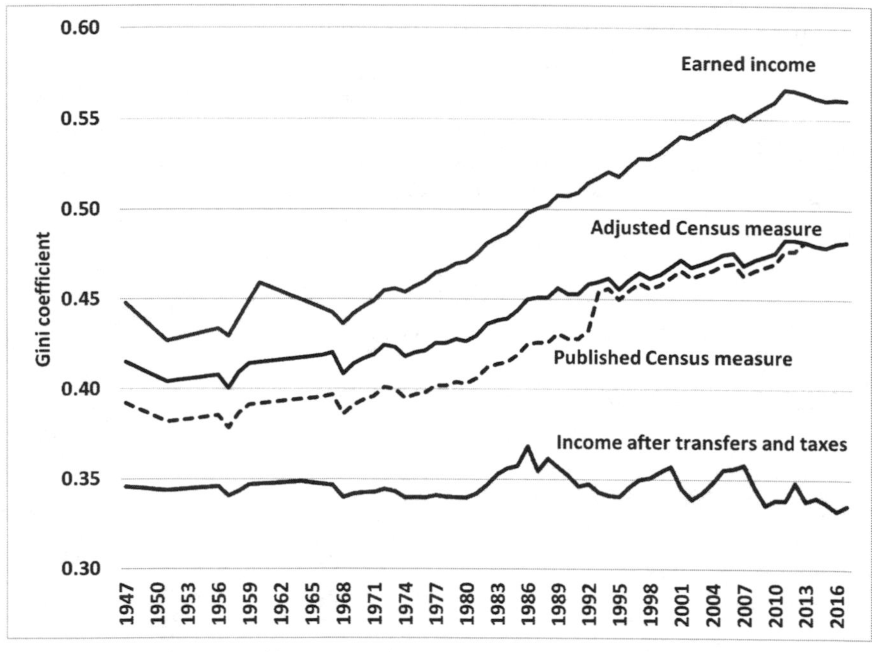

Figure 4.2. Gini coefficients of inequality for three income measures, 1947–2017.

Sources: Calculated from "The Distribution of Household Income, 2015," Congressional Budget Office, March 2018, data files "54646-additional-data-for-researchers." "Table 2.1—Receipts by Source: 1934–2022" and "Table 2.5—Composition of 'Other Receipts': 1940–2022," Office of Management and Budget, https://www.govinfo.gov/app/collection/budget/2018/BUDGET-2018-TAB. "Table 1. State and Local Government Finances by Level of Government and by State: 2016," Census Bureau, 2016 Annual Surveys of State and Local Government Finances, https://www.census.gov/data/datasets/2016/econ/local/public-use-datasets.html. "Table 3.2. Federal Government Current Receipts and Expenditures," National Bureau for Economic Analysis, National Income and Product Accounts, https://apps.bea.gov/iTable/iTable.cfm?reqid=19&step=2#reqid=19&step=2&isuri=1&1921=survey. "Table 3.3. State and Local Government Current Receipts and Expenditures," National Bureau for Economic Analysis, National Income and Product Accounts, https://apps.bea.gov/iTable/iTable.cfm?reqid=19&step=2#reqid=19&step=2&isuri=1&1921=survey. Census series from "Table H-4. Gini Indexes for Households, by Race and Hispanic Origin of Householder: 1967 to 2017," US Census Bureau, https://www.census.gov/data/tables/time-series/demo/income-poverty/historical-income-households.html. 1947–1967: computed from Census Bureau, archived tables of income distributions for individual years.

distribution data from the Census.[6] This chart of the Census Bureau estimates portrays a 22.9 percent increase in the measure of income inequality since 1947.

A careful examination of this line shows an anomaly—an unusually large jump of 4.8 percent from 1992 to 1993 that is more than seventeen times greater than the average annual increase for the entire data series. This anomaly was caused by changes that Census made to its survey methods. While the Bureau of the Census at the time published documentation about the changes, it neither calculated an overlap estimate comparing the results of the old and new methods nor revised the historical data to reflect the new methods.

The most significant change in the Census method of collecting and reporting data for 1993 was to raise the upper limit on the collected values of income. In 1992 and earlier years, when a respondent reported income greater than $249,999 from wages and salaries, investments, or some other sources, the interviewer entered only $249,999 for that income category. Census raised this artificial reporting limit to $999,999 in 1993 and subsequently eliminated it all together. This one change alone added $52.7 billion to the estimated aggregate income in 1993 of the highest-income households, thereby causing the Gini coefficient to be larger strictly as the result of changes in the way data were collected and recorded.[7] The leap in measured inequality in 1993 was almost solely the product of a change in measurement technique and did not reflect an actual increase in income inequality. Of course, income above the maximum cutoff had existed in all previous years, but it had simply not been recorded.

Census reported on the methodological discontinuity and warned, "The change in the questionnaire causes a break in the time series for some income measures. . . . Mean income, per capita income, shares of aggregate income by quintile, and the index of income concentration (Gini index) were all affected by the revisions, and caution should be used when comparing 1993 with earlier years."[8] But Census continued to publish the pre-1993 artificially lower estimates without correction in the same tables with the new estimates, effectively encouraging users to make erroneous, overstated comparisons about the growth of income inequality.

Census made another methodological change in 2013. A new set of questions in the data-collection interview were designed to probe for and encourage more complete reporting of income.[9] The rise in the Gini coefficient caused by these revised methods was smaller than the increase in 1993, but it still had a significant effect on the measured trend of income inequality. This increase was only the result of an improvement in the measurement techniques that uncovered additional inequality that had always been there, just not measured.

The combined effects of the 1993 and 2013 changes in the way the Census collected and processed data was to create the appearance of a rise in income inequality from 1947 to 2017 that was overstated by 42.1 percent—a published

22.9 percent increase versus a 16.1 percent increase in the Gini coefficients adjusted to remove the effects of the changes in methods.[10] The published Gini coefficients are charted as a dashed black line in Figure 4.2. The adjacent solid line shows the result of adjusting the Gini coefficient to eliminate the effects that come solely from changes in Census methods.

We are having an intense national debate over whether to force additional redistribution of income and in the process to change the structure of our economic system, and yet purely technical changes in the way Census collects and processes data have overstated the trend in the measure of income inequality, a key claim in the entire debate, by 42.1 percent.[11]

Other years, especially 1967 and earlier, also show relatively large changes, but these result from normal sampling variability from smaller samples in the earlier years and from using summary tabulations rather than the raw data for calculations before 1967. As a result, they quickly snap back to the overall trend line rather than staying permanently higher or lower.[12]

The income estimates in Chapter 2 avoid the problems of these discontinuities in the Census data by incorporating data from the Internal Revenue Service (IRS), Commerce Department Bureau of Economic Analysis, and Congressional Budget Office that are more complete and accurate than those in the Census estimates.[13] The Census data are derived from personal responses to an interview survey. For many years, Census arbitrarily did not record income values larger than $249,999 for individual income categories. Tax records and other public records do not have those limitations and, hence, have no discontinuities from removing or changing the limitation.

The Census personal interview survey also suffers from nonresponse and memory lapses. But public records are based on official documents, systematically audited, and often derived from actual company payroll data. As a result, they do not suffer significant deficiencies related to nonresponse or memory. The 2013 Census discontinuity resulted from changes in methods to minimize nonresponse and memory lapses, but since public sources like the IRS do not have those limitations, there have been no discontinuities associated with managing them.

The Census income measure has not counted two-thirds of transfer payments. These uncounted transfer payments constituted 59 percent of total income for households in the bottom quintile in 2017. Because those transfer payments grew 242 percent faster than earned income during the seventy years, real income after counting all transfers and taxes in the bottom quintile actually grew 49 percent faster than the average income after transfers and taxes for all households. For the second quintile, real income after counting all transfers and taxes grew 19 percent faster than the average for all quintiles. Real income after transfers and taxes for the top two quintiles grew more slowly because transfers constituted a much smaller share of their incomes and their relative tax burdens rose. This faster income growth at the bottom of the income distribution and slower growth at the top, of course, reduced income inequality.

The Gini coefficients for income after transfers and taxes are shown as the solid line at the bottom of the chart. They clearly show that income available to households after transfers and taxes has not become more unequal in the last seventy years. On the contrary, it has become more equal, with inequality declining by 3.0 percent since 1947.[14] Over that entire postwar period, greater transfers to lower-income households, combined with steeper taxes taken from higher-income households, have more than offset the rising inequality of earned income.

Chapter 2 demonstrated that income is most unequal at the point it is created—namely, earned income. The top solid line in Figure 4.2 shows the history of Gini coefficients for earned income. Not only is earned income more unequal than other measures of income, but its inequality has also risen by 25.2 percent since 1947. The causes of this notable rise in the inequality of earned income will be explored fully in Chapter 5.

International Comparisons of Income Inequality

America is the world's most prosperous large country, but critics often attempt to tarnish that achievement by claiming income is distributed less equally in the United States than in other developed countries. These critics point to data from the Organisation for Economic Co-operation and Development (OECD), which ranks the United States as having the highest level of income inequality among the seven largest developed countries. But the OECD income-distribution comparison is based on data submitted to OECD by the Census Bureau, which counts only about one-quarter of actual transfer payments, less than it counts for its published official estimates of income.[15] Unlike that used for Census publications, the OECD method does account for taxes. When the OECD data are adjusted to account for all government transfer programs, income distribution in the United States aligns closely with that in other developed countries.

Figure 4.3 shows the Gini coefficients published by the OECD for the seven largest developed countries, along with a second "complete" Gini measure for the United States, which includes all transfer payments. The Gini coefficients for these seven countries published by the OECD range from .291 for France to .390 for the United States. The OECD Gini coefficients are calculated for what OECD calls adjusted disposable income, with a definition similar to the income after transfers and taxes calculated in Table 2.4. The individual country

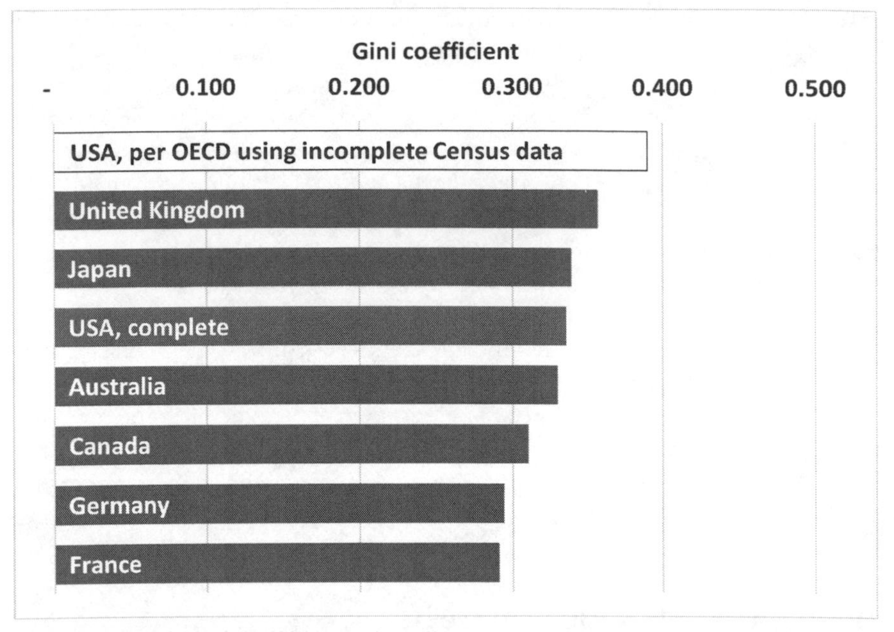

Figure 4.3. Gini coefficients for disposable income in major industrial countries, 2017.

Sources: DP_LIVE_21012020161022263, "Income Inequality," OECD, https://data.oecd.org/inequality/income-inequality.htm. "USA, complete" calculated from same sources as Table 2.4.

estimates are prepared by the respective national statistical agencies, generally following OECD guidelines in an effort to achieve some minimum level of comparability. The Census Bureau submits the data for the United States.[16]

As one might expect, there are variations in the rigor with which nations follow OECD guidelines in collecting and reporting their data. The US data submissions deviate significantly from the norm by excluding large portions of government transfers to low-income households. The Census Bureau excludes two of the three largest transfer programs—Medicare and Medicaid (including the Children's Health Insurance Program [CHIP])—which transfer more than $1.1 trillion annually, most of it to the bottom two quintiles of American households. The US data also exclude eighty-four other federal transfer programs such as Supplemental Security Income, Special Supplemental Nutrition Program for Women, Infants, and Children, and Temporary Assistance for Needy Families. Finally, states and localities directly fund another $712 billion in redistribution programs that are not included in the Census Bureau's submission. As a result of these exclusions, the data sent by the Census Bureau to OECD for the United States Gini coefficient in 2017 failed to include $2.1 trillion of annual transfer payments, $1.6 trillion of which went to low-income Americans.[17]

When the available missing data are added to the US submission to the OECD, the resulting US Gini coefficient is lowered significantly, and the United States ranks between Australia and Japan, as shown by the "USA, complete" bar in Figure 4.3. When all transfer payments are included, the United States falls well within the range of the six other large, developed nations.

The "USA, complete" result is validated further by other independent international data. OECD also publishes comparisons using national income and product accounts that show the United States spends 30.0 percent of its gross domestic product (GDP) on transfer payments, more than any other country except France, which spends 31.7 percent.[18] These data are consistent with the finding that the OECD calculation of income inequality has omitted transfer payments for the United States that are included in the calculations for other countries.

When OECD has been challenged concerning the failure of Census to submit complete data, it does not disagree with the findings that many transfer payments excluded by Census should have been included in the bureau's submission to the OECD. The only US transfer payments that the OECD has argued should not be counted are Medicaid and Medicare.[19] As a practical matter, as significant as Medicare and Medicaid are, even if they were excluded, the addition of the other missing transfer payments would still lower the US Gini coefficient sufficiently to rank the United States between Japan and the United Kingdom rather than Australia and Japan, still well within the range of other developed countries and hardly an outlier in terms of income inequality.

But OECD objections to including Medicare and Medicaid as transfer payments are still inconsistent with the organization's own definition of what qualifies as a transfer payment, and excluding them overstates US income inequality. OECD does not offer a general definition of what constitutes a "transfer payment," but its technical instructions for reporting do say to include "disability benefits, old-age cash benefits, [and] . . . all income-tested and means-tested benefits that are part of social assistance, including quasi-cash transfers given for a specific purpose."[20] That would clearly include US Medicare, Medicaid, and CHIP benefits because they pay cash to providers for specific services delivered only to low-income or aged beneficiaries. Other Americans pay for their own healthcare.[21]

Instead of applying its own published guidelines, the OECD attempted to justify the exclusion of Medicare and Medicaid by claiming that their inclusion would reduce the comparability with other nations that have government-paid medical care for all citizens.[22] But in those countries, every citizen is supposed to get the same medical coverage, so there is no redistribution of income involved except the differences in taxes paid to support these state-run programs. Since those taxes are already included in the calculations for all countries, those differences have already been captured in the OECD numbers.

With its Medicare and Medicaid exclusions, OECD seems to be making a value judgment that the United States should have socialized medicine and, since it does not, Medicare and Medicaid should not count as transfer payments. By any definition, they are and should be counted as transfers because they are government benefits targeted only to specific groups that meet income or age criteria, exactly like other programs that OECD does count. In the United States, other population groups pay for their own healthcare either out of pocket or by purchasing health insurance.[23]

International Tax Differences

Proponents of greater income redistribution in the United States often urge imposing additional taxes on higher-income households, thereby "making the rich pay their fair share," reducing the income available to the top of the income distribution, and providing more revenues to fund transfer payments to the bottom of the income distribution. They support that view with the general assertion that other large, developed countries that have higher levels of government spending also have more progressive tax systems than the United States.

The top 10 percent of households in the United States earn about 33.5 percent of all income, but they pay 45.1 percent of income-related taxes, including Social Security and Medicare taxes. In other words, their share of all income-related taxes is 1.35 times larger than their share of income. That is the most progressive income tax share of any OECD nation. In Germany, the top 10 percent earn 29.2 percent of the income and pay 31.2 percent of income-related taxes, 1.07 times their share of income. The French top 10 percent earn 25.5 percent of the income and pay 28.0 percent of the income taxes, 1.10 times their share of income.[24]

If the top earners pay a smaller share of income taxes in other countries, that means everybody else pays a greater share. In the United States, the top 10 percent of income earners pay 7.6 percent of GDP in income-related taxes, and the bottom 90 percent pay 9.2 percent. In Germany, the top 10 percent of earners pay a similar 7.4 percent of GDP in income-based taxes, but the remaining 90 percent in Germany pay 16.4 percent of GDP, 77 percent more than in the United States. In France, the top 10 percent pay 7.1 percent of GDP; the remaining 90 percent of taxpayers pay 18.2 percent of GDP, 97 percent more than in the United States. Even in Sweden, the top 10 percent of earners pay only 5.9 percent of GDP in income-related taxes, 22 percent less than in the United States; the other 90 percent of earners pay 16.3 percent, 77 percent more than in the United States.

Even these numbers understate just how progressive the total tax burden is in America. The United States collects only 35.8 percent of all tax revenues from sources other than income, such as sales and excise taxes, the smallest share of any country in the OECD. Most OECD members have large value-added taxes (VATs). These taxes are paid on most purchases by all consumers. The VAT is one of the most regressive forms of taxation, which means that the tax systems of the rest of the developed world are even less progressive than indicated by the income tax comparisons.

Artificial Increases in Measured Income Inequality Produced by Changes in the Tax Code

The Tax Reform Act of 1986 reduced the top individual income tax rate to 28 percent while eliminating numerous deductions and exemptions. As a result, more income was taxed—not only because there were fewer deductions and exemptions but also because the lower tax rate made taxable income more attractive relative to tax-exempt income. The net effect of those changes caused the average overall tax rate of the top quintile to rise from 32.8 percent in 1986 to 34.0 percent five years later.

But these tax changes had another significant effect on the Census measure of income inequality, as well as other analyses that used tax data uncritically. The new law made the marginal individual tax rate lower than the 35 percent tax rate on corporate income. This change made it advantageous for many business owners to convert their businesses from C corporations, which were taxed at the corporate rate, into so-called pass-through entities such as S corporations, limited liability companies, and partnerships, all of which were taxed at the owners' new personal income tax rate of no more than 28 percent. This reclassification of business income also avoided the double taxation on corporate dividends.

S corporations and other pass-through companies have more restrictions on them than C corporations have, such as the number and types of shareholders or partners they can have. They cannot be traded on stock exchanges. So not every company would want to adopt an S corporation or other pass-through structure. But in many cases the choice of structure is primarily determined by the effect of taxes.

Monumental changes in organizational structures followed the 1986 tax-code revisions. Before the 1986 tax law took effect, more than half of all businesses (other than individual proprietorships) were organized and taxed as

C corporations at the corporate tax rate. Within five years, after the 1986 tax reform reduced the top individual rate to 28 percent, half a million C corporations disappeared, and 870,000 new S corporations were formed. By 2013, the remaining C corporations accounted for only 17 percent of the total number of businesses other than individual proprietorships.[25]

This revision to the tax law did not change how much money businesses or their owners made, but by inducing owners to restructure their businesses, it changed where the income was reported and the tax rate that was paid. The changes in company structure inflated the personal income reported by many business owners, especially in the upper quintiles, and thereby increased the measured degree of income inequality, even though there was no actual change in income, only a change in which IRS form was used to report it. Research on this phenomenon has concluded, "Shifting between the corporate and individual tax systems has accounted for more than half of the apparent increase in the top 1 percent's income share since 1986."[26] That artificial addition to upper incomes, in turn, inflated the corresponding Gini coefficient.[27]

Unlike other deficiencies in the Census data that can be corrected readily, there is no means of precisely calculating adjustments to the Gini coefficient for these business organization effects caused by changes in the tax code. But we can be reasonably certain that during the late 1980s, when the Gini index was rising faster than during other periods, much of that increase was just a bookkeeping artifact, not a real difference in income inequality.[28]

Gini Coefficients Do Not Measure Economic Well-Being

Among the seven major developed nations, the official OECD Gini coefficients showed that France had the least income inequality, followed closely by Germany. The United States had the most. The differences in the Gini coefficients for these two countries and the United States implies that France redistributed about 9.9 percent more of its national income than the United States did and Germany 9.6 percent more. When the OECD number is corrected for the transfer payments missing from the US data submission, France's extra redistribution was only 4.4 percent more and Germany's 4.1 percent more. Other than changing the ranking of the United States from the highest level of income inequality among the seven largest developed nations to a rank close to the middle, do either of these differences in Gini coefficients imply greater economic well-being among low-income French and German citizens compared with low-income Americans?

A calculation from the Pew Research Center answers that question with a resounding no. It uses data from the Luxembourg Cross National Data Center, which generally omits the same transfer payments excluded from the Census submissions to the OECD. But even within the context of that less complete US data, it still shows that the greater income equality measured by the Gini coefficient is no indicator of a higher level of economic well-being. The Pew calculations define lower-income households as those with less than two-thirds of the national median income after transfers and taxes, adjusted for household size. Upper-income households are those with more than twice the median, and middle-income households are those in between.[29] Using each nation's own national median income, the study found that France and Germany had 17 and 18 percent of their populations, respectively, living below the low-income level, compared with 26 percent for the United States. That would be consistent with the lower OECD Gini coefficients for France and Germany. But if the low-income level for those two supposedly more equal nations were computed using the United States' median income rather than their own median incomes, then 33 percent of the population in both nations would be low income. Using a consistent cross-national standard like this one tells us that the supposedly more equal countries actually have 27 percent more of their population living at what is defined as a low-income level in the United States. They may be more equal, but they are equally poorer.

Household income in the United States differs in only one significant way from that in other nations: Americans at all levels have a lot more of it. American income after taxes and transfers is not distributed more unequally than income in some other large, developed economies. And compared to the other large, developed countries claiming more income equality, far fewer Americans have low incomes because the American economy creates more economic value, paying higher wages and salaries. Even those who rely almost exclusively on government transfer payments benefit from that higher income and the nation's higher living standard.

CHAPTER 5

Causes of the Growth in Earned-Income Inequality

The Impact of the End of the Postwar Period on Income Distribution

The United States emerged from World War II with an almost totally new industrial base, a carryover from what Franklin Delano Roosevelt had called America's wartime role as "the great arsenal of democracy." With its productive capacity intact, a modern capital base, and a well-trained and highly motivated labor force, the United States was the world's economic colossus. With much of the developed world in rubble from history's most destructive war, America was to enjoy dominance in heavy manufacturing for a quarter century.

The 1950s and 1960s are today viewed as the golden age of American manufacturing. In 1938, the United Kingdom exported more manufactured products than the United States, while Germany, France, Italy, and Japan combined exported more than twice as much as the United States. But by 1953 US manufacturing exports were nearly twice as large as the United Kingdom's and a third more than those of Germany, France, Italy, and Japan combined.[1] In the 1950s, real average hourly earnings in manufacturing leapt 50 percent—more than twice their growth rate in the 1970s.[2] US industries that dominated global trade were easily able to accede to demands for higher pay from industry-wide unions. Companies typically faced a single union covering an entire industry, which resulted in uniform wages across the industry, so individual companies were not disadvantaged by wage increases relative to their domestic competitors.

By the mid-1970s, Europe and Japan had risen from the ashes of the war, and Korea and Taiwan had become industrialized. An international system of wealth creation based on trade and market-driven economies was beginning to crush the Soviet Union, transform China, win the Cold War, and bring economic opportunity and greater prosperity to billions. But with more viable competitors, American manufacturing lost its dominance.

William Branson, for forty years a professor of international economics at Princeton University, analyzed the effects of this increased international competition on American manufacturing in the 1970s. He found that the effects of this added competition varied by industry. American manufacturing's share of international trade in consumer and automotive goods declined. But American manufacturing retained a competitive advantage in industries that required substantial physical and human capital, such as capital goods and chemicals.[3]

American manufacturers responded to the mounting competition with increased automation and the application of more efficient production methods aimed at reducing cost, increasing efficiency, and improving quality. As a result of these improvements in methods and concentration on high-end, capital-intensive production, real US manufacturing output continued to grow from 1979 until the 2008 recession, when it fell sharply; it has not, as of this writing, fully recovered. But US jobs in manufacturing peaked in 1979, declined gradually until 2000, and then in 2001 began a ten-year decline of more than 33 percent, after which they stabilized and began to grow moderately.[4]

Just as America's postwar manufacturing dominance was ending, another transformation was beginning. In 1978, China came into the world market, followed by India, Brazil, Turkey, and, after the collapse of the Soviet Union, Russia and eastern Europe. These developments significantly expanded the supply of labor available for the production of global exports.[5] As a result, the world's capital-labor ratio fell, increasing the relative returns to scarce capital while lowering the relative returns to abundant labor.[6]

Americans were the greatest beneficiaries of these changes because they owned more than one-third of the world's capital and supplied only 5.4 percent of its labor.[7] Those with college educations benefited as the value of their human capital rose.[8] And middle- and high-income households also benefited from higher returns on their savings and investments.[9]

The value of US manufactured goods continued to rise with the application of more efficient production methods and a shift to a more high-end product mix, but the demand for relatively unskilled labor grew at a slower rate.[10] According to a study led by Michael Hicks, professor of economics at Ball State University, between 2000 and 2010, the effect of automation on manufacturing jobs was 6.6 times greater than the direct effect of imports replacing domestic production.[11] Of course, one of the primary reasons for adopting more automation and other efficient methods of production was to become more competitive in the face of foreign competition. Overall, living standards in America have continued to rise. Both highly skilled and unskilled labor benefited, but the most highly skilled benefited the most, contributing to the growth in earned-income inequality. These increases in the inequality of earnings from employment were amplified by the rise in the return on capital, which disproportionately benefited upper-income Americans.

Although the difference in hourly pay between the top and the bottom earned-income quintiles grew, the standard of living for low-wage earners who continued to work improved significantly. There were still low-skill jobs in the United States that needed workers. As a result, from 1967 to 2017, real hourly earnings in both the bottom and the second quintiles rose a substantial 42 percent. Average hourly earnings in the middle quintile grew 54 percent, and hourly earnings in the fourth and top quintiles grew by 70 percent and 163 percent, respectively.[12] The rising value of human capital drove these differentials.

Over the seventy-year period from 1947 to 2017, real earned income for each quintile grew faster than it did for any of the quintiles with less earned income. But, if we look back to Figure 4.1, we can see that this long-term trend was not uniform throughout the period. During the first two decades of the postwar period, income in the bottom quintile grew faster than for the other four quintiles, which all grew at roughly the same rate. American consumers had a large backlog of demand from wartime restrictions, and wage and price controls were lifted. Limited foreign competition and strong foreign and domestic consumer demand drove up the demand for US labor. Employers needed workers to meet the demand and were able to bid up wages to attract them.

This strong demand for labor was complemented by a significant upgrading of the skill level of the American labor force. In the two decades following the close of World War II, the proportion of the adult population that had completed four years of high school rose from less than a third to more than half. The GI Bill sent record numbers to college, and the proportion of adults completing four years of college almost doubled to more than 10 percent. Increased demand combined with a more skilled labor force produced growth in wages and benefits that outstripped subsequent periods in postwar America.

In the immediate postwar years, 1947 to 1956, average hourly earnings in manufacturing, adjusted for inflation, rose at a strong annual rate of 4.7 percent.[13] While earnings for all labor grew rapidly in this period, the increased numbers of high school graduates and GI Bill college students shrank the pool of low-skilled workers, thereby helping relative earnings in the bottom quintile to rise faster than for the others.

Following the large pay raises immediately after the war, the growth in average real pay began to slow gradually. The backlog in domestic demand shrank, and foreign production began to come back online. The growth in real average hourly earnings for manufacturing gradually slowed from 4.7 percent per year during the initial ten postwar years to slightly less than 1.0 percent per year in the 1980s. For the full period since 1980, the average real earned income of each quintile has grown faster than for each of the quintiles below it. This general trend of earned income rising faster for higher quintiles, of course, has produced increasing earned-income inequality. But there have been brief exceptions within that period when bottom-quintile earned income rose relatively faster during times of strong economic growth. More recent data show that during the strong economic performance in 2018 and 2019, income for lower-earning households grew faster than for those with higher earnings.[14]

This chapter examines why earned-income inequality has expanded in America following the close of the immediate postwar period. The driving forces producing the growth in earned-income inequality are the decoupling of low-income households from the workforce, the increase in educational attainment at higher levels, the dramatic rise in the value of that education, the increase in economic participation for women, and the rise of the super two-earner household.

The Decoupling of Low-Income Households from the Workforce

The analysis of Chapter 2 showed that the primary determinant of earned-income inequality was inequality flowing from wages, salaries, and benefits earned through work. The average income flowing from work in each quintile was simply the product of the number of people who worked per household, the average number of hours each of them worked, and their average earnings per hour. Table 5.1 has been calculated from the Census Bureau's Current Population Survey, augmented by data from the Internal Revenue Service, the Bureau of Labor Statistics, and the Bureau of Economic Analysis. Its first column of data shows the average annual household earnings from wages, salaries, and benefits in each quintile. The next three columns show the magnitude of each of the three factors determining those annual earnings: average hourly earnings of those who worked, the average number of hours worked each week, and the average number of individuals in the household who worked.

The number of people working primarily depends on two factors: the number of prime work-age persons and the proportion of prime work-age persons who actually worked. Persons are defined as being of prime work age when they are between the ages of eighteen and sixty-five,[15] not a full-time student, and not retired. Table 5.1 shows, for example, that in the bottom quintile, the average household had only 0.2 workers per household, partly because 50 percent of bottom-quintile adults were retired and only 45 percent of the households had a prime work-age person.

The most significant finding shown in Table 5.1 is that among prime work-age persons in the bottom quintile in 2017, only 36 percent were actually

Table 5.1. Determinants of earned household income from employment, 2017

					For prime work-age persons at least age 18 and under age 66 who are not full-time students or early retirees			
Earned income quintile	*Average wages, salaries, and benefits (dollars)*[a]	*Average hourly earnings of workers (dollars)*	*Average hours worked per week*	*Workers per household*	*Percentage of households with prime work-age adults*	*Prime work-age adults per household with prime work-age adults*	*Percentage who worked*	*Average wages, salaries, and benefits if all prime work-age adults worked as much as top quintile (dollars)*
Bottom	4,428	11.76	17.3	0.2	44.9	1.3	36.2	16,824
Second	29,546	12.23	32.0	1.0	75.8	1.5	85.3	38,308
Middle	63,842	17.84	36.1	1.4	87.0	1.7	92.0	72,212
Fourth	107,595	24.05	37.5	1.7	91.8	2.0	96.6	113,884
Top	246,275	52.12	38.6	2.0	93.4	2.2	100.5	246,275
Total	*90,339*	*30.55*	*36.0*	*1.3*	*78.6*	*1.8*	*90.0*	*105,446*
Ratio								
Top to bottom	55.6	4.4	2.2	9.7	2.1	1.7	2.8	14.6
Top to middle	3.9	2.9	1.1	1.5	1.1	1.3	1.1	3.4
Middle to bottom	14.4	1.5	2.1	6.6	1.9	1.3	2.5	4.3

Note:
a. Includes earnings from self-employment.

Sources: Calculated from US Census Bureau, Current Population Survey, Annual Social and Economic Supplement, March 2018 (data for 2017), public-use file. "The Distribution of Household Income, 2015," Congressional Budget Office, March 2018, data files "54646-additional-data-for-researchers," which in turn relies heavily on the "SOI Tax Stats—Statistics of Income," Internal Revenue Service, https://www.irs.gov/statistics/soi-tax-stats-statistics-of-income, and Bureau of Labor Statistics, Employer Costs of Employee Compensation, https://data.bls.gov/PDQWeb/cm. Extreme-poverty adjustments based on Bruce D. Meyer et al., "The Use and Misuse of Income Data and Extreme Poverty in the United States," Working Paper no. 25907, National Bureau of Economic Research, May 2019.

working, compared with more than 90 percent for households in the middle and higher quintiles. While employment income as shown in Table 5.1 is almost 56 times larger in the top quintile than in the bottom quintile, the average hourly earnings of the top quintile are only 4.4 times larger than the average earnings of the bottom quintile. That gap in total employment income as compared to average hourly earnings resulted from the fact that only 45 percent of bottom-quintile households had a prime work-age person, and only 36 percent of the prime work-age persons in the bottom quintile actually worked. In the top quintile, only 6.6 percent of households had no prime work-age person, and the number of employed persons as a percentage of prime work-age individuals was greater than 100 percent. That level of work participation was possible because a significant number of people of retirement age in the top quintile continued to work, as did a significant number of full-time students. It is worth noting that unemployment was only 4.4 percent in 2017, one of the six lowest unemployment rates during the preceding half century, so employment for most prime work-age persons was a matter of choice.[16] The second quintile also has below-average worker engagement among prime work-age persons, with only 85 percent of its prime work-age adults working.

There were also substantial differences between the top and bottom quintiles in the average number of hours worked. For the people who were employed in the top quintile, the average number of hours worked during a week was almost 39. But for the 36 percent of prime work-age persons in the bottom quintile who were employed, the average number of hours worked per week was only 17.

The overall effect of work effort is shown in the last column of Table 5.1. It shows what the income from compensation (wages, salaries, and employer-paid benefits) would have been for each quintile if the same proportion of its prime work-age persons had been working as worked in the top quintile and if its average worker had worked the same number of hours as the average worker in the top quintile.

With the same proportion of prime work-age persons working the same number of hours as the top quintile, the average bottom-quintile household would have earned $16,824, almost four times more than the $4,428 it actually earned. The compensation disparity between the top quintile and the bottom quintile would have fallen from 56:1 to less than 15:1, a nearly 75 percent reduction in income inequality. This massive improvement comes only from the assumed increased work effort by prime work-age individuals.

The most significant factor in the growth of earned-income inequality in the last fifty years has been the sharp drop in the proportion of prime work-age persons who worked in the bottom two quintiles. In 1967, 68 percent of prime work-age adults in the bottom quintile had jobs,[17] but by 2017 that percentage had dropped by almost half to 36 percent. The percentage working in the second quintile declined from 90 percent to 85 percent. At the same time, the proportion of prime work-age persons working in the top three quintiles of households increased by 7 percent, largely from an increase in the employment of women. The huge drop in work effort among lower-income households between 1967 and 2017 cannot be explained by any reduced demand for labor or rise in unemployment. The overall unemployment rates in both 1967 and 2017 were almost identical, and both were among the lowest unemployment rates during the entire fifty-year period.[18]

Among individuals who did work in 2017, those in the bottom quintile, on average, put in far fewer hours than working individuals in the other quintiles—only 17.3 hours per week. That was up 4.6 hours from only 12.7 hours worked in 1967, but the other 80 percent of the population increased their average weekly hours of work by even more, 7.8 hours, working on average 36.0 hours per week.

Clearly, one reason for the rise in earned-income inequality was that the proportion of prime work-age persons in lower-income households who were working declined, while the proportion working in higher-income households increased. Earned income inequality rose still more because the increase in hours worked by workers in higher-income households was two-thirds greater than the increase in lower-income households.

Only one structural change can explain the major decoupling of prime work-age persons in low-income households from the world of work: the near quadrupling (in constant dollars) of government transfer payments to lower-income households. In 2017, transfer payments increased the average bottom-quintile household's income after transfers and taxes to $49,613—only $4,908 of which was earned income. The average income after transfers and taxes for the bottom quintile was only 8 percent less than the average for the second quintile and 24 percent less than the average for the middle quintile.

There has been only one significant attempt to reverse this fifty-year trend of reduced work and increasing dependency. The Personal Responsibility and Work Opportunity Reconciliation Act of 1996 (P.L. 104-193), or simply the Welfare Reform of 1996, was a bipartisan effort by President Bill Clinton and a Republican Congress. It replaced the Aid to Families with Dependent Children transfer payments with the Temporary Assistance for Needy Families. Both the old and the new programs served only households with children, about 90 percent of which were headed by a single mother. The welfare reform endeavored to wean these families off welfare and build their self-reliance by creating stronger requirements for work or training. It also set more stringent time limits on receiving aid.

The 1996 reforms were successful. The number of families receiving payments declined by more than half. Much of the decline was the result of beneficiaries finding employment. As a result, employment among low-income single parents rose.[19] Poverty for single-mother families declined and has continued to remain lower than it was before the reforms. Single-mother poverty also declined relative to poverty for other types of families and has remained lower ever since.[20]

From 1967 until the 1996 reforms, inflation-adjusted transfer payments per family in the two lowest quintiles rose at a rate of 3.9 percent annually. For the four years immediately following the reform, the growth in transfer payments slowed to an annual rate of only 0.6 percent because the reforms focused on moving families with children from total dependence on government to greater independence. But then total transfer payments reaccelerated to a 3.5 percent annual rate, almost as rapid as before. The significant and quantifiable effects from the initial reform efforts were overwhelmed by subsequent expansion of other transfer payments. For example, from 1996 to 2017, the proportion of the population receiving food stamps jumped from 9.5 percent to 13.0 percent. That increase in food stamp recipients was not the result of poorer economic conditions because the unemployment rate in 2017 was actually 18.5 percent lower than in 1996. Yet the proportion of the population receiving food stamps was 36.7 percent greater. Over the same period, the proportion of the prime work-age persons receiving Social Security Disability Insurance benefits increased by almost 50 percent.[21] This increase in disability beneficiaries occurred when work-related accidents had fallen to an all-time low, medical advances had reduced the impact of many disabilities, and the Americans with Disabilities Act had forced employers to make the workplace more accommodating to those with disabilities.[22]

The increased dependence on transfer payments in households other than families with children was created by several factors. First, laws governing transfer payments have generally granted significant discretion to administrators in implementing the programs. Administrators have had the power to increase enrollment in these programs by weakening eligibility standards, changing what is counted as income in qualifying for benefits, raising how long beneficiaries can remain eligible, and waiving any work requirements.

The Congressional Budget Office (CBO) has calculated that in one four-year period from 2007 to 2011, about 35 percent of the food stamp growth was created by administrative changes that lowered eligibility standards to make benefits easier to get.[23] Since other liberalization policies were implemented both before and after the four years studied by CBO, similar effects likely occurred over the longer period as well.[24] The weaker standards also encouraged people to stay on food stamps longer so that two-thirds of beneficiaries continued to receive food stamps for more than five years and 41 percent for more than ten years.[25]

Prior to the beginning of the twenty-first century, the mantra of US public welfare policy was to assist those in need with the stated goal of promoting their capacity to become self-supporting. It appears that both the objective and the method of outreach started to change around the turn of the twenty-first century. Government has not only raised benefits and lowered the eligibility standards but also started actively to urge people to become more dependent on government. From 2000 through 2016, the US Department of Agriculture (USDA) conducted aggressive recruitment efforts that it claimed boosted food stamp enrollment by 157 percent.[26] USDA spent $40 million annually on advertising to recruit beneficiaries, above and beyond the usual public service announcements concerning the availability of benefits. Seniors and Hispanics were targeted with the dramatized message that they were entitled to the benefits, had paid taxes for them, and should feel guilty because, by refusing to apply for them, they were hurting their families.[27]

USDA also trained state and local social service agencies to encourage their public assistance clients to enroll in food stamps. One such training module was titled "Overcome the Word 'No,'" which taught techniques for changing the attitudes and values of people preferring not to enroll in food stamps.[28] Staff were not just taught the factual content of the benefits. They also learned to promote claims such as food stamps were the same as Social Security, for which the participants had already paid, and food stamps created additional economic benefits for the community. USDA rewarded and publicized state social service agencies for their success in overcoming the "mountain pride" of potential beneficiaries "who wished not to rely on others."[29]

While the effects of these promotion programs may be difficult to measure, they are clearly and directly counter to the objectives stated by President Roosevelt in beginning the food stamp program and by President Lyndon Johnson in reviving and massively expanding the program. To the degree that these promotion programs were effective, they continued to sever low-income households from the mainstream of American economic life, lowered the probability that those receiving the benefits would escape poverty, and increased earned-income inequality.

The rapid rise in transfer payments and the accompanying decoupling of low-income prime work-age adults from the workforce began with the War on Poverty. As the War on Poverty legislation was being passed and implemented, the bottom quintile's share of total earned income was more than one-third greater than it had been twenty years earlier, and the second quintile's share was also greater, by 7 percent.[30] Johnson's stated policy objective, "to allow them to develop and use their capacities,"[31] was a commitment to strengthen this growth in earned income among the nation's lowest earners.

But the exact opposite happened. In the fifty years after the funding for the War on Poverty ramped up in 1967, the bottom quintile's share of the nation's earned income fell by more than half. Incredibly, its share in 2017 was 40 percent below what it had been in 1947.[32] The second quintile's earned-income share fell by more than a third. These incredible drops in income share were largely the result of a massive decline in the proportion of people in the bottom quintile of households who worked and a smaller decline in the proportion in the second quintile who worked. Nevertheless, the standard of living among lower-income households improved substantially from massive government subsidies. Between 1967 and 2017, these subsidies raised the bottom quintile's share of total income after transfers and taxes by more than a third and the second quintile's share by 10 percent. Dependence on government subsidies increased dramatically. Low-income Americans became less likely to "develop and use their capacities" to earn a living, and measures of inequality for *earned* income rose.

The War on Poverty significantly increased dependency and failed in its primary effort to bring lower-income people into the mainstream of America's economy. Government programs eliminated deprivation but increased idleness and stifled human flourishing. It happened just as President Roosevelt said it would in 1935: "To dole out relief in this way is to administer a narcotic, a subtle destroyer of the human spirit. It is inimical to the dictates of sound policy. It is in violation of the traditions of America. Work must be found for able-bodied but destitute workers. The Federal Government must and shall quit this business of relief."[33] Despite government's stated intention to avoid dependence, government policies have created more dependence and, in the process, dramatically increased the inequality of earned income.

Disincentives for Working

Figure 5.1 illustrates how government redistribution of income has dramatically reduced the incentive to work among low-income, nonelderly households that are not drawing Social Security old-age benefits. Although all these households were composed of prime work-age adults, in the bottom quintile, transfer payments still constituted 86 percent of their income before taxes. Only 14 percent of their total income was earned from working or saving and investing. These percentages were only slightly different from those of the entire bottom quintile, which included a large number of elderly households.

The average household with prime work-age adults in the bottom quintile earned $6,941, paid $3,512 in taxes, and received $45,377 in transfer payments, resulting in $49,488 of income after taxes. In an average household in the second quintile, more than twice as many of the prime work-age adults worked (80.8 percent versus 33.0 percent for the bottom quintile). And, on average, they worked almost twice as many hours per week (33.0 versus 18.5). As a result, they earned $31,811, or $24,870 more than the average bottom-quintile household. But because they earned so much more money, the average second-quintile household was not eligible for $18,972 in transfer payments that the average bottom-quintile household received and paid $4,212 more in taxes—mostly additional payroll taxes. So, after working more than four times as much, the average second-quintile household had only $1,686 more money for living than the average bottom-quintile household. From the additional income that they *earned* compared with the bottom quintile, the average second-quintile household got to keep only 7 cents of every additional dollar, an extremely small economic incentive to work more.

The average middle-quintile household earned $59,512 more than the average for the bottom quintile but lost $32,444 in transfer payments and $14,524 more in taxes, keeping only 21 cents of every additional dollar earned. While not as small as the incentive to work in the second quintile, that is still a small economic reward for significantly more effort.

But irrespective of the exact size of the disincentive, the evidence is clear that substantially larger transfer payments have more than doubled the proportion of prime work-age persons who do not work.

With these strong government financial disincentives to work, it is a tribute to American workers that most have not succumbed to the temptation to take a slightly lower income for a lot less work.[34]

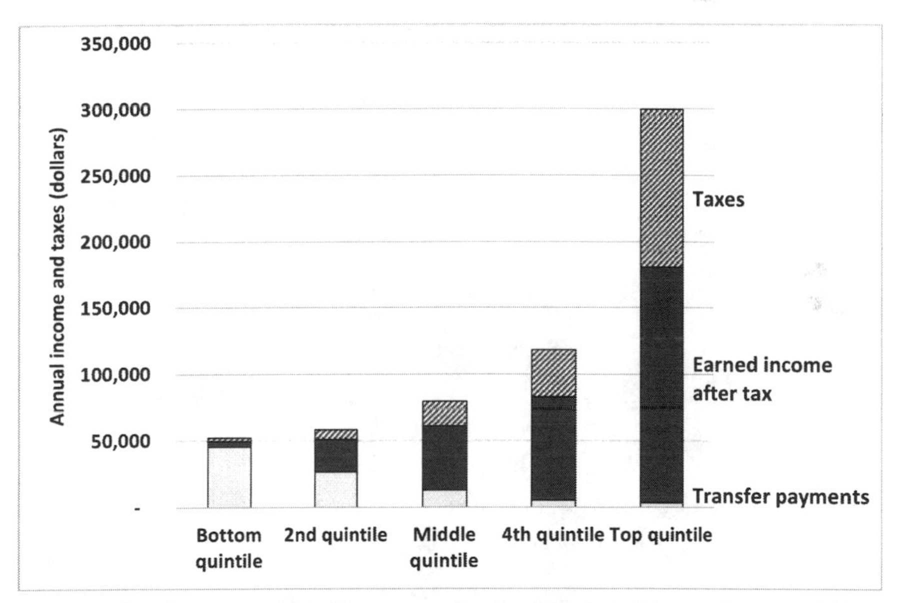

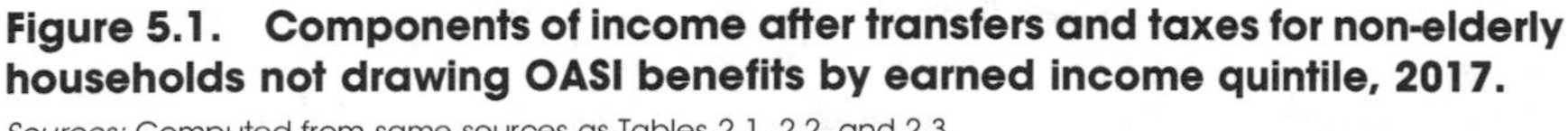
Figure 5.1. Components of income after transfers and taxes for non-elderly households not drawing OASI benefits by earned income quintile, 2017.

Sources: Computed from same sources as Tables 2.1, 2.2, and 2.3.

Education and Earned Income Inequality

The primacy of education in economic advancement is accepted across the broad spectrum of American public opinion. On average, in 2017, completing high school with no further education raised hourly earnings by 20 percent above those who dropped out. An associate's degree in an occupational program delivered a 23 percent boost in average hourly earnings above those of a high school graduate. Average hourly earnings for people with at least a bachelor's degree were 96 percent greater than for those with only a high school diploma. Among college graduates, those who went on to earn a master's degree earned, on average, 35 percent more than those who had only a bachelor's degree. Those with a doctorate such as a PhD or EdD earned 62 percent more, and those with traditional professional degrees such as doctors, dentists, and lawyers on average garnered 88 percent more than those with only a bachelor's degree.[35]

Figure 5.2 shows the level of educational attainment in each of the income quintiles. About 60 percent of adults in the bottom quintile had no postsecondary education. The percentages with no postsecondary education became smaller with each successive quintile until the top quintile, where they still constituted almost 25 percent. The relationship was reversed for college graduates, who accounted for 53 percent in the top quintile and only 13 percent in the bottom.[36]

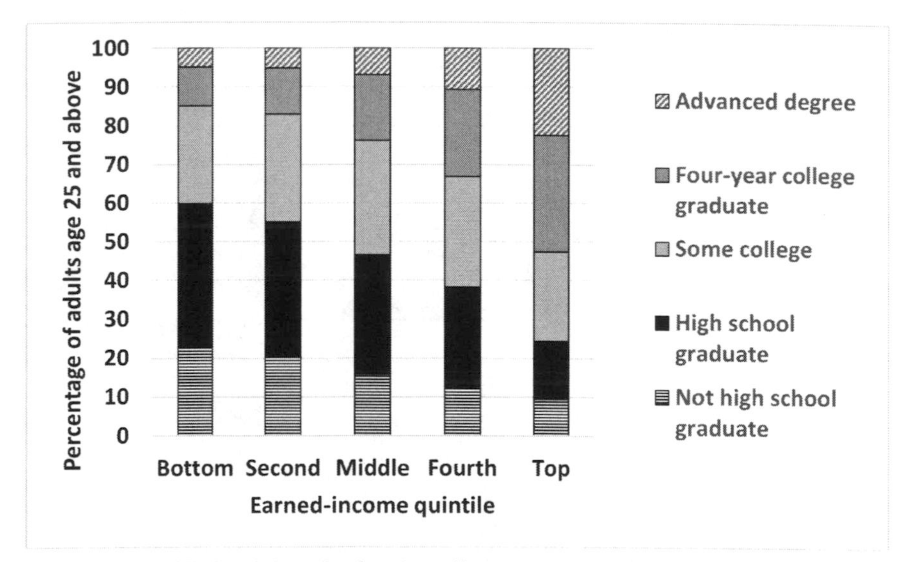

Figure 5.2. Highest level of education, age twenty-five and above, by earned-income quintile, 2017.

Source: Calculated from Census Bureau, Current Population Survey, Annual Social and Economic Supplement, March 2018, public-use micro-data files.

The data in Figure 5.2 indicate that factors in addition to education affect hourly earnings because the relationship between education and income is far from uniform. More than 6 percent of people with doctorates or professional degrees earned only in the two lowest quintiles in 2017, as did 14 percent of other college graduates, but a significant number of these people were in graduate school, professional school, internships, residencies, or other training programs. However, more than 10 percent of high school graduates with some college work but no degree earned at levels that put them in the top quintile. The top 1 percent of earners who never completed high school made more money per hour than 75 percent of earners with doctorates or professional degrees. Obviously, there are many factors other than education that affect hourly earnings. But while there are exceptions and occupational choice, experience, general intelligence, ambition, and even luck have an impact on earned income, education is the prime path by which most Americans achieve economic advancement.

More education and the growing differential between the income earned by those with and those without higher education have also created greater earned-income inequality, especially after the 1960s. Table 5.2 shows that the number of high school dropouts fell from 45 percent of the entire population in 1967 to only 15 percent in 2017. The proportion of the population that graduated from college tripled, as did the proportion going on to earn an advanced degree. College graduates were as prevalent in the middle income quintile in 2017 as they had been in the top quintile in 1967. Even though 85 percent of the population

Table 5.2. Change in share of population and in average hourly earnings by level of education, 1967–2017

	Percentage of population			*Average hourly earnings (2017 dollars)*		
Highest level of education	*1967*	*2017*	*Percentage change*	*1967*	*2017*	*Percentage change*
High school dropout	45.5	15.1	-66.8	12.11	15.94	31.6
High school diploma only	31.2	27.3	-12.5	13.63	20.46	50.1
Some college (less than BA/BS)	12.8	26.9	110.4	15.30	23.05	50.6
College bachelor's degree only	6.9	19.6	184.3	19.42	34.37	77.0
Graduate degree	3.6	11.1	209.8	23.31	48.24	107.0

Source: Calculated from the Census Bureau, Current Population Survey, Annual Social and Economic Supplement, March 1968 and March 2018, public-use datasets.

held a high school diploma or higher in 2017, the proportion of the population with only a high school diploma actually dropped slightly because there was a 59 percent increase in the proportion of high school graduates going on to at least some form of higher education.

This shift to a more highly educated workforce added significantly more college graduates to the ranks of the middle and fourth quintiles, thereby increasing the inequality of their earned income compared to the bottom quintile, where dropouts and high school graduates predominated. In addition, the top quintile added more college bachelor's and graduate degrees than the fourth and middle quintiles combined, increasing the inequality between the top and the middle quintiles. Over the last fifty years, real average hourly earnings of those with only a high school diploma rose by a healthy 50 percent, but earnings for those with a four-year college degree rose half again as fast, and earnings for an advanced degree rose at double that rate (see Table 5.2). The "college earning premium" compares the average hourly earnings for all college graduates (including those who added advanced degrees) to the earnings for those with only a high school diploma. In 1967, college graduates made, on average, 55.9 percent more than those with only a high school diploma. By 2017, that pay premium had nearly doubled to 96.2 percent.[37]

While Table 5.2 shows the growing economic value of human capital, it also shows the extraordinary economic progress of the US economy from 1967 to 2017. The growth in American productivity was sufficient to produce real hourly earnings for high school dropouts in 2017 that were higher than those earned by high school graduates with some college or technical training in 1967. High school graduates in 2017 had higher real hourly earnings than college graduates in 1967, and high school graduates with some college in 2017 earned about as much as people with advanced degrees earned in 1967.

The natural progression of economic development from human muscle power to animal power, to machine power, to knowledge power not only created more jobs requiring more education but also made education a greater differentiator in earning power, which, in turn, has increased the inequality of earned income.

More Advancement by Women Created Greater Inequality in Earned Income for American Households

One of the significant economic changes of the last one hundred years has been the reduction in barriers that formerly interfered with women being able to participate fully in the economy. In 1948, women constituted only 29 percent of the labor force, but by 2017 they were 47 percent. Labor force participation rates for men fell from 87 percent in 1948 to 69 percent in 2017, whereas those for women rose from 32 to 57 percent.[38]

Women's greater participation in the economy was part of a broad cultural and economic transformation. Attitudes about the relative roles of women and men within the household and the labor market shifted dramatically beginning with the mobilization during World War II. These changes in attitudes were accompanied and supported by the growth in innovations and conveniences such as frozen prepared foods, microwave ovens, no-iron apparel, and dishwashers, which greatly reduced the time required for housekeeping by all members of the household and generally made it easier to shift labor from household work to the labor market. More effective birth control also allowed families to regulate the size and timing of childbirth more effectively.

The details about these and other significant shifts in social norms and technology are beyond the scope of this book, but the consequences of those societal shifts are important in understanding the upward trend of inequality of earned household income during the postwar era. In the past fifty years, at the lower end of the income distribution the growth in earned income was slower than for the higher quintiles because an increasing proportion of its prime work-age people left the labor market in response to larger transfer payments that provided the things they had traditionally worked to be able to buy. At the same time, households in the upper 60 percent of the income distribution were accelerating their earnings, in large measure because women became more actively involved in the labor market. This dual dynamic increased earned-income inequality by depressing earned income at the bottom of the income distribution and increasing earned income in the middle and at the top.

Two-thirds of the increase in women's participation in the labor market occurred in the nineteen years from 1948 to 1967. While their participation rose more slowly during the subsequent fifty years, data that are available only since 1967 show that in addition to more women working, they were working longer hours and earning more. In 1967, women earned only 21 percent of the total household income from working outside the home, but by 2017 they were earning 38 percent of the total. Average hourly earnings for women rose more rapidly than for men as their skill and education levels increased more rapidly and the percentage of women in high-paying occupations grew faster. As a result, the overall earning differential between men and women declined rapidly.[39]

Women's share of bachelor's degrees earned rose consistently from 14.7 percent in 1870 to 41.3 percent in 1940. Then, although the number of women earning college degrees continued to climb, their share of the total dropped to 23.9 percent in 1950 because the GI Bill tripled the growth rate in bachelor's degrees for men. Beginning in the 1960s, women's share of new college degrees started to grow more rapidly, surpassed the number granted to men in 1982, and reached 57.2 percent of the total by the turn of the millennium. It has stayed roughly at that level for almost twenty years. The proportions of masters and doctorate degrees earned by women have followed a similar pattern. By 1987, women earned 50.4 percent of master's degrees, and that percentage hit 60.3 percent in 2007, where it stabilized. Doctorates earned by women (including advanced professional degrees in medicine and law) reached 50.1 percent in 2005 and continued to climb to 53.8 percent by 2017, the last year for which data are available.[40]

In addition to their increased participation in the workforce and higher levels of education in general, women have increasingly moved into professions that receive higher compensation. The proportion of women earning degrees in medicine, law, and business rose from less than 10 percent of the degrees granted in 1967 to almost half in 2017. In mathematics and physical sciences, they increased their share of advanced degrees by more than a factor of five but still held only about one-third of the total degrees. In biological sciences, they earned somewhat more than half of all degrees at all levels.[41] See Appendix B for a more extensive list of disciplines.

Super Two-Earner Households

Numerous social and economic studies have shown that in addition to causing work effort in lower-income households to plummet, greater transfer payments have weakened the formation of two-income households.[42] As a result, two-earner households have become a smaller proportion of the bottom two quintiles, and the inequality of earned income has increased. At the middle and upper end of the income distribution, as more women entered the labor market, they created greater household earnings by expanding the number of two-earner households. In 1967, only 50.4 percent of married women were employed, and their earnings averaged only 38.3 percent of their husbands' earnings. Fifty years later, 83.2 percent were employed, and they earned on average 57.3 percent of their husbands' earnings. In 1967, only 10.7 percent of married couples earned incomes that were within 10 percent of each other, but by 2017 that proportion had nearly doubled to 19.6 percent.[43]

Married couples accounted for 79.8 percent of two-adult households in 2017. Two-thirds of the remainder identified themselves as partners, which would have similar economic effects as being married.[44]

This general effect of married or partnered households adding to the inequality of earned income has been amplified at higher levels of education. In 1967, only 16.7 percent of prime work-age households contained at least one adult with a college degree. By 2017, the increased prevalence of college graduates in general, and of women college graduates in particular, caused that proportion to almost triple to 52.9 percent.

Highly educated women and men tend to marry or form households with those possessing similar levels of education who earn similar incomes. As a result, the rise in college graduates also has led to a sharp increase in the number of households with two highly educated people, sometimes called "super two-earner households." This increased concentration of earning power is one of the reasons for the growth in earned-income inequality.

In 1967, 14.0 percent of the prime work-age married men and 7.9 percent of prime work-age married women held a college degree. If the entire married population had married randomly without any educational preferences, only 1.1 percent of households would have had two college graduates. In fact, 5.2 percent of households had two college graduates—nearly five times as many as would have resulted from random selection of spouses. By 2017, 29.5 percent of all households were headed by two college graduates, and 74.2 percent of all college graduates were in two-graduate households. The incidence of the super two-earner households had exploded from only one in twenty households to almost one in three. This greater concentration of college-educated couples in super two-earner households alone accounted for 8.1 percent of the increase in the inequality of earned household income from 1967 to 2017.[45]

When political activists denounce the rise in earned-income inequality, they are neglecting the fact that a significant portion of the phenomenon they decry has arisen from the individual efforts of women and their greater participation in the economy. Not surprisingly, increased equality of opportunity and the attendant expansion of effort to succeed often generates more earned-income inequality.

Choice of Occupation and Experience Create Differences in Average Hourly Earnings

Occupational choice was the most important factor determining the differences in hourly earnings among individuals with the same level of education in 2017. Of the fifty-two occupational groups on which Census collects data, people without a high school diploma worked in thirty-nine, high school graduates in forty nine, and college graduates in fifty. A career as a scientist, physician, or attorney requires advanced education, at least in part because of state licensing requirements. A career in business may not require highly specialized education, but earnings in business generally will be strengthened with education in principal business disciplines such as finance, accounting, marketing, or specialized operations. Many occupational choices are dependent only on the mastery of basic high school education and the individual preferences and talents of the individual.

Three occupational groups illustrate some of the complementary effects of education and occupational choice. Food-preparation jobs paid between $12.39 per hour for high school dropouts and $16.82 for college graduates. While education raised their earnings, food preparers were either the lowest or the second-lowest occupational group for every educational level. Electricians were paid much better, averaging between $30.10 and $30.73 per hour across all levels of education.[46] Electricians earned about the same irrespective of education, but that same hourly pay placed them among the top quarter of occupations for holders of only high school diplomas and in the bottom half for college graduates. Finally, business executives without a college degree averaged between $35.18 and $39.36 per hour. Those with a college degree averaged $55.56, and those with an advanced degree, $78.36. Advanced-degree executives averaged only somewhat less than the highest-paid occupation of medical professionals and somewhat more than attorneys.

Census data show that experience also strengthened job performance. Average hourly earnings were higher for workers who had more experience. The gain from additional experience was greatest during a person's earliest years, but on average some positive effect continued until the worker retired. Differences in education on average accounted for about 30 percent of the difference in earned income from work. Occupational choice within an educational level added another 7 percent and experience accounted for about 2 percent.[47] Work effort, education, choice of occupation, and experience explained about 78 percent of the difference in earned employment income between the bottom and top quintiles of households in 2017.[48] The remaining 22 percent came from factors not captured in the Census CPS/ASEC survey, such as general intelligence, specialized talents, ambition, attitudes toward work, and random events such as luck.

The Missing "Gender Pay Gap"

Despite significant gains in earnings for women, if one compares the median annual earnings for women who worked full-time year-round in 2020 with those for men, women earned 17 cents less per dollar earned by men.[49] This difference has sometimes been labeled the "gender pay gap."

Just as for most other groups' differences in earnings, the largest factor explaining this pay gap is the amount of time that the individuals work. While the official pay-gap measure compares annual earnings for full-time year-round workers, that is not a real apples-to-apples comparison. Full-time is defined as 35 or more hours per week, but within that definition is huge variation from 35 hours to more than 80 hours. Within the full-time category, on average, men worked 2.0 hours more per week than women. If full-time women had worked the same number of hours as men without any change in their hourly earnings, then the resulting pay gap would have been 4 cents smaller.[50]

But the total effect of hours worked is even larger than that. On average, teachers report working only 38 weeks per year. But Census changes the actual weeks reported by teachers in the survey to 52 weeks per year for calculation and reporting. That converts all teachers to year-round workers, even though on average they work less than three-quarters of a year. This, of course, overstates their actual hours, so when earnings per hour are calculated, they are understated by 27 percent.[51] The majority of teachers are women, so the Census changes to reported teacher hours adds at least another 1 cent to the gender earning difference.

More detailed Bureau of Labor Statistics data also show that the pay gap existed only for those working 40 hours or more per week. Among full-time workers who worked less than 40 hours per week, women earned 4 cents *more* than men. Among part-time workers, women made 6 cents *more*.[52] So the only place where an actual "pay gap" existed was for those working 40 or more hours per week. For those working fewer hours, women made more.[53]

Just as more experience creates pay inequality in the population generally, experience accounts for a significant part of the gender pay gap. Women, on average, have worked fewer years than men of the same age. Women between the ages of forty-three and fifty-one, on average, had nearly three fewer years of work experience compared with men of the same age, giving men 13 percent more experience and adding another 5 cents to the pay gap.[54] The time lost from work for child rearing also explains why, on average, women who have not married had only a 9-cent pay gap, married women had a 22-cent gap, and those who were widowed, divorced, or separated had an 18-cent gap.[55]

As in other group comparisons, occupational choices also affect relative earnings. Women work at almost every type of job, but they are still more likely to work in occupations that on average pay less. Of course, it would be equally true that men, on average, work in the occupations that pay more. Women are, as a matter of fact, less likely to hold jobs in areas such as commission sales and finance that have greater financial risk of periods with lower earnings, although in the long run the pay may be higher.[56] Similarly, there are fewer women in jobs that entail greater physical danger and offer significant premium pay. Men are nine times more likely to hold a job with known physical risks, seventeen times more likely to hold jobs exposing them to fumes, eight times more likely to work in extreme weather, and almost five times more likely to hold jobs exposing them to high levels of noise.[57] As a result, men have twelve times the workplace fatality rate of women and 50 percent more workplace injuries.[58]

Economists June O'Neill and David O'Neill, professors of economics at Baruch College, City University of New York, calculated that overall occupational selection determined another 3 cents of the observed pay gap.[59] For those occupational choices that required a postsecondary education, the choice of college major had a significant effect. A Georgetown University study found that only one of the ten top-earning college majors had a majority of women as graduates. More women than men selected nine of the ten lowest-earning majors.[60] And two economists from the University of Michigan found that in addition to selecting courses that specifically prepare them for higher-paying occupations, men were more likely to make course selections that were associated with higher pay, with an effect large enough to account for about 1.5 cents of the pay gap.[61] Hours worked, experience, selection of occupations, and educational choices explain all but 1.5 cents of the 17-cent gender pay gap.

Because differences between men and women have narrowed on each of these factors, the gender pay gap has declined by 60 percent since 1967. Economists June O'Neill and David O'Neill have demonstrated that this strong convergence of pay between the sexes predated the Equal Pay Act and that subsequent government regulations had no major role in the reduction in observed pay differences.[62] This convergence between earnings for men and women has been consistent and broad based, with real weekly earnings for women rising faster than those for men at all educational levels.[63]

Of course, today's older workers made their choices decades ago, and their choices have already been baked into the numbers, so changes in the total have been gradual as new workers making different choices have replaced those who began working more than forty years ago. The differences in choices made by the four adult generations active in the labor market in 2019 had substantial impacts on their gender pay gaps.[64] The pay gap for Baby Boomers was 2.6 times greater than for the newest Generation Z.[65] Some of the difference reflects Gen Z's younger age, but most of the generational differences are dominated by changing educational attainment, occupational choices, and gender roles within the household. The generation-to-generation reduction in the reported gender pay gap has also been accelerating. The gap for Generation X is 11 percent smaller than for the Baby Boomers. The Millennials have a 31 percent smaller gap compared with Gen X. And the Gen Z gap has so far declined by 36 percent from the gap for the Millennials. Even if there were no further changes in the labor market, the arrival of more young adults with preferences that create smaller pay differences and the departure of their parents and grandparents would systematically and inevitably reduce the little remaining pay gap by more than half.

The data show that differences in earnings by men and women arise quite naturally from the operation of a competitive market. If employers could, in fact, hire women at 83 cents on the dollar for the same job, women would have all the jobs they wanted and no unemployment. Only extreme discriminators would pass up a bargain like that, and they would shortly go out of business. The late Gary Becker, Nobel laureate and professor of economics at the University of Chicago, established this principle in more elegant form more than forty years ago, and subsequent research has continued to strengthen his case.[66]

The Causes of Rising Earned Income Inequality

Recall from Chapter 4 that the Gini coefficient for earned-income inequality rose by 26.6 percent between 1967 and 2017, from 0.443 to 0.561. There were, of course, many economic and social changes in this fifty-year period that might affect earned-income inequality—some increasing it and others reducing it. Fortunately, this overall increase can be largely explained by three factors that are measured directly by the Census Bureau's Current Population Survey: the amount of work performed by prime work-age adults, their levels of education attainment, and the increase in the premium earned by college graduates.

The most significant factor affecting earned-income inequality was the dramatic enlargement of the difference in the amount of work performed by members of households. The proportion of prime work-age persons in the bottom quintile who worked dropped by half. A smaller decline also occurred in the second quintile. In the middle and higher income quintiles, the change was in the opposite direction, with increases in the proportion of prime work-age people who worked.

Not only did the differences among quintiles in the proportion of prime work-age adults who worked grow bigger between 1967 and 2017, but the differences in the hours they actually worked also grew. In 2017, workers in the middle and fourth quintiles worked an average of 19.6 more hours per week than workers in the bottom quintile, a difference that was 3.0 hours greater than the difference that existed in 1967. The gap between the top and bottom quintiles grew by even more, by almost four hours per week.

We can estimate the effects of these increasing disparities in work performed on earned-income inequality by taking the data for 1967 and making two changes to it. First, the percentage of the prime work-age population that was employed in each income quintile would be adjusted to the percentage that was employed in 2017. Second, the hours worked by workers in each quintile would be adjusted to the hours worked in 2017. Everything else would remain as it was in 1967. With these changes, we can see what the household income structure would have looked like in 2017 if there had been no other changes than the increased disparities in the proportion working and in the hours that they worked.

The Gini coefficient for these 1967 data, with the changes in the proportion working and the hours worked to the value for 2017, is 0.497, which is an increase of 12.3 percent from the 1967 Gini coefficient. That means that the difference in the amount of work performed by households between 1967 and 2017 accounted for almost half of the total Gini coefficient increase of 26.6 percent.

The second-largest contributor to the increase in the inequality of earned income was the increase in disparities in educational attainment. The most obvious changes were the greater proportions of college graduates and holders of advanced degrees in the top quintile and in the middle and fourth quintiles. But there were other changes as well: more high school graduates completed additional occupational and technical training. Using the same approach we applied to the changes in the amount of work, we can look at the impact of educational attainment on earned-income inequality. The Gini coefficient for earned income that has been adjusted for these changes in educational attainment, proportion of people working, and the hours worked is 0.549, an increase of 24.0 percent over the 1967 value, which means that an additional 11.7 percent increase in earned-income inequality can be explained by the increased disparities in educational attainment.

Finally, between 1967 and 2017, the premium in earnings received for having a college degree nearly doubled. We can compute the effect of that higher premium by adding the premium increase to the average hourly earnings for each quintile's college graduates. The result of all these changes to the 1967 data (proportion of people working, hours worked, educational attainment, and college premium) is a Gini coefficient of 0.572, an increase of 29.2 from 1967, which means that adding the higher college premium explains about a 5.2 percent increase in earned-income inequality.[67]

The Gini coefficient that results from all three factors combined is 2.6 percent greater than the actual 2017 Gini coefficient. That means that other factors were working to reduce earned-income inequality. Many factors have reduced earned-income inequality in specific areas and, thereby, kept the rise in overall earned-income inequality smaller than it otherwise would have been. Growth in labor productivity has contributed to higher wages for lower-skilled workers. Welfare reform has increased the work participation of women who head low-income households. Although changes in occupational classification over the last fifty years make it difficult to calculate the exact effects, more women and minorities have moved into higher-paying occupations within their education levels, thereby reducing one source of overall inequality.

In short, earned-income inequality has risen because some people have been induced to work less by the availability of greater government transfer payments, while others have worked more to promote their households' well-being. An increasing proportion of Americans have achieved higher levels of education, and the value of that education has grown. Women have entered the labor force in greater numbers, dramatically increasing the number of two-earner households in the top 60 percent of households. And highly educated high achievers have tended to marry or otherwise form households with each other.

Those who are the most vocal critics of our economic system for its growth in earned-income inequality in postwar America are also often the most committed advocates of expanding the very transfer payments to low-income Americans that have been the largest cause of the growth in earned-income inequality. They also have been the biggest promoters of the public education system that has left so many behind and the greatest critics of education reforms, such as school choice, that enable more children to raise their future earnings. But, as has been shown in this chapter, the growth of earned-income inequality has been produced by government programs that discourage work, growing equality for women, a rise in the value of education, and the free choices made by people who love each other. On any kind of factual basis, it is hard to argue that the growth of earned-income inequality in postwar America is a result of some fatal flaw in our economic system.

CHAPTER 6

Measures of Well-Being

National economic well-being is measured using official statistics such as real average hourly earnings, real median household income, real gross domestic product (GDP), productivity, and the poverty rate. These indicators of well-being are compared over extended periods and are either measured in dollars or calculated from other numbers expressed in dollars. The term "real" means that they have been adjusted for changes in the purchasing power of the dollar to prevent inflation from distorting the real trends.

The adjustments for changes in the value of the dollar over time are made using price indexes that measure the average change in prices. The accuracy of our measures of well-being are, therefore, heavily dependent on the accuracy of these price indexes. The accuracy of government consumer price indexes used for most of these adjustments has been challenged and disputed by many of the nation's most respected authorities for more than fifty years. This chapter examines those challenges and the implications they have for the accuracy of the nation's standard measures of well-being. Extraordinarily, the statistical agencies of the US government today use not one price index but five different indexes to adjust the various measures of our economic well-being for inflation experienced by consumers.

Assessing Economic Well-Being Across Time

Real average hourly earnings for production and nonsupervisory employees, as published by the Bureau of Labor Statistics (BLS), reached a peak in October 1972, after which they continued to fall for nearly twenty-two years before they began to recover their lost ground. It took another twenty-four years for the measure to return to its 1972 level in December 2018. Then, for the next sixteen months, it grew at a healthy 4.9 percent annual rate until the effects of the COVID-19 pandemic struck. These highly publicized official figures fed a polemic that "the average American today has not seen a nickel more in real wages than he or she got 45 years ago."[1]

The argument that Americas have not had a raise in almost fifty years has several problems, the first of which is that the claim is generally made by comparing only wages and salaries and therefore excluding employer-paid benefits. Neither BLS average hourly earnings nor Census income figures count employer-paid benefits. Benefits such as employer-funded health insurance and contributions to worker retirement programs have risen dramatically over the last half century, and today they add 25 percent more compensation to basic wages and salaries. Excluding these benefits distorts the picture of what has happened to total compensation. Over the period of alleged wage stagnation, employer-paid benefits alone increased total individual compensation by 6.7 percent.

Another distortion is that the numbers supporting this claim are averages for production and nonsupervisory employees and exclude more than a third of all workers—namely, the self-employed, workers in agriculture and government, and supervisory and managerial employees. Furthermore, because they are averages at a point in time, they include both brand-new workers with no experience and highly experienced workers. As new workers gain experience, acquire training, and move on to better jobs, they get raises. But these raises are partially or even totally offset in the averages by inexperienced people entering the workforce at the lower pay from which others have moved on to higher earnings.

Most of the millions of top earners started in entry-level jobs at McDonald's, Walmart, or somewhere else that launched them on the path to economic success. They may have risen to success within the same company, with a new employer, or even as self-employed entrepreneurs. Even individuals who stayed in the same occupation all their lives would gain higher pay from their experience and seniority. As documented in Chapter 2, experience accounts for 2.0 percent of the inequality of earned income, and, on average, across individuals' work lives, real earnings rise by 91 percent.[2] This growth of earnings within an occupation or from honing skills and moving on to higher pay and greater opportunity is obscured by just looking at the average compensation number.

But as important as these weaknesses are, there is a much more profound failure in the official numbers. Does wage stagnation remotely describe the life you have lived over the last five decades or in any way square with numerous other official measures of changes in the actual physical items Americans own and consume? In short, should you believe your eyes or the official government measure of real hourly earnings?

Compared to 1972, our homes today are much more spacious and modern. The proportion of homes with two or more rooms per person is 33.5 percent greater today. The proportion with two or more bathrooms has grown by 200.5 percent; 313.1 percent more have central air conditioning; and 68.3 percent more have dishwashers.[3] Most homes in 1972 had televisions, but only about half were color. Today they are all color, and most are high-definition, flat-screen TVs connected to cable or satellites.[4] Most homes in 1972 had at least one phone, but none had cell phones or internet access.

Our kitchens today are stocked with a far greater array of food products, out-of-season fruits brought from half a world away, and a vast variety of prepared foods. Remarkably, as compared to 1972, this abundance of food costs an ever-smaller portion of our families' budgets, freeing up $3,200 in 2017 that the average family can now spend on other things.[5]

Our cars last more than twice as long,[6] they are almost four times safer,[7] and many have GPS navigation and premium sound systems. No standard model lacks air conditioning or power steering. Today almost three times as many of us are college graduates.[8] Americans live 7.8 years longer,[9] partly because the death rates from cancer declined by 31 percent from 1991 to 2018.[10] Our median age is almost ten years older, and yet the proportion of people reporting poor health is 20.3 percent smaller.[11] Real median household net worth is up 172.2 percent.[12] In short, by virtually any physical definition of economic well-being, working Americans across all income levels, racial classifications, education levels, and other commonly used statistical classifications are substantially better off today than they were in 1972. So how did we obtain this massive cornucopia of prosperity without a pay raise since 1972?

Assessing Economic Well-Being Across Time: Adjusting for Price Changes

The answer to this conundrum lies in the differences between two types of statistics on well-being. One type measures physical evidence of well-being such as the spaciousness and quality attributes of our homes, our health and longevity, the physical assets we own, and the amount and quality of the goods and services we consume. Based on all available evidence of physical well-being, Americans across any broadly defined classification are far more prosperous today than they were fifty years ago.

The second type of well-being metric is based on data measured in terms of dollars, such as average hourly earnings, median annual household income, GDP, productivity, and poverty. As a result, any analysis of these currency-denominated measures across time requires accurate adjustments for changes in the purchasing power of the dollar. We all have an intuitive sense of the meaning of inflation. A young adult Millennial in 2017 might have paid $4.00 a pound for ground beef, $40.00 for a shirt, $24,000 for a new car, and $2.40 per gallon for its gasoline. Her mother, at the same age, might have paid $1.30, $30.00, $5,000, and $1.00, respectively, and her grandmother, $0.45, $5.00, $2,000, and $0.30.

We all see price inflation at work in these price differences. But these raw differences in cost may not be entirely the result of price changes. For example, today's ground beef may be low fat and the shirt no-iron, whereas Gramma's were not. Today's cars last almost twice as long, are nearly four times safer, get more miles per gallon, and pollute less. Most cars also have air conditioning, power steering, power brakes, and power windows. Today's Ford Mustang is not the same car as the 1965 model, and a Tesla did not even exist. We need unbiased measures of inflation that accurately identify pure price changes without erroneously counting quality improvements in price changes for goods and services.

Unfortunately, the price indexes used for inflation adjustments fail to meet that standard fully and, as a result, substantially overstate the true amount of inflation. These overstatements are not simple mathematical mistakes. They are the result of methods and procedures that were adopted over a long period. Some of them have since been corrected, but most have not. When price indexes that overstate price increases are used to adjust measures of well-being for inflation, they create understatements in household income, average hourly earnings, GDP, and productivity, and they cause an overstatement in the number of people living in poverty.[13] That is why the increasing prosperity we encounter in our everyday lives is consistent with the plethora of official statistics based on physical evidence of well-being, while the official statistics that are calculated from dollar values suggest stagnation.

This overstatement of inflation is a well-known problem and has been extensively documented for years by the same people who calculate the Consumer Price Index (CPI) and researchers both inside and outside government. From its inception in 1913, the CPI has been best understood, according to the Bureau of Labor Statistics (the agency that compiles it), as "an upper bound on a cost-of-living index."[14] In other words, a true cost-of-living measure will never rise any faster than the CPI and is likely to rise more slowly.

George Stigler, Nobel laureate and one of the twentieth century's top economists, chaired the 1961 Price Statistics Review Committee that found a "systematic upward bias in the price indices." In 1996, Michael Boskin, former chairman of the Council of Economic Advisors, headed another blue-ribbon commission that concluded, despite improvements, the CPI was still overstating inflation by some 1.1 percentage points per year. Alan Greenspan, then chairman of the Federal Reserve, agreed and called on Congress to correct the overstatement. And in 2010, Erskine Bowles, former chief of staff to President Bill Clinton, cochaired the Commission on Fiscal Responsibility and Reform and recommended a more accurate measure of inflation to improve government fiscal policy.[15]

These deficiencies are so important that some care must be taken to explain and illustrate them. The explanations may sound a bit technical, but they are consistent with commonsense observations about the real world. One of the fundamentals for calculating an accurate price index is that price changes must be measured by comparing the price of an apple in one time period to an apple of the same variety, grade, and size in another time period. An accurate price index always compares the price of a US Fancy, Size 100, Fuji apple in one period to the price of the exact same grade and size of Fuji apple in the next period. Price indexes should never compare the price of a Fuji apple in one period with the price of a Red Delicious apple in another. That is common sense we all can agree on. Following that principle, a price index for Fuji apples would be straightforward.

But when we are adjusting income for inflation across all consumption, we must combine the price changes of thousands of things in addition to apples—ground beef, sneakers, rent, airfare, and heart surgery, to name a few. That is where things start to get more complicated. The Bureau of Labor Statistics combines all these different items into the CPI by weighting the percentage change in prices for each item by the dollar amount consumers spent on that item in some initial reference period. In concept, this calculation would be straightforward, just a lot of number crunching. The result would be a price index that measured the change in the cost of an unchanging market basket of goods and services—the same number of apples, automobiles, swimsuits, and knee surgeries. The fixed market basket would also contain the same-size home, the same gas mileage, and the same medical treatments for our knee surgery as it did before.

If consumers purchased exactly the same things in the same quantities forever, this calculation would present no major difficulties, and there would be no overstatement of inflation. But in the real world we are always changing what we buy. For example, over the last several decades, we have substituted purchases of packaged prepared foods and meals in restaurants for much of the raw foods previously purchased to prepare meals and eat at home. When those kinds of changes occurred, the consumer expenditure weights used to combine the price changes of raw food components and prepared dishes became outdated—the weights for raw food items became too large and the weights for prepared food and restaurant food became too small.

For most of the postwar period, the relative weights representing the amount spent by American consumers for the various goods and services they purchased were as much as ten years out of date. In recent years, the expenditures for what consumers are actually buying have been updated more often, improving the price indexes' accuracy. But even now, when the market basket is updated, the new weights for what is being bought are as much as three years out of date before they are actually used, and, once introduced, they continue to become more out of date. As a result, the market baskets that are actually priced to determine what has happened to consumer prices are based on what was purchased in the past, not what is being bought currently.

In addition to the timeliness of the market baskets, the fixed-market-basket approach creates other serious issues. In the real world, changes in relative prices induce people to change the market basket of goods they buy. For example, the prices for landline phone services have risen faster than those for wireless phone services. As a result, consumers have shifted more of their consumption to wireless phones, some even dropping their landlines altogether. A true cost-of-living price index would account for consumers maximizing their standard of living by shifting more of their telephone spending from landlines to the relatively less expensive wireless services. But the traditional CPI has made no allowance for the effect of this substitution of one service for another. It has continued to apply a fixed higher expenditure weight to the faster-rising landline prices and a fixed lower expenditure weight to the slower-rising, or even falling, wireless rates. As a result, it has overstated the true average price increase for telephone services as actually experienced by consumers. This type of overstatement in the CPI is well known in the economic literature and is called "substitution bias."[16]

Besides the large, obvious substitution of relatively less expensive mobile phone service for more expensive landlines, there are thousands of other, often less dramatic substitutions that the traditional CPI fails to capture. If beef prices rise by 20 cents per pound and chicken rises by 5 cents per pound, consumers are worse off because both prices have risen, but they reduce the impact of the price increases by buying relatively more chicken and less beef. Similarly, when discount outlets open across the country and offer the same brands and varieties of electronic devices at lower prices than traditional stores, some people will switch to the discount stores. The associated effective price reduction for consumers who switch outlets is lost because the fixed market basket also keeps the outlets from which the products are purchased fixed from one time period to another. Just as the samples of items priced are updated periodically, so are the samples of outlets, but the price changes when consumers switch outlets are never measured. When the cost of flying started to fall relative to the cost of driving or taking the train, Americans, in large numbers, started to fly more. We respond to changes in relative prices constantly, and if the price index keeps the same weighting based on the things we used to buy, it misses the benefits we get from the substitutions we make.

Fortunately, the Bureau of Labor Statistics has developed and for twenty years has published an index called the Chained Consumer Price Index for

All Urban Consumers (C-CPI-U or Chained CPI) that largely solves this "substitution bias" problem. It uses the same price data collected for the basic CPI, but it makes significant improvements. First, it revises the consumption expenditure weights to reflect what was actually bought at the time the price data were collected.

Second, the computation explicitly accounts for the effects of changes in relative expenditures from one time period to the next. The traditional CPI weights price changes by the estimated expenditure for the item in first time period only. The chained index averages the price change calculated by applying the first period's expenditure weights with the price change calculated by applying the second period's weights.[17] This helps correct for the overstatement that would otherwise result from failing to account for the higher standard of living created as consumers substitute relatively cheaper items for relatively more expensive items.

The Chained CPI does not exist for periods before December 1999, but a very similar index, the Personal Consumption Expenditure Price Index (PCEPI) calculated by the Bureau of Economic Analysis (BEA) in the Department of Commerce, covers the earlier time periods.[18] The combination of these two price indexes is universally accepted by economists and the government agencies that compile them as being a far more accurate measure of consumer price change than the traditional CPI-U. The more accurate combination of Chained CPI and PCEPI rose 482 percent from 1967 to 2017, compared to a 634 percent rise in the less accurate traditional CPI-U. That means that the substitution bias in the traditional CPI-U alone overstated the increase in consumer prices over the last fifty years by 32 percent. Robert J. Gordon, professor of economics at Northwestern University and a member of the original Boskin Commission, provided an update on the commission's recommendations ten years after its report. Among other findings, which are discussed below, he noted that the results from the C-CPI-U index had not only fulfilled some of the commission's recommendations but also demonstrated that the substitution bias was even somewhat larger than anticipated in the commission's report.[19]

Unfortunately, despite having a more accurate price index available, BLS and Census continue to adjust measures of well-being such as hourly earnings, household income, and poverty using the traditional CPI rather than the more accurate Chained CPI. For example, BLS data for real average hourly earnings of production and nonsupervisory employees show an increase of only 8.7 percent over the fifty-year period from 1967 to 2017. But if the more accurate Chained CPI had been used to adjust for inflation instead of the less accurate CPI-U, hourly earnings would have been found to have increased by 31.8 percent, more than three times the increase shown in the official BLS number. This difference between the two inflation adjustments is the equivalent of an additional pay raise of $3.55 per hour in 2017 dollars. Real median household income as calculated by the Census using a traditional CPI shows an increase of 33.5 percent over the fifty-year period, but using the more accurate Chained CPI shows real median household income rose by 47.7 percent, the equivalent of $4,406 more per household than the official figure reported by the Census.[20] Current calculations of GDP and productivity and of tax brackets in the tax code already use the more accurate indexes that avoid substitution bias. But other measures of well-being in monetary terms and all indexed spending programs continue to use a traditional CPI.

The Impact of New and Improved Products on Our Measures of Inflation

A second source of overstatement in the CPI comes from new and improved items that make it impossible to continue pricing exactly the same item. Price indexes attempt to address this problem by splitting the listed prices of new or modified items into changes resulting from the market value of quality differences and changes that represent only pure price changes. For example, the price tag for a new computer tablet might be $100 higher than for the preceding model. If its greater speed had a market value of $50 and its larger memory had a market value of $40, then the pure price change would be an increase of $10. The key to making these adjustments is obtaining accurate estimates of the market value of the quality changes.

Part of the new-product bias has come from delays in capturing new products. For example, the cell phone first came on the market in 1984, but it was not included as an identifiable item in the CPI until 1998, fourteen years later. Because of that delay, the index missed the 75 percent price decline and the quality improvements that occurred over those fourteen years, as phones became smaller and lighter and the batteries lasted longer. While the CPI is now able to capture new items much more quickly, the historical indexes are permanently biased upward from the historical delay because they have not been revised to correct for the known biases.

Despite the improvements in the index, extensive technical research has demonstrated that current methods of separating quality and pure price changes for new and modified items still consistently overstate inflation because they continue to count some quality improvements as price increases. Examples of overstated price changes for new and improved products abound.

Today 224 million Americans have at their fingertips more than 2 million apps, forecasting the weather anywhere in the world and showing us how to get to wherever we want to go. We communicate immediately without stationery or stamps or driving to the post office. We get medical advice without going to the doctor's office and obtain instantaneous access to more knowledge than is in the local library. We shop from our armchairs and work for companies thousands of miles away. Improved quality of medical care has provided more than increased convenience and pleasure; it has added eight years of life itself to the average American life span.[21] Yet government consumer-price indexes do not come close to adjusting for all the value embodied in these and many other innovations.

In addition to Robert J. Gordon's analysis cited above about the ten-year progress on implementing the Boskin Commission recommendations, a more recent 2013 technical paper by Bruce Meyer and James Sullivan, professors of economics at the University of Chicago and University of Notre Dame, respectively, evaluated and adopted the Boskin approach for their improved measures of poverty. Another 2018 study by Brent Moulton, former chief of price and index number research at the Bureau of Labor Statistics, confirmed the continuing size of the price index biases and their adverse effects on measures of economic well-being. The assessments incorporate more than fifty credible studies documenting overstatements for specific sets of items in the CPI-U. For example, studies of personal electronic devices showed overstatements in price changes of between 3.6 and 5.8 percent annually because new or improved features were treated as price increases rather than as additional value for the consumer. Annual price increases for medical care were 3 percent too high because they did not account for the greater efficiency and improved outcomes of new drugs and procedures. Inflation for shelter was shown to be overstated by 0.25 percent annually because government statistical agencies ignored some of the consistent improvements in greater living space and added modern conveniences in homes.[22]

There are known solutions for these problems, but they have been implemented in official price indexes only very slowly and have never been applied to revise overstated historical price indexes. For example, BLS began implementing better methods for pricing feature changes in mobile phones in January 2018. They are now using advanced statistical techniques to calculate the market value of new features, applying an approach illustrated above with a computer tablet. Since the beginning of 2018, BLS has been able to adjust for 83.8 percent of changes in mobile phone features and more effectively separate value changes from price changes. These more extensive quality-adjustment methods were applied to only 4.5 percent of the new features that were adjusted for quality changes prior to 2018.[23] While these adjustments for new products and quality changes will be made in estimating price changes in the future, BLS has not gone back to correct for the overstatement of price increases in the past. As a result, historical data on price changes remain significantly overstated.

Pricing of medical care has also presented significant challenges, with its vast advances in both technology and methods of medical practice. Medical care price indexes in the CPI are based on prices for the components used in providing the care—a doctor visit, use of a surgical suite, days in the hospital, a bottle of pills, and so forth. But we really purchase medical care as a treatment for a condition. So, when the quality of care improves, the CPI calculation usually misses the improvement. For example, in the 1960s, patients with peptic ulcers, for whom changes in diet and antacids were not sufficiently effective, were often treated with surgery that would open up the abdomen and stomach to repair the damage. Surgery required hospitalization for several days and more days to recuperate at home.

Then more advanced prescription medications were invented that often made surgery unnecessary. Those medications finally became routinely available over the counter. So, for many patients the cost went from tens of thousands of dollars to $10 per month. Their risk from surgery disappeared, and their quality of life was better. But the improvements did not stop there. In the 1980s, a significant fraction of cases were determined to be caused by a unique bacterium that could usually be treated inexpensively with an antibiotic, again at lower cost and with better outcomes. And for those who still required surgery, the invention of laparoscopic surgery meant that their procedure was less invasive and their recovery time in the hospital was shorter and cheaper. The cost of treating peptic ulcers went down dramatically, and the medical outcomes improved exponentially, but the CPI continued to price the market basket of surgeons, surgical suites, hospital recovery, and so forth.[24]

Hundreds of other medical conditions also benefited from these types of improvements. Joint replacement has gone from rare with long recovery times and very high prices to relatively common with almost miraculous recovery at significantly lower costs. Perhaps most important are the diseases that can now be treated effectively, such as AIDS, and those that can be cured rather than merely treated, such as hepatitis C.

The failures of the CPI to account for these better medical outcomes at lower cost are well known, and BLS in concert with BEA has developed and published Disease-Based Price Indexes that implement the best methods. They price the total cost of treating a specific condition and thereby capture improvements in both efficiency and outcomes. BLS has published these disease-based indexes going back to 1999, but no statistical agency has incorporated them into other official statistics, including the most commonly used measure of inflation, CPI-U, or the two very similar indexes that eliminate the substitution bias, the Chained CPI and PCEPI. The differences are stunning. The CPI-U for medical care rose 89.7 percent from 1999 to 2017, but the aggregate Disease-Based Price Index rose less than half as much, 40.7 percent.[25] Even when official price index research conducted by the BLS has shown that the medical care price indexes at the consumer level overstate medical inflation by more than a factor of two, the indexes used to adjust economic indicators of well-being have never been corrected to incorporate this improvement.

This CPI-U overstatement of inflation in medical care has, in turn, produced a substantial understatement in the measures of economic well-being. Medical care constitutes 8.67 percent of the CPI-U market basket. Over the eighteen years for which it was available, the superior Disease-Based Price Index rose a substantial 49.0 percent less than the CPI medical care index (89.7 percent minus 40.7 percent). Simply replacing the medical care portion of the CPI with the calculations from the existing, officially published Disease-Based Price Index would reduce the measure of overall inflation by 4.2 percent (8.67 percent times 49.0 percent). The most conservative estimate of the new product bias is 7.8 percent for the eighteen years.[26] Replacing the current medical care portion of the CPI-U with an index calculated like the Disease-Based Price Index would eliminate about 54.7 percent of the upward bias in the CPI-U from the introduction of new and improved products.

While the remaining 45.3 percent of the new-product bias has not been addressed in official indexes like the Disease-Based Price Indexes, the studies described above from Boskin, Gordon, Meyer, Sullivan, and Moulton show that existing research results from more than fifty respected technical papers provide data that can be used to calculate reasonable best-practice estimates of the minimum effects from eliminating new-product bias. Combining these improved methods of valuing new and improved products with the official indexes that eliminate the substitution bias (C-CPI-U/PCEPI) produces a consumer price change of only 344 percent for the fifty years from 1967 to 2017. The CPI-U used for adjusting many measures of well-being rose almost twice as much, 634 percent, and even the indexes that eliminate substitution bias, the Chained CPI and PCEPI, rose nearly half again as much, 482 percent (see Figure 6.1).

If the inflation adjustment for real average hourly earnings for production and nonsupervisory employees were to incorporate both the Chained CPI to remove the substitution bias and more accurate adjustments for new and improved products, real average hourly earnings would have risen 74.0 percent over the last fifty years rather than the official reported number of 8.7 percent. That is an additional $7.50 per hour. A similar adjustment for median household income would result in an increase of 93.3 percent rather than 33.5 percent, making the fifty-year increase in real annual income $14,215 larger per household.

The Bureau of Economic Analysis already adjusts GDP for inflation using the methods of the PCEPI, which, like the Chained CPI, eliminates substitution bias. But the GDP and productivity measures still suffer from the overstatement

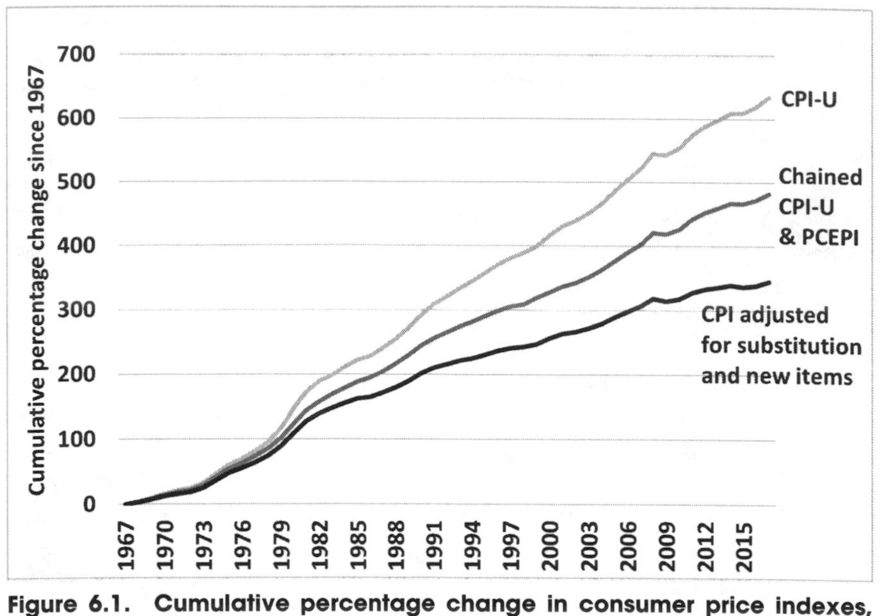

Figure 6.1. Cumulative percentage change in consumer price indexes, 1967–2017.

Sources: CPI-U: Bureau of Labor Statistics, https://data.bls.gov/PDQWeb/cu. Chained CPI and PCEPI: Chained CPI, Bureau of Labor Statistics, https://data.bls.gov/PDQWeb/su, linked to PCEPI in December 1999, Bureau of Economic Analysis, https://apps.bea.gov/iTable/iTable.cfm?reqid=19&step=2#reqid=19&step=2&isuri=1&1921=survey. CPI adjusted for substitution and new items: constructed from Bruce D. Meyer and James X. Sullivan, "Winning the War on Poverty: Poverty from the Great Society to the Great Recession," Working Paper no. 18718, National Bureau of Economic Research, January 2013, http://www.nber.org/papers/w18718; Brent R. Moulton, "The Measurement of Output, Prices, and Productivity: What's Changed since the Boskin Commission?" Brookings Institution, July 2018, https://www.brookings.edu/research/themeasurement-of-output-prices-and-productivity.

of inflation caused by undervaluing new and improved products. Official figures for real GDP show an increase of 297 percent from 1967 to 2017, but if adjustments were made to account for the value of new and improved products, GDP would have increased by 446 percent over the fifty years, or by an additional $5.3 trillion of real economic value created by the nation in 2017.[27]

Accounting more fully for the effects of new products has a similar effect on measures of labor productivity.[28] The BLS labor productivity index measures the change in the real-dollar value created by the private business sector of the economy per hour worked by its employees.[29] The official productivity estimates show an increase of 164 percent over the full fifty-year period. If the inflation adjustments had corrected for the known understated value from new and improved products, productivity would have risen 325 percent—almost twice as fast. Accounting more fully for the value of new and improved products raises the value created by an hour of work in the private sector from $35.80 to $57.80.

The effect of using a more accurate measure of inflation on the poverty rate is a bit more complicated. The poverty rate counts the number of people who live in families that have incomes that fall below a defined poverty threshold. The poverty thresholds that define poverty were intended to identify the minimum income necessary to escape poverty, and poverty was specified by official policy as "the inability to satisfy minimum needs. The poor are those whose resources—their income from all sources, together with their asset holdings—are inadequate."[30] Those resource levels that define poverty, of course, require adjustment for inflation over time, and the Bureau of the Budget (now Office of Management and Budget) issued a memorandum on August 29, 1969, directing all agencies to use the poverty thresholds developed for 1963 and adjust the thresholds by the percentage change in the CPI in subsequent years.[31]

Adhering to this directive for inflation adjustment, the Census Bureau has increased the official poverty thresholds by 701 percent from 1963 to 2017. But if a more accurate price index that avoids substitution bias, such as the Chained CPI or the PCEPI, had been used to adjust for inflation, then the thresholds would have risen only 529 percent. And if the new-product biases outlined above had also been eliminated, then the thresholds would have risen only 365 percent. Consequently, using the CPI-U, which overstates inflation, to calculate poverty thresholds has actually overstated the standard of living below which families are defined as being poor by 72 percent.

For 2017, Census compared its official measure of income to the poverty thresholds that had been adjusted by the CPI-U and calculated that 12.3 percent of the population was living in poverty, only a small decline from the 14.2 percent in poverty in 1967. If, instead, Census had adjusted the poverty thresholds using the more accurate Chained CPI, 9.1 percent of the population would have been in poverty. Incorporating the better measures of the effects of new and improved products would have lowered the poverty rate even further to 6.5 percent—a decline of more than half from 1967.

The analysis in Chapter 3 showed that the official income measure used by the Census fails to include 88 percent of government transfer payments to families classified as poor. Counting all transfer payments as income to the recipients, even using the CPI-U to adjust the poverty threshold for inflation would cause the poverty rate to fall to only 2.5 percent. Both counting the missing transfer payments and using improved price measures with reduced biases from substitution and new products would cause the poverty rate in 2017 to fall to 1.1 percent (see Figure 6.2).

Accounting for the missing transfer payments and using more accurate inflation adjustments not only reveals a much lower level of poverty overall but also sharply narrows the differences in the poverty rate among different demographic groups. The more accurate measures show that only 1.3 percent of

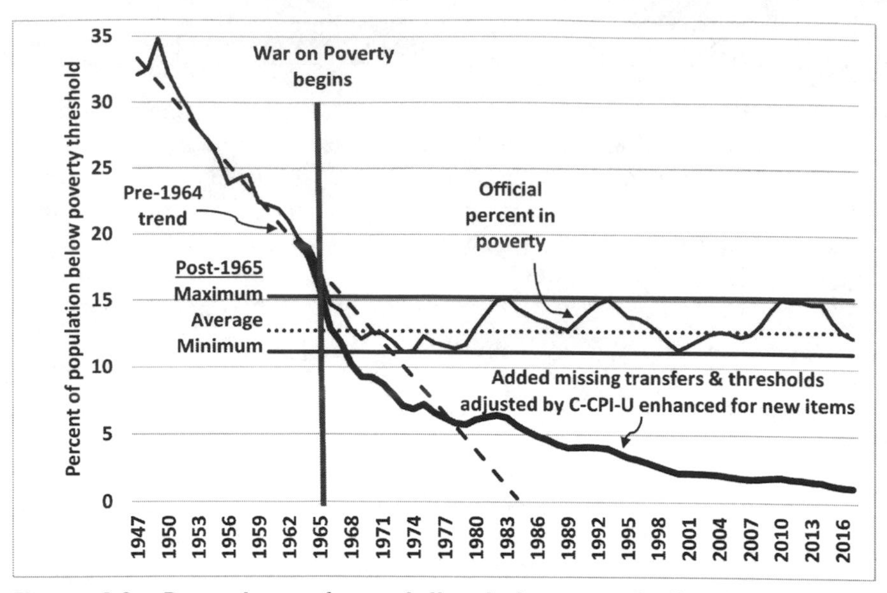

Figure 6.2. Percentage of population below poverty threshold, official and measure improved to add missing transfer payments and eliminate biases from substitution and new-product introduction, 1947–2017.

Sources: Official percentage below poverty threshold, 1959–2017: "Table B-1: Poverty Status of People by Family Relationship, Race, and Hispanic Origin: 1959 to 2017," in "Income and Poverty in the United States, 2017," US Census Bureau, https://www.census.gov/content/dam/Census/library/publications/2018/demo/p60-263.pdf. For earlier data: Gordon Fisher, "Estimates of the Poverty Population under the Current Official Definition for Years before 1959," US Department of Health and Human Services, Office of the Assistant Secretary of Planning and Evaluation, 1986. Added missing transfer payments: Calculated from US Census Bureau, Current Population Survey, Annual Social and Economic Supplement, March 2018 (data for 2017), public-use file. "The Distribution of Household Income, 2015," Congressional Budget Office, March 2018, data files "54646-additional-data-for-researchers." "Table 3.12. Government Social Benefits," "National Income and Product Accounts," US Bureau of Economic Analysis, July 31, 2018. Social Security Administration, *Annual Statistical Supplement to the Social Security Bulletin, 2017,* Board of Trustees, Federal Old-Age and Survivors Insurance and Federal Disability Insurance Trust Funds, Washington, DC, June 5, 2018. Social Security Administration, *The 2018 Annual Report of the Board of Trustees of the Federal Old-Age and Survivors Insurance and Federal Disability Insurance Trust Funds,* Washington, DC, June 5, 2018, Table II.B1, 7. The Boards of Trustees, Federal Hospital Insurance and Federal Supplementary Medical Insurance Trust Funds, *2018 Annual Report of the Boards of Trustees of the Federal Hospital Insurance and Federal Supplementary Medical Insurance Trust Funds,* Washington, DC, June 5, 2018, Table II.B1, 11. "CRS Report: Welfare Spending the Largest Item in the Federal Budget," US Senate Budget Committee, 2013. "Spending for Federal Benefits and Services for People with Low Income, FY 2001–2011: An Update of Table B-1 from CRS Report R41625," Congressional Research Service, October 16, 2012. US Census Bureau, American Housing Survey, 2017 National – Housing Costs – All Occupied Units, Tenure Filter: Renter. https://www.census.gov/programs-surveys/ahs/data/interactive/ahstablecreator.html#?s_areas=a00017&s_year=s2017&s_tableName=Table10&s_byGroup1=a1&s_byGroup2=a1&s_filterGroup1=t3&s_filterGroup2=g1&s_show=S. "Federal Student Loans: Education Needs to Improve Its Income-Driven Repayment Plan Budget Estimates," GAO-17-22, US Government Accountability Office, November 2016. "Fair-Value Estimates of the Cost of Federal Credit Programs in 2019," Congressional Budget Office, June 2018, https://www.cbo.gov/system/files?file=2018-10/54095-2019fairvalueestimates.pdf. "Disbursements 2017," Universal Services Administrative Company, https://www.usac.org/li/about/process-overview/stats/historical-support-distribution.aspx. "Table 2.1—Receipts by Source: 1934–2022" and "Table 2.5—Composition of 'Other Receipts': 1940–2022," Office of Management and Budget, https://www.govinfo.gov/app/collection/budget/2018/BUDGET-2018-TAB. "Table 1. State and Local Government Finances by Level of Government and by State: 2016," US Census Bureau, 2016 Annual Surveys of State and Local Government Finances, https://www.census.gov/data/datasets/2016/econ/local/public-use-datasets.html. Enhanced CPI adjustments to poverty thresholds calculated from price index research summarized in Bruce D. Meyer and James X. Sullivan, "Winning the War on Poverty: Poverty from the Great Society to the Great Recession," Working Paper no. 18718, National Bureau of Economic Research, January 2013, http://www.nber.org/papers/w18718; Brent R. Moulton, "The Measurement of Output, Prices, and Productivity: What's Changed since the Boskin Commission?" Brookings Institution, July 2018, https://www.brookings.edu/research/themeasurement-of-output-prices-and-productivity. Chart updated from John F. Early, "Assessing the Facts about Inequality, Poverty, and Redistribution," Policy Analysis no. 839, Cato Institute, April 24, 2018, https://www.cato.org/sites/cato.org/files/pubs/pdf/pa-839-updated-2.pdf, 18.

children and less than 0.4 percent of seniors live in poverty. For children living with married relatives, the poverty rate is a mere 0.2 percent. Poverty affects 1.7 percent of Blacks, about 92 percent fewer than shown by the Census counts. While the improved measures show that poverty among Blacks is still somewhat higher than for Whites, the difference is only 0.6 percentage points, versus the 11.5 percent difference in the Census numbers. With the improved estimates, poverty affects 1.3 percent of women and 1.0 percent of men.

The first printing of this book was released in early September 2022, just days before the Census Bureau published its poverty data for 2021. Before that, we and others had been highlighting the deficiencies in the official poverty measure with technical audiences and articles in the *Wall Street Journal*. The Biden administration knew it had a problem. Its policy response to the economic effects of the COVID-19 pandemic had been to expand government transfer payments, mostly to low-income households, by 47 percent, or $1.5 trillion, between 2019 and 2021.[32] Because most of these additional transfer payments, especially the refundable child tax credits, would not be counted by the Census Bureau as income, the official poverty rates overall and for children would likely rise, directly contradicting administration claims that child poverty would fall by half.

And sure enough, the official Census poverty rate rose between 2019 and 2021 from 10.5 percent to 11.6 percent, and the official Census child poverty measure rose from 14.4 percent to 15.3 percent.[33] But to divert attention from the obvious measurement flaws, the Census Bureau completely changed the way it released the poverty data. Ever since the War on Poverty, the annual release of household income and poverty had been combined into a single publication, but with the release of the 2021 data in September 2022, the Census split household income and poverty into two separate publications. Even more telling, it added an experimental poverty measure called the Supplemental Poverty Measure (SPM) to the official poverty release. Before that, the SPM had only been published, starting with 2011, in a separate paper as an experimental index a few days after the official poverty rate report.

One of the features of the SPM is that it counts more transfer payments as income than the official measure counts. Although it still fails to count 59 percent of all transfer payments, it does count specific programs such as the child tax credit and food stamps that had been vehicles for greatly expanded payments under the administration's pandemic stimulus initiatives. As a result, the SPM provided an alternative, more favorable view of the effects of the pandemic stimulus packages. It reported an overall poverty rate that declined from 11.8 percent in 2019 to 7.8 percent in 2021 as well as the politically advertised reduction of child poverty from 12.6 percent to 5.2 percent.[34]

With the official poverty measure discredited, the administration began pushing to adopt the experimental SPM as the new official poverty measure. That would be a serious mistake. The defective official measure fails because the Census uses incomplete data. Those gaps can be fixed readily, as we have shown, by simply counting all transfer payments and using better price indexes to update the poverty thresholds. The proposed experimental SPM also fails to count 59 percent of transfer payments, a small improvement over the official measure's omission of 67 percent; however, it is fatally flawed because it ties the poverty threshold to median income so the poverty threshold rises with general prosperity.

The poverty thresholds used in the official measure to identify poor families are the cost of a defined quantity of goods and services required by a specific size and type of family to satisfy its minimum economic needs. The official poverty thresholds have been adjusted for inflation over time, but the defined level of poverty in terms of real consumption levels remained fixed at the defined minimum necessary quantity of goods and services.

The SPM defines the poverty threshold in relative terms as the amount of income necessary to purchase 83 percent of the median family's current level of consumption of food, apparel, shelter, and utilities plus an additional 20 percent of that total for other smaller necessities. Under this relative definition of poverty, no matter how much the median household spends on food, apparel, and other necessities and no matter how luxurious those items might be, the members of families who did not have enough income to pay for the requisite percentage of that median spending amount would always be counted as poor, no matter how well-off they were.

Since its start date in 1999, the SPM thresholds have risen by 42 percent more than official poverty thresholds and at about the same rate as median income, simply because with rising income, median households have bought more and higher-quality items in categories defined by the Census as necessities.

Adopting the SPM as the official measure would ensure that economic growth, which raised the level of income and consumption across the entire economy, would not significantly reduce the poverty rate no matter how well-off low-income households became. The poverty rate would decline significantly only with additional income redistribution. In addition, Kevin Corinth, of the American Enterprise Institute, has shown that adopting the SPM as the qualification standard for welfare payments would add more than 3 million households to the welfare rolls and increase federal welfare payments by more than $124 billion over the next ten years.[35]

Improved Measures of Household Income

Chapter 4 documented the improvements in measures of income by adding items missing from the Census estimates: the missing two-thirds of government transfers, all taxes, employer-paid benefits, realized capital gains, and general underreporting of a number of smaller items. The resulting household income after transfers and taxes was adjusted for inflation using the traditional CPI-U and was displayed over a seventy-five-year period for each of the five income quintiles in Figure 4.1. Those same data have also been adjusted for inflation using the best practices described above for removing substitution and new-product biases and charted in Figure 6.3.

The improved inflation adjustment does not, of course, change the relative positions of the growth rates among the various income quintiles, but by using the more accurate inflation adjustments, all five quintiles show dramatically stronger income growth. Real household income after transfers and taxes for the bottom quintile grew the most, 681 percent, followed by second-quintile growth of 543 percent. The top quintile grew more slowly by 456 percent, followed closely by the middle quintile at 398 percent and the fourth quintile at 381 percent. The substantially faster growth by the bottom and second quintiles reflects the greater government transfer payments to lower-income households, while the top- and fourth-quintile growth was suppressed by higher taxes.

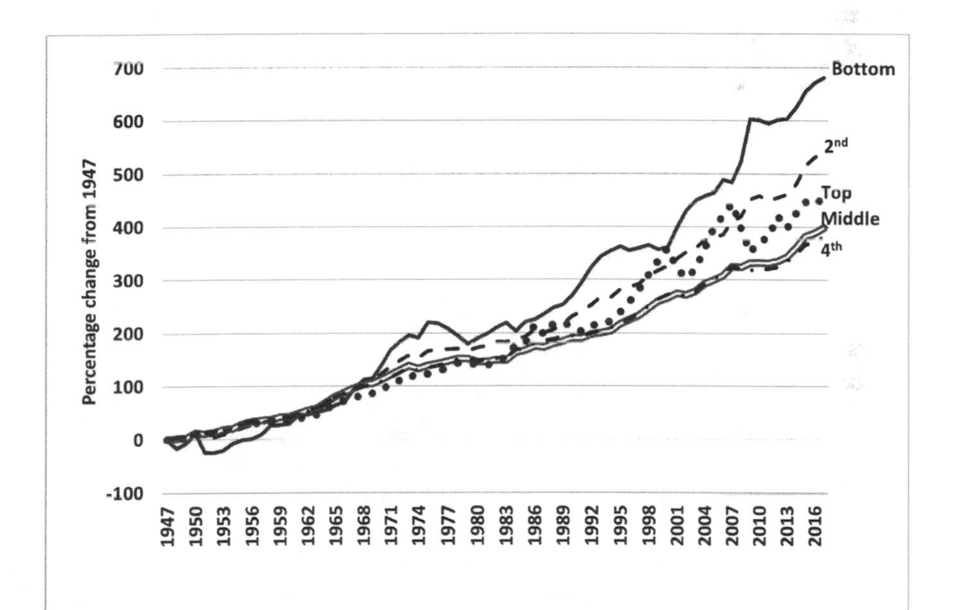

Figure 6.3. Cumulative percentage changes from 1947 in real household income after transfers and taxes by earned-income quintile, 1967–2017.

Note: Real dollars calculated using best practices described in this chapter, including using the C-CPI-U to remove substitution biases and applying research results to reduce new-product biases.

Sources: Calculated from sources in Figure 4.1 and Figure 6.1.

Fiscal Effects of Overstating Inflation

In addition to understating measures of well-being, the upward biases in consumer price indexes adversely affect the overall fiscal health of the nation. Many government payments such as Social Security and federal employee pensions are automatically increased by cost-of-living adjustments based on the percentage change in the CPI. Other programs such as Medicaid and food stamps establish eligibility based on poverty guidelines or other CPI-adjusted income levels. The upward biases in the CPI increase benefit levels by more than the true change in the cost of living and add beneficiaries who would not otherwise qualify.

From 2000 to 2018, the six largest federal benefit programs that contain automatic cost-of-living adjustments for benefit levels or eligibility spent a total of approximately $6.8 trillion providing those cost-of-living adjustments.[35] If, instead, the adjustments had been made using the more accurate Chained CPI, which eliminates substitution bias, the increase in government spending would have been $1.1 trillion smaller. And if, in addition, a price index had been available that took more complete account of the value of new and improved products, the cost-of-living adjustment might have been as much as $2.6 trillion smaller.

Ironically, while the federal government continues to use a traditional CPI for cost-of-living adjustments on entitlement spending, it now adjusts the personal income tax brackets for inflation using the more accurate Chained CPI. Because the Chained CPI removes the substitution bias, it rises more slowly than the traditional CPI, slowing the increase in income levels that define the tax brackets and accelerating the rise of income tax payments relative to what would have occurred using the traditional CPI.

Adoption of the more accurate Chained CPI for indexing tax brackets was a significant reform and improvement. If the Chained CPI had been used from 2000 to 2018 to adjust both income tax brackets and spending for the six largest programs with cost-of-living adjustments, the national debt held by the public would have been $1.4 trillion smaller than it is today. In making that change the government would be simply applying the same, more accurate price index to calculating the cost of living for entitlement spending purposes that it already uses in adjusting taxes for inflation. If a price index had been available that incorporated both the elimination of the substitution bias and more complete adjustments for the value of new and improved products, and if it had been used to adjust both spending and tax brackets for inflation, then between 2000 and 2018 tax collections would have been $1.1 trillion greater, spending would have been $2.6 trillion smaller, and the national debt would have been $3.7 trillion smaller. This reduction of the national debt would have been achieved by simply using a more accurate measure of inflation.

Getting Our Facts Straight about Measures of Economic Well-Being

Government's standard measurements of well-being are significantly understated because they use price measures that have overstated the actual rate of inflation that occurred during the last fifty years. The result is that we are having major debates based on measures of economic well-being that are demonstrably wrong. When a politician today attacks American economic performance because of high poverty rates, stagnant wages, and slow or unequal growth in household income, it is their data, not America's economic performance, that is bad. As a nation, we need to get our facts straight.

CHAPTER 7

What about the "Super Rich"?

Public discussion of income inequality has often focused on the very richest—the "billionaires" or the "400 richest." These households are the outliers, the exceptions to the overall distribution of income, but advocates for more income redistribution have sought to make these unrepresentative groups the focal point of the debate. This chapter concentrates on measuring and understanding the impact of very high income households on inequality and the overall performance of the economy. Previous chapters have looked closely at the bottom of the income distribution and found that, despite the political claims to the contrary, income redistribution has virtually eliminated poverty and most households actually receive at least middle-class incomes after transfers and taxes. This chapter examines the households at the very top of the income distribution, evaluates some of the common characterizations of them, and tries to lay out the facts about who they are, whether they pay their fair share of taxes, and how they contribute to the economic life of the nation.

Who Are the Super Rich?

So far, the analysis of high-income households in this book has focused mainly on the average income level of the 25.5 million households that constitute the top quintile of household earnings. Table 7.1 begins with the 2017 average income statistics for each of the five quintiles presented in earlier chapters. It then separates out successively higher-income groups of households within the top quintile. The double underlining below the top quintile, top 1.0 percent, top 0.1 percent, top 0.01 percent, and top 0.001 percent indicates that each is the sum of the groups immediately underneath it. The top 0.00031 percent (or top four hundred households) is the highest-income group. The first classification

Table 7 1. Average earned income and income after transfers and taxes for higher-income households, 2017

Earned-income quintile or percentile	*Households*	*Average earned income (dollars)*	*Average income after transfers and taxes (dollars)*	*Saving and investment income as percentage of earned income*	*Taxes as percentage of earned income plus transfers*	*Percentage share* of earned income*	*Percentage share* of income after transfers and taxes*
Bottom quintile	25,515,560	4,908	49,613	9.8	7.5	1.0	10.9
Second quintile	25,517,281	30,931	53,924	4.5	14.1	6.1	11.9
Middle quintile	25,518,223	66,148	65,631	3.5	22.7	13.0	14.4
Fourth quintile	25,516,785	112,563	88,132	4.4	28.4	22.1	19.4
Top quintile	25,518,304	295,904	197,034				
81–90 percentile	12,758,222	179,045	131,583	5.3	29.7	17.5	14.5
91–95 percentile	6,380,259	243,369	166,445	7.5	33.8	11.9	9.2
96–99 percentile	5,103,767	354,327	222,255	10.6	38.7	13.9	9.8
Top 1 percent	1,276,055	1,493,282	903,483				
99.1–99.9 percentile	1,148,450	803,190	480,538	27.1	40.9	7.1	4.8
Top 0.1 percent	127,606	7,527,471	4,525,441				
99.91–99.99 percentile	114,845	4,248,948	2,530,300	47.4	40.6	3.7	2.5
Top 0.01 percent	12,761	38,499,719	24,019,163				
99.99–99.999 percentile	11,484	23,592,279	14,209,803	67.3	39.8	2.1	1.4
Top 0.001 percent	1,276	175,196,962	114,899,852				
Top 0.001 percent minus top 400	876	73,014,608	43,749,434	74.3	40.1	0.5	0.3
Top 400 (0.00031 percent)	400	400,516,391	272,273,806	79.3	32.0	1.2	0.9

Note:
*Share is total for all households in the income group as a percentage of the total for the entire population.

Sources: See Table 2.5. For households with incomes in the top 1 percent, the Congressional Budget Office and Census CPS/ASEC data have been supplemented with data from "Table 3. All Individual Returns Excluding Dependents: Number of Returns, Shares of Adjusted Gross Income (AGI), Selected Income Items, Credits, Total Income Tax, AGI Floor on Percentiles, and Average Tax Rates, by Selected Expanded Descending Cumulative Percentiles of Returns Based on AGI, Tax Year 2017," Internal Revenue Service, https://www.irs.gov/statistics/soi-tax-stats-individual-statistical-tables-by-tax-rate-and-income-percentile; "Table 1—Selected Items for the Top 400 Individual Income Tax Returns with the Largest Adjusted Gross Income (AGI), Tax Years 1992–2014," in "The 400 Individual Income Tax Returns Reporting the Largest Adjusted Gross Incomes Each Year, 1992–2014," Internal Revenue Service, https://www.irs.gov/statistics/soi-tax-stats-top-400-individual-income-tax-returns-with-the-largest-adjusted-gross-incomes.

breaks down the top quintile into four groups: the lower half of the top quintile from the 81st to 90th percentiles, followed by the next fourth of the quintile from the 91st to 95th percentiles, then the 96th to 99th percentiles, and finally the top 1 percent.

The top 1 percent is divided into its bottom 90 percent, followed by its top 10 percent—namely, the 0.1 percent of all households. This group is similarly divided into its bottom 90 percent and top 10 percent to arrive at 0.01 percent of households, or the "top one percent of the top one percent." One more similar division brings us to 0.001 percent of households, which is further divided into the 400 highest-income households and the residual 876 households that complete the 0.001 percent. The top four hundred households are the highest-income group for the analysis because this group is the highest level for which the Internal Revenue Service (IRS) publishes data.

For each income group, Table 7.1 shows the number of households, the average earned income, the average income after transfers and taxes, the percentage of earned income coming from saving and investing, and taxes paid as a percentage of earned income plus transfers. The last two columns contain each group's percentage share of all household earned income and all household income after transfers and taxes.

Income from saving and investing in 2017 remained a small fraction of total earned income up to the 99th percentile of households. Even up through the 99.99th percentile, saving and investing generated less than half of household income. From there, each higher income group earned larger proportions of its income from saving and investing. But even for the top four hundred highest-earning households, wages, salaries, and benefits still created more than 20 percent of their earned income.[1]

The fact that income from work is the dominant determinate of earned income for 99.99 percent of all households in America has significant implications. Prosperity for all but a tiny outlier group of very-high-income households comes from normal, everyday work. And even most of earnings from saving and investing are the results of saving from previous work income. A recent study of millionaires (households with a net worth of more than $1 million) discovered that only 21 percent of them had received any inheritance. Only 16 percent inherited more than $100,000, and only 3 percent inherited $1 million or more.[2] Yes, a few people inherited wealth, but the vast majority earned it first and then saved it. Any significant reduction in earned-income inequality will come only from removing disincentives for more people to work and enhance their human capital and, thereby, their productivity and earning power.

This chapter's title refers to the "super rich," but there is no obvious definition for the term. In the 96th to the 99th percentiles, just below the top 1.0 percent, households earned almost 90 percent of their income from the wages and salaries they earned working. They earned an average of almost $355,000 per year and, on average, kept less than $225,000 after taxes.

Certainly, they were well off, though hardly super rich. In fact, the first households earning $1 million do not appear until percentile 99.3. These so-called millionaire earners, however, lost about 40 percent of their income to taxes, and 57 percent of them dropped below the millionaire-earner status after taxes. One could safely apply the term "super rich" to the 127,600 households in the top 0.1 percent of household earnings. On average, they earned about $7,527,000, and although they lost about 40 percent to taxes, they still averaged more than $4,525,000 in after-tax income. But within this rarified group, there were still huge differences. The bottom nine-tenths of the top 0.1 percent (115,000 households) averaged $4,249,000 in earned income and kept $2,528,000 after taxes. The top four hundred households averaged $400,500,000 in earnings and $272,300,000 after taxes—respectively, 94 and 108 times as much as the bottom nine-tenths of the top 0.1 percent of households by earnings. Some of the top four hundred earned more than $1 billion.

Even among the top 0.1 percent, work was still an important part of their income, so what did they do to earn all that money? Data from the IRS tells us that business and financial leaders of major companies constituted a substantial portion of the highest-earning population—a little less than half of the top 1 percent and about 60 percent of the top 0.1 percent. The legal and medical professions also had significant membership in the top 0.1 percent. The arts, media, sports, academia, and the sciences were among those professions well represented. Earners in other very-high-income households came from a wide array of other pursuits. Appendix D has more detailed data and analysis related to the occupations of the top 1 percent and top 0.1 percent.

Reports of celebrity pay in the general press show that many entertainers and news commentators make incomes from $10 million to over $100 million annually, squarely in the top 1 percent of the top 1 percent (0.01 percent overall), with a few even reaching $500 million and making it into the top four hundred.[3] Star players in major-league professional sports are also in the top 0.01 percent, and even the average players are in the top 0.1 percent.[4] Football coaches at major tax-payer-supported universities also fall into the top 0.1 percent.[5] Their fans obviously think they are worth it.

For those who earn very high incomes, their stay in the exclusive income groups can be short. A study of publicly available IRS data between 1992 and 2014 showed that 4,584 different households were in the top four hundred at some point over the twenty-three years. Nearly three-quarters qualified for only a single year. The average length of time a tax unit was in the top four hundred was only 2.01 years. On average, in any given year, only one-third of the four hundred had been in the group for ten or more years. Aside from the usual economic ups and downs of the marketplace, one reason for this high turnover is that more than 60 percent of income among the top four hundred comes from capital gains—that is, from selling assets. Unlike salaries, interest, or even dividends, capital gains are typically quite irregular, not only because of market forces but also because the decisions to sell assets are not usually uniform for the same individuals year after year. A household may receive a large capital gain that puts it in the top four hundred for a year and then return to more stable, lower earnings. Similar, although less pronounced, volatility is also reflected in other high-end groups. More than a quarter of the income for the top 1 percent, more than one-third for the top 0.1 percent, and half for the top 0.01 percent comes from capital gains. Income spikes from large, onetime capital gains cause households to move into and out of higher income groups for short periods.[6]

With all of the political rhetoric about the one-percenters, it is important to look more closely at the economic profile of the top 1.0 percent of households. Their incomes before taxes start at less than $600,000, which is often earned by two full-time workers. This is hardly the yacht and private-jet set. If a household at the 1 percent income level lives in San Francisco or Manhattan, it will live very comfortably but hardly lavishly. The mental model perpetuated by the political clamor about the one-percenters or the rich is generally about someone like Warren Buffett, Bill Gates, or Larry Ellison earning hundreds of millions or even billions of dollars. But they are not the top 1 percent, or 0.1 percent, or even 0.01 percent. Households in the top 0.01 percent (equal to 1 percent of the 1 percent) earn at least $9 million in annual income. The three households just mentioned earn (based on publicly available data) at least ten times that.

The CEOs of large, established US companies like IBM, Xerox, and Federal Express make about $10 million per year, falling at the lower end of the top 1 percent of the top 1 percent of households. CEOs of large financial and telecommunications companies are, on average, paid about $15 million. Healthcare CEOs on average earn about $4.6 million.[7] Of course, by the very definition of "average," there are individual entrepreneurs and unusually successful leaders who make significantly more than the average and many others who barely qualify for the distinction of being in the top 1 percent of the top 1 percent. This is huge variation, but all that variation is among the approximately twelve thousand households that produce at that level.

The Forbes 400 is the most referenced list of the richest four hundred people in the United States in a given year. For the 2021 list, each is estimated to have a total net worth of more than $2.9 billion. There were also another 353 billionaires who did not make the list.[8] Billionaires typically have annual incomes of at least $50 million. The public has a fascination with these super wealthy individuals, but at less than 0.0006 percent of all households, or fewer than six out of every million households, they are best viewed as highly productive outliers. And they are highly productive. Almost two-thirds came from poor to upper-middle-class families, including 7.0 percent from poor families that faced serious obstacles, often as immigrants. Twenty-three percent inherited significant wealth but actively managed it to grow it into the Forbes 400 class. Only 6.5 percent merely lived on the wealth they inherited.[9]

A team of three economists and mathematicians lead by investor Robert Arnott analyzed the history of the nation's super wealthy over the last one hundred years using not only the Forbes 400 list, which began in 1982, but also other lists that stretched back to the early years of the twentieth century. They discovered that while the total wealth of the wealthiest individuals grew somewhat faster than the nation's wealth, most of the growth came not from individuals who were already on the list but rather from new people who earned their way onto the list through invention, innovation, entrepreneurial risk, and personal drive. These new arrivals joined the list because they accumulated even more wealth than those who were already there. The wealth of their descendants generally fell off by half in twenty years or less. As a result, the wealthiest families from the nineteenth century are all but gone from the ranks of the wealthiest, and most of those from fifty years ago are gone as well.[10] On average, the wealth of Forbes 400 members, alumni, and their descendants grew 5 percent *less* per year than the returns that would have accrued to the typical conservative investor in stocks and bonds over the same period.[11]

While income inequality has become a staple of modern American political debate, there is little evidence that it is a major mover of votes. In 2016, income inequality was a more pronounced issue than it had been in most election years, and yet blue-collar Americans elected the richest person ever elected president since George Washington.[12] Different views on the best approach to the inequality issue are certainly debatable, but it appears convincing Americans to vote based on resentment of the rich is a hard sell.

Do the Rich Pay Their Fair Share of Taxes?

It is often asserted that rich Americans are not paying their fair share of taxes.[13] No call for an increase in taxes is complete without the demand that the rich pay their fair share. Of course, the advocate for the tax increase never defines what that "fair" share is, other than taxing more than the current assessment. Claims have even been made that rich Americans pay a smaller share of their income in taxes than do middle-income households.[14] These claims are verifiably false. Table 7.1 shows that taxes as a percentage of total income, including both earnings and transfer payments, increased steadily from 7.5 percent in the bottom quintile of households to approximately 40 percent for the top 1 percent of households. There is only one meaningful exception to these constantly increasing tax rates as incomes rise. For the top four hundred households, the average tax rate drops to 32.0 percent. This income group is miniscule—only three out of every million American households. But even with that decline in the tax rate of this miniscule group, they still pay a higher percentage of their income in taxes than 90 percent of all households. In fact, the average 32.0 percent tax rate for the top four hundred households is 41 percent larger than the average 22.7 percent tax rate for the middle quintile. Each of the top four hundred households is almost a special case given the large amounts of income from onetime asset sales. To put the economic significance of this tiny group of super-rich households in perspective, if government seized all of their after-tax income, it would fund the federal government for less than six days.

The argument that the rich do not pay their fair share of taxes often relies on cherry-picked anecdotes of specific households that, because of the way they earn and spend their income, fall far outside the norm of even other high-income households and are in no way reflective of a significant number of taxpayers. For example, Bill Gates's tax returns have never been made public, but he has reportedly given $54 billion to charity.[15] He clearly reduces his tax liability by giving away so much money. But it is his money, and it is certainly debatable whether the public would benefit if the government took the money and spent it instead of letting him give it away to what he and other people deem worthy causes.

Warren Buffett may be worth hundreds of millions of dollars a year to Berkshire Hathaway, but he pays himself only a nominal salary. Because he rarely sells assets and makes considerable charitable donations, Buffett might, as he has said, actually pay a lower effective tax rate than his secretary, who may be well compensated.[16]

In June 2021, ProPublica posted what it claimed were tax returns of the twenty-five richest filers stolen from the IRS. It used the revelation of stolen returns to claim that the wealthiest twenty-five people only paid 3.4 percent of their incomes in income taxes in recent years.[17] That claim was contrary to the actual stolen tax returns themselves and is inconsistent with the publicly available IRS data showing that the top four hundred income earners paid on average 32 percent of their income in federal income and payroll taxes. The difference arose because ProPublica engaged in a classic bait and switch. It claimed to be presenting stolen information from the IRS, but while the taxes paid may have come from the stolen documents, the income figures used to calculate the 3.4 percent were pure fiction. In addition to the actual taxable income reported on the documents, ProPublica included a guess about how much the value of assets held by these individuals might have appreciated. No one pays taxes on the appreciation of their assets such as homes, pension funds, or any other investments until they are sold and, in the process, generate income. In focusing its story on how little of Warren Buffett's wealth was taxed, ProPublica could have picked no better example of how this nation became wealthy. Like a modern-day Scrooge, Buffett has accumulated vast wealth over decades of thrift and wise investing. Famous for both being the world's greatest investor and living modestly, he eats using coupons from McDonald's, works in a cheap office, drives an old car, and lives in a modest home. No one seems to ever ask, "If Buffett is not benefiting from all his wealth in the way he lives, who is benefiting?"

Buffett has no vast vault of gold where he takes a daily swim like Scrooge McDuck. Instead, his billions, which do not seem to do him much good since he does not spend them, are invested. They enable people with good ideas and big dreams to create value. They buy plants and equipment, create jobs, and develop new goods and services that transform our lives. And when Buffett's investments generate economic activity, there is always a tax man there to take a slice in sales, payroll, income, and property taxes. When he dies, the government's death tax will take 40 percent of his life's work and, consequently, reduce the well-being of millions of Americans who now benefit from the jobs and growth his wisdom and thrift continue to create.

It is not clear that government would get more by seizing Buffett's wealth than by collecting taxes on all the economic activity his snowballing investments create. Even if it could, how can anyone believe that the American people would benefit from stopping Buffett's wealth from working for the economy so that government can spend it? Wealthy investors who accumulate wealth but do not consume it are public benefactors, for their wealth is creating jobs and promoting the general prosperity.

There is no better illustration of how wealth accumulation benefits society than the most famous and infamous wealth hoarder of Victorian literature, Ebenezer Scrooge. In Charles Dicken's *A Christmas Carol*, Ebenezer Scrooge is a caricature of a man of business in the Victorian era: a rich, obsessive wealth hoarder. The very name Scrooge has become a global synonym for stingy or miserly. Though Buffett is far sweeter and more charitable than the unreformed Scrooge, his work effort and thrift are remarkably similar to Scrooge's. Charles Dickens describes Scrooge as working in a "moldy old office" and living in "his dusty chambers" in a building so old and dreary that "nobody lived in it but Scrooge." He was "a tight-fisted, hand at the grindstone." He strove from dawn till dusk to "understand his own business" and "with his banker's-book" trudged home in the dark "to take his gruel" alone by a dying fire.

There is nothing unethical about Ebenezer Scrooge. In his view, business "is the even-handed dealing of the world," and good business fights poverty: "there is nothing on which it is so hard as poverty." His great failing, in the words of his former fiancée (whom he gave up to marry his business), was that he had become a prisoner of "the master-passion, Gain." Scrooge's obsession with gain denied him many human pleasures and the happiness that would have flowed from those pleasures. But there is no evidence that he directly harmed anyone economically. His investments created jobs and growing prosperity for others just as Warren Buffett's investments do today.

Just as many fail to see how Warren Buffett's wealth helps many besides himself, it appears that Dickens never considered the possibility that Scrooge and Jacob Marley's business in any way contributed to the common welfare of humanity. Like Scrooge, Marley created and accumulated wealth, leaving it to Scrooge, who continued to invest and accumulate. When Dickens has Scrooge's nephew say that Scrooge's wealth "is of no use to him," since he doesn't spend it, it is clear Dickens never considered to whom Scrooge's wealth was useful. Few ask the same question of Buffett's wealth today.

In 1800, no one had experienced anything resembling economic progress on a sustained basis. Based on all Dickens knew or could envision, the only hope for the poor was charity. Yet, unbeknownst to Dickens and virtually every other writer of the Victorian era, at the very moment *A Christmas Carol* was published in December 1843, the Market Revolution, funded by the thrift of Britain's Scrooges, was already enriching all humanity. What followed was a period of broad-based prosperity, the likes of which had never occurred in recorded history, and, most amazingly, the progress has never ended.

Who, then, benefited from the accumulated wealth of investors like Scrooge and Marley? First Great Britain and then all of humanity reaped the benefits. Since Scrooge and Marley never consumed the wealth they created, its use was, in reality, a gift to humanity. It funded the factories and railroads, tools and jobs that first fed and clothed millions of British people and then billions around the world. Their unspent wealth was of no use to them, but it was of great use to humanity. Even as Dickens's Ghost of Christmas Present pulled back his robe to reveal the children who embodied Ignorance and Want, the wealth accumulated by British investors like Scrooge was already beginning the long drive that would do more to end ignorance and want than all the governments and all the charities that ever existed. One point seems clear: Scrooge's wealth accumulation would have benefited far more people than anything he might have given to charity after his transformation and many times more than government would have helped had it taken his wealth and spent it.

The same would be true for Warren Buffett and his peers today. They create jobs and income for millions of other people. Their wealth is not something they have taken from others; they have created it and in the process made greater prosperity possible for us all. Wealth is also the product of entrepreneurial activity that creates new technology or discovers unique and innovative ways to produce and market existing products. The superstore, the mall concept, franchising, and e-commerce all emerged in this manner. Technology, robotics, and digital applications continue to generate today's wealth. The gig economy of Uber, Lyft, and Airbnb built on those capabilities to revolutionize transportation and hospitality. As time passes, new innovations will create the new super wealthy and displace the old, in an evolutionary process that enriches us all.

Academic Claims That the Rich Pay Less

Most claims that higher-income households do not pay enough taxes are merely anecdotal outliers like those discussed above. But one widely circulated academic study by Emmanuel Saez and Gabriel Zucman used a broader data set to make a claim that "the working class pays around 25% of its income in taxes. This rate slightly increases for the middle class and stabilizes around 28% for the upper middle class. Finally, [tax rates] fall to 23% for the 400 richest Americans."[18] Their summary chart is recreated in the top chart labeled "Saez-Zucman average tax rates on distorted scale" in Figure 7.1.

They separate earning groups by percentiles—each percentile containing 1 percent of the adult population. So, for example, P0–10 contains the 10 percent of the population with the lowest income. P99.9–99.99 contains the 0.09 percent of adults with income just below the top 0.01 percent. The fact that they count percentages of adults rather than percentages of households creates some minor differences between their data and that in Table 7.1, but those differences are small compared with other issues that produce dramatic differences.

There are two problems with Saez and Zucman's conclusions. The first is that their chart was scaled incorrectly and gives a distorted picture of the significance of the differences they claim. The much-reviled top 1 percent of the population has been drawn to consume 26.7 percent, more than one-quarter, of the total chart area. The top four hundred, which constitute a mere 0.0002 percent of the population, are portrayed as if they were 6.7 percent of the population—28,069 times greater than their actual share of the population. This makes the tax rates of the top earners appear much more important than they really are.

A properly scaled chart of the same data is displayed in the second line labeled "Saez-Zucman average tax rates on corrected scale" in Figure 7.1. For both charts, each decile on the horizontal scale up through P80–90 has the same length. But the corrected version of the chart at the bottom assigns the same length for the top decile as it does for the other deciles, whereas the upper chart assigns six times that length, grossly distorting the relationship. The corrected result gives an entirely different impression of the tax structure. The top 1 percent of households have an average tax rate of 29.9 percent, higher than for any lower-income group. Within the top 1 percent, however, there is a lot of variation, as rates rise to 33.2 percent and fall to 23.0 percent. The advertised drop in tax rates at the highest four hundred tax units is a tiny outlier even among the top 0.1 percent of earners.

With the scaling corrected, it is now possible to compare the Saez and Zucman estimates with the results in Table 7.1, which include all income received and taxes paid, as reported from IRS, Census, and Congressional Budget Office

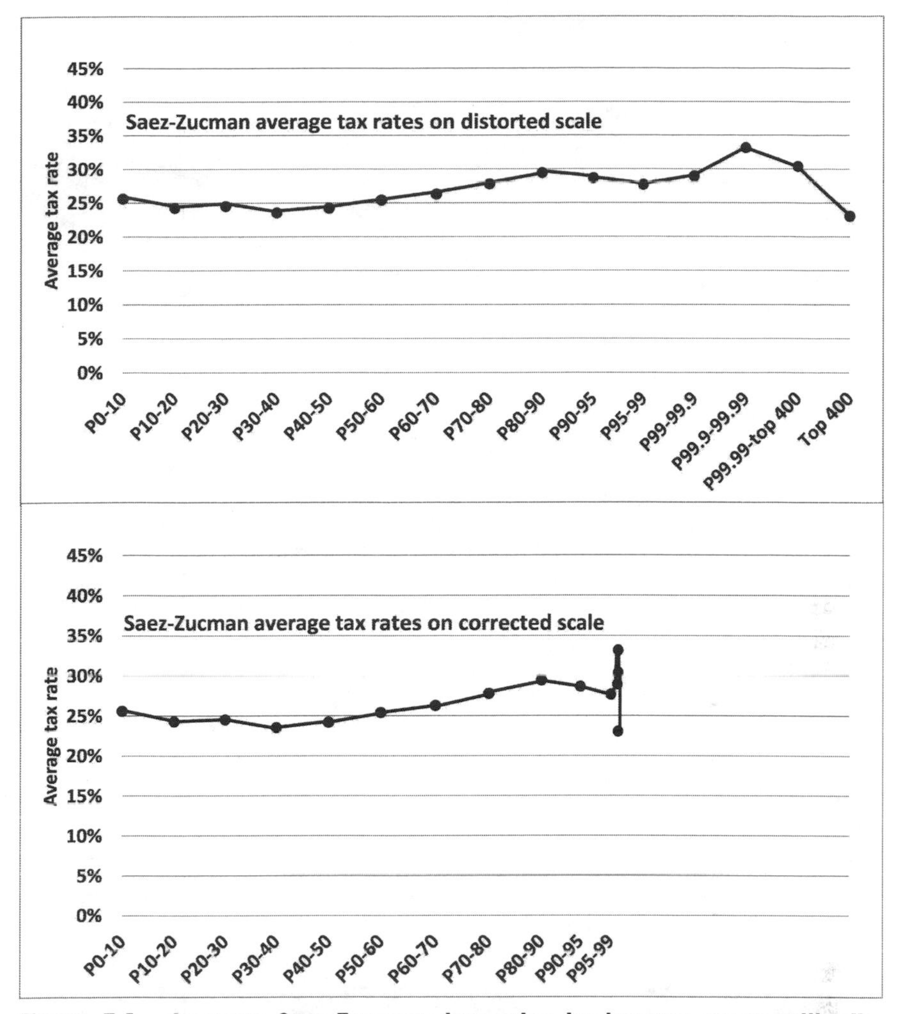

Figure 7.1. Average Saez-Zucman tax rates by income group with distorted and corrected scales, 2018.

Source: Constructed from tax rates in tab "DataF1b" and the scale in tab "F1.2" of SZ2019MainFigures.xlsx posted at https://taxjusticenow.org/#/appendix by Emmanuel Saez and Gabriel Zucman, in support of their book *The Triumph of Injustice: How the Rich Dodge Taxes and How to Make Them Pay* (New York: W. W. Norton, 2019), 13–15. Corrected scale by authors.

sources. Figure 7.2 presents that comparison. Note that from the 50th through the 90th percentiles, the results from the two data sets are essentially the same. So why are they so different at the high- and low-income ends of the income distribution?

The differences between the two sets of estimates in the lower half of the income distribution are not the result of how the taxes are counted. The actual tax numbers are in reasonable agreement with each other. The differences come

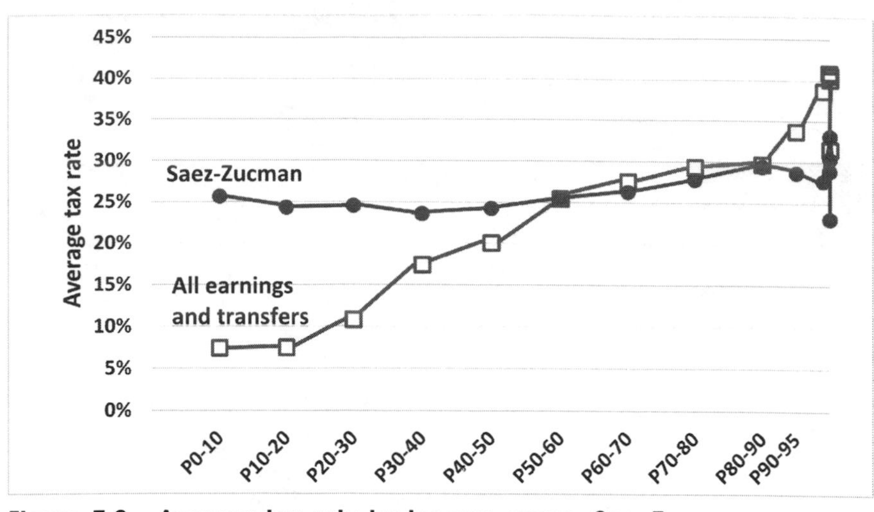

Figure 7.2. Average tax rate by income group, Saez-Zucman versus actual earnings and transfers, 2018 and 2017, respectively.

Sources: All earnings and transfers: Table 7.1. Saez-Zucman: Constructed from tax rates in tab "DataF1b" of SZ2019MainFigures.xlsx posted at https://taxjusticenow.org/#/appendix by Emmanuel Saez and Gabriel Zucman, in support of their book *The Triumph of Injustice*, 13–15.

from what Saez and Zucman count as income. They count only *earned* income. They completely ignore transfer payments that make up more than 90 percent of the income of the bottom quintile and 50 percent of the income of the second quintile. By not counting transfer payments as income to the recipient households, they grossly understate income in the bottom two-fifths of the population. So, when they then divide the actual taxes paid by an income amount that is between two and nine times smaller than the real amount, the resulting tax rates are unbelievably too high.

Not counting transfers creates a big problem for Saez and Zucman. How are people paying taxes when they earn less than they pay in taxes? Of course, in reality they pay their taxes out of transfer payments. But Saez and Zucman are ignoring transfer payments, so in the case of people who earn no income, they would be forced to divide any sales, excise, or property taxes paid by zero earned income, which is mathematically meaningless. Even with small positive amounts of earned income, Saez and Zucman's computed tax rate would be unbelievably large. They "solve" this problem by excluding individuals who have earned less than $7,250. That exclusion is strictly arbitrary and actually removes more than 80 percent of the observations from the bottom quintile. They justify this particular cutoff as being half the annual earnings of a full-time worker at the minimum wage. That, of course, is not a justification for choosing the income level but simply an arbitrary label. By dropping those earning less than $7,250, they get an average tax rate that is consistent with their story of the bottom 60 percent of the income distribution having a relatively constant average tax rate of about 25 percent. Had they used an equally arbitrary cutoff of $3,625, they would have had to explain a nonsensical tax rate of about 50 percent for the lowest income in their sample.

Saez and Zucman note in passing what we all know—namely, that low-income people pay taxes out of their transfer payments[19]—but they continue to fail to count transfer payments as income, vastly overstating the average tax rate paid by the lower end of the income distribution. By counting only earned income, they artificially raise the effective tax rate because they do not count resources like Social Security, refundable child tax credits, and Supplemental Security Income in the income from which households pay sales taxes, excise taxes, import duties, and other taxes. Saez and Zucman start counting income only when they can also add payroll taxes and some income taxes, thereby increasing the apparent tax rate, while ignoring the lower taxes for those who are not working. Had they counted all income from transfer payments, they would have computed tax rates like those in Table 7.1 for low-income taxpayers.

From the 50th through the 90th percentiles, both sets of tax rates are essentially the same because the transfer payments that Saez and Zucman ignored are relatively small in this income range. Above the 90th percentile, the Saez-Zucman average tax rates begin to decline, while those in Table 7.1 continue to rise. Again, the reason for the difference is primarily what Saez-Zucman count as income. For the lower part of the income distribution, they choose *not* to count the largest part of the actual income individuals *actually* received—namely, transfer payments. At the higher end of the distribution, Saez and Zucman decide to count *fictional* amounts that the households *never* received as income. They estimate how much assets held by individuals might have appreciated. These assets may include stock, mutual funds, retirement accounts, art collections, or homes. Then they count that amount as if it were income, although the asset owners cannot use it for consumption, savings, or paying taxes because they never received it. When the owners sell assets, their income from the sale is counted in the numbers in Table 7.1, but until then it is purely fictional. The differences between Saez-Zucman and Table 7.1 for higher-income percentiles arise almost entirely from these hypothetical additions to income. Both sources have essentially the same estimates for the taxes paid in the numerator of their tax-rate computation, but by including hypothetical, unrealized income in the denominator, Saez-Zucman artificially lower the tax rate.

In 2013, Thomas Piketty published his *Le capital au XXI siècle* (*Capital in the Twenty-First Century*).[20] Piketty and his book became something of a sensation in part because the book gave a justification to those seeking to expand dramatically the role of government. Piketty claims to have discovered new mathematical laws about the behavior of inequality that applies across all times and nations. His general thesis is that major dislocations of the first half of the twentieth century—wars and depressions—interrupted the natural forces of free markets that inherently create inequality. He claims that these interruptions caused a temporary decline in inequality, which was then reversed during the second half of the twentieth century. In his telling, inequality of wealth and income in the last half of the twentieth century and thus far in the twenty-first is reaching new extremes and is destined to be even greater.

The empirical evidence that he uses to support this thesis with respect to income inequality in the United States is the same used by Emmanuel Saez, who has often collaborated with Piketty in his research.[21] The Piketty income data do not include transfer payments, which make up a majority of the income of the bottom 40 percent of the population. His data also overstate the income of higher-income individuals by imputing to them income such as unrealized capital gains, which they do not actually receive.

His calculations show a dramatic increase in income inequality in postwar America because he ignores the massive infusion of transfer payments to the low end of the income distribution and imputes income that was never received to the high-end households. If he had included transfer payments as income to the recipients and counted only income that high-income taxpayers actually received after taxes, his empirical evidence of growing income inequality in postwar America would have collapsed.[22] As already shown in Chapter 4, when all transfer payments are counted as income to the recipients and income is measured conventionally in terms of payments actually received and retained after taxes, income inequality is lower today than it was in 1947.

Postwar Tax Rates

Another claim floated by advocates for more income redistribution financed by massive increases in the top individual income tax rates is that for thirty-five years after the end of World War II, America had a top federal personal-income tax rate of 70 percent or higher, and the nation prospered. The postwar period, they argue, is proof that very high individual tax rates are compatible with strong economic growth and general prosperity.

But before accepting this as proof by example, it is worth examining how many taxpayers actually paid those top rates and what percentage of their income high earners actually paid in taxes. Economists Gerald Auten of the Treasury Department and David Splinter of the Joint Committee on Taxation have compiled an extraordinary new database using Internal Revenue Service data on federal income and payroll taxes actually collected since 1962.[23] The top marginal income-tax rates and the taxes actually paid, including payroll taxes, as a percent-

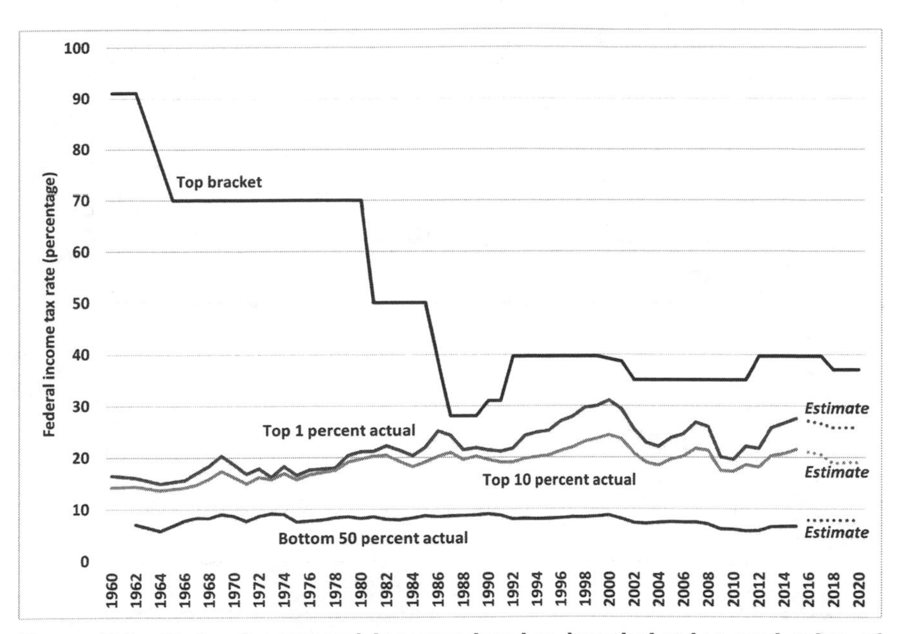

Figure 7.3. Federal personal income tax top bracket rates and rates of income and payroll taxes actually collected as a percentage of income for top 1 percent, top 10 percent, and bottom 50 percent.

Note: Data before 1962 are not available for the bottom 50 percent. Data since 2015 not yet available for actual average rates. Estimates from Microsimulation Model (version 0319-2), Urban-Brookings Tax Policy Center, https://www.taxpolicycenter.org/file/183220/download?token=sd3EIT8c.

Source: Average actual rates: Gerald Auten and David Splinter, "Income Inequality in the United States: Using Tax Data to Measure Long-term Trends," http://davidsplinter.com/AutenSplinter-Tax_Data_and_Inequality.pdf. Excel data file AutenSplinter-IncomeIneq.xlsx, Tables C9 and C9a, available through link at davidsplinter.com > Income Inequality > Online data (excel).

age of income for the top 1 percent, top 10 percent, and bottom 50 percent of income tax filers are shown in Figure 7.3, along with comparable estimates for 2016 to 2020 by the Urban-Brookings Tax Policy Center.[24]

The top income tax rate in 1962 was 91 percent. After deductions and credits, only 447 tax filers out of 71 million paid any taxes at the top rate. The top 1 percent of income earners on average paid 16.1 percent of their income in federal income and payroll taxes while the top 10 percent paid 14.4 percent and the bottom 50 percent paid 7.0 percent. This followed the pattern set by the top Depression-era and wartime tax rates. Only three filers paid any taxes at the top Depression rate, and only thirteen paid any taxes at the top wartime rate.[25] The top 1 percent of earners paid 12.6 percent and 23.5 percent of their income in federal income and payroll taxes in 1938 and 1945, respectively.[26]

President John F. Kennedy recognized that while confiscatory tax rates collected little revenue, they stifled growth as resources were squandered in the "avoidance of taxes" rather than the "production of goods."[27] When the top tax rate was reduced to 70 percent, individual income tax collections continued to grow, and the actual percentage of income paid in taxes by high-income earners remained virtually unchanged. Only 3,626 out of 75 million filers paid any taxes at the new 70 percent rate.[28] When the Reagan tax cut reduced the top rate to 50 percent, gross domestic product surged. Taxes collected from high-income earners as a percentage of their incomes were largely unchanged, and only 341,000 out of 91 million filers paid any taxes at the new 50 percent top rate.[29]

The 1986 Tax Reform lowered the top rate from 50 percent in 1986 to 38.5 percent in 1987 and, finally, to the postwar low of 28 percent in 1988. The rate reductions were accompanied by closing loopholes and other changes in the tax code, allowing income tax revenues to rise with the lower marginal rates being applied to higher taxable income.[30] More than a fifth of all tax filers paid some taxes at the 28 percent rate from 1988 to 1990.[31] The top rate was raised to 39.6 percent in 1993 and has fluctuated between 39.6 percent and 35 percent since. Only 453,000 out of a total of 123,278,000 filers paid any taxes at the 39.6 percent rate in 1993.[32]

Remarkably, as shown in Figure 7.3, while the top marginal rate fell from 91 percent in 1962 to 28 percent in 1988, the percentage of their income that the top 1 percent and 10 percent of filers actually paid in income taxes rose to 21.5 percent and 19.6 percent from 16.1 percent and 14.4 percent, respectively. As the top tax rate fell by two-thirds, the percentage of their income that the top 1 percent of tax filers paid in federal income and payroll taxes rose by a third.

Virtually no tax filer paid any taxes at either the 91 percent or the 70 percent top rate. Only three-tenths of 1 percent of filers paid any taxes at the 50 percent rate in 1985, and on average only one half of 1 percent paid any taxes at the 39.6 percent top rate. The percentage of income actually paid by the top 1 percent of earners, which the Tax Policy Center estimates to be 25.7 percent in 2020, is very close to the average rate paid during the last quarter century and almost 15 percent greater than the average since 1962. Whether the federal government could actually impose a higher top rate, such as 50 percent, on a significant number of taxpayers or actually collect much more than 30 percent of the income from the top 1 percent in income and payroll taxes without crippling economic growth is a question our postwar experience certainly does not answer.

As described in detail in Chapter 4, high-income Americans already bear a significantly greater relative share of the income-related tax burden than their peers in other developed nations. The bottom 90 percent in America pay proportionately less than in other developed nations, even before counting the regressive value-added taxes that many other nations also pay. Although the Organisation for Economic Co-operation and Development has not updated these international comparisons since 2015, the Congressional Budget Office evaluated the effects of the 2017 tax cuts and found that they made the American income taxes even more progressive, with higher-income households paying proportionately still more of the total tax burden.[33]

The Contribution of the Rich

For thousands of years, there have always been a few very rich people, whether Gates and Buffett today or stereotype investors like Scrooge in Dickens's time, the kings and queens of medieval Europe, Genghis Khan, Julius Caesar, King Xerxes of Persia, or pharaohs like Ramesses II. But there are two important differences between Buffett, Gates, and the nineteenth-century Scrooges, on the one hand, and the marauding princes, on the other. First, most of the modern wealthy became rich by creating new economic value, whereas their predecessors got wealth through government power and force of arms. Second, when Buffet, Gates, and investors like Scrooge created new economic value, they also improved the lives of others. For example, Gates personally owns only about 7 percent of the wealth created by Microsoft;[34] most of the rest is owned by pension funds, mutual funds, and insurance companies to fund annuities and insurance benefits. About ninety-six thousand people in the United States and sixty-seven thousand people in other countries hold good-paying Microsoft jobs.[35] What is more, because of the massive wealth and productivity of our modern economy, today's workers have replaced seventy hours of dangerous, intermittent, and backbreaking labor with thirty-five to forty hours per week of safe, steady, and only rarely arduous work. Despite less demanding work, they have been able to enjoy a level of abundance and luxury that in the olden days only kings could have dreamed of.

But before anyone could live like kings, someone first had to produce like gods. Workers do exactly that in our productive world that would never have existed without the miserly coppers of all the world's Scrooges and the genius of its Thomas Edisons. It would not continue without Buffett's cheap McDonald's coupons and Elon Musk's entrepreneurial drive. Before wealth could work its magic, some individuals first had to sacrifice their personal consumption and then apply those savings to investments that enabled more productive work and produced more value so humanity could live better. Paradoxically, the founders of our feast, from Scrooge to Buffett, are criticized to this day rather than praised for their contributions.

CHAPTER 8

The American Dream Is Alive and Well

The distribution of income at any point in time is often discussed as if people were assigned to a particular permanent place in the rank order of incomes. But an income distribution is a snapshot of a point in time, and as soon as it is measured, people's choices and broader economic dynamics immediately begin changing their positions in the distribution. These changes in income are typically called income mobility.

Some of these dynamics are so fundamental to our lives that we hardly notice them as anything unusual. Part of growing up is moving from earning no income, to earning minimum wage, or less, in the neighborhood cutting lawns or babysitting, to performing low-skill jobs in the formal economy like bussing tables or washing dishes. People acquire more education and training, land better jobs, and earn promotions. At retirement, incomes typically decline as older folks leave the world of work and are replaced in the job market by the next generation. These are all elements of income mobility.

Income mobility has also been a fundamental part of the American experience in the land of opportunity. Most of those who immigrated to the British colonies in North America did not arrive with fortunes. Many sought religious liberty, and many were seeking economic opportunity. They were often orphans, bastards, convicts, or younger siblings who could not inherit family land. Many came as indentured servants, including George Washington's grandmother, to pay off the cost of their passage, and some were brought as slaves. The spirit of conquering adversity and rising economically has been part of our national identity from the beginning. After the Civil War, income and wealth began to rise more rapidly for newly emancipated slaves than for Whites, from a base of nearly nothing, and the income and wealth of the two races began to converge slowly, despite discrimination and legitimate concerns about how former slaves would even survive in an age of little government and private aid.[1] Between 1880 and 1900, Black wealth per capita increased substantially, and the ratio between Whites and Blacks in terms of wealth decreased by more than half.[2] Jim Crow laws impeded significantly, but could not stop, the progress made by Black families in the last twenty years of the nineteenth century.

In the second half of the nineteenth century, ordinary people turned themselves into real-life rags-to-riches Horatio Algers. Not everyone became a John D. Rockefeller ($300+ billion in wealth in today's dollars) or a Cornelius Vanderbilt ($200+ billion), whose fortunes once exceeded those of the modern-day super rich when adjusted for inflation,[3] but more than sixteen million immigrants came to America seeking opportunity and freedom and found both.[4] Extraordinary achievement was so common that it ceased to be extraordinary.

The Vanderbilts offer an example of how ordinary people do extraordinary things in America and how the American ethos enables their success. They also illustrate another important component of the American system, sometimes called creative destruction. America encourages competition, which creatively brings new goods and services to market and rains creative destruction on inferior ones. Google, Facebook, and Amazon have demoted former giants like AT&T, Hotmail, AOL, and the Sears catalog, but who knows what will replace them? We do not know, but history assures us somebody will. Most American fortunes, including the very largest, disappear within a few generations as new entrepreneurs rise with still better ideas and the founders of fortunes often generously give away much of their wealth. In America, vast fortunes generally come and go without creating a hereditary aristocracy.

Cornelius Vanderbilt was the descendent of a Dutch farmer who immigrated to America in 1650 as an indentured worker. His father was a working man of limited means who ran a ferryboat in New York Harbor. Young Cornelius went to work for him at age eleven. From those humble beginnings, he built a railroad and shipping empire in the nineteenth century that allowed him to leave an estate worth about $100 million, approximately $200 billion in today's dollars, the second largest in American history.[5] His great-great-granddaughter, Gloria Vanderbilt, died in 2019 at the age of ninety-five and left her son most of her estate valued at less than $1.5 million, only about 0.002 percent of the value of the business Cornelius Vanderbilt created.[6] And most of her money came from her own successful entrepreneurial ventures in fashion and not as a residual of Cornelius's bequests. This dramatic decline was mostly the result of relentless competition, significant charitable donations such as the founding of Vanderbilt University, lavish spending by his early descendants, and dilution by inheritance. Despite their record-setting wealth just over one hundred years ago, no member of the Vanderbilt or Rockefeller families is on today's Forbes 400 list of the wealthiest Americans.

As with the Vanderbilts, large accumulations of wealth in America typically disappear within about four generations. Other mega-rich families like the Kluges, Hartfords, and Strohs completely disappeared so quickly that they are now known only to economic historians.[7] Chapter 7 showed that the four hundred highest-income households in America hold that status for an average of only two years before falling back to more prosaic income levels. Among other topics, this chapter looks at the broader question of the relationship of earnings across generations at all levels of the income distribution.

Measuring Income Mobility

Official statistics on income and its distribution tell us nothing about mobility, they simply compare averages for different years. For example, this book frequently compares 2017 with 1967. But in 2017, only about 3 percent of the people who were working in 1967 were still working. Mobility estimates seek to answer the question about the changes in income for individuals over time as opposed to the averages of groups that are composed of entirely different individuals at the two points in time being compared.

Two time scales are typically used to measure income mobility. The first measures the changes in the income of a single household or individual over a lifetime or some shorter period—the within-generation or intragenerational changes. The second measures the change of children's household incomes compared to their parents' household incomes—the between-generation or intergenerational changes. For either of these time scales, there can be two types of mobility comparisons. Absolute mobility is the change in real dollar income. Relative mobility is the change in the rank of a household's income compared to that of other households.

Each of these mobility types and time scales tells us something different about income dynamics. There are no official or standard reports on income mobility, but a variety of studies have been conducted on all four combinations of time scales and mobility types.

Absolute Income Mobility within a Generation

Average hourly earnings of mature adults between ages fifty-six and sixty-five in 2017 were $34.88 per hour, more than 90 percent greater than the $18.24 for young adults (ages nineteen to twenty-five), who were in starter jobs and just beginning their work lives.[8] This difference by age is almost half of the total difference in hourly earnings across earned-income quintiles shown in Table 5.1. Most people's earnings increase as they build their human capital with new knowledge, skill, and experience. On average the biggest raises come with the first promotions, which are reflected in the rise of 47 percent from $18.24 to $28.96 for the twenty-six- to thirty-five-year-olds. After that, the average raises become relatively smaller, but they continue to age sixty-five. This natural upward mobility in earnings from experience, of course, makes earnings more unequal across the population at a single point in time because new entrants to the labor market with less human capital are being compared to those who have acquired considerably more capability as they have gained experience. This freedom of individuals to build human capital and, thereby, increase their earning power is a critical element in fulfilling the American dream of rising income.

In addition to this substantial earnings mobility that individuals create for themselves, their earnings increase over time from the growth of productivity in the companies and economy within which they work. This economy-wide upward mobility is illustrated in Figure 8.1. The 2017 column in Figure 8.1 portrays the earned-income range for each of the earned-income quintiles in 2017 using a different shading for each of the five quintiles. The 1967 column shows the quintile income ranges for fifty years earlier, with the dollar values adjusted for inflation to reflect 2017 dollars. Note that the top quintile in each case is shown as fading away as a reminder that there is no absolute upper bound on income. The horizontal dashed lines mark the earned-income quintile limits that existed in 1967, in 2017 dollars.

Most notably, this chart shows that for 2017, in addition to the top quintile, the entire fourth quintile and about 18 percent of the middle quintile all earned real incomes that would have been in the top quintile 50 years earlier in 1967. This means that 44 percent of all households in 2017 had incomes that were earned only by the top quintile fifty years before. In 2017, 58 percent of the middle quintile had earnings that were in the fourth quintile in 1967. More than a third of second-quintile households in 2017 earned what middle-quintile households earned in 1967. Although 77 percent of the bottom quintile in 2017 still earned at the bottom-quintile rate for 1967, that still means that 23 percent of those formerly in the bottom quintile moved up to the second quintile, despite the fact that the proportion of prime work-age adults in the bottom quintile who chose not to work doubled between 1967 and 2017. That doubling of nonworking prime work-age adults accounts for most of those households that continued to be at the level of the 1967 bottom quintile.

The dynamic illustrated by Figure 8.1 has been characterized as an economic escalator. No matter what step of the escalator individuals begin on, the rising productivity in the economy will tend to increase their real earnings over

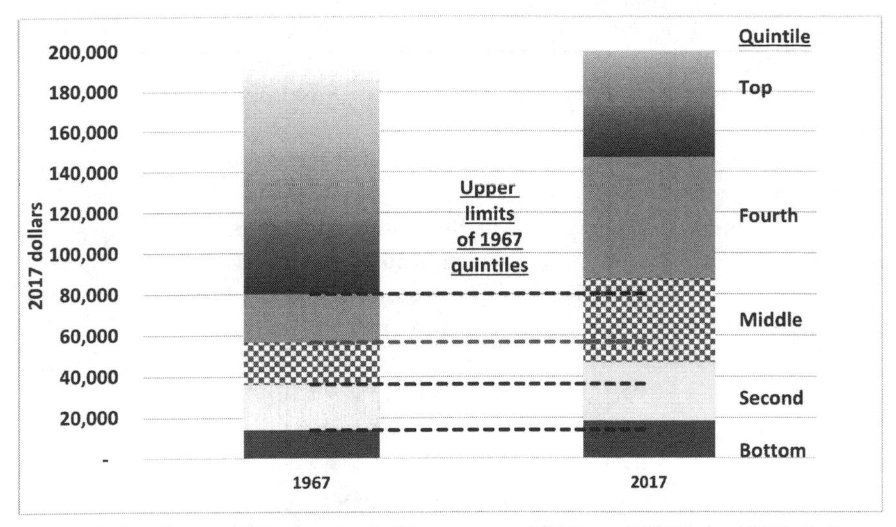

Figure 8.1. Earned-income quintile ranges, 1967 and 2017, in 2017 dollars, using the Census adjustment for inflation.

Sources: Earned income from sources in Table 2.1. Adjusted for inflation using the CPI-U-RS (research series) that the Census Bureau uses to adjust household income; Kayla Fontenot, Jessica Semega, and Melissa Kollar, "Income and Poverty in the United States: 2017," Current Population Reports, P60-263 (Washington, DC: Census Bureau, September 2018), 26.

time. Those who exert more effort are like those who climb up the escalator as it is moving. They will earn even more.[9]

With the exception of the prime work-age adults in the bottom quintile of earners who dropped out of the workforce, this is a story of extraordinary upward mobility driven by the efforts of American workers and the most prosperous economy in the history of the world. Parents' dreams for their children do not die easily in America.

The combined effects of individual effort and the productivity increases flowing from investments in technology and businesses can be measured by calculating the changes in income for the same set of individuals between the first year and last year of a time period being investigated.

These studies require special data sets that trace the same individuals over an extended period. Most of them use income definitions that are similar to the Census income measure—earned income excluding capital gains and employer-paid benefits, one-third or less of transfer payments, and no adjustment for taxes. This means, in particular, that upward mobility for lower-income individuals may tend to be understated in all the studies. Otherwise, the differences in income definition among the studies are not significant.

The US Department of the Treasury has published calculations for two different time periods using large samples of tax records to analyze changes in individual income over time.[10] The first set of calculations measured changes in income from 1987 to 1996 for a fixed set of individuals. The second measured changes between 1996 and 2005 for another set of individuals. The analysis was based primarily on tax returns, but it used a measure of income that also included tax-exempt amounts from Social Security, pensions, and bonds.

The bottom line of this Treasury research was that, on average, individuals' income rose 24.1 percent from 1987 to 1996 and 41.0 percent from 1996 to 2005. (More detailed results from these studies are contained in Appendix E.) Those increases were almost two times and more than three times greater, respectively, than the official Census estimates for personal income increases of 12.7 and 12.4 percent for the same two time periods.

Why did the Census measure miss the growth of income actually experienced by individuals? An analogy may help explain. Suppose you measured the height of all the students in an elementary school and found that they averaged fifty inches tall. The next year you go back and measure the students' height in the same school and find that the average is still fifty inches. You would not conclude that none of the students had grown because you know that after a year of growth, the fifth graders moved on to middle school, fourth graders with their year of growth were promoted to fifth grade, and new first graders arrived.

The Census calculation of the change in personal earnings is just like measuring the average height of students in a school year after year. Yet the Census numbers are cited to make implausible claims that people have not gotten a raise because folks with the most experience and human capital have retired and new workers without that experience have arrived. The Census numbers do not measure individual income raises, just like the average height of all elementary students does not measure whether individual students have grown. That is an inherent feature of the way the data are computed.

Now let us extend the school children's height analogy a little further. Suppose there were a baby boom and all of a sudden two to three times more first graders arrived than the number of last year's fifth graders who left. If we continue measuring the average student height for the whole school, we might discover that it has dropped to forty-eight inches because there are proportionately more first graders, who are naturally shorter on average than the older students. The forty-eight inches would not mean any children shrank. But that is an exact analogy to what happened in the 1987–2005 time period in the labor market. New, less skilled workers were arriving at two to three times the rate that the older, more skilled ones were leaving. The Census estimates of income growth were, consequently, much smaller than even the usual structural understatement from ignoring individual earning changes.

In addition to demonstrating the much larger individual increases of income, the Treasury Department calculations documented the significant differences in the rate of increase for different levels of income. With one minor exception, the increases in real income in both time periods were greatest for the lowest income quintiles, and the increases became smaller for each successively higher quintile. The income for the bottom quintile rose about 250 percent in the first decade and 285 percent in the second. The second quintile rose only about one-quarter as much, and the middle quintile rose still less. For the fourth quintile, real income increased by less than 16 percent. For the 1987–1996 time period, the top quintile rose even more slowly, increasing by less than 10 percent. The exception was the 25 percent increase for the top quintile for 1996 to 2005, which was greater than for the fourth quintile, but even then, the top 1 percent still posted the smallest increase of all groups.

Part of the reason for the greater increases in the lower quintiles is that they were populated disproportionately by individuals who were still early in their careers when relative increases in earnings tend to be larger. But those results are also an important part of the American mobility story.

One of the important conclusions of the Treasury Department's study was that despite advocates' claims that economic mobility had declined, "An examination of the various cells suggests that income mobility was approximately the same in almost all income groups during these time periods [1987 to 1996 and 1996 to 2005]."[11] In another study, economists at the Federal Reserve Bank of Dallas extended this conclusion back farther to the 1975–1991 period. Their study not only used data from an earlier time period and covered more years but also used a different data source, the University of Michigan's Panel Survey on Income Dynamics (PSID), which collects income data every year from the same individuals over many decades.[12] Evaluating income mobility during the sixteen years that extended into the 1990s, the Federal Reserve study concluded, "Tracking individuals' incomes over time gives a startlingly different view of the forces shaping America's income distribution. The conventional view leads us to think [people in the bottom quintile] were worse off in the 1990s. Nothing could be further from the truth."[13]

The Treasury report provided some additional details that are included in the last four columns in Appendix E. It measured the proportion of each quintile that lost more than half of their income between the beginning and the end of the decade studied and the proportion that more than doubled their income. On average, between 6 and 8 percent of people suffered a 50 percent decline in both time periods for all quintiles except the top quintile. In the top quintile, income losses were almost twice as frequent. The proportion of individuals experiencing a decline of income during each of the two decades reached more than one-third for the top 1 percent. Most declines in income were created by factors that are rather evenly spread throughout the population, such as loss of a job, illness, injury, or a decision to retire. These would account for the similar frequency of income loss for most of the population.

But different dynamics were at work among the highest earners who posted much more frequent income declines. The Treasury report explains that for these more frequent declines among the highest earners, "the likely causes include the typical life cycle of income and 'mean reversion' in which the incomes of taxpayers whose incomes were temporarily high in 1996 revert to a level closer to their long-run average."[14] Such temporary highs in earnings among the top earners are largely attributable to their greater proportion of volatile earning sources such as capital gains, dividends, and returns on self-employment.[15]

During each of the two decades studied by the Treasury Department, the proportion of people who more than doubled their income was remarkably smaller at higher incomes than at lower incomes. About half of those who began the decade in the bottom quintile more than doubled their incomes. In the top quintile, less than 10 percent succeeded in doubling theirs. Some of that difference is simple arithmetic. It is easier to double an income of $20,000 than one of $200,000. But some of it also reflects the fact that large returns from capital gains are often offset by losses. Within the top quintile, the top 1 percent of families did manage to double their incomes slightly more than 10 percent of the time, but they lost more than half their income about 37 percent of the time.

The results from the two different time periods in the Treasury studies shown in Appendix E and the third time period from the Federal Reserve study, which used an entirely different data source, are all three remarkably consistent. In all cases, the low-income individuals see their income rise faster than those with high incomes, and the average growth of an individual's income is much larger than the growth of the Census averages, which do not capture the effects of increased experience and human capital acquired by individuals over time.

Relative Income Mobility within a Generation

Absolute income mobility has produced rising real incomes for the vast majority of Americans over all extended periods of the nation's history. Relative mobility measures how individuals' incomes change compared to the income changes for others. Of course, as a relative measure, even people who benefit from significant increases in their earnings can fall to a lower rank, because other people increased their earnings by even more and moved ahead of them. For every person who rises in a relative measure like this, somebody else falls, even if both became substantially more prosperous.

The same Treasury study cited above also calculated the changes in the relative income quintile rank of people over time. It concluded that, like the measures of absolute mobility, relative mobility continued to be essentially the same in both decades (see Figure 8.2). It further concluded that members of the bottom quintile had been consistently upwardly mobile, with almost half of them moving to higher quintiles in the course of each ten-year period. Of course, members of the top quintile could go no higher, so about 60 percent of them remained at the top, while 40 percent fell to lower quintiles. At the upper end of the top quintile, mobility was far less stable. The report notes that less than half of the top 1 percent stayed where they began, while only one-quarter of the top 1/100th of 1 percent stayed at that income level.[16]

Figure 8.2 provides additional details from the Treasury report with regard to income mobility among individuals by income quintile. In both graphs, each of the five vertical bars represents the population in one of the income quintiles for the first year of the decade being analyzed. Each bar is divided into five segments, and each segment represents the proportion of those same people who ended the ten-year period in the income quintiles represented by the segment.

For example, 54.6 percent of the members of the bottom quintile in 1987 were still in the bottom quintile of the 1996 distribution ten years later. But 45.4 percent had risen to one of the higher quintiles, with 2.7 percent reaching the top quintile. For the top quintile, the results were almost an exact mirror image, with 58.4 percent of those in the top quintile in 1987 remaining in the top quintile in 1996 and 41.5 percent falling into a lower quintile, including 4.7 percent who fell all the way to the bottom quintile. The results were about the same for the 1996–2005 decade, so the following discussion relates to both.

It should not be particularly surprising that a little more than half the people who started in the bottom quintile did not see their earnings rise enough to move into a higher quintile. During both decades, income overall rose significantly, so for individuals to rise to the second or a higher quintile would have required that their earnings rise even faster than the overall increase. They would have needed to move ahead of other people who started the decade earning more than they did and, in most cases, were increasing the amount of income they earned as well. The truly amazing result is that in each ten-year period, almost half of those beginning in the bottom quintile did just that. They displaced higher earners and climbed to higher relative positions in the income distribution of the country. About one out of every thirty-five of them climbed all the way into the top quintile. Since the data for this analysis included only people over age twenty-five and thus excluded some of the greatest upward mobility created by moving from the part-time minimum-wage jobs of youth to full-time jobs after completion of education and training, the substantial upward relative mobility is even more impressive.

At the other end of the income spectrum, approximately 60 percent of those in the top quintile at the beginning of each decade stayed there, and 40 percent dropped to other quintiles. Within the 40 percent who dropped to

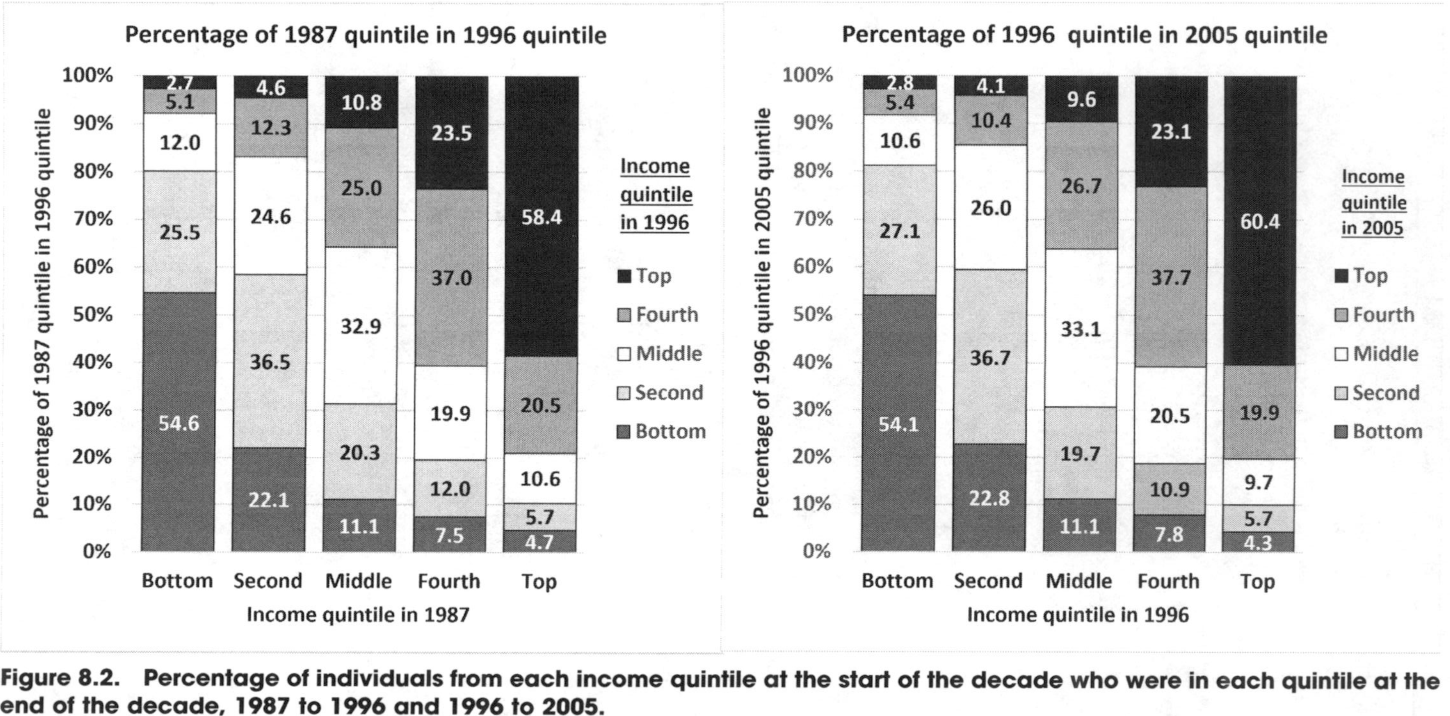

Figure 8.2. Percentage of individuals from each income quintile at the start of the decade who were in each quintile at the end of the decade, 1987 to 1996 and 1996 to 2005.

Source: "Table A.5: Income Mobility Relative to the Base Year Population, Age 25 and Over, 1987–1996 and 1996–2005," in "Income Mobility in the U.S. from 1996 to 2005," US Department of the Treasury, November 13, 2007, revised March 2008, https://home.treasury.gov/system/files/131/Report-Income-Mobility-2008.pdf.

lower quintiles were three different types of dynamics that created the declines, as described below.

First, some of the individual declines from top-income rank were the result of the same factors that caused many of the declines in other quintiles: illness, loss of jobs, the end of temporary employer payments (such as bonuses or severance pay), or retirement. Second, some individuals were in the top quintile because, as described in Chapter 7, in the first year of the study, they had received large, onetime income from sources such as large capital gains on investments, sale of personal businesses, home sales, lump-sum retirement payouts, or mandatory redemption of stock options and deferred compensation. In subsequent years, these onetime events were generally not repeated, and their income dropped back to more modest levels by the end of the decade. The combined effects of (1) income losses common to all quintiles and (2) large onetime income events in the first year accounted for about three-fifths of the declines in rank among the top quintile. In these cases, when the income of one of these individuals declined, we can visualize another individual at the top of the fourth quintile being, in effect, promoted to the top quintile. These are predictable and easily understood events. But the most interesting results lie with the third type of decline, which accounted for two-fifths of the declines in relative income among the top quintile. These decliners were all replaced by individuals who had begun the decade in the bottom, second, or middle quintiles. Folks beginning this low in the distribution would never have been merely promoted to the fifth quintile as the result of a decline by one of the top quintile's current inhabitants. Instead, each and every one of these individuals vaulted to the front of the line with extraordinary combinations of capability and drive that enabled them to create more economic value for their customers or employers, which, in turn, raised their incomes substantially.[17]

The second, middle, and fourth quintiles each retained only about a third of their original inhabitants from the beginning of the decade. More people left these quintiles during the ten-year spans because they could both rise and fall from their starting positions, unlike the top and bottom quintiles, where they had only one direction to move—down from the top quintile or up from the bottom.

On average, 26.7 percent of the people in the study fell by one or more quintiles across each of the two decades. But recall that real income for the whole nation rose strongly during those two decades, so most of those whose income rank fell to a lower quintile still experienced rising real income. Their income just rose more slowly than income for others.

Computing mobility using individual histories of earnings rather than comparing averages across groups demonstrates that there is substantial mobility and that much mobility is the perfectly understandable result of the natural progression of income over individual life cycles. But even these comparisons across decades understate the full extent of mobility. Other analyses with different data and both shorter and longer time periods have shown much more mobility than just comparing quintiles at a decade interval might suggest.

Incomes can dramatically change over short periods. For example, three economists from the Federal Reserve, Georgetown University, and the Joint Committee on Taxation published a paper with the Washington Center for Equitable Growth. It showed that even if their incomes did not grow enough to move up a full quintile, 43 percent of households in the bottom quintile and 27 percent of those in the second quintile increased their real incomes by 25 percent or more within only two years.[18]

Even over short periods, large proportions of low-income folks have made huge improvements in their incomes. In 2013, NBC (and other news outlets) reported on a number of research studies showing that 20 percent of all households in the population will be in the top 2 percent of income for at least one year during their lives.[19] And for the even higher top 1 percent, Thomas Hirschl and Mark Rank, sociologists at Cornell University and Washington University, respectively, have applied a "life course approach" to measure individual mobility across active work lives. They found that between the ages of twenty-five and sixty, 11.1 percent of the population spent at least one year in the top 1 percent, 2.2 percent spent five or more years in the top 1 percent, and over the thirty-five years analyzed, only 1.1 percent spent ten years or more in the top 1 percent. A mere 0.6 percent spent ten or more consecutive years. The authors conclude, "The findings indicate high year-to-year turnover within this category [top 1 percent]."[20] If households are rapidly moving in and out of the top 1 percent, others must, as a mathematical certainty, also be moving in and out of the lower percentiles.

Absolute Income Mobility between Generations

An important element of the American dream is that children achieve greater economic prosperity than their parents. That dream can come true for most Americans, of course, only if the economy as a whole is growing faster than the population. Without growth in the nation's per capita income, family progress becomes a zero-sum game where some have to earn less for others to earn more. Since children's progress compared to their parents occurs over a generation of thirty years or more, incomes for this analysis must be adjusted for inflation. Some studies examined here have also adjusted for household size.[21]

Using data from the Panel Survey on Income Dynamics, analysts for the Pew Charitable Trusts calculated the percentage of adult children who at an average age of forty-five lived in a family with an average family income greater than that of their parents at an average age of forty-two. The results by income quintile, shown in Figure 8.3, are quite stunning.[22]

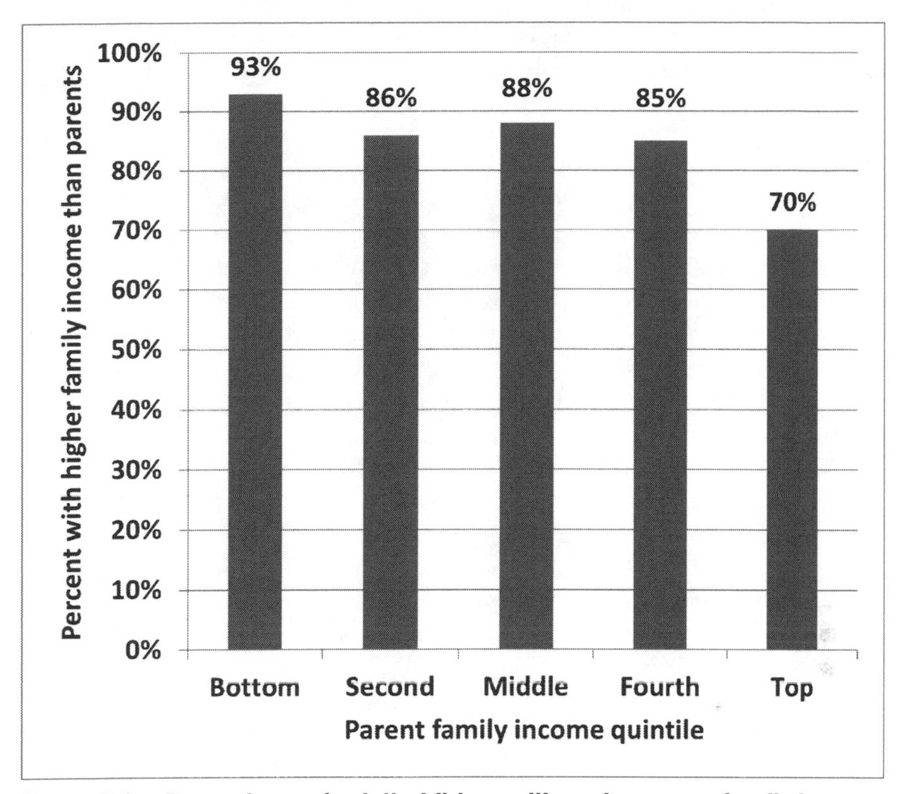

Figure 8.3. Percentage of adult children with real average family income from 2000 to 2008 that was higher than their parents' real average family income from 1967 to 1971.

Source: "Pursuing the American Dream: Economic Mobility across Generations," Pew Charitable Trusts, July 2012, https://www.pewtrusts.org/~/media/legacy/uploadedfiles/wwwpewtrustsorg/reports/economic_mobility/pursuingamericandreampdf.pdf, 4. Based on PSID, a longitudinal data set that has followed families from 1968 to 2009. Income adjusted by square root of family size. Adjusted for inflation by the CPI-U-RS and CPI-U-X1. Average ages were 41.9 for parents and 45.0 for adult children.

For children reared by parents in the bottom income quintile, 93 percent grew up to have more real income than their parents. Fewer than 7 percent did not. Many of these children and their parents worked hard to attain greater levels of education and acquire skills that allowed them to increase their earnings. But even for the considerable number who failed to complete high school or acquire additional skills, their incomes rose as a by-product of strong economic growth. These results are an extraordinary testament to the dedication of many parents, the efforts of the new generations, and the power of a growing American economy. In the three central quintiles, a substantial but slightly smaller average of 86 percent of all adult children lived in families that had a higher real income than their parents did.

A much smaller 70 percent of children reared in the top quintile grew up to have families that earned more than their parents did. These adult children benefited from the same earnings escalator of economic growth as the other four quintiles, so their smaller rate of surpassing their parents' earnings is notable. The data do not reveal the exact reasons why these children reared in the top quintile would be more than four times as likely as children from the bottom quintile to fail to earn more than their parents. But some are obvious. Their parents have set a high bar that requires a lot of effort, and to surpass that achievement, the children must survive intense competition. Some children may lack the capabilities to survive that competition. Others may elect to follow different careers that are either more interesting to them or less demanding on their time, while still paying well in the fourth quintile. Or they may simply not be as ambitious as their parents.

The Pew Charitable Trusts analysts report the facts in Figure 8.3, but they characterize the results as "Americans' absolute mobility by family income shows a glass half full."[23] They fail to explain how 93 percent of children raised in the bottom quintile surpassing their parents' income is only half a glass. Without celebrating the donut of success, they immediately jump into its hole. They claim, for example, "Blacks have a harder time exceeding their parents' family income . . . than whites."[24] But their own data show that is true only for the second quintile. Intergenerational changes in income are not statistically different by race in the bottom and middle quintiles, and their sample sizes are too small to make estimates at the fourth and top quintiles. The next chapter in this book explores differences in income by race and other demographic variables in detail.

Relative Income Mobility between Generations

In America, we can rise above the economic level where we start and keep on rising as far as our energy, talent, and desire will take us. So, why should we care whether somebody else rises still higher? How does the fact that some Americans are extraordinarily successful make the rest of us worse off? If they are highly successful under the rule of law in a market-driven economy, their higher incomes are derived from producing new and better goods and services or simply from being more efficient. We all freely buy and benefit from their contributions, which deliver a higher standard of living for us all.

Beyond the ephemeral wealth of super-rich families described at the beginning of this chapter, there has been a broad, general interest in the relationship of adult children's income and that of their parents. If parents' income had no relationship whatsoever to their adult children's future income, then the income quintile for each child would be a random result. In that case, each of the five quintiles of parental income would have children grow up to earn at levels that would put 20 percent of them in each of the five child quintiles. By contrast, if adult children's income ranks were fully determined by their parents' ranks, then all children reared within each quintile would grow up to have incomes in the same quintile as their parents.

Real-world cases fall somewhere between the income rank of the children being totally unaffected by their parents' income rank and being fully determined by it. The practical question is how close the real-world rank of adult children's income is to being either fully determined by or totally unrelated to that of their parents. Three significant research efforts have measured these actual relationships between the ranks of adult children's family incomes and the ranks of their parents' family incomes.

The first study was part of the Pew Charitable Trusts report described above, which used data from the University of Michigan's PSID. It compared the quintiles of average adult children's incomes for the period 2000 to 2008, when the children were between the ages of thirty-two and fifty-eight, with the quintile of their parents' income in 1967 to 1971, when the children were between the ages of zero and eighteen.[25]

The second study, by a team led by Raj Chetty of Harvard University, was calculated from Internal Revenue Service files of income tax returns. It compared the income rank of children in their early thirties based on their average income for 2011 to 2012 with the rank of their parents' income in 1996 to 2000, when the children were between the ages of fifteen and twenty.[26]

The third study, by Michael Strain of the American Enterprise Institute, used the same PSID source as the Pew Foundation, updated by a decade. It compared children's income rankings in their forties during the years 2013 to 2017 with their parents' rankings during the years in which their parents were also in their forties.[27]

The summary results of each of the three studies are shown in Figure 8.4. The structure of these graphs is similar to those in Figure 8.2, but instead of comparing the same individuals' income rank at the end of a decade to their income rank at the beginning of the decade, these compare the adult children's income rank to that of their parents during some portion of their childhood. Even a cursory glance at the chart in Figure 8.4 tells us that all three studies reported comparable outcomes. Clearly, the income ranking of adult children is not even close to being totally determined by the parents' rank because, in all three studies, far more than half of the children of parents in each quintile earned at levels that put them in different quintiles from their parents' quintile. However, some of the outcomes appear to be either substantially larger or smaller than the 20 percent that would result from random outcomes, so the children's incomes, as a result, show some relationship to their parental incomes.

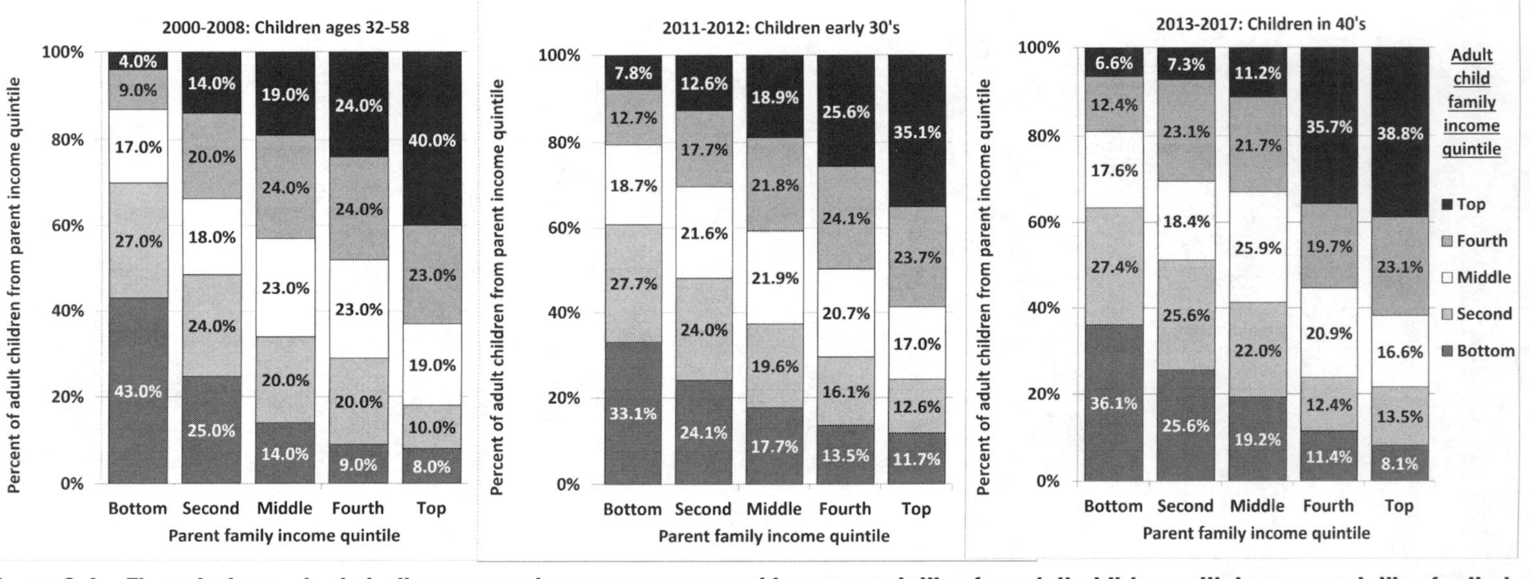

Figure 8.4. Three independent studies comparing average annual income quintiles for adult children with income quintiles for their parents.

Note: Percentages may not add exactly to 100.0 percent owing to rounding in original studies.

Sources: Children ages thirty-two to fifty-eight: "Pursuing the American Dream: Economic Mobility across Generations," Pew Charitable Trusts, July 2012, https://www.pewtrusts.org/~/media/legacy/uploadedfiles/wwwpewtrustsorg/reports/economic_mobility/pursuingamericandreampdf.pdf, 6. Children in their early thirties: "Online Appendix Table VI: National Quintile Transition Matrix: 1980–85 Cohorts," in Raj Chetty et al., "Where Is the Land of Opportunity? The Geography of Intergenerational Mobility in the United States," National Bureau for Economic Research, http://www.equality-of-opportunity.org/assets/documents/mobility_geo.pdf. Children in their forties: Figure 16 in Michael R. Strain, *The American Dream Is Not Dead (But Populism Could Kill It)* [Conshohocken, PA: Templeton Press, 2020] [as corrected after first printing].

The three studies have only small differences in their statistical results, even though there are substantial differences in the data sources, methods, and time periods studied. That is an important observation because it means the results are robust and not merely accidental or the consequence of some unique design feature in a single study. Since the results of the three studies are so similar, this analysis will proceed using an average of the three because that will give more robust estimates.[28] Figure 8.5 shows a chart of those averages positioned between two charts illustrating the possible extreme limits of the distribution.

The chart on the left of Figure 8.5 shows the random results that would indicate parents' income quintiles had no relationship to their adult children's family incomes. If the income of parents had no effect on the income of their adult children, we would expect 20 percent of the adult children's families would end up in each of the five income quintiles. This chart is labeled "Relationship = 0.0%" because it shows no relationship between parents' and children's income levels. The chart on the right shows that if the income of adult children's families were totally determined by the income of their parents, then all the adult children would have income in the same quintile as their parents. Consequently, it is labeled "Relationship = 100.0%."

The three studies shown in Figure 8.4 have been averaged together to create the center chart in Figure 8.5. It reveals that in the real world, some children from each of the parental-income quintiles grew up to have incomes in each of the five children's quintiles. It also shows that far less than half of children grew up to have income in the same income quintile as their parents, a much smaller amount than the 100 percent that would have occurred if the adult children's income were fully determined by their parents' income. While the real-world results do not show either a fully determinate or a random relationship between parental income rank and adult children's income rank, they are much closer to the 20 percent we would expect to find in each children's quintile if parental income had no effect on the income of adult children and thus are indicative of only a small parental-income effect.

The real-world averages of the three studies show that 37.9 percent of children from top-quintile families grew up to have incomes in the same quintile as their parents. Twenty percent of the children would have been expected to have income in the same quintile as their parents by random chance even if parental income had no effect on their income. So an additional 17.9 percent (37.9 percent minus 20.0 percent) of the children from the top quintile had incomes that could be said to be determined in some way by their parents' income rank. Or, looked at in a different way, the chart shows that 62.1 percent of the children reared in top-quintile families fell into a lower quintile. If parental income had fully determined their children's income, then zero, rather than 62.1 percent, would have ended up in these lower quintiles. Part of that difference included 9.3 percent falling all the way into the bottom quintile.

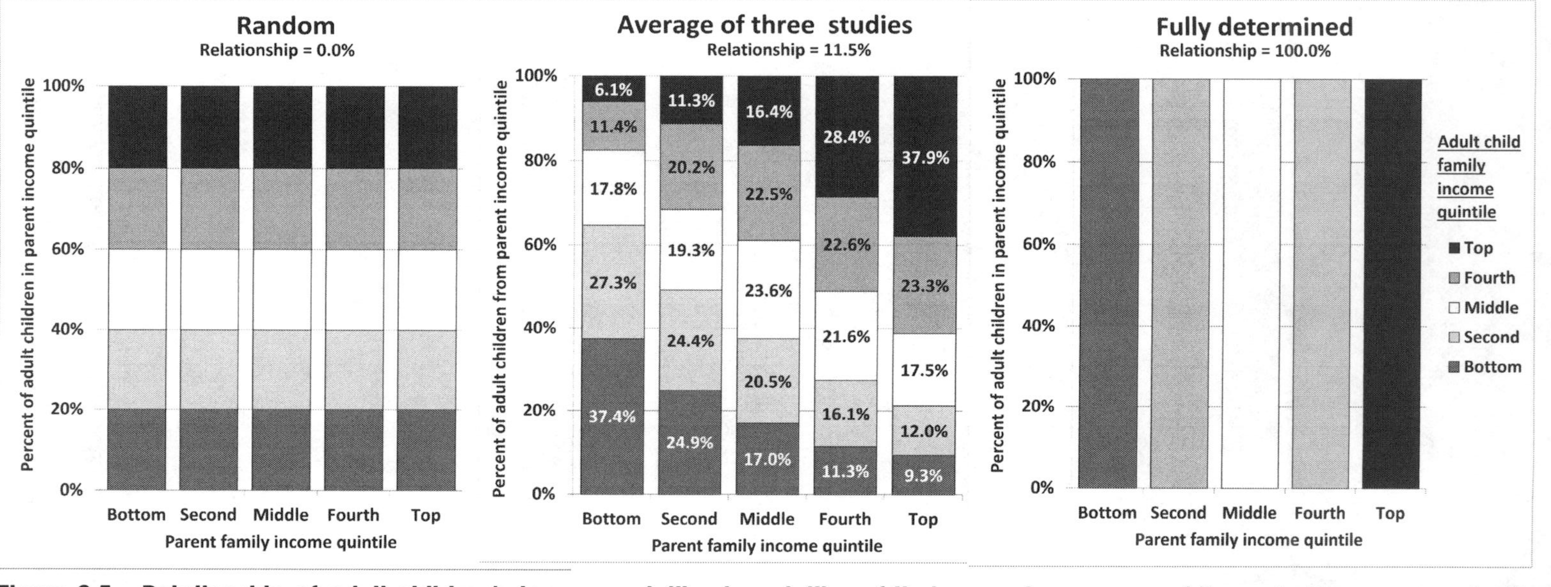

Figure 8.5. Relationship of adult children's income quintiles to quintiles of their parents, average of three studies compared with limits of possible values.

Note: Percentages may not add exactly to 100.0 percent owing to rounding in both published results of the original studies and calculation of the averages. Relationship is the difference between a parent-child distribution and the random distribution, divided by the difference between the fully determined distribution and the random distribution.

Source: Average of three studies in Figure 8.4.

So, there is some relationship between the top-quintile parents' income and the income of their adult progeny, but it is relatively weak, and other factors unrelated to their parents' income appear to be more important.

Children of bottom-quintile parents had an income distribution that was almost a mirror-image of that of children from top-quintile parents, with 37.4 percent of them growing up to have incomes in the bottom quintile of their youth. That is 17.4 percentage points (37.4 minus 20.0) more than would have been expected if there were no relationship between parents' and children's incomes, indicating a fairly weak relationship between parents' and children's incomes. The remaining 62.6 percent of those born in the bottom quintile rose to a higher income quintile, including 6.1 percent climbing to the very top. This is indicative of substantial upward mobility. If parents' income had fully determined their children's income rank, there would have been no cases of rising income ranks. The results do not mean that there is zero effect from parental income, because if the effect were zero, then the distribution would have been purely random, and 80 percent of the children of bottom-quintile parents would have grown up to higher income quintiles than their parents. The actual percentage rising was 17.4 percent less than would have occurred in a purely random model, so there was some parental effect. But 62.6 percent more children rose to income higher than their parents. That would not have occurred if adult children's income were totally determined by their parents' income, so that parental-income effect was much smaller than would have occurred in a fully determined model.

Of the children raised in the middle income quintile, 23.6 percent remained in the middle quintile, only 3.6 percentage points more than would have been there by random chance (23.6 minus 20). The rest of the adult children were almost equally divided between those who rose to a higher quintile and those who fell to a lower one. Those who rose constituted 37.5 percent of the total—just 2.5 percentage points fewer than would have risen from a purely random result with 20.0 percent in each of the two higher quintiles. Those who fell in rank were 38.9 percent of the total, only 1.1 percentage points smaller than the purely random result of 40.0 percent falling into the two lower quintiles. This overall distribution is only slightly different from a purely random result and indicative of no meaningful effects from parental income.

In the fourth parental quintile, 22.6 percent of the children grew up to earn in the fourth quintile as adults, only 2.6 percentage points more than the 20.0 percent that would have occurred randomly without any parental income-rank effect and 77.4 percentage points short of the 100.0 percent that would have occurred if child income were fully determined by parental income. Children of the fourth parental quintile did show a modest parental-income effect, with 28.4 percent of them rising to the top quintile, 8.4 percentage points more than would have been expected randomly. Forty-nine percent of adult children of fourth-quintile parents fell to an income rank less than their parents' rank, which was 11.0 percentage points fewer than the 60.0 percent that would have occurred from a random result consistent with no parental income effect and 49.0 percentage points more than would have occurred with fully determined effects. Children born in the fourth quintile stayed there about as often as would have been expected randomly. They were slightly more likely than expected to rise to a higher income quintile and less likely to fall when compared with purely random results.

Children of second-quintile parents grew up to live in the same quintile as their parents 24.4 percent of the time, only 4.4 percentage points more frequently than would have occurred randomly with no parental effects, a weak relationship. More than half of them (50.8 percent) rose to a higher income quintile. Despite this substantial upward mobility, it was still 9.2 percent fewer than would have been expected if parental income had no effect on children's income. Overall, it appears that children born in the second quintile remained there only about as frequently as would be expected from random results, and they were slightly more likely to fall below their parents' quintile than to rise above it when compared with purely random results.

On average over the five quintiles, adult children's income distributions showed that 29.2 percent of adult children stayed in the same quintile as their parents. Because a purely random result without any parental-quintile effects would have resulted in 20.0 percent of the adult children being in the same income quintile as their parents, this means that 9.2 percent of adult children (29.2 percent minus 20.0 percent) remained in the parental quintile as the result of some parental-income effects. For the parents' income to have fully determined their children's income, the remaining 70.8 percent of adult children (100 percent minus 29.2 percent) would not have left the quintile of their childhood. These numbers show strong income mobility across generations and demonstrate that parental income has a surprisingly small effect. On average, the actual income mobility of adult children is so substantial that the effects of parental income explain only 11.5 percent of the actual child quintile outcomes (the 9.2 percent average above random expectation, divided by the 80 percent distance from random to fully determined).[29]

Despite the differences in the raw data used and methods applied by the three studies, the actual quantitative results among the three were very similar. But in two cases, the authors drew strikingly different conclusions. The Pew study claims that because the proportion of children who remain in the quintile of their birth is higher for the bottom and top parental quintiles than for other parental quintiles, they are somehow "stuck" in that position. "This lack of relative mobility is called 'stickiness at the ends' because those at the ends of the income distribution tend to be stuck there over a generation. By contrast, those raised in the middle income quintile come closer to experiencing mathematically perfect mobility, in which they are equally likely to end up in each quintile of the distribution."[30]

Michael Strain's analysis, by contrast, notes the implausibility of expecting "perfect" mobility by observing, "Perfect mobility would correspond to a zero return on parental investment, or no relationship between investment and income. . . . [H]ow much more mobile should we be? How would we know?"[31]

The "stickiness at the ends" in the bottom and top quintiles is at least partly the result of confining the analysis to five quintiles. Among the children reared in the top quintile are some who will not only greatly exceed their parents' income but also exceed it by an amount that in any other parental quintile would have enabled them to rise to a higher child quintile. But there is no "penthouse" quintile above the top quintile for them to rise into. A "greater than" rank is not available to them, and they remain in the top quintile no matter how fabulously successful they are. They remain there not because they are somehow "stuck" but because of the arbitrary choice to cut off the data at five groups. That is a feature of what statisticians call a "truncated" distribution or "censored" data set. It stops at the "top."

The bottom quintile is also truncated or censored. It stops at the "bottom." Some children reared in the bottom quintile will have incomes that are significantly lower than those of their bottom-quintile parents. But there is no "basement" quintile for them to fall into, so they accumulate in the bottom quintile. Children reared in the second, middle, and fourth parental income quintiles always have at least one quintile in each direction to which they can migrate, and sometimes two or three. At least part of the apparent "stickiness" in the top and bottom quintiles is explained by the analytical structure of defining income by quintiles, not by an absence of economic mobility.

Of course, we might expect that children of economically successful parents would have greater opportunities for quality education and would receive more socialization in behaviors that tend to produce success. As a result, they might, on average, be more successful than others in their age group. But does anybody really believe that parental income alone, or even primarily, determines the capacity of parents to inspire their children, nurture them, and instill in them the desire to succeed? If so, they have not met enough American mothers. Nor are they familiar with ancient scripture: "Train up a child in the way he should go: and when he is old, he will not depart from it."[32] We have records of parents of all income levels motivating their children to succeed that go back at least twenty-seven hundred years, even in the midst of resource-poor, arid lands. The numbers are also on the side of American mothers and ancient prophets. Almost 90 percent of adult children's economic success has come from factors that are not related to the income ranks of their parents (100.0 percent for all factors minus the 11.5 percent related to parental income rank computed above). Many of the factors, both positive and negative, that can influence a child's adult income quintile are well known. The same factors that influence parents' income ranks can also influence the income ranks of their children. Of course, experience informs us to expect that children will share some similar income outcomes with their parents because they spring from the same gene pool and live together in a nuclear family with shared values and interactions. Parents and children are certainly not mere duplicates of each other, but they have closer biological and social ties than any other grouping of people on the planet. The rather modest relationship shown by the data from all three studies is surprising only in that it is so weak. Part of this weak relationship is likely explained by the fact that effective nurturing and parenting are not necessarily correlated with family income. Other factors unrelated to family income are also highly important, such as the unique characteristics of the individual children, their social interactions outside the family, and myriad other influences unrelated to family income.

The existence of some modest relationship between the income ranks of the two generations should be no surprise or cause for questioning the fairness of America. What is amazing, however, is that all three studies demonstrate extraordinary mobility that exists no matter what income level a child was born into.

Mobility Including the Effect of Economic Growth

But even these impressive numbers understate actual income mobility in America. The three studies just discussed measure relative mobility by comparing the quintile of adult children's income with the quintile of their parents' income quintile. Relative mobility is a zero-sum game—by definition, 20 percent of households are in the lowest quintile, and only 20 percent are in the highest. If one household moves to a higher quintile, another household, of mathematical necessity, moves to a lower one. But income growth is not zero-sum. In the fifty years covered by the three studies of relative income mobility, median household income rose by 93 percent.[33] In figure 8.3 we showed that the vast majority (84 percent) of adult children had significantly higher real incomes than their parents, so even if there were no changes in income rank, almost all children would still have higher real incomes than their parents.

To rise out of the bottom quintile, children's inflation-adjusted income had to increase by more than the growth of the income ceiling for the bottom quintile during the years between generations—35 percent in the Strain study. Children reared in any other quintile had to see their real income as adults rise on average by roughly 50 percent above their parents' income simply to avoid falling into a lower quintile than their parents. The climb to a higher quintile was steeper still.

Fortunately, data from the Strain study can be used to measure mobility in a way that considers the extraordinary income growth in America between the parents' generation and the adult children's generation.[34] When the inflation-adjusted income of the adult children is compared with the income of their parents using the real income quintiles of their *childhood* in 1982–1986 rather than the income quintiles of 2013–2017, measured mobility is dramatically greater. In figure 8.6 the left-side chart reproduces the mobility without the effects of economic growth for the Strain study in figure 8.4. The right-side chart shows the adult children's real income quintiles based on the inflation-adjusted income of their parents' generation.

Only 28 percent of children reared in the bottom quintile had real adult incomes that would put them in the childhood bottom quintile, and 26 percent rose all the way to the childhood top quintile, which required a minimum income of only $111,416 (in 2016 dollars) for a family of four in 1982–1986. A family of four with that inflation-adjusted income in 2013–2017 would have been in the middle quintile based on 2013–2017 income distribution. Overall, almost half (49 percent) of all the children grew up to live in families with incomes that only those in the top quintile enjoyed in their youth.

During the thirty-five years of the study, adult children who worked rode up the American economic escalator as average incomes rose dramatically. Those who climbed as the escalator rose moved up faster. Those who stood still or stumbled down rose more slowly, and those who stayed off the escalator by not working missed the ride. While the Strain study does not provide data on the employment status of households, it seems clear that many adult children who did not escape the bottom quintile they were born in did not work as adults. The mobility studies shown in figures 8.4 and 8.5 capture the effect of climbing, stumbling, and choosing not to ride, but they miss the escalator effect, which came from the growth of the American economy. Many of today's middle-income adults have a real standard of living that would have put them in the top quintile in their parents' era.

This incredible income mobility is measured only over one generation. Parents struggle and sacrifice to provide their children with education and opportunities they themselves lacked. Millions of parents have lived out their dreams through the achievements of their children, generation after generation. As a result, America's real mobility is most visible over multiple generations. Many historians believe George Washington's grandmother came to America as an indentured worker. Washington became one of the richest men in colonial America and, in the words of King George III, "the greatest man in the world."

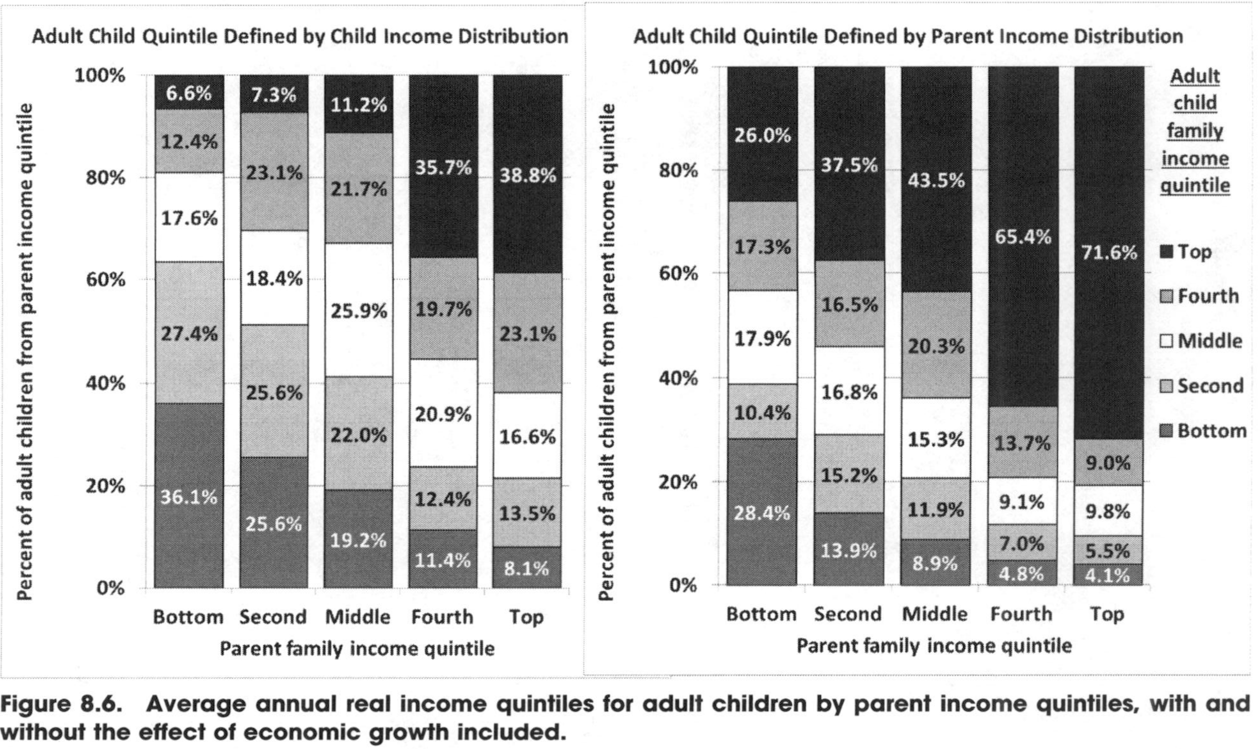

Figure 8.6. Average annual real income quintiles for adult children by parent income quintiles, with and without the effect of economic growth included.

Source: Michael R. Strain, *The American Dream Is Not Dead (but Populism Could Kill It)* (Conshohocken, PA: Templeton Press, 2020), plus additional unpublished data from the underlying study shared with the authors.

Mobility Promotes Prosperity, and Prosperity Promotes Mobility

Economic mobility is alive, powerful, and widespread in America today. While an old saying tells us it is better to be born rich, beautiful, and brilliant than to be born poor, plain, and ordinary, people who are born poor, plain, and ordinary succeed in America every day. As shown in this chapter, there appears to be a real limit to the ability of parents to purchase upward mobility for their children.

The vast majority of those born into bottom-quintile families earned more than their parents in real dollars, and 63 percent rose to a higher income quintile. But even among those who did rise, removable barriers such as attending poor schools or facing the perverse incentives of the welfare system prevented them from rising as much as their capability and drive might otherwise have enabled them. Chapter 10 looks at ways to improve mobility by eliminating barriers that stand in the way of this additional mobility. Barriers that impede mobility waste human talent that our country needs. A single undiscovered genius who might solve critical health or other human problems makes us all poorer. Increased mobility will promote greater prosperity, and greater prosperity will increase mobility.

CHAPTER 9

Fifty Years of Economic Progress

In no period of American history has the economy been more maligned than in the last fifty years. The official statistics of the US government and publications based on those statistics provide a drumbeat of economic woe. The poverty rate has remained virtually unchanged for fifty years. America has not had a pay raise in decades. Growing income inequality is now a threat to both the health of our economy and the stability of our political system.

The first eight chapters of this book have shown that those claims simply do not comport with the America we live in. The official statistics compiled by our government do not reflect the economic progress we see everywhere because those statistics are wrong. They are wrong not because of measurement error but because, by design, they don't count most government transfer payments as income to the recipients and fail to account for taxes paid as income lost to the taxpayers. The official measures of well-being also do not use the most accurate price indexes to adjust for inflation; as a result, they understate the nation's economic progress. The data needed to fix these and other design failures in our official measures of well-being are all available in plain sight from other official government sources.

Fifty Years of Progress

Figure 9.1 shows the distribution of income after transfers and taxes in 1967 on the left and that income distribution in 2017 on the right, both in 2017 dollars. The horizontal dashed lines define the upper limit of the income quintiles in 1967 and are extended to the 2017 distribution to show how the income quintiles in 2017 compare with the inflation-adjusted 1967 levels. Even though fifty years is a long time, the comparison is still startling.

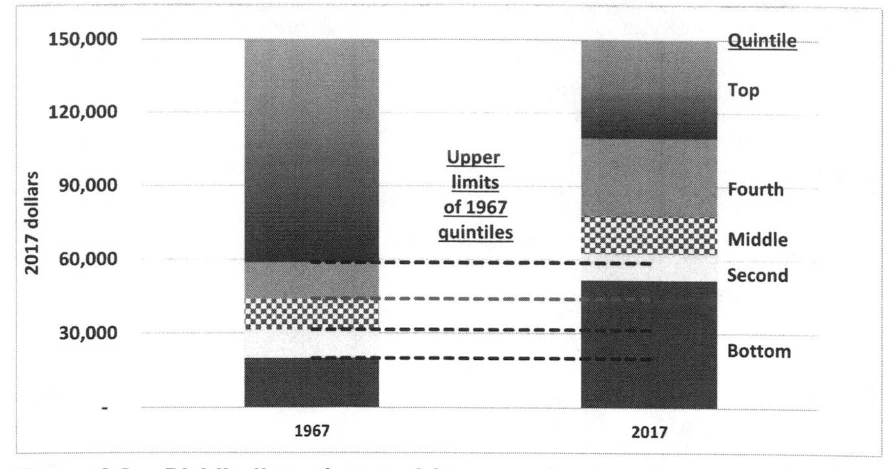

Figure 9.1. Distribution of earned income plus transfer payments minus taxes, 1967 and 2017 (2017 dollars, using the Census adjustment for inflation in income).

Note: Adjusted for inflation using the CPI-U-RS index applied by the Census Bureau for adjusting household income.

Sources: See Table 2.4 and Figure 8.1.

When all the transfer payments to households are counted as income and household income is reduced by the taxes paid, not only do both the top and the fourth quintiles in 2017 have income that would have placed them in the top quintile in 1967, but all the households in the middle quintile and almost a third of those in the second quintile also had incomes equivalent to top-quintile incomes in 1967. An extraordinary 66.3 percent of households in 2017 had incomes after transfers and taxes that would have been enjoyed only by those in the top quintile in 1967.

Twenty-five percent of households in 2017 had income that would have placed them in the fourth quintile in 1967. Only 5.4 percent of 2017 households had incomes that would have put them in the middle quintile in 1967. Another 1.7 percent had incomes in the range of the second quintile, and a mere 1.6 percent would have been in the bottom quintile.

Figure 9.1 applies the same traditional price index used by Census to adjust income for inflation. But economists and statisticians have reached a broad consensus that the traditional consumer price indexes used to adjust most well-being measures for inflation consistently overstate inflation. Even the agencies that produce the price indexes acknowledge this fact. Chapter 6 analyzed and explained the two upward biases that, in combination, have caused the Consumer Price Index for All Urban Consumers (CPI-U) to overstate inflation significantly over the last fifty years (see Figure 6.1).

Recall from Chapter 6 that the first bias comes from ignoring how consumers continually improve their well-being by substituting items that become relatively cheaper for those that have become relatively more expensive while maintaining the same level of spending. This bias is called the substitution bias. For example, between 2010 and 2011 the price of ground beef rose by 41 cents per pound, from $2.36 per pound to $2.77 per pound, while the price of chicken rose by only 3 cents per pound, from $1.26 to $1.29. At the 2010 prices, consumers were required to forego 1.87 pounds of chicken in order to buy a pound of ground beef, but in 2011 they were required to forego 2.15 pounds of chicken to get that pound of beef.[1] Obviously, we would expect that consumers would, on average, consume more chicken and less beef. And that is exactly what they did, consuming 12.4 percent fewer pounds of beef and 12.9 percent more pounds of chicken.[2] Consumers were negatively affected as the prices of both beef and chicken rose, but by buying relatively less beef and more chicken as the price of beef rose relative to chicken, they were able to reduce some of the negative impact of the price increases. The CPI-U completely ignored this dynamic and continued measuring inflation using higher-than-actual expenditure weights for the faster-rising beef prices and lower-than-actual weights for the slower-rising chicken prices. This simple example illustrates substitution bias. It happens every day in every nook and cranny of the economy, and the CPI-U ignores it.

While the total substitution bias in the Consumer Price Index (CPI) is small in a single year (an average of 0.5 percent per year for the last fifty years), official government data show that from 1967 to 2017, this bias caused the basic CPI-U to overstate inflation by 31.6 percent.[3] Since August 2002, the Bureau of Labor Statistics (BLS) has published a Chained Consumer Price Index for All Urban Consumers (C-CPI-U) that eliminates this bias beginning with data for December 1999. This improved index uses a market basket of items that reflects the actual purchases of each item at the same time as the prices were collected and also reflects the value of the substitutions that the consumer chooses to make. But this more accurate index has not been used to adjust any measures of well-being for inflation. It has been applied only to adjust personal income tax brackets in the federal tax code. A very similar official index (the Personal Consumption Expenditure Price Index [PCEPI] from the Bureau of Economic Analysis) is used in the adjustment of gross domestic product and productivity calculations for inflation. That index is available for time periods before December 1999, enabling us to look at the effect of eliminating the substitution bias over the entire fifty years.

Figure 9.2 shows the results of using the official price indexes that eliminate the substitution bias. By using the more accurate measure of price changes, we can see that almost all of the second quintile households in 2017 received incomes

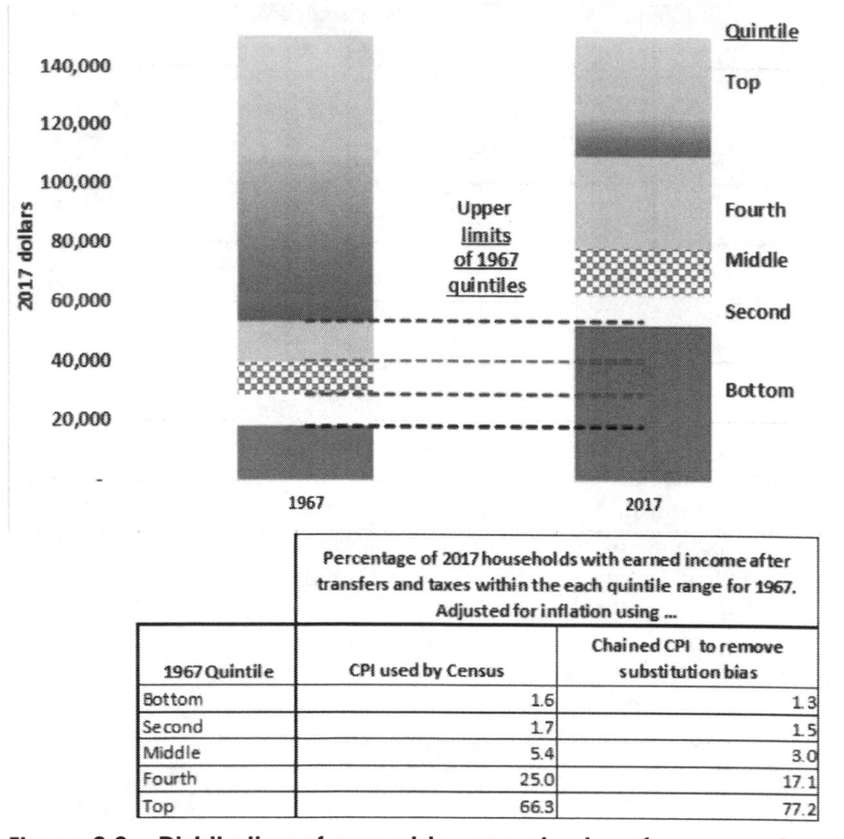

1967 Quintile	Percentage of 2017 households with earned income after transfers and taxes within the each quintile range for 1967. Adjusted for inflation using ... CPI used by Census	Chained CPI to remove substitution bias
Bottom	1.6	1.3
Second	1.7	1.5
Middle	5.4	3.0
Fourth	25.0	17.1
Top	66.3	77.2

Figure 9.2. Distribution of earned income plus transfer payments minus taxes, 1967 and 2017 (2017 dollars, adjusted to eliminate substitution bias using C-CPI-U).

Note: Adjusted for inflation using the C-CPI-U to remove substitution bias. Before December 1999, the comparable PCEPI is used.

Sources: See Table 2.4 and Figure 6.1.

after transfers and taxes that were large enough to have put them in the top quintile in 1967. An extraordinary total of 77.2 percent of all households had incomes in 2017 that were equivalent to the top quintile of 1967 in inflation-adjusted dollars. From the table below the chart, we can see that in 2017, fewer than 6 percent of households were receiving real incomes after transfers and taxes that would have put them in any of the lowest three quintiles for 1967.

As shown in Chapter 6, even correcting for the substitution bias does not eliminate the failure of our current measures of inflation to account fully for the additional value consumers receive from new and improved products. While BLS has not published an official index that corrects for most of the new-product biases as it did to correct for the substitution bias, ample official and other credible data are available to calculate reasonable, conservative estimates of the effects of new-product bias from more than fifty government and scholarly research papers. That research was incorporated into the congressionally chartered Boskin Commission report, "Toward a More Accurate Measure of the Cost of Living," and subsequent updates that were discussed in Chapter 6.[4]

Chapter 6 further showed that half of the new-product bias can be eliminated by using the existing official BLS Disease-Based Price Indexes to calculate the medical-care component of an improved CPI. It also showed that the remainder of the new-product effects can be calculated from published research by the same statistical agency that calculates the basic CPI, advisory expert commission reports chartered by government, and a growing array of academic and other research outside government. Chapter 6 presented some of the major studies, including two recent summaries that used calculations from the combined results of more than fifty studies. This research has led to some important improvements in the official CPI in recent years, but significant additional improvements are still needed, and the historical indexes continue to contain the new-product biases that existed before these improvements were made in the current CPI.

Based on comprehensive research covering a wide range of items from telecommunication equipment to medical care, researchers have developed measures of price change that quantify the effects of the value of new products that are not yet captured in any official CPI or that are partially captured in the current CPI measure but are totally missing from historical data. These measures show that the existing official indexes most likely overstate the fifty-year inflation rate by about 40 percent, in addition to the overstatement from the substitution bias. Real-dollar calculations in the remainder of this chapter have adopted these research measures that reduce new-product bias in addition to eliminating the substitution bias.

The physical evidence of the unmeasured value of new and improved products is all around us. Chapter 6 described that evidence in more detail, but a brief review can help explain why adjusting for the value of new and improved products is an important part of getting a complete picture of the growth in the purchasing power of household income over the last fifty years.

Examples of the impact of new and improved goods and services significantly enriching our lives are found throughout the last fifty years. Medical advances have added eight more years of life expectancy.[5] The CPI calculation, however, has not accounted for all of this added value. It assumes little or no value for HIV/AIDS being transformed from a disease that produced virtually certain early death into a chronic illness with long-term survival. CPI price changes do not show the change from expensive abdominal surgery to cheap over-the-counter pills to treat stomach ulcers. It has ignored how open-heart surgery has become a routine life-saving procedure and how even it has been partly replaced with microsurgery to insert stents.

Until the last few years, the extra value of having a cell phone and the expansion of its vast capabilities had not been recognized in the CPI, and it continues to be missing in the historical data. The value of larger homes with more conveniences and functionality has been underestimated. For example, the historical CPI data do not reflect fully the fact that central air conditioning has risen from being rare to almost universal, including for low-income families, and that the typical home now has two or more bathrooms rather than one. These are but a few of the striking improvements in our lives that the CPI has undervalued or ignored altogether, and, as a result, price increases are overstated.

Figure 9.3 displays the results of adding estimates for the effects of new and improved products to the price index used to adjust household income for inflation. When the inflation adjustment accounts more completely for the extraordinary improvements in our well-being from new and improved products over the last fifty years, all but 6.2 percent of households in 2017 had incomes that would have placed them in the top quintile in 1967.

As amazing as these results are, for those who have lived through this fifty-year period, the results look like common sense. Consider how in 1967 the bottom- and second-quintile levels of American households lived. In 1967, about half of all households in the bottom quintile lacked "complete" plumbing (piped hot and cold water, a flush toilet, and a bathtub or shower). Those days are gone because fewer than 2 percent of the bottom-quintile homes lack those basics today.[6] Many homes in both of the lower-income quintiles still had party-line telephones or even none at all. Now there is hardly a household without at least one smart cell phone with internet access. Fifty years ago, instances of hunger were more common in poor households. Today they exist only in isolated households run by adults who are unable to perform common daily tasks.

Even the fact that the lower income households today are economically as well off as some households in the top 20 percent of income in 1967 is easily understood. Health insurance for the top quintile would usually have covered only hospitalization in 1967, but most of the poorest households in the land now get full, first-dollar coverage without any cost sharing. Even with full coverage, the poorest today are still about 20 percent less likely to need hospitalization than their rich predecessors in 1967 because of improved treatments. When people at any income level go to the hospital, they will stay only a fraction of the time spent in 1967, are more likely to emerge fully restored, and are far less likely to be readmitted with the same complaint. An average lower-income person in 2017 will live eight years longer than a top-quintile person did in 1967.

Nobody, however rich, in 1967 had any of the services available over the internet—and only the mega rich in the top fraction of 1 percent of income could afford personal shoppers to go to the store to pick up what they wanted,

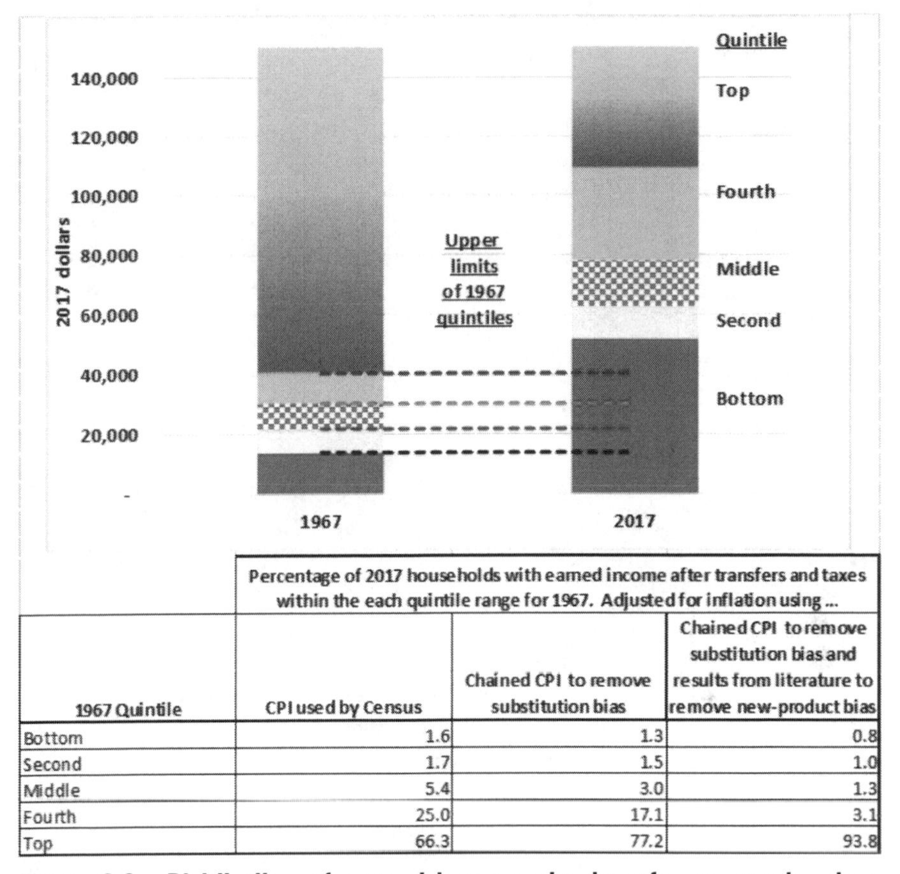

1967 Quintile	Percentage of 2017 households with earned income after transfers and taxes within the each quintile range for 1967. Adjusted for inflation using ... CPI used by Census	Chained CPI to remove substitution bias	Chained CPI to remove substitution bias and results from literature to remove new-product bias
Bottom	1.6	1.3	0.8
Second	1.7	1.5	1.0
Middle	5.4	3.0	1.3
Fourth	25.0	17.1	3.1
Top	66.3	77.2	93.8

Figure 9.3. Distribution of earned income plus transfer payments minus taxes, 1967 and 2017 (2017 dollars, calculated from C-CPI-U and summary of research literature on new-product bias).

Sources: See Table 2.4. Adjusted for inflation using the C-CPI-U and comparable PCEPI to remove substitution bias. Before December 1999, the comparable PCEPI is used. Additional adjustment for inflation used the summary results of the economic literature on the new-product biases in the various components of the CPI as described in Chapter 6.

research assistants to go to the library to dig out knowledge they wanted to have, and tax advice that even the poorest household today can access through a computer or smart phone.

Miracle fabrics that required less care and wore better were available in 1967 only to those with higher incomes. And when it came to home chores, clothes dryers were rare, and dishwashers were even rarer. Now they are almost universal. In 2017, almost every household has a color television set, and most have multiple sets with large flat screens. In 1967, only about 16 percent of households had color, and nobody had flat or LCD screens.

If you were an adult fifty years ago, think about the top 20 percent of the homes in your hometown—not the top 10 percent or the top 1 percent but the homes that were comfortable but less than mansions. They were the only homes with central air conditioning and two or more full bathrooms. Today, most families classified as poor have both.[7]

In 1967, the middle quintile might vacation in the family car or by bus; the top quintile might fly, mostly in a prop plane. Today, cheap tickets are used by people in all income brackets to jet throughout the nation and, increasingly, throughout the world. And if they choose to travel by car, the Cadillacs and Rolls-Royces of the crème de la crème in 1967 broke down ten times more often than the Ford owned by a bottom-quintile family in 2017. The Ford will also last twice as along and be four times safer.

Eating food away from home at a restaurant where somebody else prepared the meal was a hallmark of a high-income lifestyle in 1967. In the mid-1960s, households in the top quintile spent 27 percent of their food budget on food away from home. But by 2017, the average bottom-quintile household spent 34 percent of its food budget away from home, far more than the top quintile did in the mid-1960s and more than even the top 1 percent did.[8]

The more basic consumption of food at home also has shown substantial improvement in the average standard of living. In 1967, the US Department of Agriculture's "low-cost" food plan for the bottom quintile would have required the average production or nonsupervisory employee to work two hours and thirteen minutes per day during a five-day workweek to feed a family of four. In 2017, that same amount of work would have enabled the same worker to buy the "moderate cost" food plan and have earnings left over from an additional eighteen minutes of work to buy other things; an additional eight minutes of work would enable the worker to purchase the same top-grade diet consumed by the top quintile. Even in low-tech products such as food, many bottom-quintile households in 2017 could easily obtain the food consumed by the top quintile fifty years earlier.[9]

By any reasonable measure, the economic progress experienced across the board in the American economy over the last fifty years has been nothing short of extraordinary. Contrary claims are based on figures that do not count all the income households received from government and fail to use the most accurate measure of price changes.

Fifty Years of Declining Poverty by Race and Ethnicity

Table 9.1 shows the total, Black, and White poverty rates for the last fifty years. Chapter 3 already showed that the official poverty rate for the total population

Table 9.1. Percentage of population in poverty by race, 1967–2017

	Percentage of population in poverty											
	Official Census count				*Using all income*				*With all income and improved price indexes*			
Year	*Total*	*Black*	*White*	*Gap*	*Total*	*Black*	*White*	*Gap*	*Total*	*Black*	*White*	*Gap*
1967	14.2	39.3	11.0	28.3	12.9	35.7	10.6	25.1	12.2	34.7	10.3	24.4
2017	12.3	21.2	10.7	10.5	2.5	3.5	2.3	1.2	1.1	1.7	1.1	0.6
Change 1967–2017	–1.9	–18.1	–0.3	–17.8	–10.4	–32.2	–8.3	–23.9	–11.1	–33.0	–9.2	–23.8

Sources: US Census Bureau, Current Population Survey (CPS), March 2018, public-use micro-data file, calculations by authors. "Using All Income" includes all transfer payments and underreported income not in the CPS survey. "With All Income and Improved Price Indexes" also recalculates the poverty thresholds using the PCEPI before 2000 and the C-CPI-U after that and adjusting both for documented new-product biases.

simply oscillated within the relatively narrow range between 11.1 percent and 15.2 percent during the last fifty years, with no discernable trend. The official White rate varied within a similar range of 9.5 percent to 13.0 percent. The official Black rate, however, systematically declined from 39.3 percent to 21.2 percent with transient upticks during recessions. As a result, the difference between the official Black and White poverty rates was cut by more than half, from 28.3 percent to 10.5 percent.

Counting all of the $1.9 trillion in transfer payments that have been omitted by Census dramatically reduces the poverty rate. Table 9.1 shows a comparison of the official poverty rates from the Census Bureau with rates using a complete accounting of all earning and transfer payments. The Black poverty rate falls to 3.5 percent, and the White poverty rate falls to 2.3 percent in 2017, leaving a gap of only 1.2 percent. Using more accurate price indexes as described in Chapter 6 to calculate poverty thresholds causes the Black and White household poverty rates to fall to only 1.7 percent and 1.1 percent, respectively, in 2017, virtually eliminating the gap in poverty based on race. Getting the data right makes a big difference.

Data covering the full fifty-year period do not exist for other racial and ethnic groups, but in the year 2017 they show the same types of effects from using more complete data. When all transfer payments are accounted for and the most accurate estimates of consumer price change are applied, the poverty rate for Asians falls from 10.0 percent to 1.0 percent. The poverty rate for Hispanics drops from 18.3 percent to only 1.7 percent, cutting the gap with the White rate from 7.6 percentage points to 0.6 percentage points.

"Earning Gaps" by Race and Ethnicity

Discussions of differences of income and poverty by race frequently focus on differences between the White and Black populations because they are the two largest racial groups and because the lower income of the average Black household has generated substantial public policy discussion.[10] The third-largest race is Asian, with 5.3 percent of the households and a median income substantially higher than that of White households. Black and White households are also the only two races with a significant history in the Census data. Asians were identified separately beginning only in 2002 and in combination with Pacific Islanders beginning in 1987.[11] The combined populations for all other single- and multiracial groups account for less than 3 percent of all households. In addition to racial distinctions, Census identifies 13.5 percent of all households as being of Hispanic origin regardless of race. Hispanic origin has been tracked by the Census only since 1972.

The analysis of income by race begins with looking at the distribution of *earned* income. The earned-income definition has been used throughout this book and differs from the Census measure of money income because it includes employer-paid benefits, income from capital gains, and other income missed by the Census survey, and it does not include any government transfer payments.

By definition, 20.0 percent of all households are in the bottom quintile of earned income. But in 2017, 28.1 percent of all Black households were in the bottom quintile, 8.1 percent more than for the overall population. That means that, as shown in Table 9.2, they were overrepresented in the bottom quintile by 40.7 percent (8.1 divided by 20.0). They were overrepresented by 31.6 percent in the second quintile and had almost their expected share in the middle quintile. But they were underrepresented by 23.3 percent and 49.9 percent in the fourth and top quintiles, respectively. While these over- and underrepresentations were large, they were still an improvement of approximately one-third from fifty years earlier.

Because White households constituted the vast majority of all households, their differences from the overall averages within quintiles were small simply because of their large proportion of the total. And because Black households were the largest other racial group, White households differed from the average in the opposite direction from Black households, with overrepresentation in the upper two quintiles and underrepresentation in the lower two. As Black

Table 9.2. Percentage over- and underrepresentation of households in earned-income quintiles by race and ethnicity, 1967 and 2017

	Percentage by which households are over-/underrepresented in income quintile					
	White		*Black*		*Asian*	*Hispanic*
Earned-income quintile	*1967*	*2017*	*1967*	*2017*	*2017*	*2017*
Bottom	(6.3)	(5.3)	59.1	40.7	(28.2)	(13.0)
Second	(5.9)	(4.1)	55.3	31.6	(29.9)	31.2
Middle	1.0	(0.2)	(8.2)	1.0	(8.8)	21.4
Fourth	4.5	3.9	(42.8)	(23.3)	7.4	(0.2)
Top	6.6	5.8	(63.4)	(49.9)	59.5	(39.4)

Note: Numbers in parentheses are underrepresented. Those without parentheses are overrepresented. Races other than White or Black constituted 0.9 percent of households in 1967 and 8.2 percent in 2017. Households other than White, Black, or Asian were 2.9 percent in 2017. Hispanic can be of any race, and in 2017 other races of Hispanic origin represented 0.9 percent of all households. In 1967, Census data recorded any race other than White or Black as "other." Census data for 2017 recorded much more detail, including Asian, American Indian or Alaskan Native, Hawaiian Native or Other Pacific Islander, nineteen specific racial combinations, and two "other" combinations categories—one for other three races and one for four or five.

Source: Computed from US Census Bureau, Current Population Survey, March 2018 and March 1968, public-use micro data.

households became more highly represented in the upper quintiles over the fifty years, White households became less represented.

Households other than Black and White were only 0.9 percent of the total in 1967, but their proportions increased ninefold over the fifty years and were 8.9 percent of the total by 2017, with Asians contributing about two-thirds of the growth. While full historical data are not available for Asians, data for 2017 show that disproportionately more Asians earned higher incomes than any other racial or ethnic group. That is especially notable since, on average, they have arrived in the United States more recently than any of the other groups discussed here.[12]

Data for Hispanic households do not reach back to 1967, but Table 9.2 shows that in 2017 Hispanics were heavily overrepresented in the second and middle quintiles. They were underrepresented in the bottom quintile by 13.0 percent, having a smaller proportion of households in the bottom quintile than either Black or White households. They were proportionately represented in the fourth quintile and underrepresented by 39.4 percent in the top quintile.

Annual earned income for Black households averaged 40.1 percent lower than for White households in 1967. By 2017, that difference had become a somewhat smaller 36.4 percent.[13] The difference is sometimes called an "earnings gap."[14] The "gap" was actually reversed for Asian households, which on average earned 38.5 percent more than White households. Hispanic households earned 17.7 percent less than White households. The following discussion identifies some of the reasons for these differences based on data available from the Census's Current Population Survey (CPS).

The primary reason for the improvements in the relative income distribution for Black households was that average hourly earnings by Black workers (adjusted for inflation) rose by 217 percent over the fifty-year period, while hourly earnings for White workers rose by a somewhat smaller 196 percent. The proportion of prime work-age adults who were employed declined by more than 40 percent between 1967 and 2017 for both Black and White prime work-age adults in the bottom quintile and by about one-tenth that much for those in the second quintile. The proportion of White prime work-age adults working increased slightly in the middle and higher quintiles, while the proportion for Blacks decreased slightly. Although the decline in the number of prime work-age persons who were employed was the largest single cause of the overall earned-income disparity between the bottom quintile and other quintiles for the total population, the differences in the proportions working between Black and White populations in 2017 were small and explained relatively little of the earnings difference between Black and White adults.

The average Black household in 2017 earned $67,287, compared with $105,729 for the average White household, a gap of 36.4 percent and a modest improvement from the 40.1 percent gap in 1967. The earning gap between Hispanics and Whites was 23.6 percent. Earnings for Asian households were 38.5 percent higher than for Whites. This positive gap appears to have been caused mostly by the greater human capital from more education among Asians, which on average were 50 percent more likely to hold college degrees and two times more likely to hold graduate degrees than Whites. This greater education, in turn, created average hourly earnings that were one-quarter higher.

Effects of Education and Related Factors on Inequality of Earned Income among Racial and Ethnic Groups

Chapter 5 showed that the levels of education attainment constituted the second most important factor in determining differences among individual earnings. Historical data are available back to 1967 only for Whites and Blacks. It shows real progress in expanding educational attainment in both races. Figure 9.4 shows the distribution of education completed for the White and Black populations in 1967 and 2017. Both populations benefited from a huge growth in human capital created by increased education over the fifty years, which was a major reason for the respective 196 percent and 217 percent increases in real hourly earnings for Whites and Blacks. High school dropouts went from being the most frequent educational status for both races to being outnumbered by each of three groups: graduates from high school alone, high school graduates with some postsecondary training, and graduates from college. This dominance of high school and college graduates was significant among both Black and White adults. Within that larger shift, Whites were more likely to earn bachelor and graduate degrees, but the overall differences in educational attainment between the two has narrowed considerably, and the relative progress of Blacks in educational attainment has been a major reason for the one-quarter reduction in the difference for average hourly earnings between the two races. If Blacks and Whites had the same amounts of educational attainment in 2017, that would have eliminated only a little less than 10 percent of the difference in their earned income.[15]

The Asian population demonstrated even greater educational attainment, with 50 percent more college graduates than the White population, including twice as many with graduate degrees. Hispanic education lagged behind the other three groups with more than twice the incidence of high school dropouts and significantly lower proportions of college graduates.

Super two-earner households with two college graduates constituted 28.6 percent of White households and 20.3 percent of Black households in 2017, as

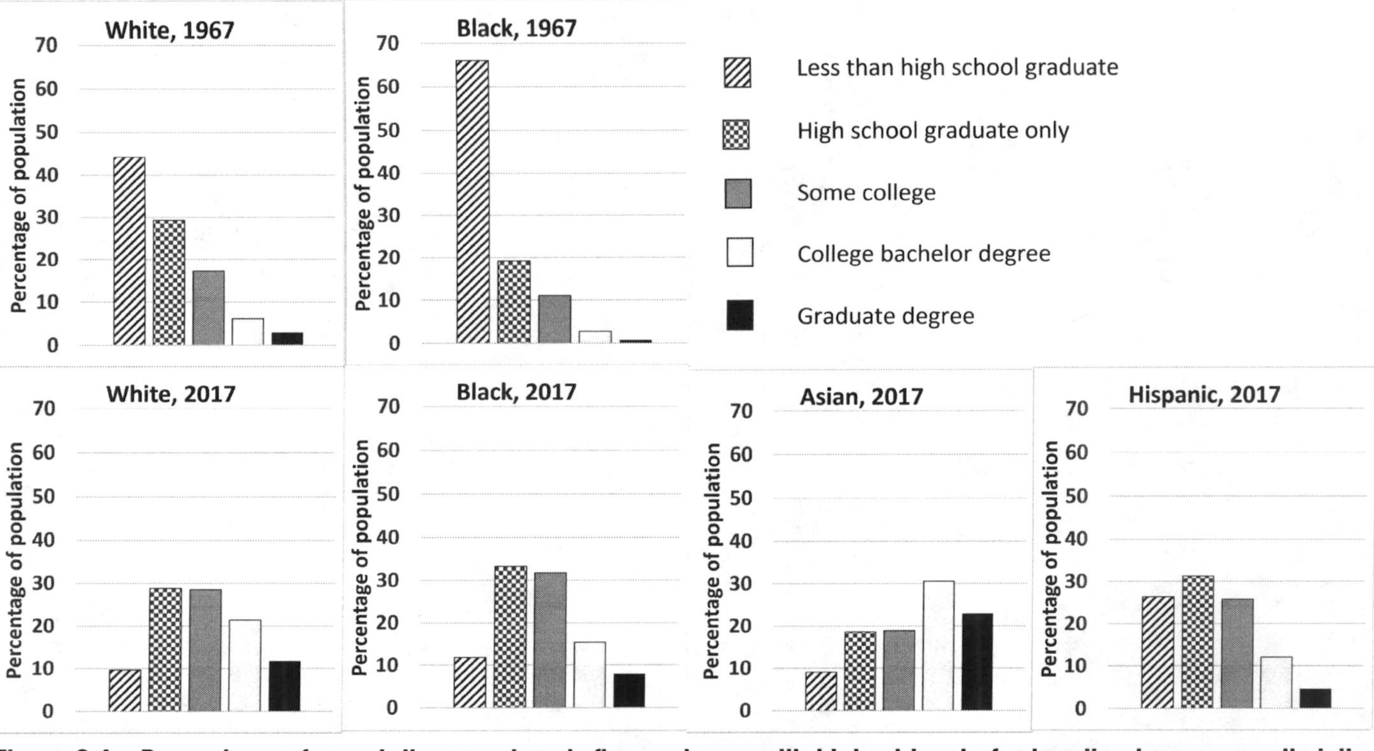

Figure 9.4. Percentage of population age twenty-five and over with highest level of education by race or ethnicity, 1967 and 2017.

Source: Computation from US Census Bureau, Current Population Survey, Annual Social and Economic Supplement, March 1968 and March 2018, public-use micro data.

compared to an average of only 5.2 percent for all households in 1967. Two college graduate earners in both Black and White households significantly increased overall income inequality, as people with higher education and earning power increasingly tended to form households together.

Asian households were more than twice as likely as White and Black households to have two college-graduate earners, at 53.4 percent. Hispanic college graduates, just like the other three groups, were more likely to form households with other college graduates. But because there were proportionately fewer Hispanic college graduates, households with two college graduates were considerably less frequent, constituting only 11.3 percent of all households.

Educational attainment of the current working population is a partial indicator of its human capital and earning capacity. But it reflects the cumulative effect of education completed over the last forty years or more by current workers, not only the current educational progress. Figure 9.5 displays the percentage of eighteen- to twenty-four-year-olds who were enrolled in college for each of four racial and ethnic groups. Twenty years ago, approximately 20 percent more White young adults compared with Hispanic young adults and 10 percent more compared with Blacks were attending college. By 2019, those differences had narrowed to less than 5 percent of each population, and at this rate of convergence, college enrollment would be essentially equal for all three groups within the next decade or so. Whether these three groups will move on to close the additional 20 percent gap with Asian young adults is another question. But as the new, more highly educated individuals enter the workforce, the average educational attainment of the total workforce for these three groups will slowly rise and converge, reducing one important source of earned-income inequality.

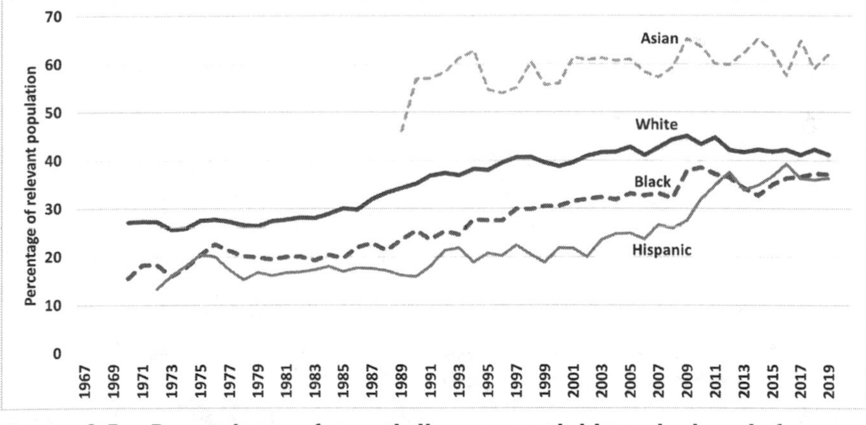

Figure 9.5. Percentage of population ages eighteen to twenty-four enrolled in college, 1967–2019.

Sources: Computed from "Table 302.60. Percentage of 18- to 24-Year-Olds Enrolled in College, by Level of Institution and Sex and Race/Ethnicity of Student: 1970 through 2019," National Center for Education Statistics, Digest of Education Statistics, https://nces.ed.gov/programs/digest/d20/tables/dt20_302.60.asp.

Chapter 5 showed that individuals with the same level of educational attainment made substantially different choices of occupation that, in turn, created significant differences in income among people with nominally the same amount of education. In addition to occupational choices that reflect different individual preferences, some occupational differences show the result of disparities in the quality of education received at the primary and secondary levels that limit access to further training and entry into occupations that earn higher incomes. As will be discussed in more detail in Chapter 10, Black and Hispanic elementary and secondary students, especially those who live in inner cities, are far more likely to attend schools that fail to provide the basic skills required for higher-paying jobs.[16]

Graduates of underperforming elementary and secondary schools often lack fundamental skills in reading, writing, and mathematics. Although these graduates may have the high school diploma required for some high-paying jobs, they may not be able to perform successfully some of the tasks that are required because they lack the fundamental skills. Even graduates of underperforming high schools who go on to additional technical training or attend college will be far less likely to successfully complete the courses of study that would produce the skills needed to earn high incomes. Differences in occupational choices within an educational level, whether the reflection of personal preferences, differences in the quality of elementary and secondary education, or other factors, accounted for about 24 percent of the earned-income gap between Black and White adults.

Hispanics have, on average, the lowest level of educational attainment of any major racial or ethnic group in the workforce, with more than twice as many high school dropouts. They often have received poorer public education than Whites and Asians. Because their much higher dropout rate disqualifies many of them from some of the higher-paying jobs that require only a high school diploma, they have a greater proportion of workers who begin in the lowest-skill jobs. In these lower-level jobs, formal education usually has less effect on performance, and other factors such as individual initiative and nonschool skills are more likely to determine success, promotion to more responsible positions, or even success with their own business. While the lack of formal education limits some of their options, Hispanics with initiative and skill are able to rise within their more limited options, earning more than would have been predicted based on their formal education alone.

Asians are the group with the highest average educational attainment. This, of course, is one of the main reasons for their higher income. But the occupations they work in are not always fully commensurate with the degrees and certifications that they have received, so their average income is somewhat less than one would predict from their education alone. One reason for this difference is that Asians in the workforce are, on average, more recent immigrants, and substantial numbers received some or all of their education, associated certifications, and licenses for their intended occupations from institutions outside the United States. They are not always able to convert these certifications quickly into American equivalents, so some newer immigrants will have lower incomes than the average for individuals with similar credential from American institutions.

The path for equal opportunity in America is most often found through education. Students who attend failing public schools too often receive poor elementary and secondary education and are consequently less likely to complete training and degree programs that produce high incomes. They are disadvantaged before they even begin to compete in the economy. As we will see in Chapter 10, test results strongly suggest that our failing public schools, especially in inner cities, represent the greatest impediment to equality of opportunity in America.

Other Factors Affecting Income Differences by Race or Ethnicity

Age and geography also have contributed to the observed differences in earned income by race and ethnicity. In the Black population, individuals under the age of thirty-six constituted a 20 percent larger proportion of the prime work-age adults than in the White population. As a result, on average, White prime working-age adults in 2017 had 2.6 more years of job experience than the average Black adult. This added experience accounts for about 3 percent of the earned-income gap between the two races.[17] Hispanic workers were even younger with more limited experience, which contributed about 6 percent to their earned-income gap with Whites. Asians had proportionately more people in the higher-earning middle years and fewer in the younger ages than Whites, which added about 5 percent to their total earned-income gap above Whites.[18]

Historically, one of the major contributors to the Black-White earning gap was geography. Black workers disproportionately lived in the South, and the South, on average, had lower pay scales for most jobs, so the national Black-White disparity was in part a reflection of that geographic difference.[19] Over time, however, this relative Black concentration in the South has become smaller, and economic differences among regions have also become smaller. As a result, the effect of geography on the Black-White pay gap has largely disappeared and in 2017 accounted for only about 1 percent of the earnings gap. Geography affected the earnings differential for Hispanics and Asians by only 1 to 2 percent as well.[20]

Table 9.3 provides a more complete analysis of income differences among racial and ethnic groups. It begins with the earned income for each group, adds

Table 9.3. Summary of contributions to household income difference by race or ethinicity, 2017

	Household income by race (dollars, 2017)				*Income gap (value for group minus value for White)*			*Income gap as percentage of White income*		
	White	*Black*	*Asian*	*Hispanic*	*Black*	*Asian*	*Hispanic*	*Black*	*Asian*	*Hispanic*
Earned income	105,729	67,287	146,448	80,821	(38,442)	40,719	(24,908)	(36.4)	38.5	(23.6)
Transfer payments	23,542	25,754	19,173	21,444	2,212	(4,369)	(2,098)			
Taxes	(36,225)	(21,743)	(51,346)	(25,701)	14,482	(15,120)	10,525			
After-tax income	93,046	71,298	114,276	76,565	(21,747)	21,230	(16,481)	(23.4)	22.8	(17.7)
Amount of income gap explained by . . .										
Education quantity					(3,407)	10,393	(13,332)			
Occupation in addition to education quantity					(9,376)	(4,433)	1,923			
Age					(1,172)	1,939	(1,546)			
Work engagement					(908)	(8,630)	(2,477)			
Geography					(340)	793	188			
Total explained from CPS data					(15,203)	63	(15,245)	(16.3)	0.1	(16.4)
Amount from other factors					(6,544)	21,168	(1,236)	(7.0)	22.7	(1.3)

Sources: Calculated from US Census Bureau and Bureau of Labor Statistics, Current Population Survey, March 2018, public-use micro-data file, and data sources in Tables 2.1, 2.2, and 2.3.

the $2.8 trillion of income from transfer payments to households that received the payments, and deducts the $4.4 trillion taken from the households that paid taxes. On average, Black households received $2,212 more in transfer payments than White households, and White households paid $14,482 more in taxes than Black households. As a result, the overall gap between Black and White household incomes after transfers and taxes was more than one-third smaller than the gap for earned income (23.4 percent versus 36.4 percent). Hispanic incomes after transfers and taxes also showed about the same difference—a 39.3 percent smaller gap with White income than existed between the earned incomes of the two. Asian earned incomes were 38.5 percent greater than White incomes, but that margin was reduced to 29.8 percent after transfers and taxes, primarily as the result of higher taxes paid on the higher Asian income.

Table 9.3 also summarizes the contributions of factors identified in this chapter that explain some of the differences in household earned income among racial and ethnic groups using data in the Current Population Survey—the quantity of education received, occupational choices within an educational level, age, the choice of whether to work, and geographic location. These five factors are listed in the table along with their contributions to the income gap for each of the groups. In sum, these five factors account for more than two-thirds of the gap in income after transfers and taxes between Black and White households. They account for more than 90 percent of the gap between Hispanic and White households. But they explain very little of the difference between Asian and White households, a topic that would require additional data and would be a fertile area for future research.

The income gap compares the average earned income for households of a specific racial/ethnic group to the average for White households. The comparison could just as well be made to any other group or even to the overall population average. This analysis adopts the convention that is widely used, including by the Bureau of the Census, of making comparisons to the largest group—namely, the White household average.[21]

Negative gaps mean that the group being compared has lower average income than White households. Positive gaps mean it has higher income. The amount of income gap explained by each of the factors can be either negative or positive as well. A negative effect means that the listed factor caused the income of the group being compared to be lower relative to White households than it otherwise would have been. For example, education quantity caused Hispanic households' income to be $13,332 lower than it would have been if Hispanic households had the same educational level as White households. The difference in education quantity was the major contributor to the Hispanic gap in income after transfers and taxes.

The effects of each of these factors on income gaps has been calculated in a similar fashion. For example, the effect of education quantity on the income gap is calculated by changing the relative proportion of each educational level within the comparison group population to the relative proportion within the White household population and computing the income and income gap with those new proportions, leaving everything else unchanged. For example, if Black households had the same proportion of their adults in each educational attainment level as White households, they would, on average, have earned $3,407 more than they actually did.[22]

The earnings effects of the differences in educational quality cannot be readily estimated directly from existing CPS data, but they are undoubtedly significant contributors to the occupational differences and to other factors that have not been measured directly. In Chapter 10, we will look at data measuring the quality of education actually received in America's primary and secondary schools.

Fifty Years of Progress in Households Headed by Unmarried Women

Historically, public assistance was focused on providing aid to households with children headed by unmarried women. Table 9.4 shows that households headed by unmarried women with children have been substantially overrepresented in the bottom and second earned-income quintiles throughout the fifty-year period, but they have made significant progress, and their overrepresentation in the bottom quintile was almost seven times smaller in 2017 than in 1967.

This substantial improvement of income for households headed by unmarried women moving out of the bottom quintile was the result of two trends. First, their incomes rose faster than the nation's average. Second, proportionately fewer of these women dropped out of the workforce. Similar improvements occurred in all other quintiles except the second, where the number of households headed by unmarried women saw their overrepresentation increase because of the large number who had earned their way out of the bottom quintile into the second quintile.

Both of these factors can be traced in large measure to the 1996 welfare reforms that included replacing the Aid to Families with Dependent Children program with a more targeted Temporary Assistance for Needy Families program that included mandatory requirements for training and work. As shown in Chapter 5, economic gains such as those for women-headed households with children flowed directly from welfare reform.

Average real earned income for households headed by unmarried women jumped 265 percent over the fifty years. Average income after transfer payments and taxes rose slightly less, by 228 percent, because of the increase in taxes paid

Table 9.4. Households with children headed by unmarried women, selected indicators of well-being

Earned-income quintile	*Percentage over-/underrepresentation in income quintile*		*Earned income (2017 dollars)*			*Income after transfer payments and taxes (2017 dollars)*		
Quintile	*1967*	*2017*	*1967*	*2017*	*Percentage change*	*1967*	*2017*	*Percentage change*
Bottom	122.4	18.1	3,749	9,071	142.0	14,808	47,854	223.2
Second	70.8	78.5	16,443	30,564	85.9	17,682	50,136	183.5
Middle	(32.2)	7.2	31,247	65,352	109.1	27,682	63,299	128.7
Fourth	(75.7)	(33.7)	45,863	109,051	137.8	37,795	86,066	127.7
Top	(85.3)	(70.2)	85,502	298,854	249.5	66,502	199,849	200.5
Average	n/a	n/a	16,268	59,369	264.9	20,175	66,121	227.7

Note: Numbers in parentheses are underrepresented. Those without parentheses are overrepresented.

Sources: See Tables 2.1, 2.2, and 2.3. See Chapter 6 for inflation adjustment.

as earned income rose. Average income after transfers and taxes for the bottom and second quintiles rose between one and a half and two times faster than earned income because of the vast increases in transfer payments to low-income households over the fifty years. The middle quintile rose slightly faster than its earned income as the result of transfer payments expanding into the middle-income levels and middle-income tax reductions. Income after transfers and taxes for the top and fourth quintiles rose substantially more slowly than their earned income because of higher taxes.

Changes in Income Inequality across Regions

Incomes vary by region within the United States. In recent years, nearly 10 percent of the population has moved their residence every year. A majority of those moves have been local, within the same county. But more than a third moved to a different county, including 1.5 percent of the population who moved to a different state.[23] That 1.5 percent may seem small, but it is for a single year. At that rate, in the course of an average work life, approximately half of all households would move to a different state at least once.[24]

This substantial rate of physical mobility has actually declined by about half since the immediate postwar years. A number of different explanations have been offered for this decline in physical migration, each with at least some data to support it, including an aging population, which tends to move less readily; smaller regional differences in earning potential, which reduces the earning incentives to move; more two-earner families, which adds the complication of moving two jobs; increased homeownership, which may increase both the economic and the noneconomic costs of moving; and increased communication capabilities that reduce the need for as much physical relocation.[25]

Data from the Current Population Survey show that in 1967, the top quintile of households was overrepresented in the Northeast by 12.3 percent, and the bottom quintile was underrepresented by 12.5 percent, a clear skew toward higher incomes in the Northeast. But fifty years later, in 2017, the top quintile was overrepresented even more, by 18.8 percent. But the bottom quintile had shifted from being significantly underrepresented to being slightly overrepresented. The 60 percent in the middle of the income distribution was underrepresented in 2017. (See Appendix F for the full set of regional data.)

The West was even more strongly skewed toward higher incomes than the Northeast in 1967, but by 2017 its income distribution became less skewed toward the top and looked more like the Northeast had been in 1967. The Midwest shifted away from a modest overrepresentation at higher incomes in 1967 to an underrepresentation in 2017. The bottom and second quintiles in the Midwest both shifted from being substantially underrepresented to being essentially the same as the national average. In short, the Midwest became relatively less prosperous.

The South had, by far, the lowest income distribution of the four regions in 1967, with very large overrepresentations in each of the two lowest quintiles and a large underrepresentation in the top two highest quintiles. By 2017, the South still had the lowest income of the four regions, but it experienced the greatest increase in its earned income, adding a greater proportion of its households to the two highest quintiles and losing more from the lower two quintiles than any of the other regions. These shifts reduced the South's gaps with the other regions by more than half.

Fifty Years of Stunning Progress

Over the last fifty years, the American economy has outperformed all other large, developed economies. Within the broad framework of strong economic growth, the benefits of this national prosperity have been widely shared. Income differentials that existed fifty years ago on the basis of race, ethnicity, sex, age, and region have narrowed. The much-maligned last half century has been a period of astounding progress that, in any country except America, would warrant the title of a golden age.

CHAPTER 10

Policy Implications and Conclusions

When Thomas Jefferson wrote in the Declaration of Independence that "all men are created equal, that they are endowed by their Creator with certain unalienable Rights," he laid the cornerstone of equality before the law in the foundation of American government, planted the seed that would end slavery in America, and ignited a worldwide liberty revolution that rages to this day. But neither he nor any Founder believed that all people had equal ability or equal ambition or that government could or should seek equal outcomes in the efforts of its people to succeed. The Founders' view seems to have been captured by historians Will and Ariel Durant in their *Lessons of History*: "Nature smiles at the union of freedom and equality in our utopias. For freedom and equality are sworn and everlasting enemies, and when one prevails the other dies. Leave men free, and their natural inequalities will grow almost geometrically."[1]

Knowing that some people had extraordinary amounts of both ability and ambition, the Founders set about to build a government where the talented and ambitious could not seize control and use the power of government to endanger the freedom and property of others. They equally feared both the man on the white horse and the enflamed masses who, by either force or the ballot box, might seize the power of government and use it to destroy the rule of law. To avoid crashing the ship of state on either Scylla or Charybdis, they installed a government of strictly limited and enumerated powers, and those powers were separated into three equal branches so that they would check and balance each other.

America's Founders wisely rejected the concept that humans could ever be perfected and tried to construct a constitutional system that would withstand and redirect genius, boundless ambition, and self-interest to promote the greatest public good—namely, general prosperity. While perhaps less than perfect, this constitutional system has served us well for 233 years and counting. The very rich among us became rich not by seizing control of the government but, with very few exceptions, by providing goods and services that have enriched us all.

Inequality has been a source of social upheaval throughout recorded history. Plato, in an era when ownership of land was the principal source of income inequality, called for redistribution of land. But in a keen insight into the future of collectivist societies, Plato foresaw that a state powerful enough to redistribute land (wealth) would become corrupt and would ultimately serve its own interest and the interest of those who controlled it.[2]

Antiquity and the world that would spring from it are replete with examples of self-serving leaders who obtained power in the name of redistribution only to serve their own interests. Plutarch saw the struggle for power in the name of income and wealth redistribution as the "inveterate disease."[3] The golden age of Athenian democracy had begun in a bloody class struggle. Pericles, an aristocrat, gained the confidence of the people and expanded the voice of ordinary citizens in Athens's democracy while largely preserving the sanctity of property.[4] This balance, according to Will Durant, was the source of progress and stability: "Greek civilization was at its best when democracy had grown sufficiently to give it variety and vigor and aristocracy survived sufficiently to give it order and taste."[5] Variety, vigor, competition, and upward mobility combined with the rule of law have remained the source of economic success and human happiness ever since.

It is important to understand that in the ancient world, the major source of income and wealth was the ownership of land, and the quantity of land in the city state (polis) was fixed. The competition for land was therefore a zero-sum game. For one person to acquire property or wealth, another person had to lose it. Increasing the size of the economic pie was largely an alien concept in the ancient world.

Under Roman law, the Mediterranean world became one vast free trade area, and land was far more abundant. A small, at least by modern standards, level of economic growth over significant periods made it possible for a very few with extraordinary talent and ambition to become "new men" and even part of the governing elite, senators, but progress was achieved over generations. After the fall of Rome, economic progress on any kind of broad basis in the Western world stopped for a thousand years.

The dawn of the Enlightenment brought a fundamental change in the wellspring of wealth creation. The Enlightenment affirmed labor and capital as private property, not communal property to be shared with the crown, church, guild, and village. The concept of labor and capital as private property, protected from leeching by communal "stakeholders," was the fundamental economic contribution of the Enlightenment upon which the modern world was built. The Industrial Revolution grew out of the Enlightenment, and it powered the rapid ascent of all people, especially workers. The plethora of goods and services grew beyond human imagination, and the zero-sum world came to an end. An increase in one person's income and wealth did not require a decrease in another's, as new wealth could be continually created. This fundamental change, conveniently neglected by collectivists of various stripes throughout the ages, created a new world—a world where wealth can be created instead of redistributed.

The wealth of a nation and its people came from enhanced productivity. Greater output per capita led to higher wages and incomes, greater consumption, and increased capital accumulation. This virtuous process, led by entrepreneurs and innovators, would swell production, granting anyone and everyone at least a chance to prosper. Today the first-generation college graduate and Jeff Bezos do not rise economically by taking something away from somebody else. They create their own income and wealth by producing goods and services that others willingly, even eagerly, buy, enriching both seller and buyer. Democracy, which Plato had seen as "a bazaar of constitutions and charters," was to him the most attractive state among the options that actually existed, but he believed that it was unstable.[6] Envy and the lust for equality made it unstable and prone to tyranny and dictatorship. The attempt to impose equality where it does not exist and cannot be sustained was seen by Plato as the Achilles' heel of democracy. Rulers gained political advantage by promising to take income and wealth and redistribute it, but in the ensuing struggle, often the wealth and democracy itself were destroyed. Plato could not have envisioned a post-Enlightenment world, as described by Adam Smith. The very concept of creating income and wealth rather than taking it from someone else was totally foreign to him and his contemporaries. In the non-zero-sum world we live in, it does not follow that democracy is necessarily unstable and must lead to tyranny.

In a world of sustained economic growth, progress is promoted and stability is maintained by providing greater equality of opportunity. Through what Abraham Lincoln called "an open field and a fair chance for your industry, enterprise, and intelligence,"[7] ordinary people have been able to do extraordinary things in America. Like equal justice before the law, greater opportunity for everyone to pursue their own happiness is the American dream, and that goal should animate America's economic and social policy.

Pursuing Opportunity

Not only has this book shown that the way we collect and report statistics has significantly overstated inequality and understated national well-being, but it has also shown that the explosion of transfer payments following the War on Poverty has caused a significant number of prime work-age persons to become detached from the economy. That disengagement from the world of work has denied them the opportunity to benefit from the extraordinary economic progress that has occurred in the last fifty years and is the largest single cause of income inequality in postwar America.

The second-largest source of income inequality has been differences in both the quantity and the quality of educational attainment. The failure of public primary and secondary education, especially in inner-city schools, has become a major impediment to educational and economic opportunity. The path to the open field and fair chance that America has promised can best be found by getting all Americans back to work, dramatically improving the quality of our primary and secondary schools, and removing artificial impediments to competition.

Getting Our Facts Straight

As noted in the introduction, this book is an effort not to end a debate but to begin a debate. A constructive public policy debate on inequality, poverty, and our national and individual well-being requires a comprehensive overhaul of how we collect and report national economic statistics. The truth can make us free only if we know the truth.

Throughout this book, the analysis of all available data has shown that the official statistics of the United States have overstated inequality and poverty and have understated well-being, thereby biasing the public policy debate. The official statistics are wrong because they explicitly measure the wrong things. They do not include two-thirds of government transfer payments as income for the recipients and do not count taxes paid as income lost to the taxpayers. Official statistics also omit employer-paid benefits, capital gains, and a variety of other underreported income items.

Ironically, President Joe Biden, House Speaker Nancy Pelosi, and Senate Majority Leader Chuck Schumer all proclaimed in the fall of 2021 that their proposed monthly child tax credit costing $1.6 trillion over a decade would "cut child poverty in half."[8] They were, by definition, absolutely wrong. The official poverty rate does not count the refundable portion of tax credits as income, even though the benefits are paid with a check from the Treasury. And the same mismeasurement problem also invalidated their original claim that the transfer payments were needed in the first place owing to high childhood poverty. That claim was invalid because the official child poverty rate was five times larger than it would have been had the Census merely counted all transfer payments as income to the recipient—only 3.1 percent versus the official 17.5 percent.[9]

This story of incorrect data misdirecting policy is hardly unique. This book has shown in detail that the official income measures show levels of inequality that are overstated by a factor of four. Income inequality has fallen, not risen, in postwar America. Poverty has declined dramatically and almost disappeared, not remained largely static for half a century as Census data show. The ability to climb the economic ladder to success is alive and well in America, with children routinely making more than their parents and upward mobility being the norm, not the exception. The vast improvement in economic well-being during the last half century has been broadly shared across race, ethnicity, gender, and region, not just enjoyed by the privileged few.

In the fall of 2021, those disconnects between official statistics and reality were on full display. The administration and majority leadership in Congress were calling for huge additional increases in federal transfer payments on top of an unprecedented 45 percent increase in 2020.[10] The Census Bureau was preparing for the scheduled release of household income and poverty figures. After the government spending spree to boost household income, the Census Bureau leadership was confronted with a problem: the official statistics for median household income showed a 2.9 percent decline, which suggested that all that big spending didn't help those households that received the transfer payments. Of course, that decline shown in the official statistics occurred because most of those extra transfer payments have never been counted as income by the Census Bureau.

So, for the first time ever, in the same publication alongside the official numbers, the Census Bureau issued a second set of estimates that included the types of transfer payments that the government had been making all along but that Census had never counted before. By counting some of these missing transfer payments, median household income miraculously rose 4.0 percent rather than falling 2.9 percent, as the official data showed.[11]

The official poverty rate for 2020 increased by 1.0 percentage point. But for the first time in its primary poverty release, Census explicitly referenced the experimental Supplementary Poverty Measure, which included some of the missing transfer payments and showed that the poverty rate declined by 2.6 percentage points.[12] Clearly, the official data need to be fixed and not just adjusted ad hoc when the information they convey is obviously not credible.

All the procedures that distort the measurement of income and poverty are administratively prescribed and could be repaired by changing administrative policy. But getting our facts straight is too important to rely merely on changes in administrative procedures. Legislation is required to assure that the statistical agencies of the federal government measure income, poverty, and income inequality in ways that are complete and meaningful. The legislation should also specify that these improved data must be used to adjust the eligibility for and the size of government transfer payments.

Legislation should mandate that the statistical agencies count all earned income, including capital gains and all employer-paid benefits like health insurance premiums and employer contributions to worker retirement plans. All government transfer payments must be counted as income to the recipients, including not only the so-called cash benefits that are currently counted but all benefits such as Medicare, Medicaid, food stamps, refundable tax credits, public housing, loan subsidies, loan forgiveness, and free services to low-income households such as free community clinics. All federal, state, and local taxes must be counted as income lost to the taxpayer.

Agencies should be directed to use multiple survey sources and administrative agency records such as those from the Internal Revenue Service and Social Security as needed to fill any data gaps. Survey responses should be adjusted to equal known administrative totals for actual transfer payments made and taxes collected. For example, the sum of all food stamp payments reported in Census household surveys should be reconciled with the actual record of the value of food stamps that were issued. The total of all income taxes, sales taxes, and residential property taxes reported in household surveys should be reconciled against the known total of taxes actually collected by governments.[13] Much of the foundational data needed to add the improvements to survey data on economic well-being already exist in multiple government surveys and databases, and any impediment to using that data should be removed.

Current and historical estimates for all measures of well-being that are adjusted for inflation, including poverty thresholds, should immediately begin using the most accurate existing price indexes that eliminate substitution bias (the Chained Consumer Price Index for All Urban Consumers from 2000 forward and the Personal Consumption Expenditure Price Index for earlier periods). The same indexes should be used to deflate all indexed spending programs as they are now used to index portions of the tax code.

There is no existing official index that corrects for the failure of the consumer price indexes to take adequately into account the value of new and improved items. The Bureau of Labor Statistics (BLS) is already using appropriate advanced methods for selected items such as mobile telephones, and it needs to expand these practices to all items. The existing official Disease-Based Price Indexes from BLS should be integrated into the Consumer Price Index (CPI) as a replacement for the existing medical-care indexes. The methods for adjusting price indexes for the value of new and improved products are well known and have been the subject of numerous public and private studies, including extensive work by the BLS itself. These improved methods should be incorporated into the calculation of all official price indexes as soon as they are available.

Most of the improved methods described here should be in place and applied to all official current measures of well-being within one year. Since historical price indexes that eliminate substitution bias already exist, they should be applied within one year for all inflation adjustments to official statistics. The work to implement more accurate methods to adjust for new and improved products in the CPI should begin immediately, be incorporated into the price index as improvements are made on an item-by-item basis, and be completed within three years. All historical measures related to individual, family, and household income and to poverty and other measures of well-being should be recomputed back to 1947 to incorporate the requirements for counting all earned income, transfer payments, and taxes and using the most accurate available price indexes to adjust those measures for inflation.

Remove Government Disincentives to Work

The current welfare system was created in the 1930s during the Great Depression. At the time President Franklin Roosevelt explicitly warned, "Work must be found for able-bodied but destitute workers. The Federal Government must and shall quit this business of relief."[14] When President Lyndon Johnson greatly expanded welfare with his Great Society programs in the mid-1960s, he likewise warned, "The War on Poverty is not a struggle simply to support people, to make them dependent on the generosity of others. It is an effort to allow them to develop and use their capacities."[15]

All Americans have been poorly served by the failure of the government to live up to those pledges. In the bottom two income quintiles today, eighteen million prime work-age adults live in whole or in significant measure on government transfer payments. They have been induced to give up their opportunity to "develop and use their capacities," as President Johnson promised. Today public assistance continues to grow faster than the earned income of taxpayers, with the average nonretired household in the bottom quintile receiving more than $41,000 in government transfer payments, while employers cannot find people willing to work in their eleven million vacant jobs. Taxpayers pay more to fund transfer payments that discourage work, and everyone suffers the consequences. Most importantly, by providing transfer payments that allow nonworkers to live a middle-income lifestyle, public policy has induced millions of prime work-age persons to drop out of the labor market and, as a result, to lose access to the opportunities for economic advancement that are generated by the American economy.

In the 1990s, officeholders from both political parties began to recognize that the welfare system was a failure. Recipients were caught in a "trap," becoming dependent on these subsidies, which gave the able-bodied little incentive to find work and be part of the economic system. The bipartisan consensus that those transfer payments were at the heart of a failed welfare system led to passage of the Personal Responsibility and Work Opportunity Reconciliation Act, or the Welfare Reform Act, of 1996. That reform has been the sole significant and successful effort to stem the tide of withdrawal from work by incentivizing self-reliance with stronger requirements for work or training in the Temporary Assistance for Needy Families program. The results of the reform were very encouraging, increasing employment among recipients and reducing their incidence of poverty.

Unfortunately, the reform did not apply to other welfare programs, and the benefits of those other programs, such as food stamps and unemployment insurance, continued to increase, creating additional incentives not to work. The work requirements in the welfare reform program were also subsequently weakened by granting states waivers that allow them to stop enforcing the work requirements. Casey Mulligan, professor of economics at the University of Chicago, has shown, based on existing research, that while the reform program promoted work and reduced subsidies, over time, the expansion of other welfare programs with no work requirements and the weakening of work requirements in the welfare reform program itself caused work effort to decline dramatically. The higher transfer amounts per person, combined with the increased number of people not working, significantly increased total transfer expenditures.[16] The largest source of earned-income inequality today is that most of the prime work-age adults in the bottom quintile and a growing number in the second quintile are largely detached from the labor market and have not shared in the broad-based opportunities for advancement that have occurred in the last half century.

Chapter 5 introduced income data for nonelderly households by excluding those that were receiving Social Security retirement benefits or were above the full-retirement age.[17] Those data show that at the current level and design of transfer payments, there is little economic incentive for people in low-income households to work. The bottom 20 percent of households with one or more prime work-age earners and no Social Security retirement benefits received on average more than $41,000 in government transfer payments, which enabled them to consume at middle-income levels. At these high subsidy levels, most beneficiaries have little or no incentive to take a job since they are receiving about as much for not working as they could earn working. At the current high benefit levels, if they work more, they lose almost as much in reduced subsidies and higher taxes as they gain in additional earnings. At the current level of subsidies, a work requirement is an indispensable first step in incentivizing low-income Americans to join the world of work and benefit from the opportunities it provides.

For the economic health of both low-income households and the nation as a whole, work requirements need to be restored in those programs where they have been weakened or eliminated and implemented where they never existed. States should no longer be allowed to waive or weaken work requirements in programs using federal funds, and states themselves should implement work requirements for their own public assistance programs. These requirements should apply to all prime work-age persons receiving welfare benefits. While there should be work requirements for all means-tested programs, educational activity could, in special cases, be substituted for work requirements, allowing the welfare recipient to acquire literacy training, a GED, technical training, or an associate's degree.

By excluding most transfer payments instituted since the War on Poverty from its measures of income, the Census Bureau has consistently overstated the poverty rate and understated many measures of individual and household well-being. We do not know whether Americans would have knowingly provided more than $41,000 worth of transfer payments to the average low-income household with adults of working age. But we do know the consequences of providing that level of support without any work requirement. The proportion of work-age adults in the bottom quintile who do not work has doubled, and millions of Americans have lost their opportunity to "develop and use their capacities."

Reengaging low-income, prime work-age persons in the labor market and, therefore, providing them on-the-job training and opportunities that will allow them to join the economic mainstream of American life starts with mandatory work requirements as a condition for receiving welfare payments. Those work requirements will lower the cost of welfare transfers and lower measured income inequality, but, most importantly, they will provide access to the American dream to millions of people who are today idled by a well-meaning but destructive public policy.

Unfortunately, more Americans continue to drop out the labor force as transfer payments increase. We have all seen an additional significant decline in labor force participation produced by the explosion of transfer payments in response to the COVID shutdown. After transfer payments to households jumped 30 percent from the first quarter of 2019 to the third quarter of 2021,[18] no one should have been surprised that over the same period 1.5 percent of the civilian labor force, or about 2.5 million people, simply dropped out of the labor force.[19] With 11 million job openings and a booming economy, these 2.5 million people did not come back to work.

Reform Elementary and Secondary Education for Success

For most Americans, economic success has come through education. But by any objective standard, America's government-run primary and secondary schools, especially those in inner cities, today often fail to deliver the basic skills needed to find rewarding careers or go on to college.

The National Assessment of Educational Progress (NAEP) test in reading and mathematics is administered periodically by the US Department of Education to a large statistical sample of public schools across the nation.[20] The "proficient" achievement level "represents solid academic performance for the given grade level."[21]

The test results are a stark indictment of the failure of America's public schools. Only one-quarter of high school seniors are proficient in mathematics and only one-third in reading. Even more startling is that the proficiency in mathematics actually declines the longer the child is in school. On average, attending school longer appears to increase the gap between what is actually being learned and the standard expected by grade level. Sending more people to college is not the solution because these data show that even among those headed to college, many still lack proficiency in high school skills. In fact, such poor preparation for college often increases the probability of failure in college or at least reduces the economic value of the education received.

As shown in Figure 10.1, the results for Black and Hispanic students are even more disturbing. Asian seniors were about 8 percent more likely to be proficient in reading than White seniors. Both groups were a little less than 3 times more likely to be proficient than Black seniors and about 2 times more likely than Hispanic seniors. The differences were even greater for mathematics. Asian seniors were more than 7 times more likely to be proficient than Black seniors, 4.5 times more likely than Hispanic seniors, and 65 percent more likely than White seniors. White seniors were 4.5 times more likely to be proficient than Black seniors and 2.5 times more likely than Hispanics. Student performance also varies by family economic conditions. High school seniors from families with incomes greater than 180 percent of the poverty threshold were twice as likely to be proficient in reading and 3 times as likely to be proficient in mathematics as students with household incomes below that level.[22]

Children from low-income households are disproportionately subjected to poor government schools and are consequently more likely to have academic deficiencies that will preclude access to higher-paying jobs and success in college and technical training. Even in the occupations for which they are nominally qualified with a high school diploma, they are more likely to be ill prepared to perform well.

A long-standing excuse for the deficiencies in public education is that we do not spend enough money. But that narrative is false. Figure 10.2 shows that from 1952 to 2018, the real average expenditure per pupil rose by 343.9 percent. Since these are in inflation-adjusted dollars, that means that on average every elementary and secondary student in 2018 had 4.5 times as many resources

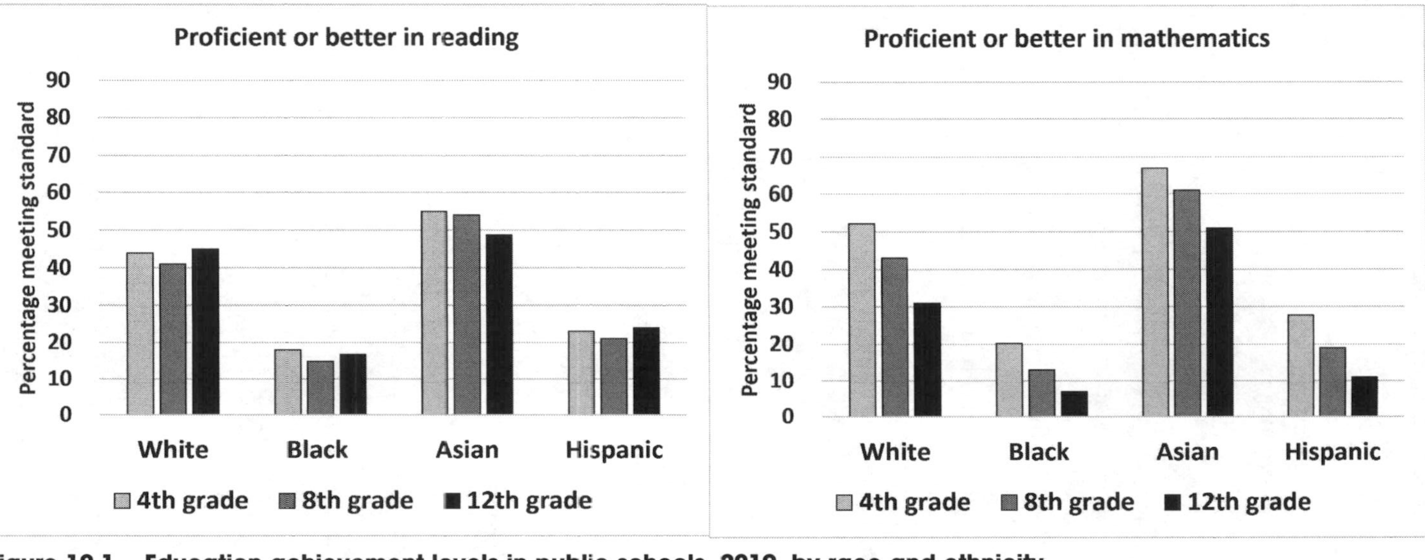

Figure 10.1. Education achievement levels in public schools, 2019, by race and ethnicity.

Note: "Proficient" achievement "represents solid academic performance for the given grade level."

Source: US Department of Education, National Center for Education Statistics, National Assessment of Educational Progress, The Nation's Report Card, Data Tools, NAEP Data Explorer, 2019, https://www.nationsreportcard.gov/ndecore/xplore/NDE.

provided for their education as students did in 1952. With that overwhelming increase in resources spent on educating our children, what did we get in return?

Performance on the Scholastic Aptitude Test (SAT) was essentially unchanged for a dozen years beginning in 1952, but then it dropped by 8.0 percent from 1963 to 1980. Inflation-adjusted expenditures per pupil rose 83.8 percent during the seventeen years. Has there ever been a more tragic waste of money, spending almost twice as much per pupil and getting 8.0 percent less education in return? Over the next thirty-six years, the SAT scores hardly improved at all, regaining less than 10 percent of the score they had lost, while real expenditures per pupil nearly doubled again.

The NAEP examinations from the Department of Education have been added to the chart because they relate to *all* students in twelfth grade, while the SAT scores relate only to college-bound students. The NAEP tests did not begin until 1972, after most of the decline in SAT scores had occurred, but since then the trends in the two tests have been very similar. From their beginning, the NAEP scores have been largely unchanged—declining by a statistically insignificant 0.1 percent—while real spending per student has grown by 123.7 percent, more than doubling the resources expended on each student with nothing to show for it.

The total disconnect between educational spending and educational outcomes over time is also confirmed by comparing the NAEP test scores and per-pupil spending among states. The expenditures are adjusted by the Department of Education's measure of regional cost differences. Examining these data shows no relationship between higher spending and better educational outcomes. For example, the state with the lowest per-pupil expenditure spent 42 percent less than the average state, but its test scores were above average. However, the state with the lowest average test scores spent 33 percent more than the average. Statistically, less than 7 percent of the variation in test scores among states can be explained by variation in their spending, and the relationship is so weak that formal statistical tests cannot distinguish the actual relationship from zero.[23]

International comparisons reinforce these findings. The United States spent 38.2 percent more per student than the average of all developed nations in the Organisation for Economic Co-operation and Development, adjusted for cost differences among countries. Yet it ranked thirty-first out of thirty-seven in mathematics performance by its students. In reading, it ranked ninth. All eight countries that performed better than America in reading spent less on education per student, averaging 27 percent less.[24] The relationship between educational spending and outcomes is even weaker for these international comparisons than it is for the variation among states, with the international variation in spending explaining only less than 3 percent of the variation in results, a value that is not statistically significant.[25]

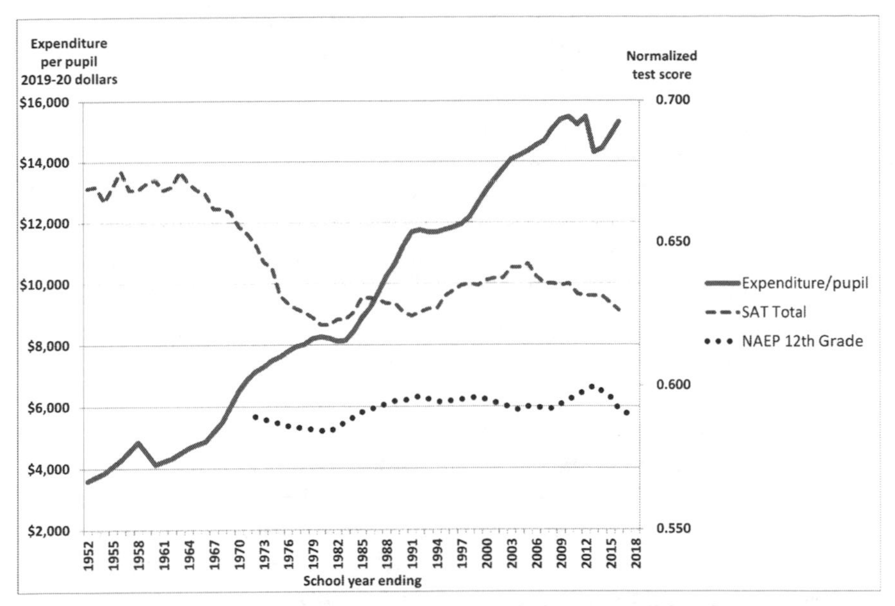

Figure 10.2. Real expenditure per public school pupil in elementary and secondary schools compared with test scores, 1952–2018.

Note: The SAT and NAEP tests are scored on different scales, so the two have been standardized to a common scale reflecting the percentage of the total range of possible scores for each.

Sources: Expenditures per pupil in 2019–2020 dollars: "Table 201.10. Historical Summary of Public Elementary and Secondary School Statistics: Selected Years, 1869–70 through 2017–18," US Department of Education, National Center for Education Statistics, Digest of Education Statistics, December 2020, https://nces.ed.gov/programs/digest/d20/tables/dt20_201.10.asp. SAT (formerly Scholastic Aptitude Test and Scholastic Assessment Test) scores: "Table 135. SAT Score Averages of College-Bound Seniors, by Sex: 1966–67 through 2006–07," supplemented with other years for other editions of the digest. Note that after 2016, SAT scoring changed radically and is not included here. National Assessment of Education Performance. US Department of Education, National Center for Education Statistics, National Assessment of Educational Progress, The Nation's Report Card, Data Tools, NAEP Data Explorer, 2019, https://www.nationsreportcard.gov/ndecore/xplore/NDE.

We should not be surprised that an educational monopoly established and operated by government performs ineffectively and inefficiently. When parents and children from higher-income households are caught in a poorly performing government school district, many are able to make the *choice* of sending their children to different schools. Generally, lower-income parents lack the means to make that choice and are captives of the failing monopoly. But in recent years, a small number of parents and children from low-income households have benefited from being able to make such choices too because they have had access to charter schools or private schools with scholarships from taxpayer funding or generous donors making tax-advantaged donations. When given the choice, these children are often outstanding exceptions to the disheartening academic performance among disadvantaged students.

The first charter school—St. Paul, Minnesota's City Academy—opened its doors in 1992. Charter schools are publicly funded, tuition-free schools that operate with a much greater degree of autonomy than traditional public schools and are frequently operated by not-for-profit organizations focused on educational success. These schools are held much more accountable for improved student achievement. There are now some seventy-five hundred charter schools serving some 3.3 million students.

Minority and low-income students attending charter schools or private schools on scholarships do not merely equal the performance of students in higher-income school districts; they often surpass them. For example, the fifth graders in a Harlem Success Academy, a charter school attended almost exclusively by low-income minority students, outperformed every other class in the entire state of New York in mathematics.[26] Of course, this is an extraordinary success story, and other school-choice programs have not equaled that achievement level, but, nonetheless, results from school choice in both charter schools and private schools with scholarships and vouchers are stunningly positive.

Because many more students apply for these opportunities for school choice than there are openings available, students are usually accepted into these programs by a random drawing from a large pool of applicants. As a result, evaluation of these programs can be unbiased and statistically very powerful. With two randomly selected groups from the same population, the performance of those accepted can be validly compared with that of those who were not because any differences in native capability, past experience, and parental engagement will be equally and randomly assigned between the two samples. Those comparisons meet the highest standards of valid statistical comparison.

The education foundation EdChoice evaluated multiple studies of the educational outcomes of publicly sponsored scholarship programs to private schools. Each of the evaluated studies used two randomly assigned samples from the same population to measure performance. Sixty-five percent of the studies found significant improvements in academic performance for those students who were randomly selected for the programs.[27] Seventy-one percent produced students who had greater educational attainment in completing high school, enrolling in college, and graduating from college than their peers who had applied but had not been selected randomly for the programs.[28]

Similar positive results have also been found for charter schools. While charter schools are public, they are free of many of the government regulations that inhibit traditional public schools. As with scholarship programs, admission to charter schools is also almost always by random selection, so comparing the outcomes of those selected with those left behind is relatively straightforward and the most accurate form of research assessment.

At charter schools run by Success Academy in New York City, 94 percent of the students are non-White, and three-quarters are poor enough to qualify for the free school lunch program. Yet they scored in the top 1 percent of all New York State schools in math and in the top 3 percent in English. Among fourth and eighth graders in these schools, 100 percent passed the state science test, and 90 percent scored at the highest level of excellence. Among Black students at Success Academy, 94 percent passed the math exam, and 96 percent of Hispanic students passed. Citywide, only 56 percent of White students passed.[29]

Mathematica Policy Research studied the performance of students in the Knowledge Is Power Program (KIPP), a network of 125 schools with forty-one thousand students in twenty states and DC. The students were 96 percent Black or Hispanic, with 80 percent from households qualifying for subsidized school lunch. Before admission to the KIPP schools, on average, they had scored at the forty-fifth percentile level in district-wide reading and math exams. After three years, KIPP students were eleven months ahead of local noncharter schools in math, eight months ahead in English, fourteen months in science, and eleven months in social studies.[30]

Stanford University's Center for Research on Education Outcomes reported on Uncommon Schools, another New York City charter network with fifteen schools and thirty-nine hundred students. By the end of a single year, 87 percent of the students in these schools scored at the "advanced" or "proficient" level in mathematics—twenty-seven points above the city average. More than half scored as advanced or proficient in English—eight points above the city average.[31]

The Stanford Center also conducted research on charter schools in Michigan. The charter school enrollments were 70 percent from poverty households versus only 43 percent in local noncharter public schools. On math examinations, 42 percent of classes in the charter schools outperformed classes in noncharter public schools in math, and only 6 percent underperformed; 37 percent outperformed in reading, and only 2 percent underperformed. In statewide rankings of school performance, 82 percent of charter schools increased their rank relative to other schools.[32] In its 2015 follow-up study, the Stanford team showed that charter-school students on average gained an additional two months of learning in math and reading for each year they attended a charter school when compared to the government-operated schools. In Detroit, they gained three months.[33]

In what may be the most telling evaluation of all, a paper in the *Journal of Policy Analysis and Management* reported that charter school pupils are not only more likely to graduate from high school and attend college but also more successful in their college studies and after graduation make higher salaries than their peers who remained in traditional public schools.[34]

EdChoice also evaluated studies that measure the impact of voucher and scholarship programs on the performance of students who remained behind in the public schools from whence the scholarship recipients came. An overwhelming 93 percent of the studies found that the students who remained in the original schools also posted improvements in their educational outcomes.[35] This particular finding is especially important because it suggests that when there is competition and choice, everyone benefits. When parents and dedicated teachers are shown evidence of significant progress from schools that are run on a different model, they begin to demand change and work to make improvements in the way their government schools are conducted; thus, even those who remain in traditional public schools can benefit.[36]

If we are as a nation serious about providing all children with a good elementary and secondary education as a basis for them to develop their own potential, then we need to let the money follow the children and let them and their parents decide how to spend it on the educational experience that best meets their needs and gives them the best opportunity to succeed in school and prosper in life. The experience with charter schools, vouchers, tax-advantaged scholarship funds, and even homeschooling have all shown that school choice can deliver superior results and do so at lower costs. If we are providing tax money to educate the nation's children, then, instead of funding the education bureaucracy, why shouldn't parents have the right to use their children's share of that money to send their children to parochial, private, or charter schools if they believe their children will get a better education there? After all, we do not allow government to select the car we drive, pick the breakfast fruit we eat, or decide what movies we watch, so why should we continue to allow government to force any parent to accept the teacher, textbooks, or extracurricular activities for our most precious responsibility as parents: preparing our children for a productive and happy life? If some parents believe the public schools are best, of course they can send their money and children there, but who has a better claim to the right to choose how children are educated than their parents? Surely there are but a few who would have the hubris to argue that teachers, administrators, and elected officials love our children as much as we do.

Education reform is difficult politically because the public school system is the largest employer in many American counties. School boards, superintendents, and teachers' unions are well organized, well funded, highly centralized, and powerful not just in local government but also in the nation's state legislatures and in Washington, DC. Education policy has become a typical political power play. On the one hand are the entrenched interests who view government-run schools as their domain, and maintaining control of them has become their major objective. On the other hand, in this unequal battle, are low- and middle-income parents fighting individually and in small local groups for the equal opportunity promised to their children. The outcome of the struggle will determine whether schools are run for the benefit of those who run them or for the benefit of the students who attend them. This conflict will also determine whether equality of opportunity in the American creed is a hollow promise. No amount of welfare, quotas, or set-asides can compensate for a failure to give our children a real opportunity to find their intellectual legs in elementary and high school and have an open field and a fair chance in life.

Government as a Barrier to Opportunity

In addition to disincentivizing work and failing to provide adequate primary and secondary education to promote equal opportunity, government has restricted opportunity in other ways. State licensing requirements erect artificial barriers to economic success by imposing unnecessary requirements that limit the earning potential for some while granting privileges to others. These suppressions of individual initiative are modern versions of the old guild system from the Middle Ages, imposing government licensing requirements to limit competition and letting government tilt the competitive scales in favor of its chosen cronies. Unfortunately, unlike most medieval holdovers that have been systematically rooted out by the Enlightenment and the Industrial Revolution, this one has become even more oppressive. In the 1950s, only one in twenty workers faced government licensing requirements as a condition for holding their job, but by 2012 more than one in four faced government restrictions on their ability to earn a living.[37] There are at least 102 lower- to middle-income occupations that require licensing in one or more states. On average, they require almost a full year of specialized preparation to receive a license.[38]

Licensing requirements usually hide behind dubious pleas for public health and safety. It might seem plausible that emergency medical technicians would need the approximately one month of training required, on average, by states, but seventy-three other occupations require more.[39] One is hard pressed to imagine the compelling need for licensing hair braiders, auctioneers, manicurists, waste haulers, animal breeders, animal trainers, taxidermists, upholsterers, florists, forest workers, home entertainment installers, itinerant wholesale produce dealers, bartenders, or street entertainers.[40]

There is little or no evidence that we are a safer society as a result of the proliferation of state licensing requirements. The mere fact that only 23 of the 102 low- to middle-income jobs required licensing in more than forty states indicates the lack of compelling public value in many of the licenses. Yet the practice continues and grows. New York State recently added a new requirement that entry-level shampoo assistants in beauty parlors and barber shops must complete a five-hundred-hour training course at an average cost of $13,240 before they can practice this complex art that most of us perform daily without mishap. Of course, three of the four regulators issuing this requirement have economic interests in companies that sell the required training.[41]

Cronyism is a system practiced at all levels of government where the politically powerful grant valuable favors and privilege to boost earnings of the privileged without creating value in the marketplace. The result of cronyism is to override merit and raise the income of those granted favor at the expense of the rest of us. Of course, government favor is granted in the name of some high "public purpose" rather than explicitly to benefit a crony interest. Quotas, preferences, set-asides, noncompetitive bidding, and the granting of monopolies, subsidies, and tariffs are fertile areas for cronyism.

As Washington has become not only the center of political power but also a massive dispenser of privilege and wealth, it has become the epicenter of cronyism in America. You would think the richest counties in the United States might be near centers of technology like Silicon Valley, inhabited by big financial tycoons in or near the nation's financial center in New York City, or near vast natural resources, like Houston. But today all five of the highest-income counties in the entire nation are suburbs of Washington, DC.[42] Should that not be a source of concern?

If high-income individuals were clustered around Silicon Valley or Wall Street, it would be because those were the locations where market forces generate vast amounts of economic value. The richest counties are now clustered around the center of government power, suggesting that government power is a leading source of income. Eliminating cronyism will not just benefit citizens, consumers, and taxpayers; it will also open the gateway for merit, competition, and equality of opportunity.

Equality through Self-Sufficiency

This book has demonstrated that failing to count all government transfer payments as income to the recipients, not treating taxes as income lost to the taxpayer, and using price indexes that are acknowledged by the very government agencies that produce them to overstate inflation has caused our official statistics to understate consistently the extraordinary ability of ordinary people to succeed, to overstate income inequality, and to understate well-being. These misleading indicators, in turn, have skewed the political debate on spending, taxing, and the role of government in American society. As a nation, we need to get our facts straight. Based on those facts, we can then decide what kind of America we want.

Ronald Reagan laid out the case for change that we still struggle to fulfill: "How can we love our country and not love our countrymen; and loving them, reach out a hand when they fall, heal them when they're sick, and provide opportunity to make them self-sufficient so they will be equal in fact and not just in theory?"[43]

America's promise is centered on opportunity. When we as individuals lend a helping hand, we help others up. But if all our government does is provide subsidies to those who have fallen, it is letting them down and too often keeping them down. America promised them much more, a chance to develop their God-given abilities and put them to work for themselves and their families. Our goal must be an America where people can rise as high and go as far as the sweat of their own brows will take them and know the triumph of that achievement, whether it be large or small, belongs uniquely to them and those who love them.

Appendix A

FEDERAL GOVERNMENT TRANSFER PROGRAMS

The following list of federal transfer programs comes from the US Senate Budget Committee, "CRS Report: Welfare Spending the Largest Item in the Federal Budget," Washington, DC, 2013, and the Congressional Research Service (CRS), "Spending for Federal Benefits and Services for People with Low Income, FY 2001–2011: An Update of Table B-1 from CRS Report R41625," October 16, 2012. The updated dollar values used in the main text come from the Bureau of Economic Analysis, National Income and Product Accounts, which, however, do not include so-called unattributable benefits in the CRS report. Attributable transfers tie each dollar to a specific person's name; unattributable transfers often have client lists of who receives benefits, but the individual value of the benefit is not tracked. The original list of programs has been augmented by so-called social insurance programs, Affordable Care Act (ACA) subsidies, student loan interest subsidies, and Lifeline telephones. The "social insurance" programs and student loans were simply out of scope for the CRS inquiry since they were already documented. The ACA subsidies were not yet active at the time of the report, and the Lifeline program is funded through Federal Communication Commission fees and not under Senate Budget Committee purview. The original list has been rearranged to show which programs are included in the Census money income and Congressional Budget Office (CBO) estimates.

At Least Partially in Both Census Money Income Estimates and CBO Estimates

1. Social Security Old-Age and Survivors Insurance
2. Social Security Disability Insurance
3. Unemployment Insurance

4. Workers' Compensation
5. Supplemental Security Income (SSI)
6. Temporary Assistance for Needy Families (TANF) (cash aid)
7. Transitional Cash for Refugees

At Least Partially in Census Money Income Estimates but Not CBO

8. Federal Pell Grants

At Least Partially in CBO Estimates but Not Census

9. Medicare
10. Medicaid
11. Earned Income Tax Credit (refunded component)
12. Additional Child Tax Credit (refunded component)
13. Supplemental Nutrition Assistance Program (SNAP)
14. State Children's Health Insurance Program (CHIP)
15. National School Lunch Program (free/reduced price components)
16. School Breakfast Program (free/reduced price components)
17. Section 8 Housing Choice Vouchers
18. Section 8 Project-Based Rental Assistance
19. Miscellaneous other housing assistance
20. Low-Income Home Energy Assistance Program (LIHEAP)
21. Voluntary Medicare Prescription Drug Benefit—Low-Income Subsidy
22. Payments for cost-sharing reduction under Affordable Care Act (effective 2014)

Attributable Transfers Not in Census or CBO Estimates

23. Special Supplemental Nutrition Program for Women, Infants, and Children (WIC)
24. Single-Family Rural Housing Loans
25. Rural Rental Assistance Program
26. Temporary Assistance for Needy Families (TANF) (social services)

Unattributable Transfers Not in Census or CBO Estimates

27. Public Housing
28. Family Planning
29. Consolidated Health Centers

30. Transitional Medical Services for Refugees
31. Ryan White HIV/AIDS Program
32. Breast/Cervical Cancer Early Detection
33. Maternal and Child Health Block Grant
34. Indian Health Service
35. Child and Adult Care Food Program (lower-income components)
36. Summer Food Service Program
37. Commodity Supplemental
38. The Emergency Food Assistance Program (TEFAP)
39. Nutrition Program for the Elderly
40. Indian Education
41. Adult Basic Education Grants to States
42. Federal Supplemental Educational Opportunity Grant
43. Education for the Disadvantaged—Grants to Local Educational Agencies (Title I-A)
44. Title I Migrant Education Program
45. Higher Education—Institutional Aid and Developing Institutions
46. Federal Work-Study
47. Federal TRIO Programs
48. Education for Homeless Children and Youth
49. 21st Century Community Learning Centers
50. Gaining Early Awareness and Readiness for Undergraduate Programs (GEAR-UP)
51. Reading First and Early Reading First
52. Rural Education Achievement Program
53. Mathematics and Science Partnerships
54. Improving Teacher Quality State Grants
55. Academic Competitiveness and Smart Grant Program
56. Water and Waste Disposal for Rural Communities
57. Public Works and Economic Development
58. Supportive Housing for the Elderly
59. Supportive Housing for Persons with Disabilities
60. Community Development Block Grants
61. Homeless Assistance Grants
62. Home Investment Partnerships Program (HOME)
63. Housing Opportunities for Persons with AIDS (HOPWA)
64. Indian Housing Block Grants
65. Neighborhood Stabilization Program
66. Grants to States for Low-Income Housing in Lieu of Low-Income Housing Credit Allocations
67. Tax Credit Assistance Program
68. Indian Human Services

69. Older Americans Act Grants for Supportive Services and Senior Centers
70. Older Americans Act Family Caregiver Program
71. Child Support Enforcement
72. Community Services Block Grant
73. Child Care and Development Fund
74. Head Start HHS
75. Developmental Disabilities Support and Advocacy Grants
76. Foster Care
77. Adoption Assistance
78. Social Services Block Grant
79. Chafee Foster Care Independence Program
80. Emergency Food and Shelter Program
81. Legal Services Corporation
82. Supplemental Nutrition Assistance Program (SNAP) (employment and training component)
83. Community Service Employment for Older Americans
84. Workforce Investment Act (WIA) Adult Activities
85. Workforce Investment Act (WIA) Youth Activities
86. Social Services and Targeted Assistance for Refugees
87. Temporary Assistance for Needy Families (TANF) (employment and training)
88. Foster Grandparents
89. Job Corps
90. Weatherization Assistance Program

Other Programs Out of Scope for the CRS Report

91. Student Loan Rate Subsidies
92. Federal Communication Commission Lifeline (free telephones)
93. Federal Fellowship Grants
94. Bureau of Indian Affairs Benefits
95. Federal Education Exchange Benefits
96. Compensation for Survivors of Public Safety Officers
97. Compensation of Victims of Crime
98. Pension Guarantee Benefits
99. Disaster Relief Benefits
100. Radiation Exposure Compensation
101. Any other program with less than $100 million in annual spending

Appendix B

PERCENTAGE OF DEGREES BY ACADEMIC DISCIPLINE EARNED BY WOMEN

Table B.1. Degrees earned by women as percentage of the total degrees by academic discipline and level, 1967 and 2017

	Bachelor's degree		Master's degree		Doctorate* degree	
Academic discipline	*1967*	*2017*	*1967*	*2017*	*1967*	*2017*
All	43.4	57.3	35.8	59.4	7.8	53.3
Medicine (MD)	n/a	n/a	n/a	n/a	7.9	47.4
Dentistry	n/a	n/a	n/a	n/a	1.4	47.9
Law	n/a	n/a	n/a	n/a	3.9	49.6
Business and management	8.7	47.1	3.4	47.3	3.1	44.3
Mathematics	37.1	41.8	24.0	43.7	5.5	27.1
Physical sciences	13.6	39.6	11.5	38.1	5.2	32.5
Biological sciences	27.8	61.0	28.1	58.0	15.8	52.4
Architecture	4.3	46.5	5.0	49.3	6.6	49.8
Engineering	0.6	21.5	0.7	24.8	0.4	23.6
Industry and technology	0.7	18.7	0.0	30.3	0.0	23.0
Journalism and communication	40.7	65.4	26.3	70.9	15.6	66.2
Nursing	98.7	87.4	98.6	87.9	100.0	87.3
Education	75.9	81.1	51.5	77.2	5.6	68.4
Military science	0.0	14.5	n/a	n/a	n/a	n/a
Other healthcare	54.8	79.7	24.5	77.9	6.9	61.2
Foreign languages and literature	72.7	68.5	57.4	64.3	28.9	59.0
Social sciences	36.4	55.9	31.4	68.3	12.2	49.3
Psychology	42.1	78.2	33.3	79.7	22.6	74.8
Library science	90.3	89.9	79.7	82.6	31.8	69.0
English and literature	67.3	70.4	56.6	66.8	26.6	61.5
Fine and applied arts	59.3	61.3	43.6	56.8	18.9	54.2
Geography and culture	21.8	72.6	16.0	65.4	2.1	65.6
Religion and philosophy	24.3	34.2	20.7	35.1	3.3	26.2
Family and consumer science	97.3	87.9	94.7	86.8	71.8	75.7
Agriculture and natural resources	3.2	52.8	4.3	55.6	1.9	48.4
Other and miscellaneous	31.3	55.8	23.1	53.1	9.8	54.5

Notes:

*Including professional such as MD, DDS, and JD.

n/a = not applicable.

Sources: Calculated from Table 112 in Kenneth A. Simon and W. Vance Grant, *Digest of Education Statistics, 1969 Edition* (Washington, DC: National Center for Education Statistics, 1969), 82, https://files.eric.ed.gov/fulltext/ED035996.pdf. Table 318.30 in Thomas D. Snyder, Cristobal de Brey, and Sally A. Dillow, *Digest of Education Statistics, 2018*, 54th ed. (Washington, DC: National Center for Education Statistics, 2019), 308, https://nces.ed.gov/pubs2020/2020009.pdf. Because the two years used different criteria to categorize the disciplines, they had to be combined in ways that were roughly consistent across the years. Academic disciplines are arranged approximately from highest to lowest earnings by holders of the degree. The ranking is approximate because no standard source exists for earnings of many of the heterogeneous discipline categories, and many degrees map poorly into occupational earnings data.

Appendix C

PERCENTAGE CHANGE IN MEASURES OF WELL-BEING WITH DIFFERENT PRICE ADJUSTMENTS, 1967–2017

Figure C.1 summarizes the effects of improved price measurement on the fifty-year trends in major measures of well-being. The percentage increase in average hourly earnings almost quadruples when the Chained Consumer Price Index for All Urban Consumers (C-CPI-U) and Personal Consumption Expenditure Price Index (PCEPI) are used for inflation adjustment to eliminate substitution bias. It more than doubles yet again when improved adjustments are made for the effects of new products on the inflation measure. The growth in median household income is increased by almost half when corrected for substitution bias and almost doubles beyond that when more accurate new-product adjustments are applied.

Real gross domestic product and productivity are already calculated to avoid substitution bias, but they respectively grow 50 percent and 100 percent faster with better adjustments for new-product effects. The poverty rate is cut by a third when the C-CPI-U and PCEPI are used to reduce substitution bias. It is cut in half again with more accurate new-product adjustments. When the missing transfer payments are added to the income used to determine the poverty rate, it declines by 92 percent over the last fifty years.

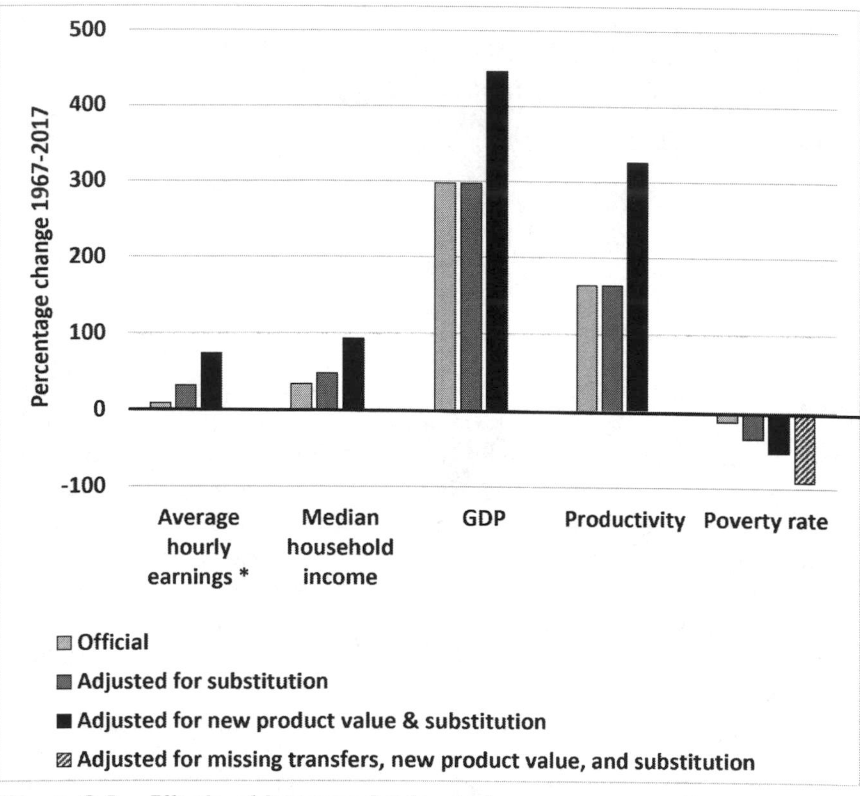

Figure C.1. Effects of improved price index measurements on measures of well-being, 1967–2017.

*For production and nonsupervisory employees.

Sources: Average hourly earnings for production and nonsupervisory employees and productivity from Bureau of Labor Statistics. Median household income from Bureau of the Census, adjusted for 2003 and 2013 discontinuities. Gross domestic product (GDP) from Bureau of Economic Analysis. Substitution adjustments are not required for GDP and productivity. Substitution adjustment for average hourly earnings and median household income calculated from Personal Consumption Expenditure Price Index and Chained Consumer Price Index for All Urban Consumers. New product value calculated from Bruce D. Meyer and James X. Sullivan, "Winning the War on Poverty: Poverty from the Great Society to the Great Recession," Working Paper no. 18718, National Bureau of Economic Research, January 2013, http://www.nber.org/papers/w18718; Brent R. Moulton, "The Measurement of Output, Prices, and Productivity: What's Changed since the Boskin Commission?" Brookings Institution, July 2018, https://www.brookings.edu/research/themeasurement-of-output-prices-and-productivity. Missing transfers calculated from Bureau of the Census, Current Population Survey, Annual Social and Economic Supplement, various years, and Table 2.2.

Appendix D
OCCUPATIONS OF HIGH EARNERS

Table D.1 shows the percentages of tax filers who claimed different occupations on their income tax filings for the top 1.0 percent and the top 0.1 percent of filers by income. In general, they show that the vast majority of the highest-income filers worked in a wide variety of occupations across the economy for their income. Very few simply lived off their wealth.

Interpreting these data requires a few technical notes. The occupations were identified by taxpayer self-reporting, which in turn was coded by the Internal Revenue Service into several dozen job titles, which were further combined by the researchers into categories. As a result, one should not attribute too much to fine distinctions. A professor of mathematics might have been put in the "math" slot or the "professor" slot depending on some combination of her specific self-identification and at least two further levels of coding and concatenation.

"Occupation" is an inconsistent combination of the conventional classifications of three different dimensions: occupation, function, and industry. Hence, the chief legal officer of a corporation might identify himself as either a lawyer or an executive. And if the firm is a financial firm, the classification scheme might put him in the financial category.

The "Other known professions" classification includes very disparate items and has greater detail for the 1 percent than for the 0.1 percent. This particular study combines all occupational, functional, and industrial classifications related to finance into one category rather than splitting out executive, operational, technical, and sales functions like in other industries. This process overstates the role of finance compared to others.

Because these are personal income tax data, the income reported is not homogeneous across the occupations. In particular, the totals include both wage and salary income and so-called pass-through income. A CEO, lawyer, doctor, accountant, or farmer hired by a corporation and paid a salary will get a W-2 form

Table D.1. Percentage of top income tax filers by occupation

Occupation (ordered by proportion of top 0.1 percent)	*Top 1 percent*	*Top 0.1 percent*
Executives, managers, supervisors (nonfinance)	31.0	42.5
Financial professions, including management	13.9	18.0
Lawyers	8.4	7.3
Medical	15.7	5.9
Not working or deceased	4.3	3.8
Real estate	3.2	3.7
Arts, media, sports	1.6	3.0
Entrepreneurs, not elsewhere classified	2.3	3.0
Computer, math, engineering, technical (nonfinancial)	4.6	2.9
Business operations (nonfinancial)	3.0	2.9
Other known professions	4.8	2.7
Blue-collar, miscellaneous service	*3.8*	*n/a*
Government, teachers, social services	*0.8*	*n/a*
Pilots	*0.2*	*n/a*
Skilled sales (except finance or real estate)	4.2	2.3
Professors and scientists	1.8	0.9
Farmers and ranchers	0.5	0.6
Unknown	0.9	0.5

Note:
n/a = not available because of confidentiality restrictions.

Source: Tabulation of public-source IRS data for 2005 by Jon Bakija, Adam Cole, and Bradley Heim, "Jobs and Income Growth of Top Earners and the Causes of Changing Income Inequality: Evidence from U.S. Tax Return Data," IDEAS, 2008, https://ideas.repec.org/p/wil/wileco/2010-22.html.

and report the income as wage and salary income. But if that same CEO, doctor, accountant, or farmer is the sole owner of or a partner in a company, then the income reported includes not only his or her personal income but also a share of the earnings of the proprietorship or partnership, even if some of those earnings are retained by the company for investment, operating capital, or reserves.

With these cautions in mind, we can still draw a few relevant conclusions about the income sources for the highest-income households. The vast majority of high-income people earn their money from working hard as business leaders, technical experts, or both. Despite the methodology that exaggerates the financial services count, finance folks are still only a reasonable fraction of the total. The wealthy are hardly dominated by Wall Street.

Only the "Not working or deceased," "Entrepreneurs, not elsewhere classified," and "Unknown" categories could include some people who are only clipping coupons or otherwise just living off accumulated wealth. These three categories are about 7.5 percent of both the 1 percent and the 0.1 percent groups. Considering that this 7.5 percent includes people who died during the tax year and people who are retired, one can reasonably conclude that the "rich but not earning it" category could be no more than 5 percent of the 1 percent.

Appendix E

INTRAGENERATIONAL MOBILITY BY INCOME QUINTILE

Table E.1. Percentage change in individual cash income for the years 1987 to 1996 and 1996 to 2005, for the same individuals by income quintile in the first year of each time period, adjusted for inflation

Quintile of individual cash income in first year	*Percentage change*		*Percentage decreasing more than 50 percent*		*Percentage increasing more than 50 percent*	
	1987 to 1996	*1996 to 2005*	*1987 to 1996*	*1996 to 2005*	*1987 to 1996*	*1996 to 2005*
Bottom	247.5	284.6	8.7	6.8	47.3	53.5
Second	53.9	82.6	6.0	6.6	20.6	26.8
Middle	30.9	52.5	7.0	6.0	11.2	18.3
Fourth	15.6	15.6	8.1	6.7	6.6	10.7
Top	9.6	25.0	14.2	12.5	7.5	8.2
Top 10 percent	10.3	25.8	18.0	16.4	8.9	8.9
Top 5 percent	9.4	27.7	23.2	22.6	10.2	10.4
Top 1 percent	1.6	13.6	37.0	36.7	10.7	12.6
Average of all	24.1	41.0	9.0	7.9	17.0	22.0
Census average	12.7	12.4				

Sources: Table A.6 in "Income Mobility in the U.S. from 1996 to 2005," US Department of the Treasury, November 13, 2007, revised March 2008, https://home.treasury.gov/system/files/131/Report-Income-Mobility-2008.pdf, 22. The data for 1987 to 1996 were originally published in Gerald E. Auten and Geoffrey Gee, "Income Mobility in the U.S.: Evidence from Income Tax Returns for 1987 and 1996," Office of Tax Analysis Paper 99, US Department of the Treasury, May 2007. Census averages calculated from "Table P-7. Region—All People (Both Sexes Combined) by Median and Mean Income: 1974 to 2019," US Census Bureau, https://www.census.gov/data/tables/time-series/demo/income-poverty/historical-income-people.html.

Appendix F

INCOME DISTRIBUTION BY GEOGRAPHIC REGION

Table F.1. Over- and underrepresentation of earned-income quintiles in geographic regions

Earned income quintile	*Percentage by which households are over-/underrepresented in income quintile*							
	Northeast		*Midwest*		*South*		*West*	
	1967	*2017*	*1967*	*2017*	*1967*	*2017*	*1967*	*2017*
Bottom	(12.5)	1.2	(8.0)	(0.6)	20.9	7.9	(4.5)	(13.7)
Second	(8.9)	(8.6)	(8.7)	0.4	22.6	7.0	(11.5)	(5.5)
Middle	5.3	(7.5)	2.5	2.8	(3.3)	1.6	(5.9)	0.5
Fourth	3.9	(3.9)	11.8	4.3	(15.4)	(4.3)	1.4	6.1
Top	12.3	18.8	2.4	(6.9)	(24.7)	(12.2)	20.5	12.6

Note: Numbers in parentheses are the percentage underrepresented. Others are the percentage overrepresented. Regions are defined according to the standard Census definitions.

Sources: Calculated from Bureau of Census, Current Population Survey, Annual Social and Economic Supplement, March 1968 and March 2018, public-use micro data, supplemented with additional sources in Table 2.1.

Notes

CHAPTER 1. INTRODUCTION: OFFICIAL STATISTICAL MEASURES UNDERSTATE AMERICA'S WELL-BEING

1. The sentiment is certainly consistent with Mark Twain, but there is no known documentation that he actually said it, and he is only one of several people to whom similar quotations are attributed. For a little history see "It Ain't What You Don't Know That Gets You into Trouble. It's What You Know for Sure That Just Ain't So," Quote Investigator, https://quoteinvestigator.com/2018/11/18/know-trouble.

2. "Have the Top 0.1% of Americans Made Out like Bandits since 2000?" *The Economist,* May 7, 2020, https://www.economist.com/united-states/2020/05/07/have-the-top-01-of-americans-made-out-like-bandits-since-2000?frsc=dg%7Ce.

3. Bernie Sanders, "The Week in Review, Friday, March 7, 2014," Bernie Sanders, US Senator for Vermont, https://www.sanders.senate.gov/newsroom/recent-business/the-week-in-review-030714.

4. "Table H-3. Mean Household Income Received by Each Fifth and Top 5 Percent, All Races: 1967 to 2017," and "Table H-4. Gini Ratios for Households, by Race and Hispanic Origin of Householder," US Census Bureau, https://www.census.gov/data/tables/time-series/demo/income-poverty/historical-income-inequality.html; "Table 2. Poverty Status of People by Family Relationship, Race, and Hispanic Origin: 1959 to 2018," US Census Bureau, https://www.census.gov/data/tables/time-series/demo/income-poverty/historical-poverty-people.html.

5. Drew DeSilver, "For Most U.S. Workers, Real Wages Have Barely Budged in Decades," Pew Research Center, August 7, 2018, https://www.pewresearch.org/fact-tank/2018/08/07/for-most-us-workers-real-wages-have-barely-budged-for-decades.

6. Basic source: "Table 3.12. Government Social Benefits," and "Table 1.1.9. Implicit Price Deflators for Gross Domestic Product," US Bureau for Economic Analysis, National Income and Product Accounts, https://apps.bea.gov/iTable/iTable.cfm?reqid=19&step=2#reqid=19&step=2&isuri=1&1921=survey. See Table 2.2 for a more complete set of supplementary sources.

7. Emily A. Shrider et al. "Income and Poverty in the United States: 2020," Current Population Reports, P60-273 (Washington, DC: Bureau of the Census, September 2021), 1.

8. Shrider et al., "Income and Poverty in the United States: 2020," 71–72; Liana E. Fox and Kalee Burns, "The Supplemental Poverty Measure: 2020," Current Population Reports, P60-275 (Washington, DC: US Census Bureau, September 2021), www.census.gov/library/publications/2021/demo/p60-275.html.

9. "Table H-3. Mean Household Income Received by Each Fifth and Top 5 Percent, All Races: 1967 to 2017," US Census Bureau, Current Population Survey, Annual Social and Economic Statistics Supplement, Historical Tables, https://www.census.gov/data/tables/time-series/demo/income-poverty/historical-income-households.html.

10. "Table 1101. Quintiles of Income before Taxes: Annual Expenditure Means, Shares, Standard Errors, and Coefficients of Variation," US Bureau of Labor Statistics, Consumer Expenditure Surveys, 2017, https://www.bls.gov/cex/tables/calendar-year/mean-item-share-average-standard-error/cu-income-quintiles-before-taxes-2017.pdf. Excel tables available at "Calendar Year Means, Shares across All Items, and Coefficients of Variation by Demographic Characteristics," US Bureau of Labor Statistics, Consumer Expenditure Surveys, https://www.bls.gov/cex/tables/calendar-year/mean-item-share-average-standard-error.htm#cu-income.

11. Thomas Piketty, *Capital in the Twenty-First Century* (Cambridge, MA: Harvard University Press, 2014), 9.

12. William Blake, "London," *Songs of Experience* (1794).

13. Gregory Clark, "The Condition of the Working Class in England, 1209–2004," *Journal of Political Economy* 113, no. 6 (2005), 1307–40.

14. Clark, "The Condition of the Working Class," 1324–25.

15. N. F. R. Crafts, "Economic Growth in France and Britain, 1830–1910: A Review of the Evidence," *Journal of Economic History* 44, no. 1 (March 1984): Table 1, 51.

16. "How Has Life Expectancy Changed over Time?" Office of National Statistics, September 9, 2015, https://www.ons.gov.uk/peoplepopulationandcommunity/birthsdeathsandmarriages/lifeexpectancies/articles/howhaslifeexpectancychangedovertime/2015-09-09.

17. Thomas E. Jordan, "An Index of the Quality of Life for Victorian Children and Youth, the VICY Index," *Social Indicators Research* 27 (1992): 257–277. https://doi.org/10.1007/BF00300464.

18. Jordan, "An Index of the Quality of Life," 257–77.

19. Clark Nardinelli, *Child Labor and the Industrial Revolution* (Bloomington: University of Indiana Press, 1990), 115.

20. Chelsea Follett, "Scrooge and the Reality of the Victorian Home: Why, for Young Women Especially, Factory Work Was Preferable to Domestic Labor in Dickensian Times," *Human Progress*, December 2018, https://humanprogress.org/article.php?p=1619.

21. Judith Flanders, *Inside the Victorian Home: A Portrait of Domestic Life in Victorian England* (New York: W. W. Norton, 2005).

22. An anonymous woman who ran a lodging house reported by Jessie Boucherett, "Legislative Restrictions on Woman's Labour," *Englishwoman's Review*, 1873, who in

turn was cited by Flanders, *Inside the Victorian Home*, and Follett, "Scrooge and the Reality of the Victorian Home."

CHAPTER 2. INEQUALITY IN PRODUCING AND CONSUMING IN AMERICA

1. An earlier food stamp program during the Depression was ended in 1943.

2. Calculated from US Census Bureau, Current Population Survey, Annual Social and Economic Supplement, March 2018 (data for 2017), public-use file. "The Distribution of Household Income, 2015," Congressional Budget Office (CBO), March 2018, data files "54646-additional-data-for-researchers." "Table 3.12. Government Social Benefits," US Bureau of Economic Analysis, National Income and Product Accounts, July 31, 2018. Social Security Administration, *Annual Statistical Supplement to the Social Security Bulletin, 2017*, Board of Trustees, Federal Old-Age and Survivors Insurance and Federal Disability Insurance Trust Funds, Washington, DC, 2018. Social Security Administration, *The 2018 Annual Report of the Board of Trustees of the Federal Old-Age and Survivors Insurance and Federal Disability Insurance Trust Funds*, Washington, DC, June 5, 2018, Table II.B1, 7. The Boards of Trustees, Federal Hospital Insurance and Federal Supplementary Medical Insurance Trust Funds, *2018 Annual Report of the Boards of Trustees of the Federal Hospital Insurance and Federal Supplementary Medical Insurance Trust Funds*, Washington, DC, June 5, 2018, Table II.B1, 11. "CRS Report: Welfare Spending the Largest Item in the Federal Budget," US Senate Budget Committee, Washington, DC, 2013. "Spending for Federal Benefits and Services for People with Low Income, FY 2001–2011: An Update of Table B-1 from CRS Report R41625," Congressional Research Service, October 16, 2012. US Census Bureau, American Housing Survey, 2017, National—Housing Costs—All Occupied Units, Tenure Filter: Renter. https://www.census.gov/programs-surveys/ahs/data/interactive/ahstablecreator.html. "Federal Student Loans: Education Needs to Improve Its Income-Driven Repayment Plan Budget Estimates," GAO-17-22, US Government Accountability Office, November 2016. "Fair-Value Estimates of the Cost of Federal Credit Programs in 2019, June, 2018," Congressional Budget Office, https://www.cbo.gov/system/files?file=2018-10/54095-2019fairvalueestimates.pdf. "Disbursements 2017," Universal Services Administrative Company, https://www.usac.org/li/about/process-overview/stats/historical-support-distribution.aspx. "Table 2.1—Receipts by Source: 1934–2022" and "Table 2.5—Composition of 'Other Receipts': 1940–2022," Office of Management and Budget, https://www.govinfo.gov/app/collection/budget/2018/BUDGET-2018-TAB. "Table 1. State and Local Government Finances by Level of Government and by State: 2016," US Census Bureau, 2016 Annual Surveys of State and Local Government Finances, https://www.census.gov/data/datasets/2016/econ/local/public-use-datasets.html.

3. See Table 2.4 later in this chapter.

4. Households can consist of a single individual, nuclear families, extended families, or any number of unrelated individuals, so long as they live in the same premises. People living in group quarters such as rooming houses, military barracks, or institutions are not households. The household unit of analysis is almost universally used in compiling

summary data about income. The chief exceptions are data on poverty, which are compiled on a family and unrelated individual basis. Families differ from households in that families must be related by blood, marriage, or legal arrangement like adoption. For the United States, household data began in 1967. Before that, all data were on a family and unrelated individual basis. Of course, this analysis will also look at some data on an individual basis as part of the picture in compiling the household summaries. The household unit is also almost universally applied by other nations. Quintiles are used as the principal grouping by income for most American and many international statistical agencies, although others such as deciles and percentiles are also used. Most Census Bureau data on income by quintile define the quintile based on the total "money income" of the household, which is defined to include most earned income plus some transfer payments. Household quintiles in this book are defined by the amount of earned income. This approach allows for a straightforward, clear understanding of how much income is earned by members of the household, how much is transferred to the household from government subsidies and from private charities, and how much is lost to taxes.

5. Mark Robert Rank, Thomas A. Hirschl, and Kirk A. Foster, *Changing the American Dream: Understanding What Shapes Our Fortunes* (Oxford: Oxford University Press, 2014), 105.

6. As a detailed technical matter, a household rising to a higher quintile may create a very small increase in the original quintile average income if the household that is then forced into the lower quintile has an income that is higher than the original income of the one that earned the promotion. But these changes, when they happen at all, will at most be extremely small and less than rounding error in the published numbers. The important point is that the new increased (or reduced) household income is in a different quintile and does not affect the average of the original quintile.

7. The official government measure for income inequality comes from the Census Bureau and is based on its "money income" measure. See Kayla Fontenot, Jessica Semega, and Melissa Kollar, "Income and Poverty in the United States: 2017," Current Population Reports, P60-263 (Washington, DC: Census Bureau, September 2018), 25–26 and "Table A-2: Selected Measures of Household Income Dispersion: 1967 to 2017," 35. Additional computations from public-use micro files US Census Bureau, Current Population Survey, Annual Social and Economic Supplement, March 2018 (data for 2017), the public-use micro-data source for the published Census data.

This research improved on the Census wage and salary components estimates by incorporating data from the "The Distribution of Household Income, 2015," Congressional Budget Office, November 2018, "54646-additional-data-for-researchers," public-use data files. The CBO estimates have been enhanced from the Internal Revenue Service Statistics of Income to add items omitted by Census or adjust underreporting in its Current Population Survey. CBO improvements added more than $55,000 of average earned household income to the top quintile—mostly from including capital gains omitted by Census and capturing more complete counts of incentive compensation. The bottom quintile average picked up less than $200 from the CBO improvements. Census excludes most employer-paid benefits, the largest being employer pretax contributions to medical insurance. CBO incorporates those benefits—adding about $24,300 to the top quintile average and $500 to the bottom.

Finally, the measures presented here are adjusted to reflect the intensive audit by University of Chicago economists and Census Bureau staff on underreporting of income among very-low-income respondents in Census surveys. Those adjustments increased average earned income in the bottom quintile by a little less than $1,800. See Bruce D. Meyer et al., "The Use and Misuse of Income Data and Extreme Poverty in the United States," Working Paper no. 25907, National Bureau of Economic Research, May 2019.

8. "Databases, Tables & Calculators by Subject," Bureau of Labor Statistics, https://www.bls.gov/data/#wages. "Employer Cost for Employee Compensation" for 2017 showed that medical insurance constituted 8.3 percent of total compensation, followed by 7.4 percent for legally required payments such as Old-Age, Survivors, and Disability Insurance, Medicare, unemployment insurance, and worker compensation. Employer contributions to retirement plans were 5.4 percent of compensation. Premiums for life and disability insurance were 0.5 percent of compensation. Paid leave accounted for 7.0 percent, and premium supplemental pay such as overtime and shift differentials accounted for 3.1 percent. Leave and premium-pay values would be included in the Census estimates for wages and salaries because they collect actual paid amounts, including paid leave and any pay premiums.

9. "The Distribution of Household Income, 2016," Congressional Budget Office, July 2019, 55413-CBO-data-underlying-figures.xlsx, describes the methods used in March 2018, data files "54646-additional-data-for-researchers."

10. Meyer et al., "The Use and Misuse of Income Data and Extreme Poverty in the United States."

11. Medicaid and some other programs include some state funding to qualify for matching grants. To keep the program totals meaningful, both state and federal funding for these programs are included in a single program total under the federal column. The state and local transfers are for exclusively state and local efforts and exclude state contributions to the cooperative federal-state programs.

12. Calculated from "Section 2: Old Age, Survivors, and Disability Insurance" and "Appendix D: Computing a Retired-Worker Benefit," in Social Security Administration, *Annual Statistical Supplement to the Social Security Bulletin, 2017*, Board of Trustees, Federal Old-Age and Survivors Insurance and Federal Disability Insurance Trust Funds, Washington, DC, June 5, 2018, supplemented by minimum wages from US Department of Labor. Effect includes taxes on higher benefits calculated from IRS tax tables. These taxes are returned directly to Social Security for further subsidies of lower-income benefits.

13. National Safety Council, *Accident Facts* (Itasca, IL: National Safety Council, 1994), 46–56. "Census of Fatal Occupational Injuries 2013," US Department of Labor, Bureau of Labor Statistics, September 11, 2014. Andrew Biggs, "Averting the Disability-Insurance Meltdown," *Wall Street Journal*, February 24, 2015. *Social Security Disability Programs: Improving the Quality of Benefit Award Decisions*, Permanent Subcommittee on Investigations of the Committee on Homeland Security and Governmental Affairs, US Senate, September 13, 2012. Nicole Maestas, Kathleen J. Mullen, and Alexander Strand, "Disability Insurance and the Great Recession," *American Economic Review Papers and Proceedings* 105, no. 5 (May 2015): 177–82.

14. The reader might notice that the average Medicaid transfers for all households is slightly larger than the average household transfers for Medicare. That does not seem to

be consistent with the fact that Medicare is the larger program and spends more money annually. There are two principal reasons for average Medicaid transfers to households being larger. First, Medicaid patients pay no premiums or cost sharing, while 80 percent of Medicare patients pay some premiums, deductibles, and coinsurance, which come from their own funds and are not transfer payments. Also, Medicare is often for single-person households and almost never for a household with more than two Medicare beneficiaries. Medicaid, by contrast, covers entire households. Even CHIP frequently covers multiple children in the same household.

15. These include families being enrolled in Medicaid or CHIP during a spell of unemployment followed by several months of a high-paying job, so they have both during the year. Also benefits can be paid to eligible individuals not in the householder's immediate family living in high-income households. Expansions to Medicaid under the Affordable Care Act have also created scenarios that result in Medicaid enrollment at higher incomes. Charles J. Courtemanche, James Marton, and Aaron Yelowitz, "Medicaid Coverage across the Income Distribution under the Affordable Care Act," Working Paper no. 26145, National Bureau of Economic Research, August 2019, https://www.nber.org/papers/w26145?utm_campaign=ntwh&utm_medium=email&utm_source=ntwg1&mod=article_inline. Brian Blase and Aaron Yelowitz, "ObamaCare's Medicaid Deception: States Cover Millions Who Exceed Income Thresholds, Some Quite Well-Heeled," *Wall Street Journal*, August 15, 2019, A15, https://www.wsj.com/articles/obamacares-medicaid-deception-11565822360. "New York Incorrectly Claimed Enhanced Federal Medicaid Reimbursement for Some Beneficiaries," US Department of Health and Human Services, Office of the Inspector General, Audit A-02-1501023, August 20, 2019, https://oig.hhs.gov/oas/reports/region2/21501023.asp. Chris Jacobs, "Medicaid Expansion Has Louisianans Dropping Their Private Plans," *Wall Street Journal*, June 8, 2019, https://www.wsj.com/articles/medicaid-expansion-has-louisianans-dropping-their-private-plans-11559944048.

16. The Earned Income Tax Credit and Child Tax Credit are refundable; that is, if the credit exceeds the income taxes owed, the filer gets the balance in cash, in addition to paying no income tax. On average, the refundable tax credits eliminated all income tax liability in the bottom and second quintiles and delivered an average cash payment of $1,884 and $1,231 to households in the respective quintiles in 2017. Most of these credits are paid on federal income tax returns, but 2.7 percent come from refundable state and local income tax credits.

17. At one time, some argued that food stamps could not be counted because they could be spent only on food, and if a poor family had received cash instead, they might have spent it on something else that was more valuable to them. That argument has largely disappeared because it is prima facie invalid. First, even if the family would have made different choices, that is an indictment of the design of the program, not a measure of the value actually transferred. Second, the dollar value is the amount taken from taxpayers to give the benefit, so in assessing income inequality and poverty, the money taken to pay the benefit must be given full value. Third, the default position of counting food stamps as worth zero is far more ridiculous than any minor loss of utility from limitations to food. Finally, and most important, the construct is purely hypothetical. Food stamp values are set based on the US Department of Agriculture Thrifty Food Plan,

which is computed as the lowest possible cost of food consumption for different family sizes and compositions that still delivers adequate nutrition. For 2017, the maximum food stamp allotment to a family of four was $649.00 per month for families with no earned income. This maximum was reduced for higher eligible incomes ("SNAP—Fiscal Year 2017 Cost-of-Living Adjustments, Memorandum to All Regional Directors, Supplementary Nutrition Assistance Program," August 10, 2016, https://fns-prod.azureedge.net/sites/default/files/snap/SNAP-Fiscal-Year-2017-Cost-of-Living-Adjustments.pdf). This benefit is almost identical to the $642.50 mid-year cost for the Thrifty Food Plan and substantially less than the $845.70 cost of the Economy Food Plan, $1,053.30 for the Moderate Cost Plan, and $1,280.70 for the Liberal Plan ("Official USDA Food Plans: Cost of Food at Home at Four Levels, U.S. Average," July 2017, https://fns-prod.azureedge.net/sites/default/files/CostofFoodJul2017.pdf). It is highly implausible that households would have elected to spend less on food than the minimum nutritionally necessary at the Thrifty Food Plan level.

18. The totals for most government transfers are from "Table 3.12. Government Social Benefits," Bureau of Economic Analysis, National Income and Product Accounts. These payments are the amounts actually given to the individuals or paid to the provider who delivered the service in the beneficiary's name. Transfers exclude the costs for program management and distribution. See Bureau of Economic Analysis (BEA), Concepts and Methods of the US National Income and Product Accounts, 9–10; Appendix, 5; and Glossary, 13–14, https://www.bea.gov/resources/methodologies/nipa-handbook. Major programs such as Social Security and Medicare are included in the BEA reports, but these calculations also use the annual official program reports to provide more detailed analysis. These reports invariably separate the benefits paid from cost of administration. Medicare is a special case because about 80 percent of aged beneficiaries must pay premiums for their coverage. When reporting Medicare transfers, we have subtracted the premium and reported only the true transfers of benefit payments net of premiums. Because deductibles and coinsurance are paid by beneficiaries directly to providers with their own funds, transfers include only the payment from government funds. All transfers are explicitly reported as the amounts going to the beneficiaries and do not include administrative costs.

19. Unattributable transfers are not included in the National Income and Product Accounts Social Benefits but are separately accounted for by US Senate Budget Committee, "CRS Report: Welfare Spending the Largest Item in the Federal Budget," 2013, and the Congressional Research Service, "Spending for Federal Benefits and Services for People with Low Income, FY2008–2011: An Update of Table B-1 from CRS Report R41625," October 16, 2012.

20. Administrative and overhead costs are accounted for separately and not included in transfers reported here. Administrative and overhead costs would add less than 1 percent to the total taxpayer cost for large, administratively simple programs like Social Security, almost 2 percent for Medicare, and more than 7 percent for food stamps. Social Security Administration, *Annual Statistical Supplement to the Social Security Bulletin, 2017*, Board of Trustees, Federal Old-Age and Survivors Insurance and Federal Disability Insurance Trust Funds, Washington, DC, June 5, 2018. Social Security Administration, *The 2018 Annual Report of the Board of Trustees of the Federal Old-Age*

and Survivors Insurance and Federal Disability Insurance Trust Funds, Washington, DC, June 5, 2018, Table II.B1, 7. The Boards of Trustees, Federal Hospital Insurance and Federal Supplementary Medical Insurance Trust Funds, *2018 Annual Report of the Boards of Trustees of the Federal Hospital Insurance and Federal Supplementary Medical Insurance Trust Funds*, Washington, DC, June 5, 2018, Table II.B1, 11. "Policy Basics: The Supplemental Nutrition Assistance Program (SNAP)," Center for Budget and Policy Priorities, https://www.cbpp.org/research/food-assistance/policy-basics-the-supplemental-nutrition-assistance-program-snap.

21. The overall average was calculated from service-specific percentages in Trudy Millard Krause, Maria Ukhanova, and Frances Lee Revere, "Private Carriers' Physician Payment Rates Compared with Medicare and Medicaid," *Texas Medicine* 112, no. 6 (June 2016): 1. The Medicare–private fee differences vary widely by the particular service and also vary by geography and carrier. The differences have also grown over the last two decades. Compare S. Norton and S. Zuckerman, "Trends in Medicaid Physician Fees, 1993–1998," *Health Affairs* 19, no. 4 (2000): 222–32; M. E. Miller, S. Zuckerman, and M. Gates, "How Do Medicare Physician Fees Compare with Private Payers?" *Health Care Finance Review* 14, no. 3 (1993): 25–39; W. Fox and J. Pickering, "Hospital and Physician Cost Shift: Payment Level Comparison of Medicare, Medicaid and Commercial Payers," *Milliman Report* (December 2008), https://www.aha.org/aha/content/2008/pdf/081209costshift.pdf; and J. Clemens and J. Gottlieb, "Bargaining in the Shadow of a Giant: Medicare's Influence on Private Payment Systems," Working Paper no. 19503, National Bureau of Economic Research, October 2013. Medicare and Medicaid are government-run insurance companies. Market insurance policies include not only the cost of the medical bills they pay but also the cost of administering the insurance policies, preventing fraud, and bearing the risk with sufficient capital. All of these market elements of health insurance are excluded from the transfer payments.

22. US Senate Budget Committee, "CRS Report: Welfare Spending the Largest Item in the Federal Budget," 2013. Congressional Research Service, "Spending for Federal Benefits and Services for People with Low Income, FY 2001–2011: An Update of Table B-1 from CRS Report R41625," October 16, 2012. US Census Bureau, *American Housing Survey, 2017*, National—Housing Costs—All Occupied Units, Tenure Filter: Renter. "Table 3.12. Government Social Benefits," US Bureau of Economic Analysis, National Income and Product Accounts, July 31, 2018, https://apps.bea.gov/iTable/iTable.cfm?reqid=19&step=2#reqid=19&step=2&isuri=1&1921=survey.

23. The definition of "money income" originates with the release of the 1946 income estimates from the Census Bureau's Survey of Population, Labor Force, and Housing, April 1947, in which transfer payments are given only the following brief definition: "Social Security, unemployment compensation, workmen's compensation, nonveteran Federal State, and local pensions and assistance, etc." from "Current Population Reports: Consumer Income," Series P-60 No. 1 Rev., January 28, 1948, Washington, DC, 4. The designation of "etc." is not particularly clear or compelling. The only earlier Census estimates were for 1939 from the 1940 Decennial Census and an earlier prototype survey for 1944, neither of which included transfer payments. Because, except for Social Security, transfer payments were rare and very small, their definition and justification were given little attention, whereas the same document goes into great detail on how to treat wages,

salaries, the operating costs for farms, and dozens of other components of income. So far as our research shows, there was never any systematic consideration of what should be included in transfer payments, and the 1946 definition was largely unchanged for the next seventy-one years. Since there were no food stamps, public housing, energy subsidies, or healthcare transfers in 1946, naturally they were not mentioned, and Census never stopped to consider, so far as we can tell, that these should be added when they entered the income stream. (Note that we use 1947 as our base year rather than 1946 because the later survey was more robust and had more of the detail we needed to maintain some continuity with the later estimates.)

24. The overall average was calculated by the author from service-specific percentages in Krause, Ukhanova, and Revere, "Private Carriers' Physician Payment Rates Compared with Medicare and Medicaid," e1. The Medicare–private fee differences vary widely by the particular service and also vary by geography and carrier. The differences have also grown over the last two decades. Compare Norton and Zuckerman, "Trends in Medicaid Physician Fees, 1993–1998," 222–32; Miller, Zuckerman, and Gates, "How Do Medicare Physician Fees Compare with Private Payers?" 25–39; Fox and Pickering, "Hospital and Physician Cost Shift"; and Clemens and Gottlieb, "Bargaining in the Shadow of a Giant."

25. See Table 2.2 and Table 2.4.

26. "The Distribution of Household Income, 2015," Congressional Budget Office, March 2018, data files "54646-additional-data-for-researchers"; "Table 3.12. Government Social Benefits," US Bureau of Economic Analysis, National Income and Product Accounts, July 31, 2018. US Senate Budget Committee, "CRS Report: Welfare Spending the Largest Item in the Federal Budget," 2013. Congressional Research Service, "Spending for Federal Benefits and Services for People with Low Income, FY 2001–2011." US Census Bureau, *American Housing Survey, 2017*. "Federal Student Loans: Education Needs to Improve Its Income-Driven Repayment Plan Budget Estimates," GAO-17-22, US Government Accountability Office, November 2016. "Fair-Value Estimates of the Cost of Federal Credit Programs in 2019," Congressional Budget Office, June 2018, https://www.cbo.gov/system/files?file=2018-10/54095-2019fairvalueestimates.pdf. For the Federal Communication Commission, see "Disbursements 2017," Universal Services Administrative Company, https://www.usac.org/li/about/process-overview/stats/historical-support-distribution.aspx. "Table 2.1—Receipts by Source: 1934–2022" and "Table 2.5—Composition of 'Other Receipts': 1940–2022," Office of Management and Budget, https://www.govinfo.gov/app/collection/budget/2018/BUDGET-2018-TAB. "Table 1. State and Local Government Finances by Level of Government and by State: 2016," US Census Bureau, 2016 Annual Surveys of State and Local Government Finances.

27. Jeffrey C. Moore, Linda L. Stinson, and Edward J. Welniak Jr., "Income Measurement Error in Surveys: A Review," US Bureau of the Census, 1997, https://www.census.gov/content/dam/Census/library/working-papers/1997/adrm/sm97-05.pdf. Erik Hurst, Geng Li, and Benjamin Pugsley, "Are Household Surveys Like Tax Forms: Evidence from Income Underreporting of the Self-Employed," Finance and Economics Discussion Series, Divisions of Research & Statistics and Monetary Affairs, Federal Reserve Board, Washington, DC, 2010, https://www.federalreserve.gov/pubs

/feds/2011/201106/201106pap.pdf. Bilal Habib, "How CBO Adjusts for Underreporting of Means-Tested Transfers in Its Distributional Analyses," Working Paper no. 2018-07, Congressional Budget Office, July 2018, www.cbo.gov/publication/54234. Where possible, totals are benchmarked and adjusted against reported program totals—for example, Social Security Administration, *Annual Statistical Supplement to the Social Security Bulletin, 2017*, Board of Trustees, Federal Old-Age and Survivors Insurance and Federal Disability Insurance Trust Funds, Washington, DC, June 5, 2018. Social Security Administration, *The 2018 Annual Report of the Board of Trustees of the Federal Old-Age and Survivors Insurance and Federal Disability Insurance Trust Funds*, Washington, DC, June 5, 2018, Table II.B1, 7. The Boards of Trustees, Federal Hospital Insurance and Federal Supplementary Medical Insurance Trust Funds, *2018 Annual Report of the Boards of Trustees of the Federal Hospital Insurance and Federal Supplementary Medical Insurance Trust Funds*, Washington, DC, June 5, 2018, Table II.B1, 11.

For a catalog of international practice on adjustment to coherence, see country-specific detailed meta-data information at the OECD Income Distribution Database (https://www.oecd.org/social/income-distribution-database.htm).

28. "Gross Domestic Philanthropy: An International Analysis of GDP, Tax and Giving," Charities Aid Foundation, January 2016, https://www.cafamerica.org/4397-2. Americans donated almost twice as much in relation to GDP as the second- and third-place charitable-giving nations, New Zealand and Canada. Charitable donations in America were almost three times the level in Great Britain and approximately ten times more than in Germany, Sweden, France, or Norway.

29. Computed from US Census Bureau, Current Population Survey (CPS), Annual Social and Economic Supplement, March 2018 (data for 2017), public-use file. Giving Institute, *Giving USA: The Annual Report on Philanthropy, 2018*, https://nonprofits source.com/online-giving-statistics/#Charitable. A little more than half of private transfers were from child support, alimony, and regular payments from family reported in the CPS. The remainder was from private charitable institutions.

30. "Gross Domestic Philanthropy."

31. The estimates for federal taxes in Table 2.3 come primarily from the CBO, supplemented with data from OMB for the approximately 5 percent of taxes not included by CBO. State and local taxes are calculated from the Census Bureau, *2017 Annual Surveys of State and Local Government Finances.*

32. Fontenot, Semega, and Kollar, "Income and Poverty in the United States: 2017," 35.

33. The Congressional Budget Office publishes another official government measure of income inequality, but it generally receives less attention. It is more complete than the Census measure because it includes items that are missing from the Census calculations. It includes employer-paid benefits and capital gains as earned income. It also more than doubles the amount of transfer payments counted as income, compared to Census. And it reduces income by the amount of federal taxes paid. As a result, it shows that the average household in the top quintile had 6.1 times the income of the average household in the bottom quintile. The CBO ratio of top-to-bottom income is 63 percent smaller than the Census measure but still 52 percent greater than the ratio when using the more complete numbers in Table 2.4 because CBO still omits about

one-quarter of transfer payments and does not adjust for state and local taxes. "The Distribution of Household Income, 2016," Congressional Budget Office, July 2019, https://www.cbo.gov/publication/55413.

34. The OECD, CBO, and a number of other nations adjust income for household size by dividing by the square root of the number of people in the household. Census uses a somewhat more complex adjustment it calls an "equivalence scale." Recall from elementary school that the square root of a number is another number that, when multiplied by itself (squared), gives the original number. The square root of 2, for example, is 1.4142. The formulas for the equivalence scale are as follows: one and two adults: scale = $(\text{adults})^{0.5}$; single parents: scale = $(\text{adults} + 0.8 \times \text{first child} + 0.5 \times \text{other children})^{0.7}$; all other families: scale = $(\text{adults} + 0.5 \times \text{children})^{0.7}$. The superscripts are fractional powers. For the mathematically curious, see Liana Fox, "The Supplemental Poverty Measure: 2017," Current Population Reports, P60-265, US Census Bureau, September 2018, www.census.gov/library/publications/2018/demo/p60-265.html. The practical results of the different adjustments are shown below:

	Adjustment factors		
	Divide income by . . .		
Type of adjustment	*Number of persons (per capita)*	*Square root of number of persons*	*Equivalence scale*
Type of household			
One adult	1.000	1.000	1.000
Two adults	2.000	1.414	1.414
One adult, one child	2.000	1.414	1.509
One adult, two children	3.000	1.732	1.791
Two adults, one child	3.000	1.732	1.899
Two adults, two children	4.000	2.000	2.158

CHAPTER 3. POVERTY IN AMERICA

1. Lyndon B. Johnson, "Special Message to Congress Proposing a Nationwide War on the Sources of Poverty," Teaching American History, March 16, 1964, https://teachingamericanhistory.org/library/document/special-message-to-congress-proposing-a-nationwide-war-on-the-sources-of-poverty.

2. The "economical" was the least expensive of four different diets developed by the US Department of Agriculture. All four met or exceeded the minimum daily requirements for all established nutrients. The differences existed in terms of the variety and grade of items consumed. High-cost diets also included more food away from home and a greater percentage of prepared dishes.

3. While the three-times food consumption was applied for most cases, the Social Security Administration made upward adjustments for one- and two-person families and for families with senior citizens. Also note that a number of other research projects at

the same time had arrived at similar family budget numbers for poverty. See Gordon M. Fisher, "The Development of the Orshansky Poverty Thresholds and Their Subsequent History as the Official U.S. Poverty Measure," Department of Health and Human Services, May 1992, http://aspe.hhs.gov/poverty/papers/hptgssiv.htm.

4. US Census Bureau, Current Population Survey, Annual Social and Economic Supplement, March 2018 (data for 2017). Excluded transfers: calculations on US Census Bureau, Current Population Survey, Annual Social and Economic Supplement, March 2018 (data for 2017), full public-use micro-data file, and "The Distribution of Household Income and Federal Taxes, 2015," Congressional Budget Office, www.cbo.gov/publication/54646. Correcting underreporting: in addition to CBO improved estimates, also incorporated: Bruce D. Meyer et al., "The Use and Misuse of Income Data and Extreme Poverty in the United States," Working Paper no. 25907, National Bureau of Economic Research, May 2019. See Social Security Administration, *Annual Statistical Supplement to the Social Security Bulletin, 2018*, Washington, DC, https://www.ssa.gov/policy/docs/statcomps/supplement/2018/index.html, for Social Security, Medicare, unemployment benefits, workers' compensation, and black lung. US Senate Budget Committee, "CRS Report: Welfare Spending the Largest Item in the Federal Budget," 2013. Congressional Research Service, "Spending for Federal Benefits and Services for People with Low Income, FY2008–2011: An Update of Table B-1 from CRS Report R41625," October 16, 2012. For poverty thresholds: Kayla Fontenot, Jessica Semega, and Melissa Kollar, "Income and Poverty in the United States: 2017," Current Population Reports, P60-263 (Washington, DC: Census Bureau, September 2018), 43. Calculations by authors. Note that all calculations are at the level of forty-eight family types. The summary income and threshold values are the rolled-up results of those calculations.

5. US Census Bureau, Department of Commerce, "Income and Poverty in the United States: 2013," Current Population Reports, P60-249 (Washington, DC: Bureau of the Census, September 2014), 4. These data come from the Survey of Program Participation (SIPP) from the Bureau of the Census, which provides information on different time frames. Data relate to the 2009–2011 period, during which time the average poverty rate was 14.8 percent. Computations from reported Census data.

6. Computed from the US Census, Current Population Survey, Annual Social and Economic Supplement, March 2018, public-use micro files.

7. Meyer and Sullivan used improved consumer price indexes much like the ones that will be discussed in Chapter 6.

8. Bruce D. Meyer and James X. Sullivan, "Annual Report on U.S. Consumption Poverty: 2017," University of Chicago and University of Notre Dame, October 31, 2018. The foundational research is from Bruce D. Meyer and James X. Sullivan, "Winning the War on Poverty: Poverty from the Great Society to the Great Recession," Working Paper no. 18718, National Bureau of Economic Research, January 2013, http://www.nber.org/papers/w18718. Earlier research by others has reached similar conclusions: Daniel T. Slesnick, *Consumption and Social Welfare: Living Standards and Their Distribution in the United States* (New York: Cambridge University Press, 2001), 154 ff, and Dirk Krueger and Fabrizio Perri, "Does Income Inequality Lead to Consumption Inequality?" *Review of Economic Studies*, March 2006. A compendium of earlier views is in Orazio Attanasio, Erich Battistin, and Hidehiko Ichimura, "What Really Happened

to Consumption Inequality in the U.S.?" in *Measurement Issues in Economics—the Paths Ahead: Essays in Honor of Zvi Griliches*, ed. E. Berndt and C. Hulten (Chicago: University of Chicago Press, 2005).

9. Data on housing of poor households are taken from the US Census Bureau, "American Housing Survey for the United States: 2011," Current Housing Reports H150/11, September 2013, https://www.census.gov/content/dam/Census/library/publications/2013/demo/h150-11.pdf, with additional analysis by Robert Rector and Rachel Sheffield, "The War on Poverty after 50 Years," *Backgrounder* no. 2955 (Washington, DC: Heritage Foundation, September 15, 2014), except for items otherwise noted.

10. John Quigley and Steven Raphael, "Is Housing Unaffordable? Why Isn't It More Affordable?" *Journal of Economic Perspectives* 18, no. 1 (winter 2004): 191–214. Furthermore, the inadequate housing is concentrated primarily in public housing units run by governments like New York City. Daniel Henninger, "America's New Nihilism," *Wall Street Journal*, June 4, 2020, https://www.wsj.com/articles/americas-new-nihilism-11591225713. "America's Progressive Slumlord," *Wall Street Journal*, June 15, 2018, https://www.wsj.com/articles/americas-progressive-slumlord-1529019608.

11. Henninger, "America's New Nihilism"; "America's Progressive Slumlord."

12. Unless noted otherwise, the following list is based on data from the US Department of Energy. Physical amenities in poor households are calculated from the Residential Energy Consumption Survey (RECS), 2009, as summarized and reported by Robert Rector, "How the War on Poverty Was Lost," *Wall Street Journal*, January 8, 2014, and by Rector and Sheffield, "The War on Poverty after 50 Years."

13. US Census Bureau, *American Housing Survey for the United States: 2016* (Washington, DC: Bureau of the Census, 2017). Count is households with less than $25,000 annual income, the closest available approximation for the poor.

14. US Census Bureau, "American Housing Survey for the United States: 2011."

15. "A Short History of SNAP," US Department of Agriculture, Food and Nutrition Service, https://www.fns.usda.gov/snap/short-history-snap.

16. Gerald M. Oppenheimer and I. Daniel Benrubi, "McGovern's Senate Select Committee on Nutrition and Human Needs versus the Meat Industry on the Diet-Heart Question (1976–1977)," *American Journal of Public Health* 104, no. 1 (January 2014): 59–69, https://www.ncbi.nlm.nih.gov/pmc/articles/PMC3910043. In 1969 and 1970, one of the authors (Early) served on Senator McGovern's staff as a legislative assistant and worked on many of these initiatives.

17. Except as otherwise cited, data on food consumption and hunger among the poor are calculated from the US Census Bureau, "Current Population Survey, December 2009, Food Security Supplement," and analysis of the primary source by Rector and Sheffield, "The War on Poverty after 50 Years," and John F. Early, "Technical Appendix I: Independent Data Demonstrating the Upward Bias of Published Poverty Measures," in "Reassessing the Facts about Inequality, Poverty, and Redistribution," Policy Analysis no. 839, April 24, 2018, https://object.cato.org/sites/cato.org/files/pubs/pdf/pa-839-technical-appendixes.pdf.

18. Katherine S. Tippett et al., "Food and Nutrient Intakes by Individuals in the United States," US Department of Agriculture, Agricultural Research Service, Washington, DC, September 1995, updated by Rector and Sheffield, "The War on Poverty after 50 Years."

19. "Table 3. Nutrient Intakes from Food and Beverages: Mean Amounts Consumed per Individual, by Family Income (in Dollars) and Age, in the United States, 2013–2014," in "What We Eat in America," US Department of Agriculture, National Health and Nutrition Examination Survey, 2013–2014.

20. Alisha Coleman-Jensen et al., "Household Food Security in the United States in 2017," Economic Research Report Number 256 (Washington, DC: Economic Research Service, US Department of Agriculture, September 2018), Table 1A, 7.

21. Robert Paarlberg, "Obesity, the New Hunger," *Wall Street Journal*, May 11, 2016, A11, reports that even reporting that forty-nine million people (in 2013 the most current number available at the time) suffer from this food insecurity is an exaggeration because the government report reveals, among its obscure technical details, that on any single day fewer than three million are insecure about their food.

22. James Bovard, "How the Feds Distort Their 'Food Insecurity' Numbers," *Wall Street Journal*, September 4, 2014, A15.

23. Johnson, "Special Message to Congress Proposing a Nationwide War on the Sources of Poverty."

CHAPTER 4. TRENDS IN INCOME INEQUALITY

1. "Have the Top 0.1% of Americans Made Out like Bandits since 2000?" *The Economist*, May 9, 2020. After that introduction, the article goes on to cite a number of studies showing the contrary.

2. Comparative rates of growth for these aggregates were calculated from the National Income and Product Accounts: US Department of Commerce, National Bureau for Economic Analysis, National Income and Product Accounts, "Table 2.1. Personal Income and Its Disposition," "Table 3.12. Government Social Benefits," and "Table 3.1. Government Current Receipts and Expenditures," https://apps.bea.gov/iTable/index_nipa.cfm.

3. "Table H-3. Mean Household Income Received by Each Fifth and Top 5 Percent, All Races: 1967 to 2017," US Census Bureau, https://www.census.gov/data/tables/time-series/demo/income-poverty/historical-income-households.html. Before 1967, data are not strictly comparable, but using archived Census tabulations, it is possible to construct reasonably consistent data. For 1947, see "Income of Families and Persons in the United States: 1947," Current Population Reports, Consumer Income, Series P-60, No. 5, US Bureau of the Census, February 7, 1949, https://www2.census.gov/prod2/popscan/p60-005.pdf. For the first strictly comparable data in 1967, Census shows a ratio of 11.1, and the more complete estimate after transfers and taxes shows 5.1.

4. Over the period there were a number of tax changes, but from beginning to end, the net effect was lower taxes on low earners and both higher effective tax rates and more income subject to taxation for top earners. After twenty years of only modest tax changes following World War II, there was a sharp shift in the effects of taxes after 1967 from several sources. Government increasingly relied on income taxes for revenue with their typical progressive rates taking proportionately more from higher earners. The income tax system itself became increasingly progressive, with both federal and state taxes

imposing higher rates and reducing deductions and exclusions that disproportionately applied to higher incomes. One of the consequences was that virtually no household in the bottom two quintiles paid any income tax in 2017. The Medicare payroll tax was changed in 1993 to eliminate the upper taxable income limit, so all employment incomes were taxed. Later, an additional Medicare surcharge on higher incomes was included, as were extra taxes on investment income. The so-called Alternative Minimum Tax, which was originally designed to impose a tax on a few hundred extremely wealthy investors who managed to structure their investments to avoid some significant taxes, eventually grew to impose additional taxes on several hundred thousand households spread across the top two quintiles.

Some reductions in tax rates actually increased the taxes paid. For example, lower capital gains taxes reduced a barrier to selling appreciated assets, thereby increasing the number and value of asset transactions and increasing the concomitant tax. The highly publicized federal income tax rates in excess of 90 percent in earlier years are largely irrelevant. First, they were only the marginal rates at very high income levels, not the average rates we are looking at here. Second, only a very few people (fewer than one hundred) actually paid these very high rates owing to the various income exclusions that accompanied them. When the rates were lowered, many exclusions were also eliminated so that the actual amount of tax collected often increased. The Tax Cuts and Jobs Act of 2017, which lowered some of the top rates, did not affect the data for 2017 presented here.

5. Footnotes 1 and 2 to "Table H-4. Gini Indexes for Households, by Race and Hispanic Origin of Householder: 1967 to 2017," US Census Bureau, https://www.census.gov/data/tables/time-series/demo/income-poverty/historical-income-households.html.

6. The old tables show income distributions for families and unrelated individuals. The universe of families and unrelated individuals included the same people as household used from 1967 forward; it just divided them into reporting units somewhat differently. Using these archived tables, we were able to construct reasonable estimates of the Gini coefficients for the Census income measure back to 1947. While the 1967 changes made it impossible to push the household approach back to earlier times, we could still calculate a 1967 Gini based on the older tabulation methods. We then calculated the percentage difference from 1967 to earlier years on that old basis and then "back-casted" the earlier year by applying the percentage change from the older tabulations to the published 1967 number. One of the challenges with this method was that the income ranges used in the old income distribution tables changed over time as income rose, so income ranges that were arranged in $500 steps one year might be in $1,000 or even $5,000 steps in other years. To deal with these discontinuities, adjacent years with different ranges were collapsed (and sometimes expanded, based on available information) to a common structure, and the relative link between the two years was calculated on that comparable basis, followed by resuming use of the shared published structure for other years.

7. "Appendix C. Conversion to a Computer-Assisted Questionnaire," in "Income: Poverty, and Valuation of Noncash Benefits: 1993," Current Population Reports, Consumer Income, Series P60-188, US Census Bureau, February 1995. This change alone accounted for about 40 percent of the 1992–1993 increase.

Other rather technical changes also contributed the remainder of the outlier effects for 1993: (1) Prior to 1993, not only was the amount of income collected for each individual in the household limited, but there were also limits on the number of people in the household for which data was collected. After 1993 there was no practical limit on the number of reported earners. For households with extended families and those with income-earning children or parents, this change raised the level of income reported, causing the Gini index to rise. (2) Most income items, such as Social Security, pensions, wages, and salaries, are collected on a basis easiest for the respondent (weekly, monthly, or annually) and later converted to annual. After the data collection was completed for 1993, the Census found that the use of their new computer-based interview tool had caused monthly or weekly amounts to be reported as annual, especially for Social Security. This, of course, led to an underestimate of income for many lower-income households and a higher Gini coefficient because more households were shifted into lower incomes. While Census made ad hoc adjustments to refine the final estimates, it is inherently unknowable how much upward bias in the Gini coefficients may remain. (3) Members of a family living in a group quarters such as a nursing home or college dormitory before 1993 were included as members of the family household during data collection, but beginning with 1993, they were counted as unrelated individuals. If these individuals had any income, whether earned or unearned, it was included in the totals for 1992, but for 1993 it was excluded because they were no longer in the household. Since group-quarter living arrangements are more frequent at lower income levels, this change would depress lower incomes, increase the income spread, and raise the Gini coefficient.

These differences are rather technical and there are no independent estimates of their total effects, such as we had for the 2013 changes.

The top coding of high income levels in the basic Census data at the time of data collection described here differs from the top coding Census uses in public-use files like the ones used in this analysis. Top coding in public-use files combined with some randomization techniques is used to ensure confidentiality of respondents and usually has minimal or no effect on aggregates. This analysis has used additional data from the Congressional Budget Office ("The Distribution of Household Income, 2015," Congressional Budget Office, March 2018, data files "54646-additional-data-for-researchers"), the Internal Revenue Service ("Table 3. All Individual Returns Excluding Dependents: Number of Returns, Shares of Adjusted Gross Income (AGI), Selected Income Items, Credits, Total Income Tax, AGI Floor on Percentiles, and Average Tax Rates, by Selected Expanded Descending Cumulative Percentiles of Returns Based on AGI, Tax Year 2017, and Other Years," Internal Revenue Service, https://www.irs.gov/statistics/soi-tax-stats-statistics-of-income), and National Income and Product Accounts ("Table 2.1. Personal Income and Its Disposition," https://apps.bea.gov/iTable/index_nipa.cfm) to supplement our estimates to minimize this understatement.

8. "Appendix C. Conversion to a Computer-Assisted Questionnaire," in "Income: Poverty, and Valuation of Noncash Benefits: 1993," Current Population Reports, Consumer Income, Series P60-188, US Census Bureau, February 1995, C-2. The change to computer-assisted collection created an unanticipated set of reporting errors that were attributed to inadequate training and performance by the field representatives. In particular, income items, such as Social Security or unemployment insurance, that might be reported on one or more different timings (such as weekly, monthly, or annually) were sometimes confused and reported at the wrong frequency. Editing of the collected data

reduced that source of error, but it appears to have left some residual underreporting in lower income levels—and hence a higher Gini coefficient.

9. Footnotes 1 and 2 to "Table H-4. Gini Indexes for Households, by Race and Hispanic Origin of Householder: 1967 to 2017." "Appendix D: Facsimile of ASEC Supplement Questionnaire," in US Census Bureau, *Current Population Survey 2018 Annual Social and Economic (ASEC) Supplement*, D-1 ff, www.census.gov. Sometimes respondents refuse or are unable to answer a question about how much they or somebody else in the household received from a source of income such as annual wages and salaries. The old method simply recorded that they refused or did not know the amount. With the new method, the interviewers ask additional questions to identify, if possible, a range for that income, such as (1) less than $45,000, (2) between $45,000 and $60,000, or (3) over $60,000 (Question Q48aarn1 from the automated question script of the interviewer, *Technical Documentation: Current Population Survey 2018 Annual Social and Economic (ASEC) Supplement*, p. D-10). When a respondent is unable or unwilling to provide an income estimate, standard operating procedures for the Current Population Survey use statistical techniques to adjust for this nonresponse. The ranges allow for a more precise adjustment because they at least give the general direction from the median response. Without the ranges, the adjustments for nonresponse were more likely to produce estimates closer to the median value. With the ranges, a wider dispersion of valid adjusted values was possible. As a result, the Gini coefficient using the new method was 1.3 percent higher than the old method for 2013, a difference that was more than four times greater than the average annal rate of change over the full fifty years.

10. The adjustment began by setting the 2013–2017 values as the benchmark values for the level of the Gini coefficient because they incorporate all the technique changes and are, according to Census documentation, the most inclusive for their published definition of income.

The 2013 discontinuity has the advantage that Census published the year 2013 on both the original and the new methods, so that there is a clear measure of the discontinuity. We used this measure to correct the coefficient for 2012 by applying the percentage difference between 2013 and 2012 in the original series to the benchmarked 2013 level, thereby eliminating the effects of the changes in the method while preserving the trend in the published estimates. We continued that same type of adjustment back through the year 1993.

In this way, the discontinuity of 1.3 percent measured by Census at the 2013 methodological change was eliminated while the trend of the original series was maintained at the corrected level.

The adjustment for the 1992–1993 discontinuity is a little more complicated because Census did not have overlap estimates for the different methods in the same year, although the technical notes from Census provide some indication of the type of discontinuity to expect. Excluding the two anomalies we have noted, the Census Gini coefficient rose an average of 0.3 percent per year. It averaged that same rate for the twenty-five years before the discontinuity and for the nineteen years that followed it before the next discontinuity, so using 0.3 percent would be a conservative estimate for the 1992–1993 change excluding the mechanical effects of methodology. By this calculation, in 1992, the Gini coefficient would have been 4.6 percent higher, had Census applied the new methods and techniques earlier. Then we applied the actual trend of the old series from 1992 back to 1967, just as we did for the earlier discontinuity.

We do know independently that the removal of the artificial limits on the amount of reported income was large enough to account for about 40 percent of that total adjustment. We do not have independent data on the effects of lifting the limits on the number of household members allowed to report income, the reassignment of family members in group quarters, and the processing errors in converting monthly and weekly amounts to annual, but if they each contributed only half as much as the change of income limits, that would be enough to account for the entire estimated methodological effects.

11. Although ignored by most politicians, the press, and many analysts, these methodological discontinuities and their effects have been documented in specialist segments of the academic literature, including by economists with very different views in the debate over inequality. Generally, these academics have made the simpler, but somewhat less conservative, assumption that the 1992–1993 and 2012–2013 changes were caused entirely by the methodological change. See, for example, Richard V. Burkhauser et al., "Recent Trends in Top Income Shares in the USA: Reconciling Estimates from March CPS and IRS Tax Return Data," *Review of Economics and Statistics* 94, no. 2 (2012), 371–88; Anthony B. Atkinson, Thomas Piketty, and Emmanuel Saez, "Top Incomes in the Long Run of History," *Journal of Economic Literature* 49, no. 1 (2011): 3–71.

12. The change from 1967 to 1968 may also appear a little unusual, but it is primarily the result of sampling variability from the much smaller samples in the 1960s. The 1993 and 2013 anomalies are each associated with a change in the methods used by Census to collect and process the data. There were no method changes between 1967 and 1968. The coefficient for 1968 is lower than for 1967 by a statistically significant 0.011 (based on the statistical error published in Kayla Fontenot, Jessica Semega, and Melissa Kollar, "Table 2. Income Distribution Measures Using Money Income and Equivalence–Adjusted Income: 2016 and 2017," in "Income and Poverty in the United States: 2017," Current Population Reports, P60-263 [Washington, DC: Census Bureau, September 2018], and adjusted for the smaller sample sizes in 1967–1968 and applying the standard business criterion of 95 percent confidence). But the series immediately snaps back, and the two-year change from 1967 to 1969 is not statistically significant. This suggests that 1968 is the outlier and that 1969 returned to the normal trend, followed by 1970 on the long-term trend line. We cannot test this hypothesis more thoroughly, however, because Census did not calculate the Gini coefficient prior to 1967. In both the 1993 and the 2013 anomalies, the upward shift is a permanent feature of the ongoing series and does not return to the long term. The one-year drop from 1967 is immediately reversed itself, and the trend was not shifted downward.

13. "The Distribution of Household Income, 2015," Congressional Budget Office, March 2018, data files "54646-additional-data-for-researchers." Extreme poverty adjustments based on Bruce D. Meyer et al., "Table 3. All Individual Returns Excluding Dependents: Number of Returns, Shares of Adjusted Gross Income (AGI), Selected Income Items, Credits, Total Income Tax, AGI Floor on Percentiles, and Average Tax Rates, by Selected Expanded Descending Cumulative Percentiles of Returns Based on AGI, Tax Year 2017," in "The Use and Misuse of Income Data and Extreme Poverty in the United States," US Department of Treasury, Internal Revenue Service, Statistics

of Income, https://www.irs.gov/statistics/soi-tax-stats-individual-statistical-tables-by-tax-rate-and-income-percentile; "Table 1. Selected Items for the Top 400 Individual Income Tax Returns with the Largest Adjusted Gross Income (AGI), Tax Years 1992–2014," in "The 400 Individual Income Tax Returns Reporting the Largest Adjusted Gross Incomes Each Year, 1992–2014," Internal Revenue Service, https://www.irs.gov/statistics/soi-tax-stats-top-400-individual-income-tax-returns-with-the-largest-adjusted-gross-incomes.

14. These additions to the Census estimates are the same as those made in the analysis of 2017 data in Chapter 2. As with those adjustments, all transfer payments are valued at the money spent by the government for the actual transfer. This does not include the administrative and delivery costs. Transfer payments are not adjusted upward for the higher market prices paid in the private economy for the same services such as Medicare, Medicaid, and Lifeline cell phones. Similarly, they are not adjusted downward for the theoretically lower value produced by "fungibility" calculations that estimate how much recipients would spend on the particular in-kind items had they been given cash instead. Using the actual monetary spending that is transferred is symmetrical with the treatment of taxes since it represents the cash taken from taxpayers to fund the transfer. In short, this valuation method is a commonsense conservative approach free from theoretical and debatable assumptions.

15. Although the magnitude of the transfer exclusions for the OECD estimates is slightly greater than that excluded from the Census money-income estimates, the difference is a net value because some programs are excluded by OECD but included in the Census estimates and others are included in the OECD estimates but excluded from the Census estimates. For example, Census money includes the following transfers that are excluded from the OECD estimates: Supplemental Security Income (SSI), Temporary Assistance for Needy Families (TANF) cash aid, Refugee Transitional Cash Assistance, and Pell Grants for college. Conversely, the OECD estimates includes some programs that are not in Census money income, for example, the refund component of the Earned Income Tax Credit and the Additional Child Tax Credit, the Supplemental Nutrition Assistance Program, and school lunch and breakfast programs.

16. The Census Bureau has kindly shared with us its detailed submission to the OECD (US Census Bureau, OECD 2016-Wave 7.xlsx), provided by Jonathan Rothbaum, chief, Income Statistics Branch, Social, Economic, and Housing Statistics Division. In addition, we have retrieved and analyzed the detailed metadata descriptions submitted by each nation to OECD ("Income Distribution Database," OECD.Stat, https://stats.oecd.org/viewhtml.aspx?datasetcode=IDD&lang=en#).

17. Our review of the available metadata for the other six nations shows that the United States has systematically failed to report transfer payments that are of the same type being reported by others, so while some other nations may also have undocumented underreporting, the available documentation suggests that the United States has significant underreporting compared to most.

The exclusion of most state and local transfers in the US submission uniquely biases it. Of the top seven countries, Canada is the only one with a significant federal system, and even there most of the revenue is collected centrally and allocated for local administration. Nevertheless, some of the countries—for example, Great Britain—report explicit tax breaks for local taxes as a transfer payment. The US submission does include state-refundable earned-income and child-tax credits, but there is no reason to exclude the other state transfers.

The United Kingdom counts the subsidies of mortgage interest rates underwritten by government, like Federal Housing Authority loan subsidies in the United States. These subsidies are entirely appropriate to include, but neither the Census submission nor the "more complete" estimates described below include them. The British also count the rebates of some local taxes.

Some other nations report items that don't belong as government transfers. France includes private pension plans as government transfers because it claims it cannot separate them from the social security plans, thereby inflating its government transfer numbers. (While the French classification exaggerates the size of government transfers, the ultimate disposable income is probably not affected.)

One of the best practices documented in the OECD terms of reference (TOR) is to test and adjust for "coherence"—namely, to adjust survey results so that transfer payment totals closely approximate the total amounts actually paid out by government. France makes this adjustment, raising its transfer payments to 95 percent of the independent aggregates from government accounting. The US Census does not, leaving reported transfers at only 26 percent of the government accounting total.

The one exception where the OECD claims other nations may be omitting transfers similar to those included in the "complete" estimates for the United States is government-provided health insurance. This case is discussed in detail in the main text. For a more detailed analysis, see John F. Early and Phil Gramm, "Data Details Supporting 'the Myth of American Inequality,' Wall Street Journal, August 10, 2018," Working Paper no. 180801, Vital Few, August 2018, https://img1.wsimg.com/blobby/go/96c33073-4042-4e15-a6cc-939becb21710/downloads/1d2ghakii_396672.pdf?ver=1574645672105.

18. "Net Social Expenditure Aggregated Data in Percentage of Gross Domestic Product, 2015," OECD.Stat, https://stats.oecd.org/Index.aspx?datasetcode=SOCX_REF. Net social expenditures are approximately the same as transfer payments.

19. Martine Durand, chief statistician and director, Statistics and Data Directorate, OECD, "Many Data Sets Show High U.S. Inequality," *Wall Street Journal*, August 24, 2018. See also Phil Gramm and John F. Early, "OECD's View of U.S. Inequality Is Mistaken," *Wall Street Journal*, August 28, 2018. The OECD response does make some other points, even though the exclusion of Medicare and Medicaid (including CHIP) is the only one that directly affects the results. Most of the comments are references to unarticulated "international standards," which seem to be just renaming of their own procedures. There is no such thing as a generally recognized international standard for these calculations. Nevertheless, our analysis in that paper was that the Census data submissions excluded many transfer payments that should have been reported under the OECD's own TOR. Its critique claims, for example, that "a broader income definition would consider not only in-kind transfers to people on low incomes but also capital gains, which would make the distribution even more unequal. Improved statistics would address underreporting across the entire distribution, not just for lower incomes." The statement is true but irrelevant. Our analysis, in fact, includes not only capital gains but also adjustments to eliminate other types of underreporting of investment income and added employer-paid benefits such as health insurance.

The "in-kind" comment is a diversion. For reasons that are not documented, Census estimates for OECD do not count programs like SSI and TANF, which are pure cash payments, but do count school lunches, which would be in-kind. Most nations' documentation of their metadata, in fact, includes in-kind transfers.

20. "Terms of Reference: OECD Project on the Distribution of Household Incomes, 2017/2018 Collection," OECD, http://www.oecd.org/els/soc/IDD-ToR.pdf.

21. According to more general definition from the financial community, "A transfer payment is a one-way payment to a person who has given or exchanged no money, good, or service for it. . . . It is a process used by governments as a way to redistribute money through programs such as old age or disability pensions, student grants, and unemployment compensation. . . . In the U.S., Social Security, Medicaid, and unemployment insurance are common types of transfer payments. . . . Medical benefits are the second most common form of transfer payments." That would seem to nail it. The OECD instructions are broad enough to include Medicare, Medicaid, and CHIP, and the general-purpose financial definition explicitly includes them. See Troy Segal, "Transfer Payment," Investopedia, June 25, 2019, https://www.investopedia.com/terms/t/transferpayment.asp.

22. Durand, "Many Data Sets Show High U.S. Inequality."

23. As a matter of detail, some, but not all, Medicare beneficiaries pay premiums for their Medicare insurance. The value of the Medicare transfer payments are net of those premiums, so the transfer payments are actually government payment of a portion of the Medicare insurance premium. Furthermore, these premiums are means-tested, making Medicare also a means-tested and not just an aged transfer payment. Some, but not all, Medicare beneficiaries pay deductibles and coinsurance. The value of the transfer payments is only the Medicare share of the payments. In addition, whether deductibles and coinsurance are charged is a means-tested benefit, again reinforcing the transfer-payment nature of these programs.

24. "Growing Unequal? Income Distribution and Poverty in OECD Countries," OECD, https://read.oecd-ilibrary.org/social-issues-migration-health/growing-unequal_9789264044197-en#page109; "Tax on Personal Income," OECD, https://data.oecd.org/tax/tax-on-personal-income.htm.

25. "SOI Tax Stats—Integrated Business Data," Internal Revenue Service, https://www.irs.gov/statistics/soi-tax-stats-integrated-business-data.

26. Alan Reynolds, "Has U.S. Income Inequality Really Increased?" Policy Analysis 586, Cato Institute, January 8, 2007, 5. For an even more in-depth analysis, see Alan Reynolds, "Misuse of Top 1 Percent of Income Shares as a Measure of Inequality," Working Paper no. 9, Cato Institute, October 4, 2012, https://www.cato.org/working-paper/misuse-top-1-percent-income-shares-measure-inequality.

27. Actual before-tax earnings did not change; only the bookkeeping changed. Profits that had previously been recorded on corporate books now showed up as individual income. The actual earnings were no different; they were only recorded differently for tax purposes. The measures of income for business owners soared because the company earnings formerly retained at a corporation for investment, operating capital, and reserves were now reported as personal income of the owners. The owners had no added income for consumption or savings.

This tax-code distortion has the greatest impact on the estimates by some researchers who base their income calculations soley on reports from IRS tax records. The most widely cited works of this variety include Thomas Piketty and Emmanuel Saez, "Income Inequality in the United States, 1913–1998," *Quarterly Journal of Economics* 118, no. 1 (2003), updated at the website http://elsa.berkeley.edu/~saez, and, more recently, Emmanuel Saez and Gabriel Zucman, *The Triumph of Injustice: How the Rich Dodge Taxes and How to Make Them Pay* (New York: W. W. Norton, 2019). But the tax-reporting effects are also a problem (if somewhat smaller) for the Census income measures discussed here. When higher-income households shifted some of their C corporate holdings to LLCs and partnerships, Census captured at least a significant portion of this income as an increase in individual earnings, even though it was only a change in where the earnings were recorded, not a real increase in earnings. Census definitions would seem to exclude S corporate income from personal income, but in neither its technical documents nor its survey instructions does it explicitly prescribe a treatment for these earnings, and without that direction, respondents would likely have included them in the reported totals. Partnership and LLC earnings are clearly included in the Census definition of earnings and rose in response to business reorganizations motivated by the 1986 changes in the tax code.

In 1986, before the top marginal individual tax rate was reduced to 28 percent from 50 percent, half of all businesses in America, other than individual proprietorships, were organized and taxed as C corporations. The next year, 118,000 C corporations disappeared, and 302,000 new S corporations were born. Within five years, half a million C corporations disappeared to be replaced by 872,000 new S corps. By 2013 (the most recent data available), nearly 1 million C corporations were gone, and 3.4 million new S corporations had begun business. In a complete reversal of the business landscape, only 17 percent of businesses in America were taxed as C corporations, and 83 percent were organized as pass-through entities ("SOI Tax Stats—Integrated Business Data"). In 1986, "business" or "self-employed" income constituted 11.1 percent of the income among the top 1 percent of income earners. By 1988, it had almost doubled to 21.2 percent and continued to rise to 28.4 percent by 2004 (Reynolds, "Has U.S. Income Inequality Really Increased?"; Reynolds, "Misuse of Top 1 Percent of Income Shares as a Measure of Inequality").

Beginning in 2018, the corporate tax rate was reduced to 21 percent compared with the top individual rate of 37 percent. Given the dramatic changes that occurred after the individual rate was reduced below the corporate tax rate in 1986, if the 21 percent corporate tax rate remains in place, a reorganization of the structure of American business will likely occur as businesses move from structures where they are taxed at the individual rates back to structures where they are taxed at the corporate rate. This change, if it occurs, will lower the measured Gini coefficient just as the 1986 change raised it. Those effects, of course, would not have appeared in the data discussed here.

28. The Census measure actually rose most rapidly around 1993 when a change in method by the Bureau of the Census enabled the surveys to get more complete income information than before. This change in method increased the Gini coefficient for 1993 because the survey captured more complete data for upper-income households, not because there was any real increased income. If the data are adjusted for that technical issue, the Census figures also rose more rapidly in the late 1980s than at any other time.

29. Rakesh Kochhar, "Appendix D: Income Tiers Defined Using the U.S. Median Disposable Household Income," in "Middle Class Fortunes in Western Europe," Pew Research Center, April 24, 2017, https://www.pewresearch.org/global/2017/04/24/western-europe-middle-class-appendix-d.

CHAPTER 5. CAUSES OF THE GROWTH IN EARNED INCOME INEQUALITY

1. Tables XI, XII, XIV, XV, XXII, and XXIII in "International Trade Statistics 1900–1960," United Nation's Statistics Division, May 1962, https://unstats.un.org/unsd/trade/imts/Historical%20data%201900-1960.pdf.

2. "Average Hourly Earnings, Manufacturing," Bureau of Labor Statistics, https://www.bls.gov/data/#employment. Adjusted for inflation using the improved methods presented in Chapter 6.

3. William Branson, "Trends in United States International Trade and Comparative Advantage: Analysis and Prospects," in *International Policy Research, Papers and Proceedings of a Colloquium held in Washington, D.C. October 3,4, 1980* (Washington, DC: National Science Foundation, 1980), III-20–III-48.

4. Bureau of Labor Statistics, Current Employment Survey, All Employees, Manufacturing, https://data.bls.gov/PDQWeb/ce.

5. Richard B. Freeman, "The Great Doubling: The Challenge of the New Global Labor Market," Chapter 4 in *Ending Poverty in America: How to Restore the American Dream*, ed. John Edwards, Marion Crain, and Arne Kalleberg (New York: The New Press, 2007). Figure 8 in Wayne M. Morrison, "China's Economic Rise: History, Trends, Challenges, and Implications for the United States," Congressional Research Service, June 2019, https://www.everycrsreport.com/files/20190625_RL33534_088c5467dd11365dd4ab5f72133db289fa10030f.pdf. Judith Banister, "Manufacturing Employment in China," *Monthly Labor Review*, Bureau of Labor Statistics, July 2005.

6. Freeman, "The Great Doubling."

7. Computed from "Gross Fixed Capital Formation (% of GDP)," World Bank, https://data.worldbank.org/indicator/NE.GDI.FTOT.ZS?view=chart. Gross fixed capital formation, 2000: global = $6.551 trillion, US = $2.373 trillion; US = 36 percent. Global labor force, 2000 = 2,762 million, US labor force = 149 million; US = 5.4 percent.

8. In 1967, college graduates earned 55.9 percent more than those with only a high school diploma. In 2017, they earned 96.2 percent more. Computed from US Census Bureau, Current Population Survey, March 1968 and 2018, public-use micro data.

9. Middle-quintile households increased saving and investment income from 2.7 percent to 3.5 percent of their earned income. The fourth quintile increased theirs from 2.4 percent to 4.4 percent, and the top quintile increased theirs from 5.5 percent to 16.8 percent. US Census, Current Population Survey, Annual Social and Economic Supplements, March 1968 and March 2018, calculated from associated public-use micro files, supplemented by "The Distribution of Household Income, 2015," Congressional Budget Office, March 2018, data files "54646-additional-data-for-researchers."

10. "Real Wage Trends, 1979 to 2019" (R45090), Congressional Research Service, December 28, 2020, https://crsreports.congress.gov/product/details?prodcode=R45090, 2.

11. Computed from Michael J. Hicks and Srikant Devaraj, "The Myth and Reality of Manufacturing in America," Ball State University, Center for Business an Economic Research, April 2017, 6.

12. Computed from public-use micro data from the US Census Bureau, Current Population Survey, Social and Economic Supplement, March 1968 and March 2018.

13. Bureau of Labor Statistics, Average Hourly Earnings in Manufacturing, current dollars, https://www.bls.gov/data/#employment. Change in constant dollars calculated following the methods in Chapter 6 to remove substitution and new-product bias.

14. Although the more complete data in Figure 4.1 are not available for 2019, other data show the shift—for example, "Table H-3. Mean Income Received by Each Fifth and Top 5 Percent of All Households: 1967 to 2019," Census Bureau, https://www.census.gov/data/tables/time-series/demo/income-poverty/historical-income-households.html.

15. The full retirement age for Social Security was age sixty-six in 2017.

16. The primary role of choice in this withdrawal from work is further supported by the fact that almost 86 percent of prime work-age persons without jobs in the bottom quintile made no effort to engage in even minimal activity to look for a job. Calculated from Bureau of the Census, Current Population Survey, Social and Economic Annual Supplement, March 2018, public-use micro-data file. For the survey reference week including March 12, 2018, 8.9 percent of the nonworkers during the previous year had taken a job, and another 5.4 percent had engaged in at least some activity to find a job.

17. Calculated from Census Bureau, Current Population Survey Annual Social and Economic Supplement, March 1968, public use micro data.

18. Unemployment in 1967 was 3.8 percent, and in 2017 it was 4.4 percent. That places both years among the lowest six unemployment rates for the entire fifty-year period. Furthermore, among the 64 percent of prime work-age adults in the bottom quintile who did not work in 2017, 86 percent had done nothing to try to find a job. (US Census Bureau, Current Population Survey, Annual Social and Economic Supplement, March 2018, public-use micro data.)

19. Robert Rector and Patrick F. Fagan, "The Continuing Good News about Welfare Reform," *Backgrounder* no. 1620, Heritage Foundation, February 6, 2003, http://thf_media.s3.amazonaws.com/2003/pdf/bg_1620.pdf. More details and updated information are in Robert Rector and Jamie Hall, "Did Welfare Reform Increase Extreme Poverty in the United States?" Welfare Report, Heritage Foundation, August 21, 2016, https://www.heritage.org/welfare/report/did-welfare-reform-increase-extreme-poverty-the-united-states.

20. Percentage of families in poverty from "Table 4. Poverty Status of Families, by Type of Family, Presence of Related Children, Race, and Hispanic Origin: 1959 to 2018," US Bureau of the Census, https://www.census.gov/data/tables/time-series/demo/income-poverty/historical-poverty-people.html. Poverty rates are from published Census calculations and have not been adjusted to correct the overstatements cited elsewhere in this document.

21. Increased from 4.1 percent of the workforce to 6.1 percent. "Table IV.B3—Covered Workers and Beneficiaries, Calendar Years 1945–2095," *The 2018 Annual Report of*

the Board of Trustees of the Federal Old-Age and Survivors Insurance and Federal Disability Insurance Trust Funds (Washington, DC: Social Security Administration, June 5, 2018), 61, https://www.ssa.gov/OACT/TR/2018/.

22. National Safety Council, *Accident Facts* (Itasca, IL: National Safety Council, 1994), 46–56; "Census of Fatal Occupational Injuries 2013," US Department of Labor, Bureau of Labor Statistics, September 11, 2014. Andrew Biggs, "Averting the Disability-Insurance Meltdown," *Wall Street Journal*, February 24, 2015. *Social Security Disability Programs: Improving the Quality of Benefit Award Decisions*, Permanent Subcommittee on Investigations of the Committee on Homeland Security and Governmental Affairs, US Senate, September 13, 2012. Nicole Maestas, Kathleen J. Mullen, and Alexander Strand, "Disability Insurance and the Great Recession," *American Economic Review Papers and Proceeding* 105, no. 5 (May 2015): 177–82.

23. "The Supplemental Nutrition Assistance Program," Congressional Budget Office, April 2012, https://www.cbo.gov/sites/default/files/112th-congress-2011-2012/reports/04-19-snap.pdf.

24. Various adjustments to the administrative rules reduced the reported income that determined eligibility and the size of the benefits. More and more assets were also excluded from the counts that determined eligibility. By 2017, weaker standards approximately doubled the number of non-senior, able-bodied adults without dependents (ABAWDs) on the food stamps to more than 3 million at an annual cost of about $6 billion per year. More than half of them did not work during the month, and one-quarter worked less than 30 hours. See Robert Rector and Katherine Bradley, "Reforming the Food Stamp Program," *Backgrounder* No. 2708 (Washington, DC: Heritage Foundation, 2012), 9, as well as Robert Rector, Jamie Bryan Hall, and Mimi Teixeira, "Five Steps Congress Can Take to Encourage Work in the Food Stamps Program," Issue Brief No. 4840 (Washington, DC: Heritage Foundation, 2018), https://www.heritage.org/sites/default/files/2018-04/IB4840_1.pdf.

The state of Maine began requiring work, job training, or public service from ABAWDs, which resulted in an 80 percent drop in ABAWD beneficiaries within three months (Robert Rector, Rachel Sheffield, and Kevin D. Dayaratna, "Maine Food Stamp Work Requirement Cuts Non-Parent Caseload by 80 Percent," *Backgrounder* no. 3091, Heritage Foundation, February 8, 2016, https://www.heritage.org/welfare/report/maine-food-stamp-work-requirement-cuts-non-parent-caseload-80-percent). But the federal government generally took an opposite approach and encouraged states to use vague standards to qualify even more able-bodied adults to take food stamps ("Food Stamps in Good Times," *Wall Street Journal*, December 5, 2019, https://www.wsj.com/articles/food-stamps-in-good-times-11575505774).

Bureaucrats set up rules that allowed people to get food stamps automatically when granted other forms of welfare, under so-called broad-based categorical eligibility. Not only did this situation evade the statutory requirements for food stamps, but the controls were so poor that when people lost eligibility for the program that initially qualified them for food stamps, they continued to receive food stamps indefinitely. (Gene Falk and Randy Alison Aussenberg, "The Supplemental Nutrition Assistance Program: Categorical Eligibility, Report for Congress" [Washington, DC: Congressional Research Service March 2, 2012]. Explained in fuller detail in Rector and Bradley, "Reforming the Food

Stamp Program," 5–8 and Appendix Table 1.) Similarly, state and federal bureaucrats coordinated efforts to exclude significant parts of beneficiary assets and income beyond those already excluded by law when calculating their eligibility (Report 112-470, Sequester Replacement Reconciliation Act of 2012, Report of the Committee on the Budget, US House of Representatives, to Accompany H.R. 5652, 112th Cong., 2nd Sess., May 9, 2012, 20, www.gpo.gov/fdsys/pkg/CRPT-112hrpt470/pdf/CRPT-112hrpt470.pdf). While some states have worked hard to slow the abuse, others have actively undermined efforts to apply even the modest controls that exist. Food stamp regulations allow certification of households solely on the basis of their receiving home heating-oil assistance from the state. Typically, the resulting food stamp benefit will be far larger than the value of the heating oil subsidy. The 2014 Farm Bill implemented a few modest reforms that were expected to reduce total food stamp spending by about 1 percent. One of these changes was to set a minimum state heating-oil subsidy required for qualification. Since food stamps are an "entitlement" benefit, the actual spending level is not subject to congressional appropriation. Short of a fundamental overhaul of the law, spending can be controlled only by changing the rules for eligibility. So, after Congress tightened the eligibility rules modestly, New York, Connecticut, and Pennsylvania immediately increased their home heating-oil assistance by just enough to assure eligibility under the new home heating-oil rule ("States Finding Ways to Skirt Cuts in Food Stamps, Frustrating Congressional Goals," *Washington Post*, March 9, 2014, https://www.washingtonpost.com/politics/states-finding-ways-to-skirt-cuts-in-food-stamps-frustrating-congressional-goals/2014/03/09/bf9d2620-a7c5-11e3-b61e-8051b8b52d06_story.html).

25. Robert Rector, "Reforming Food Stamps to Promote Work and Reduce Poverty and Dependence," testimony before the Committee on Agriculture, US House of Representatives, Heritage Foundation, June 27, 2001, http://www.heritage.org/research/testimony/reforming-food-stamps-to-promote-work. Compiled from US Department of Labor, National Longitudinal Survey of Youth.

26. US Department of Agriculture, Food and Nutrition Service, April 5, 2019, https://www.fns.usda.gov/pd/supplemental-nutrition-assistance-program-snap. Tami Luhby, "Government Wants More People on Food Stamps," *CNN Money*, June 25, 2012, https://money.cnn.com/2012/06/25/news/economy/food-stamps-ads/index.htm.

27. Radio Novella Spanish Language Episode 4, US Senate Budget Committee, https://www.budget.senate.gov/imo/media/doc/radio%20novela%20ep%204.pdf. One set of ads targeted senior citizens. These ads urged people to take money because they were entitled to it. Direct monitoring of the advertising by the authors is supplemented by information from Caroline May, "USDA Suggests Food Stamp Parties, Games to Increase Participation," *Daily Caller*, June 27, 2012, https://dailycaller.com/2012/06/27/usda-suggests-food-stamp-parties-games-to-increase-participation. *SNAP Failure: The Food Stamp Program Needs Reform*, Policy Analysis No. 738 (Washington, DC: Cato Institute, Fox News, October 17, 2013).

28. "Addressing Barriers and Challenges," US Department of Agriculture, Supplemental Nutrition Assistance Program, http://budget.senate.gov/republican/public/index.cfm/files/serve/?File_id=8668af80-3da7-40b4-b483-2256175120f8.

29. "2011 Hunger Champions Awards," US Department of Agriculture, Food and Nutrition Service, Supplemental Nutrition Assistance Program, http://budget

.senate.gov/republican/public/index.cfm/files/serve/?File_id=7bb4f0e6-a589-48b0-8b25-ca2ccd115918.

30. In 1967, bottom-quintile households earned 2.2 percent of all household income in the nation, up from only 1.6 percent in 1947. Their share of earned income, however, then dropped to less than 1.0 percent in 2017.

31. Lyndon B. Johnson, "Special Message to Congress Proposing a Nationwide War on the Sources of Poverty," Teaching American History, March 16, 1964, https://teachingamericanhistory.org/library/document/special-message-to-congress-proposing-a-nationwide-war-on-the-sources-of-poverty.

32. Census Bureau, "Current Population Reports: Consumer Income, Series P-60, No. 5, February 7, 1949," Table 1.—Distribution of Families and Individuals by Money Income Level, for the United States, Urban: 1947, 15.

33. Franklin D. Roosevelt, "Annual Message to Congress," January 4, 1935, American Presidency Project, University of California, Santa Barbara, https://www.presidency.ucsb.edu/documents/annual-message-congress-3.

34. Other research studies have reached complementary conclusions. David Altig et al. ("Marginal Net Taxation of Americans' Labor Supply," Working Paper no. 27164, National Bureau of Economic Research, May 2020, http://www.nber.org/papers/w27164) used different data sources and looked at more detailed individual cases rather than averages and the effects on income inequality. The authors found that one in four low-earning individuals with one or more of the more common government subsidies lost more than $700 in transfer payments as a result of earning an additional $1,000. But the design and administration of these subsidies was so inept that among the lowest-earning individuals, some would lose more than $2,000 for earning $1,000 more, while others with similar income would gain $500 from the government in addition to their added earnings.

35. Computed from public-use files from US Census Bureau, Current Population Survey, Annual Social and Economic Supplement, March 2018.

36. Computed from public-use files from US Census Bureau, Current Population Survey, Annual Social and Economic Supplement, March 2018.

37. The data by education in this discussion relate to all adults age twenty-five and older. Computed from US Census Bureau, Current Population Survey, March 1968 and 2018, public-use micro data. These estimates agree well with other estimates using a different method and published by David H. Autor, Claudia Goldin, and Lawrence F. Katz, "Extending the Race between Education and Technology," Working Paper no. w26705, National Bureau of Economic Research, January 2020, https://www.nber.org/papers/w26705. Their results are expressed in terms of the natural logarithm of the ratio of earning for individuals with college degrees to those with only a high school diploma. Converted to the percentage premium in the text above, their results were almost identical at 92.6 percent for 2017 and 49.2 percent for 1979.

38. US Bureau of Labor Statistics, Labor Force Statistics from the Current Population Survey, https://www.bls.gov/data/#unemployment.

39. Forty-eight percent of the increased contribution to household income came from greater numbers of women being employed. Another 45 percent came from the greater increase in the number of hours they worked relative to men, and the remaining

7 percent was the result of women's hourly earnings rising faster than men's. Calculated from US Census Bureau, Current Population Survey, Annual Social and Economic Supplement, March 1968 and March 2018, public-use micro data.

40. Table 318.10 in Thomas D. Snyder, Cristobal de Brey, and Sally A. Dillow, *Digest of Education Statistics, 2018*, 54th ed. (Washington, DC: National Center for Education Statistics, 2019), 308, https://nces.ed.gov/pubs2020/2020009.pdf. The drop in the share of college degrees earned by women following World War II reduced the proportion of college-educated women in the population for more than a generation. In 1947, women constituted 43.1 percent of people age twenty-five and over with a four-year college degree. Women's share of the college-educated population slipped over the next twenty years, reaching a postwar low of 35.5 percent in 1967. After that, women's share of college degrees in the population climbed steadily but did not regain its 1947 proportion until 1995, after which it continued to climb until it reached a majority of 50.7 percent in 2017. US Census Bureau, Current Population Survey for respective years, assembled and republished at "Percentage of the U.S. Population Who Have Completed Four Years of College or More from 1940 to 2020, by Gender," Statista, https://www.statista.com/statistics/184272/educational-attainment-of-college-diploma-or-higher-by-gender.

41. Table 112 in Kenneth A. Simon and W. Vance Grant, *Digest of Education Statistics, 1969 Edition* (Washington, DC: National Center for Education Statistics, 1969), https://files.eric.ed.gov/fulltext/ED035996.pdf, 82. Table 318.30 in Snyder, Brey, and Dillow, *Digest of Education Statistics, 2018*, 308; see Appendix B of this book for a comprehensive listing for both years.

42. The analysis in this book is presented in the context of the history and economics of government redistribution of income. Others have reached similar conclusions from entirely different analytical frameworks. See, for example, Myron Magnet, *The Dream and the Nightmare: The Sixties Legacy to the Underclass* (New York: William Morrow, 1993); Nicholas H. Wolfinger and W. Bradford Wilcox, *Soul Mates: Religion, Sex, Love, and Marriage among African Americans and Latinos* (Oxford: Oxford University Press, 2016); Kathleen Kovner Kline and W. Bradford Wilcox, *Gender and Parenthood: Biological and Social Scientific Perspectives* (New York: Columbia University Press, 2013). The famous and controversial report by Patrick Moynihan, *The Negro Family: The Case for National Action* (Washington, DC: Office of Policy Planning and Research, US Department of Labor, 1965), was an underlying document in designing the War on Poverty. His framework was sociological. Among other things, he emphasized the urgency of bringing African American men into the workforce. The irony is that the programs he helped launch had exactly the opposite effect.

43. US Census Bureau, Current Population Survey, Annual Social and Economic Supplement, March 1968 and March 2018, calculated from public-use micro-data files. Table 112 in Simon and Grant, *Digest of Education Statistics, 1969 Edition*, 82. Table 301.20 in Snyder, Brey, and Dillow, *Digest of Education Statistics, 2018*, 220.

44. In 1967, 96.8 percent of two-adult households were married couples, but information as to whether the remaining 3.2 percent were partners or merely roommates sharing housing was not collected. While we cannot make direct historical comparisons on the more expanded partner basis, the effects that we identify in this discussion of married households would likely be larger if we had the historical data on a partner basis as well.

45. This 8.1 percent contribution to income inequality from the rise in super families is included in the overall estimate of education contributing 45 percent of the increase. The contribution was calculated from sources in Tables 2.5 and 3.4. In 2017, the ratio of earned income for the top quintile to the earned income for the bottom quintile across all households was 60.3. The same ratio was 56.7 for households that did not have two spouses with college degrees. That was 6.0 percent less. In 1967, the two ratios were, respectively, 21.3 and 20.9, indicating that super families accounted for merely 2.1 percent of the inequality. The total-population ratio increased by 39.0 across the fifty years, and the ratio excluding super families increased by 35.8. The difference of 3.8, or 8.1 percent, between the two is an estimate of the contribution of increasing concentrations of super families to the rise in earned income inequality.

46. For high school dropouts, electricians averaged an eye-popping $69.99 per hour. The sample is incredibly small for this anomaly, so is probably not a good representative of the universe, but the few cases do illustrate an important point. It is virtually impossible to become an electrician without a high school diploma, but some do because they work incredibly hard and are likely also much more skilled than their education would indicate. This above-average effort and/or skill of a few resulted in their extraordinary earning power—either as a stand-alone professional or even as head of an electrical service company.

47. Computed from public-use files from US Census Bureau, Current Population Survey, Annual Social and Economic Supplement, March 2018.

48. Calculated from the public-use micro data from the US Census Bureau, Current Population Survey, Annual Social and Economic Supplement, March 2018, and augmented from sources listed in Table 2.1.

49. Table A-7 in Emily A. Shrider et al., "Income and Poverty in the Unites States: 2020," Current Population Reports, P60-273 (Washington, DC: Census Bureau, September 2021), 46.

50. Women working full-time, year-round, earned $50,982, and men working full-time, year-round, earned $61,417. That yields a pay gap of 17 cents: (61,417 – 50,982) / 61,417. Full-time, year-round women worked an average of 42.1 hours per week versus 44.1 hours per week for full-time, year-round men. Had women worked the same number of hours as men without any change in their hourly earnings, then their annual earnings would have been $53,434: (44.1/42.1) × ($50,982), computed with unrounded numbers. The earnings gap with the same number of hours worked is then only 13 cents: (61,417 – 53,434) / 61,417. That is 4 cents smaller than the gap with different hours worked.

51. Michael Podgursky and Tuttaya Tongrut, "(Mis-)measuring the Relative Pay of Public School Teachers," *Education Finance and Policy* 1, no. 4 (fall 2006): 425–40.

52. Table 4 in "Highlights of Women's Earnings in 2019," Report 1089, Bureau of Labor Statistics, December 2020, https://www.bls.gov/opub/reports/womens-earnings/2019/home.htm.

53. One might reasonably ask whether the higher frequency of workweeks less than forty hours among women is the result of their personal choices (the supply side of the transaction) or the expectations of their employers (the demand side). Multiple studies using different methods and data have shown that the selection of part-time work is

based on women's preferences, which in turn reflect the differences between mothers and fathers in how they believe their time should be divided between earning a living, caring for children, and housework. For example, the overwhelming majority (80 percent) of part-time women with children under age eighteen prefer their part-time choice. More strikingly, almost half of full-time women would prefer a part-time job over a full-time job (29 percent) or no job at all (21 percent). June E. O'Neill and Dave M. O'Neill, in *The Declining Importance of Race and Gender in the Labor Market: The Role of Employment and Discrimination Policies* (Washington, DC: AEI Press, 2013), 223–28, review and summarize several studies. The numbers they cite on page 225 are from "Fewer Mothers Prefer Full-Time work," Pew Research Center, July 12, 2007, https://www.pewresearch.org/social-trends/2007/07/12/fewer-mothers-prefer-full-time-work.

54. O'Neill and O'Neill, *The Declining Importance of Race and Gender in the Labor Market*, 231–33. Their "wage gap" is on hourly earnings, so not affected by hours worked like the "pay gap" for annual earnings.

55. Table 1 in "Highlights of Women's Earnings in 2019."

56. Mark J. Perry and Andrew G. Biggs (respectively, a professor of economics at the University of Michigan–Flint and a resident scholar at American Enterprise Institute), "The '77 Cents on the Dollar' Myth about Women's Pay," *Wall Street Journal*, April 8, 2014, A15.

57. O'Neill and O'Neill, *The Declining Importance of Race and Gender in the Labor Market*, 231–32.

58. Bureau of Labor Statistics, Occupational Safety and Health, Fatalities and Injuries by Sec, www.bls.gov/data/home.htm#injuries.

59. O'Neill and O'Neill, *The Declining Importance of Race and Gender in the Labor Market*, 228–43.

60. Anthony P. Carnevale, Jeff Strohl, and Michelle Melton, "What's It Worth? The Economic Value of College Majors," Georgetown Center on Education and the Workforce, www.cew.georgetown.edu/whatsitworth: Tables 12 and 13, p. 15, cross-referenced with detailed major characteristics on pp. 55, 91, 114, 115, 125, 136, and 137.

61. Charles Brown and Mary Corcoran, "Sex Based Differences in School Content and Male/Female Wage Gap," Working Paper no. 5580, National Bureau of Economic Research, May 1996, https://www.nber.org/papers/w5580.pdf, 20; also published in *Journal of Labor Economics* 15, no. 3: 431–64. This additional effect would add about $0.010 to $0.015 to explanation of the gender pay gap.

62. O'Neill and O'Neill, *The Declining Importance of Race and Gender in the Labor Market*, 228–43.

63. "Highlights of Women's Earnings in 2019." The Bureau of Labor Statistics (BLS) reports are based on the same Current Employment Survey that BLS jointly manages with Census. However, the Census pay gap, which is the one most frequently publicized, is based on an annual supplement that collects data for the previous year's earnings. The BLS data are based on weekly earnings gathered throughout the year from each sample in its last month in the survey. Households in the Current Population Survey sample are interviewed several times during a year. The samples are replaced on a continuous rotating basis to minimize bias and optimize the accuracy of trends. The topside estimates of

the two sets of data are very comparable but differ slightly owing to sampling variability and collection method. The BLS source enables more detailed analysis.

64. Constructed from Table 1 in "Highlights of Women's Earnings in 2019." The naming designations of generations are somewhat arbitrary, and the definitions of the relevant birth years vary a bit among sources, but the same consistent decline occurs even if one looks at other designations such as decades of birth or even individual birth years.

65. The naming of generations is not an exact science, and different commentaries use slightly different definitions. Even the length of a generation is not always constant in the same document. In this report, the generations are defined by their birth years as follows: Baby Boomers: 1946–1963; Generation X: 1964–1978; Millennials (or Generation Y): 1979–1995; and Generation Z: 1996–2012.

66. Gary S. Becker, *The Economics of Discrimination* (Chicago: University of Chicago Press, 1971).

67. Calculated from US Census Bureau, Current Population Survey, Annual Economic and Social Supplement (CPS/ASEC), 1968 and 2018, public-use micro data, augmented with missing earned income from employer-paid benefits, capital gains, and underreported earnings as described in Chapter 2 using data from the Internal Revenue Service, Congressional Budget Office, Bureau of Labor Statistics, Bureau of Economic Analysis, and the Census-University-of-Chicago audit of the CPS extreme poor. The 29.2 percent increase from these factors includes not only the direct effect of each factor but also any interactions among them.

CHAPTER 6. MEASURES OF WELL-BEING

1. Senator Bernie Sanders, candidate in the Democratic primary, on CNN with similar comment on MSNBC, May 31, 2019, as reported by Lor Robertson, "Are Wages Rising or Flat?" FactCheck.Org, June 28, 2019, https://www.factcheck.org/2019/06/are-wages-rising-or-flat.

2. US Census Bureau, Current Population Survey, Annual Social and Economic Supplement, March 2018, calculated from public-use micro data.

3. US Census Bureau and US Department of Housing and Urban Development, "Annual Housing Survey: 1973," Current Housing Reports Series H-150-70A (Washington, DC: US Government Printing Office, July 1975). American Housing Survey, table creator: https://www.census.gov/programs-surveys/ahs/data/interactive/ahstablecreator.html#?s_areas=a00000&s_year=n2017&s_tableName=Table1&s_byGroup1=a1&s_byGroup2=a1&s_filterGroup1=t1&s_filterGroup2=g1&s_show=S (accessed October 7, 2018).

4. "Television History—a Timeline 1878–2005," Tarlton Law Library, https://tarltonapps.law.utexas.edu/exhibits/mason_&_associates/documents/timeline.pdf. "The Color Revolution: Television in the Sixties," Television Obscurities, https://www.tvobscurities.com/articles/color60s/.

5. Eva Jacobs and Stephanie Shipp, "How Family Spending Has Changed in the U.S.," *Monthly Labor Review* (March 1990): 20–27. Bureau of Labor Statistics, https://

data.bls.gov/PDQWeb/cx (accessed October 8, 2018). Before 1984, the consumer unit was defined as a family with a single earner. To avoid overstating the change, the authors computed the change from 1972–1973 to 1984 (on the old definition) and the change from 1984 (on the new definition) to 2017 separately and combined them.

6. Average age 5.7 years in 1972 per National Highway Administration, https://www.fhwa.dot.gov/ohim/onh00/line3.htm. Average age in 2017 was 11.7 years per Hedges & Company, https://hedgescompany.com/blog/2022/02/how-old-are-cars/.

7. "Quick Facts 2016," National Center for Statistics and Analysis, https://crashstats.nhtsa.dot.gov/Api/Public/ViewPublication/812451; "Trends in Non-Fatal Traffic Injuries: 1996–2005," National Center for Statistics and Analysis, https://crashstats.nhtsa.dot.gov/Api/Public/ViewPublication/810944; and other releases from same source.

8. "Percentage of the U.S. Population Who Have Completed Four Years of College or More from 1940 to 2020, by Gender," Statista, https://www.statista.com/statistics/184272/educational-attainment-of-college-diploma-or-higher-by-gender.

9. "Table 4. Life Expectancy at Birth, at Age 65, and at Age 75, by Sex, Race, and Hispanic Origin: United States, Selected Years 1900–2017," Centers for Disease Control and Prevention, National Center for Health Statistics, https://www.cdc.gov/nchs/hus/contents2018.htm#004.

10. "Facts & Figures 2021 Reports Another Record-Breaking 1-Year Drop in Cancer Deaths," January 12, 2021, American Cancer Society, https://www.cancer.org/latest-news/facts-and-figures-2021.html.

11. Census Bureau, Survey of Income and Program Participation, https://www.census.gov/programs-surveys/sipp/data/datasets.html. *Extended Measures of Well-Being: Selected Data from the 1984 Survey of Income and Program Participation*, Current Population Reports, Household Economic Studies, April 1992, P70-26. *Health Status and Medical Services Utilization: 2013*, Current Population Reports, August 2018, P70-153.

12. Robert B. Avery et al., "Survey of Consumer Finances 1983: A Second Report," Federal Reserve Bulletin, December 1984, 857–68.

13. The real income changes described in Chapters 3 and 4 were not adjusted by improved price indexes that we present below. Improved estimates of real income follow.

14. "Consumer Price Index Frequently Asked Questions," US Bureau of Labor Statistics (BLS), https://www.bls.gov/cpi/questions-and-answers.htm.

15. The mentioned reports and other literature include Price Statistics Review Committee (George Stigler, chair), "The Prices Statistics of the Federal Government," National Bureau of Economic Research, January 1961, https://www.nber.org/books-and-chapters/price-statistics-federal-goverment. Advisory Commission to Study the Consumer Price Index (Michael Boskin, chair), "Toward a More Accurate Measure of the Cost of Living, Final Report," Report to the Senate Finance Committee, Social Security Administration, December 4, 1996, https://www.ssa.gov/history/reports/boskinrpt.html. The National Commission of Fiscal Responsibility and Reform, "The Moment of Truth," Social Security Administration, December 2010, https://www.ssa.gov/history/reports/ObamaFiscal/TheMomentofTruth12_1_2010.pdf. Robert J. Gordon, "The Boskin Commission Report, a Retrospective One Decade Later," Working Paper no. 12311, National Bureau of Economic Research, June 2008, http://www.nber.org/papers/w12311. Bruce D. Meyer and James X. Sullivan, "Winning the War on Poverty: Pov-

erty from the Great Society to the Great Recession," Working Paper no. 18718, National Bureau of Economic Research, January 2013, http://www.nber.org/papers/w18718. Brent R. Moulton, "The Measurement of Output, Prices, and Productivity: What's Changed since the Boskin Commission?" Brookings Institution, July 2018, https://www.brookings.edu/research/themeasurement-of-output-prices-and-productivity.

16. For a more comprehensive explanation of this substitution bias and methods that have been used to eliminate it in other price indexes, see Robert Cage, John Greenlees, and Patrick Jackman, "Introducing the Chained Consumer Price Index, Seventh Meeting of the International Working Group on Price Indices, Paris France, May 2003," Bureau of Labor Statistics, https://www.bls.gov/cpi/additional-resources/chained-cpi-introduction.pdf.

17. The C-CPI-U uses a Tornqvist formula from the family of superlative index numbers. For a summary of the overall C-CPI-U methods, see "An Introductory Look at the Chained Consumer Price Index," Bureau of Labor Statistics, https://www.bls.gov/cpi/additional-resources/chained-cpi-methodology.pdf. More comprehensive background can be found in Cage, Greenlees, and Jackman, "Introducing the Chained Consumer Price Index."

18. The PCEPI uses most of the same detailed price movements as the CPI-U and chained CPI. It differs from the chained CPI primarily because it is the price deflator for the final sales of all consumer goods and services, while the chained CPI relates to the slightly more limited consumer out-of-pocket expenditures. The actual differences between the two are very minor. The two have small random differences of about 0.1 percent per year. The C-CPI-U relates out-of-pocket expenditures by consumers and is calculated by the Bureau of Labor Statistics. The PCEPI from the Department of Commerce, Bureau for Economic Analysis, relates to a somewhat broader class of consumer expenditures that include, for example, expenditures on behalf of consumers by their employers for healthcare. The weights in PCEPI are derived from final business sales of consumer goods and services, while the C-CPI-U weights come from the Consumer Expenditure Survey. This difference in weights is small and random. The PCEPI uses a slightly different formula with multiplicative rather than exponential averaging, but it also eliminates the substitution bias.

19. Robert J. Gordon, "The Boskin Commission Report: A Retrospective One Decade Later," Working Paper no. 12311, National Bureau of Economic Research, June 2008, http://www.nber.org/papers/w12311.

20. Median household income is adjusted for discontinuity in Census methods as described in Chapter 4. The effects of these discontinuities on the median are relatively smaller because they had very little effect on the middle-income ranges. Census also uses the CPI-U-RS (for research series) to adjust median household income for inflation rather than the basic CPI-U. The CPI-U-RS has incorporated into the historical data some of the improvements that have been made to the CPI-U on a current basis. This is an improvement over the CPI-U, which is never revised historically, but it does not correct for the substitution bias or new-product bias discussed in this chapter.

21. "Table 21. Life Expectancy, by Age, Race, and Sex: Death-Registration States, 1900–1902 to 1919–1921, and United States 1929–1931 to 2017," in Elizabeth Arias and Jiaquan Xu, "United States Life Tables, 2017," *National Vital Statistics Reports* 68, no. 7 (June 24, 2019): 53, https://www.cdc.gov/nchs/data/nvsr/nvsr68/nvsr68_07-508.pdf.

22. Gordon, "The Boskin Commission Report"; Meyer and Sullivan, "Winning the War on Poverty"; Moulton, "The Measurement of Output, Prices, and Productivity."

23. "Measuring Price Change in the CPI: Telephone Hardware, Calculators, and Other Consumer Information Items," Bureau of Labor Statistics, https://www.bls.gov/cpi/factsheets/telephone-hardware.htm. Augmented with communications to John Early from Robert Cage, assistant commissioner, Bureau of Labor Statistics, September 24, 2020. BLS has not developed an estimate of the effects of this improvement, but other research has shown they are likely significant; for example, Erik Brynjolfsson et al., "GDP-B: Accounting for the Value of New and Free Goods in the Digital Economy," Working Paper no. 25695, National Bureau of Economic Research, March 2019, http://www.nber.org/papers/w25695.

24. Of course, over time the expenditure weights in the CPI would reflect this change in resource consumption, but the CPI prices did not show the decline in resources as a decline in price even though the use of fewer resources produced superior outcomes. Because peptic ulcer treatment was really the item consumed (not surgery, medicine, nurses, etc.), the drop in the overall cost of treatment should have been measured as a price decline. It wasn't.

25. "Disease-Based Price Indexes: Results and Data" at "Price and Index Number Research," Bureau of Labor Statistics, https://www.bls.gov/pir/diseasehome.htm#results%20and%20data.

26. The original Boskin Commission estimates of the overall upward bias of the CPI (including both substitution and new product) was 1.3 percent per year before 1996 and 1.1 percent after that. Meyer and Sullivan's and Gordon's conservative most-recent ten-year estimates are 0.8 percent per year. Gordon also urged a reexamination that suggested it might be as large as 1.0 percent. Moulton calculates 0.85 percent. We adopt the most conservative 0.8 percent, 15.4 percent for eighteen years. The C-CPI-U shows a substitution bias for the period of 7.6 percent, leaving 7.8 percent of new-product bias.

27. The GDP correction covers not only personal consumption expenditures, as in average hourly earnings and median household income, but also improvements to pricing gross private domestic investment and net exports of goods and services. No changes were made to government consumption expenditures since there is no relevant market valuation of changes in products. Adjustments follow those of Moulton, "The Measurement of Output, Prices, and Productivity."

28. GDP includes output from private business, government, and the nonprofit sectors. The output used for productivity measures uses only private business output. Since government and nonprofit real output are not estimated by price index adjustments, they are not affected by improvements in price measurement. As a result, the effect of improved price measurement on productivity measures is relatively larger because they are not diluted by the unaffected government and nonprofit components.

29. For more details, see "Chapter 10. Productivity Measures: Business Sector and Major Subsectors," Bureau of Labor Statistics, https://www.bls.gov/opub/hom/pdf/msp-19970714.pdf, supplemented by "Technical Information about the BLS Major Sector Productivity and Costs Measures," Bureau of Labor Statistics, March 11, 2008, https://www.bls.gov/lpc/lpcmethods.pdf.

30. *Economic Report of the President Together with the Annual Report of the Council of Economic Advisers* (Washington, DC: Executive Office of the President, January 20, 1964), 62.

31. Gordon M. Fisher, "The Development and History of the Poverty Thresholds," *Social Security Bulletin* 55, no. 4 (1992): 16. The substance of this memorandum was incorporated into Office of Management and Budget (OMB) Statistical Policy Directive 14, May 1978, and continues as the official basis for the calculation. This definition was administratively determined by OMB.

32. Bureau of Economic Analysis, National Income and Product Accounts, "Table 3.12. Government Social Benefits," https://apps.bea.gov/iTable/?reqid=19&step=2&isuri=1&categories=survey&_gl=1*z6jo7j*_ga*NDIxOTMxNzkwLjE2OTYyNjUxNDM.*_ga_J4698JNNFT*MTcwMDAwMTc4MS41LjEuMTcwMDAwMTc5MS4wLjAuMA..#eyJhcHBpZCI6MTksInN0ZXBzIjpbMSwyLDNdLCJkYXRhIjpbWyJjYXRlZ29yaWVzIiwiU3VydmV5Il0sWyJOSVBBX1RhYmxlX0xpc3QiLCIxMTAiXV19

33. John Creamer, Emily A. Shrider, Kalee Burns, and Frances Chen, *Poverty in the United States: 2021, Current Population Reports*, P60-277, September 2022, "Table A-4. Poverty Status of People by Family Relationship, Race, and Hispanic Origin: 1959 to 2021" and "Table A-5.Poverty Status of People by Age, Race, and Hispanic Origin: 1959 to 2021," https://www.census.gov/data/tables/2022/demo/income-poverty/p60-277.html.

34. Creamer et al., *Poverty in the United States*, "Table B-2. Number and Percentage of People in Poverty Using the Supplemental Poverty Measure by Age, Race, and Hispanic Origin: 2009 to 2021," https://www.census.gov/data/tables/2022/demo/income-poverty/p60-277.html.

35. Kevin Corinth, "The Consequences of Redrawing the Poverty Line," Statement before the House Committee on Ways and Means, Subcommittee on Work and Welfare, October 24, 2023, https://www.aei.org/research-products/testimony/testimony-the-consequences-of-redrawing-the-poverty-line.

36. Social Security Old-Age, Survivors, and Disability Insurance; Supplemental Security Income (federal only); Medicare; Children's' Health Insurance Program; Supplemental Nutrition Assistance Program; civilian federal employee pensions; and armed forces pensions.

CHAPTER 7. WHAT ABOUT THE "SUPER RICH"?

1. Data up through the top 1 percent are based on the same Congressional Budget Office, Census, and other supplementary sources as used throughout the analysis in this book. The estimates for more detailed higher-income groups incorporate additional information from "All Individual Returns Excluding Dependents: Number of Returns, Shares of Adjusted Gross Income (AGI), Selected Income Items, Credits, Total Income Tax, AGI Floor on Percentiles, and Average Tax Rates, Classified by Selected Expanded Descending Cumulative Percentiles of Returns Based on AGI, Tax Year 2017," Internal

Revenue Service, https://www.irs.gov/statistics/soi-tax-stats-individual-statistical-tables-by-tax-rate-and-income-percentile; "Table 1—Selected Items for the Top 400 Individual Income Tax Returns with the Largest Adjusted Gross Income (AGI), Tax Years 1992–2014," in "The 400 Individual Income Tax Returns Reporting the Largest Adjusted Gross Incomes Each Year, 1992–2014," Internal Revenue Service, https://www.irs.gov/pub/irs-soi/14intop400.pdf.

2. "Did Millionaires Inherit Their Money," Ramsey Solutions, August 26, 2021, https://www.ramseysolutions.com/retirement/how-many-millionaires-actually-inherited-their-wealth.

3. "Who Are the Highest-Paid News Anchors?" *The Street*, https://www.thestreet.com/lifestyle/highest-paid-news-anchors-15062420. "The World's Highest-Paid Hosts 2019," *Forbes*, https://www.forbes.com/sites/maddieberg/2019/12/19/the-worlds-highest-paid-hosts-2019-dr-phil-tops-the-list-with-95-million/?sh=6a44f7f437dd. "Bruce Springsteen Tops 2021's Highest-Paid Musicians List, Jay-Z Comes In Second—without Selling Catalog," *New York Daily News*, January 14, 2022, https://www.nydailynews.com/snyde/ny-bruce-springsteen-jay-z-2021-rolling-stone-highest-paid-musicians-list-20220115-eea3xh56frcubamloh2423j2wq-story.html. "2021's Highest-Paid Movie Roles, Ranked," *Style*, December 26, 2021, https://www.scmp.com/magazines/style/celebrity/article/3160938/2021s-highest-paid-movie-roles-ranked-dwayne-johnson.

4. Sportrac (https://www.spotrac.com). "NBA Salaries Analysis (1991–2022)," Run-Repeat, https://runrepeat.com/salary-analysis-in-the-nba-1991-2019. "Here's What the Average NFL Player Makes in a Season," *CNBC*, February 1, 2019. https://www.cnbc.com/2019/02/01/heres-what-the-average-nfl-players-makes-in-a-season.html. Associated Press, "Average MLB Salary at $4.17 Million, Down 4.8% from 2019," *ESPN*, April 16, 2021, https://www.espn.com/mlb/story/_/id/31270164/average-mlb-salary-417-million-48-2019.

5. Monte Burke, "College Coaches Deserve Their Pay," *Wall Street Journal*, August 31, 2015, A13.

6. "Table 1—Selected Items for the Top 400 Individual Income Tax Returns with the Largest Adjusted Gross Income (AGI), Tax Years 1992–2014."

7. Megan Knowles, "Healthcare CEOs Made $4.6 Million on Average in 2017," *Becker's Hospital Review*, November 6, 2018, https://www.beckershospitalreview.com/compensation-issues/healthcare-ceos-made-4-6m-on-average-in-2017.html.

8. Jennifer Wang, "The American Billionaires Too Poor to Make the 2021 Forbes 400 List," *Forbes*, October 5, 2021, https://www.forbes.com/sites/jenniferwang/2021/10/05/the-american-billionaires-too-poor-to-make-the-2021-forbes-400-list/?sh=443b47773888.

9. Rachel Sandler, "The Forbes 400 Self-Made Score 2021: From Silver Spooners to Bootstrappers," *Forbes*, October 5, 2021, https://www.forbes,com/sites/rachelsandler/2021/10/05/the-forbes-400-self-made-score-2021-from-silver-spooners-to-bootstrappers/?sh=1808638830c2.

10. Robert Arnott, William Bernstein, and Lillian Wu, "The Myth of Dynastic Wealth: The Rich Get Poorer," *Cato Journal* 35, no. 3 (fall 2015): 447–85.

11. Arnott, Bernstein, and Wu, "The Myth of Dynastic Wealth," 469.

12. Michael B. Sauter and Grant Suneson, "The Net Worth of the American Presidents: Washington to Trump," *24/7 Wall St.*, last updated March 20, 2020, https://247wallst.com/special-report/2019/02/26/the-net-worth-of-the-american-presidents-washington-to-trump-2. Since archived as https://web.archive.org/web/20190410142809/https://247wallst.com/special-report/2019/02/26/the-net-worth-of-the-american-presidents-washington-to-trump-2 (accessed April 27, 2021).

13. See, for example, "Van Hollen, Beyer Introduce New Millionaires Surtax to Invest in Working Families" Chris Van Hollen: US Senator for Maryland, November 7, 2019, https://www.vanhollen.senate.gov/news/press-releases/van-hollen-beyer-introduce-new-millionaires-surtax-to-invest-in-working-families.

14. For the most extensive academic claim on that point, see Emmanuel Saez and Gabriel Zucman, *The Triumph of Injustice: How the Rich Dodge Taxes and How to Make Them Pay* (New York: W. W. Norton, 2019), 14 and elsewhere.

15. "Foundation Fact Sheet," Bill & Melinda Gates Foundation, https://www.gatesfoundation.org/about/foundation-fact-sheet.

16. For Buffett on his taxes compared to his secretary, see Graeme Wearden, "Warren Buffett Says Rich Should Pay More Tax," *The Guardian*, June 28, 2007, https://www.theguardian.com/business/2007/jun/28/usnews.money. For reporting about how much the secretary may make, see Alex Crippen, "Does Warren Buffett's Secretary Really Make over $200,000?" last updated September 13, 2013, *CNBC*, https://www.cnbc.com/2012/01/26/does-warren-buffetts-secretary-really-make-over-200000.html.

17. Jesse Eisinger, Jeff Ernsthausen, and Paul Kiel, "The Secret IRS Files: Trove of Never-Before-Seen Records Reveal How the Wealthiest Avoid Income Tax," *ProPublica*, June 8, 2021, https://www.propublica.org/article/the-secret-irs-files-trove-of-never-before-seen-records-reveal-how-the-wealthiest-avoid-income-tax.

18. Saez and Zucman, *The Triumph of Injustice*, 14.

19. Saez and Zucman, *The Triumph of Injustice*, 202.

20. Thomas Piketty, *Capital in the Twenty-First Century*, trans. Arthur Goldhammer (Cambridge, MA: Harvard University Press, 2014).

21. The income calculation methods used by Piketty in *Capital in the Twenty-First Century* was published jointly with Saez before the book. Thomas Piketty and Emmanuel Saez, "The Evolution of Top Incomes: A Historical and International Perspective," Working Paper no. 11955, National Bureau of Economic Research, 2006, https://www.nber.org/papers/w11955; Thomas Piketty and Emmanuel Saez, "The Evolution of Top Incomes: A Historical and International Perspective," *American Economic Review* 96, no. 2 (May 2006): 200–205; Thomas Piketty and Emmanuel Saez, "Income Inequality in the United States, 1913–1998," as updated at http://emlab.berkeley.edu/users/saez.

22. Martin Feldstein, "Piketty's Numbers Don't Add Up," 73–76, and Richard Burkhauser, "The Rich, and Everyone Else, Get Richer," 77–80, et passim, in *Anti-Piketty: Capital for the 21st Century*, ed. Jean-Philippe Delsol, Nicolas Lecaussin, and Emmanuel Martin (Washington, DC: Cato Institute, 2019).

23. Gerald Auten and David Splinter, "Income Inequality in the United States: Using Tax Data to Measure Long-Term Trends," February 18, 2022, http://davidsplinter.com/AutenSplinter-Tax_Data_and_Inequality.pdf.

24. "Table T20-0100: Distribution of Federal Payroll and Income Taxes by Expanded Cash Income Percentile, 20171," Urban-Brookings Tax Policy Center, Microsimulation Model (version 0319-2), https://www.taxpolicycenter.org/file/183220/download?token=sd3EIT8c.

25. "Statistics of Income for 1938, Part 1," Internal Revenue Service, https://www.irs.gov/pub/irs-soi/38soireppt1ar.pdf, 102; "Statistics of Income for 1945," Internal Revenue Service, https://www.irs.gov/pub/irs-soi/45soireppt1ar.pdf, 69. Compare income ranges with top tax bracket of $5 million and above for 1938 and $2 million and above for 1945 at "Federal Individual Income Tax Rates History," Tax Foundation, https://files.taxfoundation.org/legacy/docs/fed_individual_rate_history_nominal.pdf.

26. See Thomas Piketty, Emmanuel Saez, and Gabriel Zucman, "Distributional National Accounts: Methods and Estimates for the United States," "TG2B" tab, http://gabriel-zucman.eu/files/PSZ2020AppendixTablesII(Distrib).xlsx.

27. President John F. Kennedy, "Special Message to Congress," American Presidency Project, University of California, Santa Barbara, January 24, 1963, https://www.presidency.ucsb.edu/documents/special-message-the-congress-tax-reduction-and-reform.

28. David Splinter, "U.S. Tax Progressivity and Redistribution," "5-Top" tab, September 10, 2020, http://davidsplinter.com/TaxProgressivity-Splinter.xlsx.

29. Splinter, "U.S. Tax Progressivity and Redistribution," "5-Top" tab.

30. "Table 3.2. Federal Government Current Receipts and Expenditures," Bureau of Economic Analysis, National Data: National Income and Product Accounts, https://apps.bea.gov/iTable/iTable.cfm?reqid=19&step=2#reqid=19&step=2&isuri=1&1921=survey. Personal income tax revenue grew at a 4.5 percent annual rate from 1986 to 1989, adjusted for inflation using the Consumer Price Index for All Urban Consumers, compared with 3.6 percent for the previous three-year period.

31. David Splinter, "U.S. Tax Progressivity and Redistribution," *National Tax Journal* 73, no. 4 (December 2020): 1005–24; numbers from backup workbook, "5-Top" tab, available at http://davidsplinter.com/TaxProgressivity-Splinter.xlsx.

32. Splinter, "U.S. Tax Progressivity and Redistribution," "5-Top" tab.

33. "Table B-3: Income Groups' Shares of Total Income, Means-Tested Transfers, and Federal Taxes, 2016 and 2021," in "Projected Changes in the Distribution of Household Income, 2016 to 2021," Congressional Budget Office, https://www.cbo.gov/system/files/2019-12/55941-CBO-Household-Income.pdf.

34. As of May 3, 2021, Bill Gates was reported to be worth approximately $131 billion: "Bill Gates," *Forbes*, https://www.forbes.com/profile/bill-gates (accessed May 3, 2021). That is only 7 percent of the $1.97 trillion market capitalization of the Microsoft company he founded: Jonathan Ponciano, "Microsoft Nears $2 Trillion Market Value—Second Only to Apple in the U.S.," *Forbes*, April 26, 2021, https://www.forbes.com/sites/jonathanponciano/2021/04/26/microsoft-nears-2-trillion-market-value-second-only-to-apple-in-the-us.

35. "Number of Employees of the Microsoft Corporation in Fiscal Year from 2018 to 2021* (in 1,000s), by Location," Statista, https://www.statista.com/statistics/1032154/microsoft-employees-by-location.

CHAPTER 8. THE AMERICAN DREAM IS ALIVE AND WELL

1. Robert Higgs, *Competition and Coercion: Blacks in the American Economy, 1865–1914* (Cambridge: Cambridge University Press, 1977).

2. Robert Higgs, "Accumulation of Property by Southern Blacks before World War I," *American Economic Review* 72, no. 4 (September 1982): 725–37.

3. For Rockefeller, see Kat Eschner, "John D. Rockefeller Was the Richest Person to Ever Live. Period," *Smithsonian Magazine*, January 2017, https://www.smithsonianmag.com/smart-news/john-d-rockefeller-richest-person-ever-live-period-180961705. For Vanderbilt, see note 5.

4. "Immigration to the USA: 1820–1860," Spartacus Educational, https://spartacus-educational.com/USAE1820.htm.

5. "Cornelius Vanderbilt [1794–1877]," New Netherland Institute, https://www.newnetherlandinstitute.org/history-and-heritage/dutch_americans/cornelius-vanderbilt. Arthur T. Vanderbilt II, *Fortune's Children: The Fall of the House of Vanderbilt* (New York: Harper Collins, 1991), 49.

6. Caroline Hallemann, "Gloria Vanderbilt Leaves Her Son Anderson Cooper $1.5 Million in Her Will," *Town & Country*, July 9, 2019, https://www.townandcountrymag.com/society/tradition/a28261059/gloria-vanderbilt-anderson-cooper-will-inheritance.

7. Esther Trattner, "How 5 of America's Richest Families Lost It All," *MoneyWise*, July 3, 2019 https://moneywise.com/a/how-5-of-americas-richest-families-lost-it-all.

8. US Census Bureau, Current Population Survey, Annual Social and Economic Supplement, March 2018, calculated from public-source micro survey data. Age is for March 2018. Average hourly earnings are the average for the year 2017.

9. Used in this context by "Income Mobility in the U.S. from 1996 to 2005," US Department of the Treasury, November 13, 2007, revised March 2008, https://home.treasury.gov/system/files/131/Report-Income-Mobility-2008.pdf, 3. It credits the original idea to Joel Slemrod and Robert E. Litan, "Expanding the Winners' Circle: A Guide for Increasing Upward Mobility," Brookings Institution, December 1, 1999.

10. "Income Mobility in the U.S. from 1996 to 2005." The income definition used is similar to that for Census money income, with the major exception that it includes capital gains, which the Census does not count, and excludes a few transfer payments included by Census, such as Supplemental Security Income and Temporary Assistance for Needy Families. Like the Census, it excludes the Earned Income Tax Credit and a majority of government transfer payments. The calculations are before taxes.

11. "Income Mobility in the U.S. from 1996 to 2005," 13.

12. W. Michael Cox and Richard Alm, "By Our Own Bootstraps: Economic Opportunity and the Dynamics of Income Distribution," 1995 Annual Report, Federal Reserve Bank of Dallas, https://www.dallasfed.org/~/media/documents/fed/annual/1999/ar95.pdf, 2–24. More detail in W. Michael Cox and Richard Alm, *Myths of Rich and Poor: Why We're Better Off Than We Think* (New York: Basic Books, 1999). In this survey, income is defined in the same way as money income is defined in the Census income estimates.

13. Cox and Alm, "By Our Own Bootstraps," 6.

14. "Income Mobility in the U.S. from 1996 to 2005," 9; additional details in Gerald Auten and Geoffrey Gee, "Income Mobility in the U.S.: Evidence from Income Tax Returns for 1987 and 1996," OTA Paper 99, US Treasury Department, May 2007.

15. Retirement was not a cause of a significant drop in earnings in these studies because the prevalence of ages for early and full retirement from Social Security (ages sixty-two to sixty-five) are essentially the same for the middle, fourth, and top quintiles (6.1 percent, 5.7 percent, and 5.9 percent, respectively). Calculated from the US Census Bureau, Current Population Survey, Annual Social and Economic Supplement, March 2018, public-use micro-data files.

16. "Income Mobility in the U.S. from 1996 to 2005," 4.

17. The top quintile lost 41.5 percent and 39.6 percent of its members in 1996 and 2005, respectively. Falling members would create a vacancy in the top quintile that would be replaced by the highest earners in the fourth quintile, so at least some of the fourth quintile people rising to the top quintile did so merely because somebody in the top fell. But those rising from the bottom, second, and middle quintiles to the top did so because their incomes increased so fast that they bypassed somebody still in the top quintile (or somebody in the fourth quintile who would have otherwise risen). These bottom-second-middle risers constituted 16.5 percent and 18.1 percent of their respective years, or 40.0 percent and 45.7 percent of the loss of top-quintile earners.

18. Jeff Larrimore, Jacob Mortenson, and David Splinter, "Income and Earnings Mobility in U.S. Tax Data," Working Paper no. 2016-06, Washington Center for Equitable Growth, April 2016, http://equitablegrowt.org/income-and-earnings-mobility-in-us-tax-data.

19. Hope Yen, "Who's the Biggest Barrier to Income Inequality? The '2 Percent,'" Associated Press, NBC News, December 9, 2013, https://www.nbcnews.com/business main/whos-biggest-barrier-income-inequality-2-percent-2d11708457.

20. Thomas A. Hirschl and Mark R. Rank, "The Life Course Dynamics of Affluence," *PLOS ONE*, January 28, 2015, https://journals.plos.org/plosone/article?id=10.1371/journal.pone.0116370.

21. In the reporting of results of other research, adjustments for inflation are those used by the original authors, unless otherwise specified.

22. "Pursuing the American Dream: Economic Mobility across Generations," Pew Charitable Trusts, July 2012, https://www.pewtrusts.org/~/media/legacy/uploadedfiles/wwwpewtrustsorg/reports/economic_mobility/pursuingamericandreampdf.pdf, 4.

23. "Pursuing the American Dream," 4.

24. "Pursuing the American Dream," 19.

25. "Pursuing the American Dream," 6.

26. Raj Chetty et al., "Online Appendix Table VI, National Quintile Transition Matrix: 1980–85 Cohorts," in "Where Is the Land of Opportunity? The Geography of Intergenerational Mobility in the United States," Equality of Opportunity Project, June 2014, http://www.equality-of-opportunity.org/assets/documents/mobility_geo.pdf.

27. Figure 16 in Michael R. Strain, *The American Dream Is Not Dead (but Populism Could Kill It)* (Conshohocken, PA: Templeton Press, 2020).

28. Combining the three studies reduces the sampling error by about half and also cuts by about half the nonrandom estimation error arising from the wide range of times

used by the Chetty group. A more involved meta-analysis weighting of the three studies was explored, including a sensitivity analysis of different weights, but since the percentage determined varied by only 0.4 points depending on the weight selection, we avoided the unnecessary complexity and uncertainty of weighting and used a simple average.

29. The 9.2 percent of adult children who were in their parent's quintile, in addition to the 20.0 percent from random results, represent 11.5 percent of the 80.0 percent difference between the random results of 20.0 percent and the fully determined results of 100.0 percent.

30. "Pursuing the American Dream," 11.

31. Strain, *The American Dream Is Not Dead*, 89.

32. Hebrew scriptures, Proverbs 22:6, circa 700 BCE. King James translation, 1611.

33. On page 93, we show that when adjusted for inflation using price indexes that avoid substitution and new-item biases, median household income rose by 93.3 percent rather than the official 33.5 percent. In the latest release for 2022 data, the Census began using the C-CPI-U to adjust for inflation from 1999 forward, which raised the official measure to 40.0 percent.

The Census has yet to use the similar PCEPI to adjust the entire earlier series without substitution bias. And the BLS still needs to update the CPI series to remove the remaining new product bias. Similar improvements are still missing from the poverty thresholds, average hourly earnings, and other series.

34. Our thanks to Michael Strain and Duncan Hobbs from the American Enterprise Institute for sharing this previously unpublished data from the study underlying Michael R. Strain, *The American Dream Is Not Dead (but Populism Could Kill It)* (Conshohocken, PA: Templeton Press, 2020).

CHAPTER 9. FIFTY YEARS OF ECONOMIC PROGRESS

1. Bureau of Labor Statistics, Consumer Price Average Prices, US City Average, https://data.bls.gov/PDQWeb/ap. Unweighted annual averages of monthly data.

2. Bureau of Labor Statistics, Consumer Expenditure Survey, https://data.bls.gov/PDQWeb/cx.

3. Consumer Price Index for All Urban Consumers compared with the Chained Consumer Price Index for All Urban Consumers from December 1999 to 2017, linked to the Personal Consumption Expenditure Price Index for 1967 to December 1999.

4. Advisory Commission to Study the Consumer Price Index (Michael Boskin, chair), "Toward a More Accurate Measure of the Cost of Living, Final Report," Report to the Senate Finance Committee, Social Security Administration, December 4, 1996, https://www.ssa.gov/history/reports/boskinrpt.html. Robert J. Gordon "The Boskin Commission Report, a Retrospective One Decade Later." Working Paper no. 12311, National Bureau of Economic Research, June 2008, http://www.nber.org/papers/w12311. Bruce D. Meyer and James X. Sullivan, "Winning the War on Poverty: Poverty from the Great Society to the Great Recession," Working Paper no. 18718, National Bureau of Economic Research, January 2013, http://www.nber.org/papers/w18718. Brent R. Moulton, "The Measurement of Output, Prices, and Productivity: What's Changed

Since the Boskin Commission?" Brookings Institution, July 2018, https://www.brookings.edu/research/themeasurement-of-output-prices-and-productivity.

5. "Table 21. Life Expectancy, by Age, Race, and Sex: Death-Registration States, 1900–1902 to 1919–1921, and United States 1929–1931 to 2017," in Elizabeth Arias and Jiaquan Xu, "United States Life Tables, 2017," *National Vital Statistics Reports* 68, no. 7 (June 24, 2019): 53, https://www.cdc.gov/nchs/data/nvsr/nvsr68/nvsr68_07-508.pdf.

6. Decennial Census 1960, 1970, US Census Bureau, https://www2.census.gov/programs-surveys/decennial/tables/time-series/coh-plumbing/plumbing-tab.txt; 1967 interpolated between 1960 and 1967. US Census Bureau, American Community Survey 2017, 1-year, https://www.census.gov/acs/www/about/why-we-ask-each-question/plumbing. "American Community Survey: DP04 Selected Housing Characteristics: 2019: ACS 1-Year Estimates Data Profiles," US Census Bureau, https://data.census.gov/cedsci/table?tid=ACSDP1Y2019.DP04.

7. US Census Bureau and US Department of Housing and Urban Development, "Annual Housing Survey: 1973," Current Housing Reports Series H-150-70A (Washington, DC: US Government Printing Office, July 1975). American Housing Survey, table creator: https://www.census.gov/programs-surveys/ahs/data/interactive/ahstablecreator.html (accessed October 7, 2018).

8. Computed from "Table B-9. Summary of Family Expenditures, Income, and Savings by Income Class, All Urban and Rural Families and Single Consumers, United States," in "Appendix B. Supplementary Tables," Bureau of Labor Statistics, https://www.bls.gov/cex/csxstnd.htm#196061; "Table 1. Selected Family Characteristics, Annual Expenditures, and Sources of Income Classified by Family Income Before Taxes, United States, All Urban and Rural Families and Single Consumers, 1972," Consumer Expenditure Survey, Bureau of Labor Statistics, https://www.bls.gov/cex/1973/Standard/income.pdf; "Table 1110. Deciles of Income before Taxes: Annual Expenditure Means, Shares, Standard Errors, and Coefficients of Variation, Consumer Expenditure Survey, 2019," Bureau of Labor Statistics, https://www.bls.gov/cex/tables/calendar-year/mean-item-share-average-standard-error/cu-income-deciles-before-taxes-2019.pdf.

9. Computed from US Department of Agriculture, "Official USDA Food Plans: Cost of Food at Home at Four Levels, US Average," June 2017, https://fns-prod.azureedge.us/sites/default/files/media/file/CostofFoodJun2017.pdf. Bureau of Labor Statistics, *Three Standards of Living for an Urban Family of Four Persons, Spring 1967*, Bulletin no. 1570-5 (Washington, DC: US Government Printing Office, 1967), 6. https://books.google.com/books?id=7UIvAAAAMAAJ&pg=PA41&lpg=PA41&dq=USDA+food+plan+1967&source=bl&ots=M-dRhmJ6q5&sig=ACfU3U3K6nqlEd3BmNlprPdUp1v3S0cX9Q&hl=en&sa=X&ved=2ahUKEwivs4m80rz0AhX6RDABHeG3DUEQ6AF6BAgfEAM#v=onepage&q=USDA%20food%20plan%201967&f=false. Bureau of Labor Statistics, Current Employment Statistics, Average Hourly Earnings for Production and Nonsupervisory Employees, https://www.bls.gov/data/home.htm#employment.

10. The Census Bureau classifies the race, ethnicity, retirement status, age, and other personal characteristics related to a household according to the characteristics of its "householder." A householder is a person who owns or pays for the shelter used by the

household. Married couples are assumed to share that role. When a household includes more than one person meeting the definition of householder, the Census Bureau classifies the household based on the characteristics of the householder who talked with the Census interviewer. Before 1980, the Census Bureau used the concept "head of household," which had a similar meaning except that for married couples, it was always the male. To look at comparable data for the entire fifty years, this analysis classifies household based on the characteristics of the "maximum earner," the person with the highest earned income within the household.

11. The classification of people by race is something of a fraught topic that is beyond the investigation here. This chapter investigates the reasons why average incomes differ between the sets of people as designated by Census titles and definitions, which are almost universally used in the press and most other publications. It offers no analysis on the reasonableness or appropriateness of those definitions and application. Note that, in addition to the three races mentioned here, Census has in recent years coded race according to twenty-six different identities and combinations of identities. Hispanic is an "ethnic" identifier rather than a race. Individuals must identify one of the racial categories in addition to their Hispanic ethnicity, and any race can identify as Hispanic. Hispanic identification did not begin until 1972.

12. Computations from US Census Bureau, Current Population Survey, Annual Social and Economic Supplement, March 2018, public-use micro-data file, show that 77 percent of Asians were born outside the United States, and of those born in the country, 78 percent had one or both parents foreign born. Hispanics were 45 percent born outside the United States, with 23 percent having one or both parents born elsewhere. Whites and Blacks both had 16 percent born in another country, with 10 and 7 percent, respectively, having foreign-born parents.

13. The 36.4 percent difference in average earned income is almost the same as the 38.3 percent difference in median Census money income between the two races that was cited at the beginning of the chapter. The Census number includes a few transfer payments such as Social Security and unemployment insurance, which are not earned income. It excludes some income items such as employer-paid benefits, capital gains, and some underreporting on the survey. The more complete numbers are derived for earned income only and include the earned items excluded by Census.

Census also typically presents household incomes in terms of medians—that is the middle value across the range of values for all the relevant households. That choice is reasonable for press releases, but the research presented here usually uses averages, called "means" by statisticians, because, along with other statistics, they are more appropriate for analysis of the variation within income distributions that is the topic of this book. In typical "bell-shaped" distribution averages (means) and medians are approximately the same, but in distributions like incomes where the upper end of values has virtually no limit while the bottom is limited to zero, medians tend to be smaller than means. Within quintiles, averages and medians will tend to be relatively close together because the values are bounded top and bottom—except in the top quintile, where the averages will usually be larger. The relationship of Black income to White income is essentially the same for both medians and averages (means).

The differences between means and medians are important for the substantive analysis that follows, but they have only minor effect on the starting point for that analysis—the relationship between the income for Black household income and that for White households. Both measures show a similar, significant gap, with a 36.4 percent gap in means from the improved estimates versus a 38.3 percent in Census reports of median money income. The major difference from Census is that this analysis provides a more inclusive and relevant view of all the components of the after-tax income that determine the well-being of the household. It also digs into the data to find the causes of those differences.

14. The "earnings gap" in this context is typically stated in terms of the difference between White households and households of other races or ethnicities. One could also compare all groups to the overall average, which would be equally valid, but this analysis simply follows the common convention since it seems to be used most frequently in policy discussions. The only caution for these comparisons is to always compare to the same reference; otherwise the analysis becomes confused.

15. This effect is calculated from the Census Bureau Current Population Survey, Annual Social and Economic Supplement, March 2018, public-use micro-data files, supplemented with other data sources documented in Table 2.1. The average earned income was calculated for each combination of educational attainment and race. When those detailed averages are averaged for a single race using the weights of the number of people in that combination, one gets, of course, the average income for that race. When the average income for Blacks in each educational attainment cell is weighted by the proportion of the White population for that educational attainment, the result is the average income that Blacks would have had if they had the same educational attainment as Whites. The difference between the two is a little less than 10 percent of the difference between the overall incomes of Blacks and Whites.

16. Black and Hispanic students receive, on average, significantly poorer elementary and secondary education. "Table 221.20. Percentage of Students at or above Selected National Assessment of Educational Progress (NAEP) Reading Achievement Levels, by Grade and Selected Student Characteristics: Selected Years, 2005 through 2019," and "Table 222.20. Percentage of Students at or above Selected National Assessment of Educational Progress (NAEP) Mathematics Achievement Levels, by Grade and Selected Student Characteristics: Selected Years, 2005 through 2019," US Department of Education, National Center for Education Statistics, National Assessment of Educational Progress. Chapter 10 discusses this point in more detail.

17. Computed from US Census Bureau, Current Population Survey, Annual Social and Economic Supplement, March 2018, public-use micro-data files.

18. Computed from US Census Bureau, Current Population Survey, Annual Social and Economic Supplement, March 2018, public-use micro-data files.

19. June E. O'Neill and Dave M. O'Neill, in *The Declining Importance of Race and Gender in the Labor Market: The Role of Employment and Discrimination Policies* (Washington, DC: AEI Press, 2012), 143–50, discuss details of this dynamic over time and between men and women as well.

20. Calculated from US Census Bureau, Current Population Survey, Annual Social and Economic Supplement, March 2018, public-use micro-data files.

21. The Census Bureau in recent years has often used the more limited "non-Hispanic Whites" as the basis for comparisons. But in this section the analysis includes longer-term historic comparisons for which that classification does not exist.

22. This calculation is straightforward, but there is one small complication. We are looking for the individual contributions from five factors (education quantity, occupation, age, work engagement, and geography) to the total gap. But these factors have a certain amount of overlap with each other. High school dropouts are also more likely to have disengaged from the workforce. So, if we add those two effects on household income, some of the same effects will be counted in both the education and work-engagement effects. This double counting will overstate the total effects, so each factor's effect is also adjusted to account for its overlaps with other factors. In the case of education quantity for Black households, the first estimate of the effect was $3,718. Adjustments to remove the overlap with the other factors lowers the effect to the $3,407 shown in Table 9.3. These adjustments are all less than 10 percent of the estimate and can also add to the magnitude when the signs are different.

23. "Table A-1. Annual Geographic Mobility Rates, by Type of Movement: 1948–2020," in "CPS Historical Migration/Geographic Mobility Tables, August 2021," Bureau of the Census, https://www.census.gov/data/tables/time-series/demo/geographic-mobility/historic.html.

24. Computing the number of interstate moves over longer periods is straightforward. At 1.5 percent of the population moving, over ten years, moves would equal 16.1 percent of the population. Over twenty years they would equal 34.7 percent, and over forty years, 81.4 percent. But the number of households moving (movers) during that period will be smaller because some households move more than once. If one-third of movers in any one year had also moved in a previous year (a very conservative assumption), then about half of all households would make an interstate move during the adults' work life.

25. Patrick J. Purcell, "Geographic Mobility and Annual Earnings in the United States," *Social Security Bulletin* 80, no. 2 (2020): 1–24, https://www.ssa.gov/policy/docs/ssb/v80n2/v80n2p1.pdf. This article offers a good overview of the existing research and uses Social Security records as a novel source for estimates. In addition to providing an excellent overview of the literature, he concludes, "I find that the relative difference in earnings between movers and nonmovers changed little during the observation period. Although some researchers have suggested that declining labor mobility has resulted from a decline in the earnings gains workers can realize by moving, this finding suggests that such a link is unlikely." The result is interesting but does not vitiate the earlier findings that reduced geographic differences in earnings may have slowed migration by reducing one incentive to move. He merely showed that among those who did move in recent years, the difference in their earnings compared with nonmovers was essentially the same as in previous years. But that is fully consistent with other findings of regional differences being smaller because he is measuring only those who did find reason to move. If the interregional differences were smaller, there would still be individuals moving to those jobs that were offering more. Fewer would find such jobs (which is what the original findings were), but there is no reason why the movers would necessarily be going for lower earnings. Just fewer of them would move.

CHAPTER 10. POLICY IMPLICATIONS AND CONCLUSIONS

1. Will Durant and Ariel Durant, *Lessons of History* (New York: Simon and Schuster, 1968), 20.

2. Plato, *The Republic*, trans. Desmond Lee, 2nd ed. (London: Penguin Books, 1987), 386.

3. Plutarch, "Lycrurgus," in *Plutarch's Lives*, trans. John Dryden (Boston: Little, Brown, 1906), http://classics.mit.edu/Plutarch/lycurgus.html.

4. Will Durant, *The Life of Greece* (New York: Simon and Shuster, 1939), 283.

5. Durant, *The Life of Greece*, 249.

6. Plato, *The Republic*, trans. Desmond Lee, 2nd ed. (London: Penguin, 1974), 373–77. See Plato's description and analysis of democracy as the most "attractive" of all societies. It was composed of great diversity, a positive characteristic, but that attribute was outweighed by the instability of the democratic form of government that led to dictatorship.

7. Abraham Lincoln, "Speech to the 166th Ohio Regiment," American Presidency Project, University of California, Santa Barbra, August 22, 1864, https://www.presidency.ucsb.edu/documents/address-the-166th-ohio-regiment.

8. "Remarks: Joe Biden Provides an Update on His Economic Agenda—October 28, 2021," Factbase, https://factba.se/biden/transcript/joe-biden-remarks-economic-agenda-update-october-28-2021. Similar comments explicitly claiming a reduction of child poverty by half were made by Speaker Nancy Pelosi ("Rep. Gomez, Speaker Pelosi Announce Start of Monthly Child Tax Credit Payments," Representative Jimmy Gomez: California's 34th District, July 15, 2021, https://gomez.house.gov/news/documentsingle.aspx?DocumentID=2467) and Leader Chuck Schumer (Isabella Colello, "Schumer: Child Tax Credit Expansion to Benefit 86% of New York Children," *News 10*, last updated July 16, 2021, https://www.news10.com/news/schumer-child-tax-credit-expansion-to-benefit-86-of-new-york-children). Cost estimate: "Table 1. Analysis of Potential Modifications to Selected Sections of H.R. 5376," in letter from Phillip L. Swagel, Congressional Budget Office, to Honorable Gary J. Palmer, US House of Representatives, "Re: Budgetary Effects of Making Specified Policies in the Build Back Better Act Permanent," Congressional Budget Office, December 21, 2021, https://www.cbo.gov/system/files/2021-12/57706-BBBA-Palmer-Letter.pdf.

9. The official poverty rate for children in 2017 was 17.5 percent. Counting all transfer payments as income for the recipients drops the rate to only 3.1 percent. Using the improved price indexes described in Chapter 6 reduces it further to only 1.3 percent. For children living with married relatives, the poverty rate was a mere 0.2 percent.

10. "Table 3.2. Federal Government Current Receipts and Expenditures," Bureau of Economic Analysis, https://apps.bea.gov/iTable/iTable.cfm?reqid=19&step=2#reqid=19&step=2&isuri=1&1921=survey.

11. Emily A. Shrider et al., "Income and Poverty in the United States: 2020," Current Population Reports, P60-273 (Washington, DC: Census Bureau, September 2021), 1, 71–72.

12. Since 2011, Census has prepared a second research measure of poverty called the Supplemental Poverty Measure in addition to the official poverty rate. Because this

special index counts many of the transfer payments excluded by the official estimate, it fell by 2.6 percentage points. While this special index had been prepared for ten years, the Census publication of the official poverty rate for 2020 featured it along with the official index on p. 1 of the primary data release. Shrider et al., "Income and Poverty in the United States: 2020," 1. Also see Liana E. Fox and Kalee Burns, "The Supplemental Poverty Measure: 2020," Current Population Reports, P60-275, US Census Bureau, September 2021, www.census.gov/library/publications/2021/demo/p60-275.html.

13. Benefits actually paid would need to be those paid to households and, for example, exclude Social Security paid to institutionalized beneficiaries. This approach of benchmarking and adjusting the survey totals to known administrative totals is a well-known and widely used method—for example, in the Current Employment Survey and the National Income and Product Accounts. The Organisation for Economic Co-operation and Development (OECD) recommends this approach (which it calls "coherence") in its terms of reference for reporting household income. See "Terms of Reference: OECD Project on the Distribution of Household Incomes, 2017/2018 Collection," OECD, www.oecd.org (in search box enter "IDD country-specific detailed metadata" and select it from results list); country-specific detailed meta-data information, Wave 7 definition, https://www.oecd.org/social/income-distribution-database.html, Country-specific detailed information for latest year and Wave 7 (71 pages, .xlsx), lines 112 and 113.

14. Franklin D. Roosevelt, "Annual Message to Congress," January 4, 1935, American Presidency Project, University of California, Santa Barbra, https://www.presidency.ucsb.edu/documents/annual-message-congress-3.

15. Lyndon B. Johnson, "Special Message to Congress Proposing a Nationwide War on the Sources of Poverty," Teaching American History, March 16, 1964, https://teachingamericanhistory.org/library/document/special-message-to-congress-proposing-a-nationwide-war-on-the-sources-of-poverty.

16. Casey B. Mulligan, "Has the 1996 Welfare Reform Been Reversed?" *Economix*, April 4, 2012, https://economix.blogs.nytimes.com/2012/04/04/has-the-1996-welfare-reform-been-reversed. This article summarizes the research showing that the expansions in safety net programs have reduced the rewards for working and increased the benefits for not working.

17. This discussion does not pursue one aspect of workforce withdrawal—namely, early retirement. Although the full retirement age for Social Security has been slowly moved up from age sixty-five to age sixty-seven, the early retirement age at which an individual can begin receiving reduced Social Security benefits has remained fixed at age sixty-two. Not only has this early retirement age remained unchanged, but the life expectancy has also risen sharply, adding almost ten years of benefits since the program began.

More than one-third (37.5 percent) of Social Security retirement beneficiaries actually start drawing at the earliest possible date. Another 28.5 percent take early retirement between age sixty-two and the full retirement age. Only 1.5 percent delay Social Security until age seventy, at which time they receive a substantially higher monthly benefit. Social Security Administration, *Annual Statistical Supplement to the Social Security Bulletin, 2013* (Washington, DC: Social Security Administration, 2014), Tables 6.B3 and 6.B5.

Clearly, increasing lifetime benefits has reduced work among people age sixty-two and over, but this discussion does not extend to that additional important loss.

18. "Table 3.2. Federal Government Current Receipts and Expenditures, Seasonally Adjusted at Annual Rates," Bureau of Economic Analysis, https://apps.bea.gov/iTable/iTable.cfm?reqid=19&step=3&isuri=1&1921=survey&1903=87#reqid=19&step=3&isuri=1&1921=survey&1903=87.

19. Bureau of Labor Statistics, Civilian Labor Force, https://www.bls.gov/data/#unemployment.

20. The survey includes both public and private schools, but private schools constitute less than 10 percent of the sample and also have very low response rates, so constitute an even smaller proportion of the received sample. Public schools are tabulated separately, and only public schools are shown here.

21. "NAEP Technical Documentation: Achievement Levels," National Center for Education Statistics, National Assessment of Educational Progress, https://nces.ed.gov/nationsreportcard/tdw/analysis/describing_achiev.aspx.

22. US Department of Education, National Center for Education Statistics, National Assessment of Educational Progress, "The Nation's Report Card," Data Tools, NAEP Data Explorer, 2019, https://www.nationsreportcard.gov/ndecore/xplore/NDE.

23. Calculated from US Department of Education, National Center for Education Statistics. Average of reading and mathematics test scores for eighth grade from "State Performance Compared to the Nation: Grade 8 | Reading | 2013," The Nation's Report Card, https://www.nationsreportcard.gov/profiles/stateprofile?chort=2&sub=RED&sj=AL&sfj=NP&st=MN&year=2013R3; "State Performance Compared to the Nation: Grade 8 | Mathematics | 2013," The Nation's Report Card, https://www.nationsreportcard.gov/profiles/stateprofile?chort=2&sub=MAT&sj=AL&sfj=NP&st=MN&year=2013R3. Expenditures from "Table 236.65. Current Expenditure per Pupil in Fall Enrollment in Public Elementary and Secondary Schools, by State or Jurisdiction: Selected Years, 1969–70 through 2017–18," in US National Center for Education Statistics, *Digest of Education Statistics, 2019*, NCES 2021-009. Expenditure adjusted for geographic cost difference using CWI_State_2005_1a.xls from http://nces.ed.gov/edfin/adjustments.asp. Test scores are for eighth grade because twelfth-grade scores are not available for all states. Least squares linear regression yields an R^2 of 6.4 percent, with a P-value of 0.068.

24. Computed from "Table 602.40. Average Reading Literacy, Mathematics Literacy, and Science Literacy Scores of 15-Year-Old Students, by Sex and Country or Other Education System: Selected Years, 2009 through 2018," National Center for Education Statistics, Digest of Education Statistics, https://nces.ed.gov/programs/digest/d19/tables/dt19_602.40.asp; "Table 605.10. Gross Domestic Product per Capita and Expenditures on Education Institutions per Full-Time-Equivalent (FTE) Student, by Level of Education and Country: Selected Years, 2005 through 2016," National Center for Education Statistics, Digest of Education Statistics, https://nces.ed.gov/programs/digest/d19/tables/dt19_605.10.asp. Expenditures adjusted for purchasing power parity.

25. Least squares linear regression yields an R^2 of 2.8 percent, with a P-value of 0.350.

26. Thomas Sowell, "Charter Schools' Enemies Block Black Success," *Wall Street Journal*, June 19, 2020.

27. "The 123s of School Choice: What the Research Says about Private School Choice Programs in America," EdChoice, April 14, 2021, https://www.edchoice.org/123s.

28. "The 123s of School Choice."

29. Eva S. Moskowitz, "The Myth of Charter-School 'Cherry Picking,'" *Wall Street Journal*, February 9, 2015, A11. Eva Moskowitz, "The Charter-School Windfall for Public Schools," *Wall Street Journal*, November 29, 2014, A11.

30. Nina Rees, "Will Obama's Budget Recognize Charter Schools?" *Wall Street Journal*, March 27, 2013.

31. Rees, "Will Obama's Budget Recognize Charter Schools?"

32. Michael Van Beek, "What Michigan's Charter Schools Can Teach the Country: The Secrets of Reform Success Include Liberal Chartering Rules and Freedom from Teacher Tenure," *Wall Street Journal*, May 18, 2013.

33. "Who's Afraid of Betsy DeVos? Trump's Education Nominee Is the Top Democratic Target," *Wall Street Journal*, January 17, 2017.

34. Tim R. Sass et al., "Charter High Schools' Effects on Long-Term Attainment and Earnings," *Journal of Policy Analysis and Management* 35, no. 3 (summer 2016): 683–706.

35. "The 123s of School Choice."

36. As compelling as these successes are, it is also important to learn lessons from those few cases that were not successful. For example, the Friedman Foundation evaluated eighteen published empirical studies of school choice voucher programs. Two of those studies showed some negative effects, both from the state of Louisiana. These failures resulted from the state's imposition of restrictions on how the participating private schools must do their work. As a consequence, only about one-third of private schools in the state participated. Most of the better private schools were in general interested in participating, but they declined when they discovered they would need to discard some of the principles that they had shown to produce better educational outcomes. As a result, most of the schools participating in the state voucher initiative were of lower quality and already losing enrollment to higher-performing institutions. These lower-quality schools were willing to accept the state's requirements in order to fill their seats. "School Choice Deniers: Critics Hype a Pair of Studies while Ignoring Other Evidence on Education Vouchers," *Wall Street Journal*, January 14, 2017. This report made the important contribution of demonstrating how simply making superficial changes will not be effective. Fundamental changes must free schools to compete for students in ways that both liberated schools and parents think best.

Although the fundamental motivation to establish school choice is to provide an opportunity for a quality education to more children, the change is also economically and fiscally sound. Because schools run by private organizations must compete with others providing the same services, those that are inefficient will be forced to improve their efficiency or stop providing the service. Ben Scafidi, professor of economics and director of the Education Economics Center at Kennesaw State University, and Martin F. Lueken, director of fiscal policy and analysis at the EdChoice foundation, analyzed sixteen state private school voucher programs. They found that, in addition to producing better educational outcomes, vouchers to private schools saved taxpayers an average of $3,400 per student compared with the cost of running the government schools. A similar analysis of ten tax-credit scholarship programs showed savings of $1,400 per student. None of the private schools or charter schools cost more than government-run schools. Martin F. Lueken and Benjamin Scafidi, "Myth: School Choice Siphons Money from Public Schools and Harms Taxpayers," Chapter 6 of *School Choice Myths: Setting the Record Straight on*

Education Reform, ed. Corey A. DeAngelis and Meal P. McCluskey (Washington, DC: Cato Institute, 2020), 83–89.

37. M. M. Kleiner and A. B. Krueger, "Analyzing the Extent and Influence of Occupational Licensing on the Labor Market," *Journal of Labor Economics* 31, no. 2 (2013): 173–202.

38. Dick M. Carpenter II et al., *License to Work: A National Study of Burdens from Occupational Licensing*, 2nd ed. (Arlington, VA: Institute for Justice, November 2017), https://ij.org/wp-content/themes/ijorg/images/ltw2/License_to_Work_2nd_Edition.pdf. Note that all the licenses studied are for occupations with below-average earnings. They are also a subset of that total since there were practical considerations that foreclosed including some. Even more limiting, however, is the fact that these are only state regulations. Many localities tack additional occupational requirements onto the same occupations or include additional occupations. For example, Baltimore places requirement on twenty-six low- to middle-income occupations that are not included among the fifty-nine regulated by the state of Maryland. We are not aware of a complete inventory of these local barriers, but some substantial examples are included at http://www.ij.org (enter "barriers to entrepreneurship" in the search box to get dozens of detailed examples).

39. Carpenter et al., *License to Work*.

40. Carpenter et al., *License to Work*.

41. Jon Levine, "Barber Bill Would Require Licenses . . . to Shampoo!" *New York Post*, August 16, 2020, 4–5.

42. US Bureau of the Census, American Community Survey, Table S1901_C01_012E, 2017–2013, https://data.census.gov/cedsci/, and Annual Estimates of the Resident Population for Counties in the United States: April 1, 2010, to July 1, 2019, CO-EST2019-ANNRES, https://www.census.gov/data/tables/time-series/demo/popest/2010s-counties-total.html. In addition, eleven of the top twenty surround the seat of federal power, housing the politicians, bureaucrats, and lobbyists for the big cronies. These 11 counties constitute only 0.3 percent of the 3,148 counties in the nation and 1.2 percent of the population. But they create approximately 4.2 percent of all income inequality among counties, by far the greatest concentration of high incomes in America. Percentage effect from the eleven counties on the Gini coefficient across counties computed from these data by the authors. The effect computed here on inequality between county averages is a distinct understatement of the full effect of cronyism because it misses the inequality generated within counties by the preferential income streams flowing to cronies and their patrons in government. Nevertheless, this lower-bound estimate is still evidence of significant inequality arising from government favoritism and payoffs to preferred cronies. The eleven counties include the eighth highest-earning county, Los Alamos County, New Mexico, as a crony center because it is totally dominated by the federal government's biggest energy laboratory, which owns 90 percent of the land. The county was created from parts of two other counties to house the Manhattan nuclear project and was for many years run as a federal territory.

43. Ronald Reagan, "Inaugural Address, January 20, 1981," Ronald Reagan Presidential Foundation & Institute, https://www.reaganfoundation.org/media/128614/inaguration.pdf.

Index

Page references for figures and tables are italicized.

About the Authors

Phil Gramm served six years in the US House of Representatives and eighteen years in the US Senate, where he was chairman of the Banking Committee. Gramm is a visiting scholar at the American Enterprise Institute. He was vice chairman of UBS Investment Bank and is now vice chairman of Lone Star Funds. He taught economics at Texas A&M University and has published numerous articles and books. Gramm lives in the Texas Hill Country.

Robert Ekelund was professor and eminent scholar in economics at Auburn University, having begun his career at Texas A&M University. He is the author of more than twenty books and several hundred peer-reviewed articles on the history of economic theory, economic history, and economic policy in the specific areas of art, religion, and regulation. He died on August 17, 2023, in Auburn, Alabama.

John Early is a mathematical economist who began working as a legislative assistant to a US senator and assistant commissioner at the Bureau of Labor Statistics. He has served in senior leadership positions in global consultancies on quality and financial performance and as chief customer and strategy officer for a Fortune 100 company. His publications include improving measurements of price change, labor force dynamics, and improving healthcare. He lives joyfully in Charleston, South Carolina.